1998

LANGUAGE,
METAPHYSICS,
AND DEATH

LANGUAGE, METAPHYSICS, AND DEATH

Second Edition

Edited by

JOHN DONNELLY

FORDHAM UNIVERSITY PRESS
New York
1994

Copyright © 1978, 1994 by FORDHAM UNIVERSITY PRESS
All rights reserved.
LC 94–27750
ISBN 0–8232–1581–4 *(hardcover)*
ISBN 0–8232–1582–2 *(paperback)*
First edition 1978
Second edition 1994

Library of Congress Cataloging-in-Publication Data

Language, metaphysics, and death / edited by John Donnelly. — 2nd ed.
   p.   cm.
   ISBN 0–8232–1581–4 (hard). — ISBN 0–8232–1582–2 (pbk.)
   1. Death.   2. Immortality (Philosophy)   I. Donnelly, John, 1941–   .
BD444.L377   1994
128'.5—dc20   94–27750
                                                    CIP

Printed in the United States of America

CONTENTS

PREFACE

THIS SECOND EDITION of *Language, Metaphysics, and Death* deletes eight essays from the first edition, retains nine, and adds eleven. The authors of the twenty essays analyze various fundamental themes inherent in a metaphysics of thanatology, involving the meaning and nature of death and dying and the prospects for survival and postmortem existence.

Despite Epicurus' admonition in his *Letter to Menoeceus* that we "become accustomed to the belief that death is nothing to us," most of us are skeptical about his caveat and even a few of us, in his words, "crave for immortality." The volume's contributors are at one with Plato, who reminds us in the *Phaedo* that true philosophers are regularly occupied in the practice of dying. Construed as a descriptive statement about the philosophical life, the Platonic view is no doubt false, yet interpreted as a regulative prescription, it would appear profoundly insightful. In facing foursquarely our own mortality and reflecting on the meaning of death and dying formally analyzed as the irreversible loss of those characteristics that are essentially significant to a living human being, we are simultaneously enabled to ponder the meaning of life and living.

Metaphysics is a difficult subject to study and to teach. And a course that explores the metaphysical issues inherent in thanatology is perhaps even more pedagogically burdensome, not just because of its somewhat rarefied themes and puzzles, but also due to the fact that typical undergraduate students are often reluctant to engage in serious reflection upon death-related issues. Granted: abortion, euthanasia, suicide, and capital punishment pass conventional muster as highly discussable socio-moral issues involving public policy (and staples of undergraduate courses in applied ethics); but as Tolstoy reminds us in his novella *The Death of Ivan Ilych*, a young person can easily grasp the hackneyed example of a paradigmatic deductive argument that Socrates is a human being, human beings are mortal, therefore Socrates is mortal, yet not realize that this now-trite example is not really so vacuous after all. Somewhat repressing the thought of a first-person account of death, a young person often vicariously acknowledges that, of course, Socrates in the abstract was mortal, but I'm not Socrates but a creature quite set apart. Feeling invincible, if not immortal, young people see death as something that happens to others. Unfortunately, death is no stranger to even the young, as but witness the tragedies of AIDS, suicides, accidental deaths, and personal and institutional forms of killing.

In general, human beings are both fascinated and horrified by the topic of death. What Kierkegaard said about dread we might also say of death—namely, that toward it we have a sympathetic antipathy and an antipathetic sympathy. We are somewhat perversely intrigued by the behavior of serial killers, the media reports of random killings in our streets and neighborhoods, and our children's high-tech glee over the video game "Mortal Kombat," etc. Despite the surrealism of it all, we are also repulsed by death, often sheltering the young from witnessing the death of relatives, adamant that legal executions not be televised, and so ever fretful about mortal dangers that we arm ourselves to the hilt, etc.

We often prettify death, euphemistically referring to relatives and friends that have "passed away," "been called home," no doubt as the result of a "negative patient outcome" at a hospital or nursing home. Among college students, sex is hardly a taboo subject, but direct language about the metaphysical aspects of death is surely muted, however ironically bountiful in non-thanatological vernacular contexts, as in "I was dead drunk at the party," "The Professor's lecture was deadly," or "I sat next to a drop-dead redhead in class."

In the years between these two editions of *Language, Metaphysics, and Death*, death has certainly been no stranger to me. I have lost my beloved parents, my two Jesuit uncles John and Philip Donnelly, my uncle Harold Norton, and my aunts Evelyn Norton and Gladys Cove. I learned much from their character and courage in facing their human mortality, and dedicate this volume to their memory. And amid the sadness and bereavement of death, I have been blessed by the births of my beloved son and daughter, Colin and Maria Donnelly, whose integrity and scholastic and athletic skills never cease to amaze and delight me.

I am grateful to those students in my "Death and Dying" course at the University of San Diego who have wrestled with me on various thanatological problems (despite the pernicious Southern California ethos that would vaporize death), and I wish to acknowledge the fine secretarial assistance I have received from Leeanna Cummings, Vivian Holland, and Monica Wagner.

JOHN DONNELLY
University of San Diego

Introduction

John Donnelly

> As the captive animal paces around its cage every day . . .
> so I measure the length of my chain every day by turning
> to the thought of death—for the sake of movement and in
> order to endure living.
>
> Søren Kierkegaard, *Journals and Papers*, No. 720

In Plato's *Phaedo*, Socrates in his prison cell says to Simmias and Cebes: "I am afraid that other people do not realize that the one aim of those who practice philosophy in the proper manner is to practice for dying and death."[1] Taking *memento mori* to heart, the contributors to this volume attempt to do philosophy in the proper manner. This collection of essays analyzes certain basic linguistic and metaphysical issues inherent in a philosophy of death; the themes dealt with are fundamental to a philosophical analysis of thanatology, involving both the meaning of death and the prospects for immortality.

In the opening essay, Thomas Nagel raises the question as to why death is regarded as an evil. His answer is that it involves the loss of life, the deprivation of all human possibilities,[2] so that no matter how inevitable it is, death remains the grand evil, for it removes all possibilities of continued life.

But there are several philosophical objections to the view that death is an evil. First of all, do evils exist such as death which consist solely in the selfless, unexperienced deprivation of good? Moreover, there seems to be a difficulty attached to picking out a subject of misfortune, for if Juan exists, Juan has not yet died, and if Juan has died, Juan no longer exists, so how is death *qua* the grand misfortune ascribed to Juan? Finally, there is an apparent asymmetry between our attitude toward posthumous nonexistence, which is characteristically negative, and our attitude toward prenatal nonexistence, which is usually value neutral.

Nagel attempts to answer these objections and to show that death remains rightly classified as an evil. Though he admits some hesitation about his counter of the last objection (see his discussion of Nozick's spore case), he feels that the first two objections are misplaced, because he believes primarily that it is arbitrary to restrict goods and evils to nonrelational properties ascribable to persons at various times. He argues, instead, that a person's history and possibilities count more than that person's momentary categorical state.

> There are goods and evils which are irreducibly relational; they are features of the relations between a person, with spatial and temporal boundaries of the usual sort, and circumstances which may not coincide with him either in space or in time. . . . If death is an evil it must be accounted for in these terms, and the impossibility of locating it within life should not trouble us.

But Nagel is not entirely satisfied with his dismissal of the various objections. For one, he realizes that "we still have to set some limits on *how* possible a possibility must be for its nonrealization to be a misfortune." For another, he questions whether death can be classified as an evil if it is inevitable, that is, normal to the species, so that human existence is not an open-ended possibility.

James Cameron, whose metaphysical perspective on eschatalogical matters is quite different from Nagel's, tries to convey a sense of death's horror, as he attempts to recapture the nobility found in a genuinely Christian death, especially the faith-based hope in the resurrection of the entire psychophysical person.

For the greater part of the twentieth century, any priest officiating at a Roman Catholic funeral mass wore dark-colored vestments, usually black or purple. If there was musical accompaniment at the service, it was usually the Gregorian chant of *Dies Irae*. Today, by contrast, the priest wears brighter garments, and the music is decidedly upbeat. Mozart, who died composing his *Requiem*, is not to be heard. Aesthetics aside, there is a revealing metaphysical paradigm shift in such a funeral ritual. Death is now presented as a not unpleasant rite of passage—even a joyous event. The impression is conveyed that persons are naturally immortal, and when this impression is combined with the rather popular theological demagoguery of the universal salvation thesis, heaven is viewed as a person's rightfully deserved final destiny. Cameron bemoans the cultural shift that has so prettified death.

So-called "Irish wakes" and the euphemisms of the funeral business notwithstanding, the traditional Judaeo-Christian view of human mortality is insistent that death is both terrible and terrifying. Preferring the Genesis and Ash Wednesday message of "for dust thou art, and unto dust thou shalt return," Cameron disavows metaphysical talk of ethereal bodies, discarnate personalities, or any of the trappings of Platonic dualism. Instead, he opts for the Thomistic doctrine that *an-*

ima mea non est ego, and the belief in and hope for the theistic hypothesis of resurrection without which there can be no immortality of the person. In short, assurances of personal survival of biological death rest on theology, not parapsychology or esoteric spirituality.[3]

Many contemporary philosophers would claim that we have no awareness of death in any privileged metaphysical way—where death is viewed as the complete cessation of experience, an experiential blank—with the result that death as a phenomenal state apparently characterizes absolutely nothing. Does it then still make sense to talk of death? Many philosophers would answer affirmatively, inasmuch as the concept of death serves as a limit that acts as an ordering function to guide our conceptual inquiries. Much as we can speak of the limit of the visual field as unseeable, so too we can speak of death as unexperienceable.[4]

Of course, even to raise a question about the linguistic appropriateness of death-talk would strike an existentialist as but another example of linguistic philosophy's opacity. But, Paul Edwards suggests, there are a considerable number of muddles in continental writings on death. For example, death is often compared with deep sleep, an identification Edwards finds as ludicrous as the suggestion that an empty soda bottle is saturated with ethereal liquid. Existentialists, in response, claim that they are approaching the study of death on an ontological level. That is, they are asking: What is death like to the dead? Accordingly, Edwards turns to a conceptual analysis of some ontological accounts of death, specifically those of Paul Tillich, José Ferrater Mora, and John Macquarrie.

Edwards engages in the exercise of deflationary critique. He tries to show that the existentialist ontological quest into the nature of death, far from producing profound insights, actually yields either cognitively meaningless claims, or vacuous ones, or just plain false discoveries.

The ontological view of death regards it as a state that is either unknowable (Tillich) or partially knowable (Mora and Macquarrie). But such a quest for a phenomenological insight into death is absurd, Edwards believes, for these existentialists are really asking "What kind of an experience does a person have who no longer has any experiences?"! We might note here that ontological, thanatological inquiries are distinct from the more metaphysical questions "Is there life after death?" or "Why does death occur?" Edwards writes:

> while feeling the coolness of the night, reaching the last stop of a journey, arriving in a strange country from which one will never return, sleep, and rest, sustaining losses . . . , undergoing pain and torture, feeling isolated and all alone and even finding oneself surrounded by impene-

trable darkness are states or experiences of living human beings, death is not a state.

Edwards contends that it is philosophically worthwhile to raise various *psychological* questions about death (e.g., "How should I prepare myself for death?" or "How can I relieve my suffering over my father's demise?") but not worthwhile (and indeed nonsensical) to continue to seek some phenomenological insight into what death is like from the inside. Edwards points out other alleged muddles in existentialist writings on thanatology, such as the facile equation of death with dying, and constructively points out how many existential claims interpreted as statements properly about dying, *and not death*, are meaningful and possibly true (e.g., a person could find himself or herself in dying but not in death). Edwards also suggests that the doctrine of the privacy of death (that no one can understand any other person's death or dying but his or her own) is either trivial or, if significant, false.[5]

In his essay Michael Slote criticizes various strategies that seek to prevent a person from authentically contemplating his or her impending mortality. For instance, some philosophers stoically claim no fear of death, because living world-historically they expect to overcome death by attaining immortality through their works. Slote sees this stoic dodge as a paradigm of self-deception, for such philosophers reveal "an unconscious defense mechanism of the ego that protects [them] from conscious fear about death by repressing that fear and counterbalancing it in such a way that it for the most part remains unconscious." Slote also finds the view self-defeating, inasmuch as it somewhat inconsistently posits the person as both living and not-living.

Slote here is doing existential psychoanalysis. He wishes to take seriously the existentialist's claim that the quality of a human's life is intimately associated with his or her attitudes on his or her eventual mortality. To be sure, by getting involved in what Kierkegaard calls "busyness," or becoming absorbed in what Heidegger terms the "they" (i.e., chatter, gossip, idle talk), or even simulating a Sartrean form of "bad faith," we may allay somewhat our own fear of dying. But such dodges or diversions in which we objectify ourselves as unfree things serve only to mask our real anxiety and add confirmatory weight to the view that anxiety concerning death is a fundamental characteristic of the human condition. People who want part of their life over with, and who never are fully aware of why this is so, seem to have an unconscious desire to be dead. Slote writes: "The view that it is irrational, and not courageous, to fear death, because death is no evil, may well be motivated, in many of those who propound it, by the fear of death itself, a fear that they are consequently able to repress, but not to get rid of." Indeed such self-trickery, assuming that it is true that the quality of a person's life is causally connected with his or her attitudes on his or her own death, might well explain the psychic ills of our or any age.

Some philosophers want to claim that death is *nothing* to a reasonable person. But what is the sense of "nothing"? *Nothing* may mean that which is insignificant, of no value or importance to a reasonable person, as in the sentence "nothing you say interests me." Or *nothing* may denote a nonexistent state of affairs, as in the locution "there is nothing in the room." The Epicurean claim may be true (given its metaphysical presuppositions) in the latter sense, but is surely false in the former usage.

Unlike Epicurus, who wrote in his *Letter to Menoeceus* that "there is nothing terrible in life for the man who has truly comprehended that there is nothing terrible in not living,"[6] most philosophers prudently recognize that life contains its trials and tragedies, so that even if thanatophobia could be eradicated, few if any persons could sustain a life of only catastematic and kinetic pleasures. But, like Epicurus, some philosophers do seem to think that the fear of that which is not bad for one is groundless. But isn't such a belief false? For example, theists justifiably fear the will of God, yet it is not evil; similarly, most people understandably fear an upcoming operation that is designed to cure or alleviate their medical condition.

Is it not rational, then, to fear death because of its emotionally compelling survival value? Because of that fear, we take appropriate precautions, such as monitoring our health, buying insurance policies, and so on. To fly in the face of what is often constructive anxiety over death seems to demonstrate a lack of a robust sense of reality. We might agree that the matter of our first-person attitudes toward death often embroils us in an epistemological quagmire. A hard, transcendental posture toward our mortality seems to reveal that it is both rational and irrational to fear it. The fear of death is often quite functional. Fear in itself may not be desirable or even always rational or cognitive, but as a motivational attitude it often safeguards us against harm. We need to be reminded that it is often difficult to epistemically demarcate a fear of death from a fear of serious but not terminal illness.

Our fear of death may involve an attitude toward the facticity of human mortality, and not toward a private, experiential reality. But death remains, in Mary Mothersill's words, the ultimate "deadline for all my assignments." I may not finish my assignments, but that failure to complete will have its effects and consequences, its harms and benefits, so that even thinking clearly about death does not normally allay our fear of it.

Amélie Rorty, like Slote, also addresses our human fears about and anxieties over death. On the supposition that death marks the irreversible annihilation of our personhood, it would seem not rational to fear being dead, since it has no "psycho-ontological status." Yet, while we are alive, we do fear death's consequences. There is a valuable, functional aspect to our fearing death, for death *qua* limit enables us to form our lifeplans and often discloses to us what we take to be essential to our premortem lives. We also fear death as the permanent deprivation of life's goods, and the threat that death poses to the meaningfulness of our lives. Nonetheless, the fear of death can be functional even if it is not rational, much as pain may be an undesirable yet useful aversion-mechanism that alerts us to harm. Whether fear be acquired or innate, it can often be valuable for its "safeguarding effects." Rorty claims:

> If fear were a relatively muted pastel sort of emotion that, like nostalgia, stayed in the background of our attention, it would not be efficacious as a reaction to danger. It is precisely because fear is unpleasant, because it is insistent and disturbing, and because it is often pre-rational in its occurrence and in its effects, that it helps move us out of harm's way.

To be sure, fear is so reactive that it often does not involve any fine-tuned discrimination of the objects that prompt it. However, a more purely cognitive recognition of danger would lack the resultant motivational assent provided by the fear of death. Ultimately, Rorty avers, we are left with an attitudinal dilemma: namely, that fear of death *qua* metaphysical anxiety over nonbeing is irrational, and yet fearing death is often functional and basic to our constitution as embodied creatures.

Much like Paul Edwards, Stephen Rosenbaum draws a distinction between the concepts of *dying, death,* and *being dead.* Only the latter notion is part of a person's history but not of her life.

Rosenbaum reconstructs and defends Epicurus' famed argument that death is not to be feared since it is "the privation of all sentience." That Epicurean thesis—often known as the existence-requirement thesis—maintains that in order for a state of affairs to be bad for someone that person must exist at the time to experience it. In short, Rosenbaum contends that a state of affairs *s* is bad for Jasmine only if Jasmine can experience *s* at some time *t*. But Jasmine can experience *s* at *t* only if *s* begins before Jasmine's death. And Jasmine's being dead is not an *s* that begins before Jasmine's death. So Jasmine's being dead cannot be experienced by Jasmine. Therefore, Jasmine's being dead is not bad for Jasmine. Of course, the Epicurean argument does not rule out, for example, that Jasmine's dying or even her death-moment is an evil for her, or an evil for other people (now including her even being dead).

Rosenbaum comments on the open-textured nature of the word "experience." A state of affairs can causally affect a person only if it begins before that person's death. And in response to the claim of Nagel et al. that persons can be harmed unaware (the so-called deprivation theory which holds that death is an evil or misfortune even if it is an experiential void because it deprives a person of life's goods), Rosenbaum attempts to show how a person can be harmed without consciously experiencing something, provided that person could at some time experience it. But Rosenbaum disallows that a person can be harmed unaware where there is no possibility that that person could ever experience it. Unlike a (living) person losing his wallet, death cannot be a loss to a person if that person no longer exists.

Rosenbaum also addresses Lucretius' symmetry argument about our somewhat perplexing attitudes toward our prenatal nonexistence and our posthumous nonexistence. He defends Lucretius against Nagel, contending that being dead is no worse than not yet having been born. Moreover, Rosenbaum argues against Harry Silverstein's novel thesis that treats with parity spatially distant events and temporally distant events, so that allegedly a person can experience posthumous events that happen to him or her because such events exist atemporally. Rosenbaum insinuates there is a confusion in Silverstein's account between the *existence* of an event and the *occurrence* of an event, so that it has not been shown how a person can experience an event that does not *occur* before his or her death.

Fred Feldman enters the fray postulating a possible-worlds ontology and a basic axiological assumption of hedonism in which the value of a possible world for a person is determined by summing up the totals of pleasures and pains. He seeks to show how, even on an Epicurean axiology, death could be an evil. The overall welfare value of a state of affairs for someone is the product of subtracting the value for that person of the nearest world where, say, death does not occur from the value for that same person of the nearest world where death does occur. Feldman favors a form of the deprivation thesis in which death is said to be an evil where the welfare of the individual is lower in the nearest possible world where it occurs than in the nearest possible world where it does not occur. On Feldman's view, something is bad for a person whether it occurs in life or prenatally or posthumously.

Pace Rosenbaum, Feldman argues that it may be true that nothing intrinsically bad can happen to a person when she does not exist, but something that is bad overall for a person can happen even when that person does not exist, provided her welfare level at the nearest world where the evil occurs is lower than her welfare level at the nearest world where it does not occur. Feldman also addresses the Lucretian symmetry thesis, especially the problem of late birth *vs.* premature death. He concludes, anti-Lucretius, that there can be an asymmetry here, so that early death can be worse than late birth.

Recently, there have been several philosophers (Nagel and Feldman are but two of them) who want to maintain that (1) death marks the irreversible annihilation of human life such that there is no form of postmortem survival of a discarnate personality or a resurrected psychophysical person, etc., and yet simultaneously uphold the pretheoretic intuition that (2) the deceased can be harmed or benefited. In my paper, I try to argue that (1) and (2) are a pair of inconsistent beliefs such that those philosophers must either abandon their metaphysical materialistic framework or dismiss the pretheoretic intuition.

Since the debate is usually focused on the negative aspects of death—i.e., the harms, misfortunes, and wrongs that allegedly accrue to the deceased—first I try to show that those contemporary philosophers who hold both (1) and (2) are prone to several errors, often conflating a deceased person's reputation (which can fluctuate and be tarnished) with the posthumous thwarting of that person's interests and desires. The result is that interests and desires have become so reified, so metaphysically displaced from the wants-based formerly sentient persons whose interests or desires they were, that the subject of harm becomes those transcendent, free-floating interests or desires, or the bare logical skeleton of the antemortem person after death.

Second, I try to offer some appealing counterexamples to the otherwise plausible claim that if the living can suffer harm unaware, then so too can the dead. Third, I develop the notion of anticipatory harms or misfortunes that begin to occur in part before a person's death—and are harmful in life—but do not become fully actualized until after that person's death. Fourth, I respond to Barbara Levenbook's trenchant claim that to reject the pretheoretic intuition is to lose the ability to explain the harm of any murder or instantaneous killing. Finally, I suggest that materialists have to face the hard metaphysical data that the moral deference for the dead they so cherish by upholding the pretheoretic intuition is largely a matter of law and custom—a useful fiction, no doubt—but is not philosophically sustainable. By analogy, much as law and custom have eroded respect for the fetus *qua* potential person, so the cultural pendulum now swings toward the deceased *qua* former person.

To be sure, most people have a *prima facie* bias for life. Without it, none of the *praemia vitae* could be pursued or bestowed. Indeed most people like living so much that they yearn for immortality, preferring it to enormous amounts even of premortem wealth, fame, or po.ver. Miguel de Unamuno captures well this desire to be immortal when he writes: "I do not want to die . . . I want to live for ever and ever and ever . . . and therefore the problem of the duration of my soul . . . tortures me."[7]

Bernard Williams begs to disagree. Death is sometimes an evil, but not always. *Pace* Price, Donnelly, Davis, and Clarke (all of whom defend versions of personal postmortem existence), Williams argues that any survival hypothesis that seeks to retain personal identity and offer fulfillment of persons' categorical desires in light of their premortem character is meaningless: "From facts about human desire and happiness and what a human life is, it follows both that immortality would be, where conceivable at all, intolerable, and that (other things being equal) death is reasonably regarded as an evil." One is reminded here of Achilles' advice to Odysseus that it is better to be a poor laborer on earth than king among the dead. Williams bases his view on a consideration of the (fictitious) case of Elina Makropulos who, having taken an elixir, is now 342, having been 42 for 300 years. Despite the panacea, she finds her endless life a bore (her categorical desires have ceased) and suicide the only tolerable way out. Williams contends that it is not just a contingent fact about a person that her categorical desires are finite in number.

Williams' article would provide a caveat to the bio-technical use of cryonic storage or the development of a cyborg person as poignantly as does the legendary case of Tithonus, who according to Greek myth was granted immortality by Aurora, but who soon longed for death, since he was not also given eternal youthfulness. Williams would warn even every youthful neo-Tithonian that boredom may be a greater evil than death, and that one may be *felix opportunitate mortis*.

The next three essays explore the metaphysical issue of whether there are any nonphysical characteristics or incorporeal substrata behind the human person as a biological entity. Richard Taylor, in a delightfully sardonic essay "De Anima," narrates the fable of Walter's amoebiary in which are described the various futile attempts of Walter, the keeper of the amoebiary, to determine the lineage of his amoebae so that he might more effectively influence the breeding of future amoebae.

As is well known, amoebae reproduce by splitting in two. Naturally, the inevitable metaphysical question arises, who is the parent and who are the offspring? Attempts to formulate an answer to this query by various criteria of markings, size, behavioral traits, etc., all seem to fail. The result is that Walter soon realizes that his problem was a pseudo-problem, for he had overlooked the essential metaphysical aspects of the problem. What he had failed to realize and now does realize is that amoebae lack souls and souls are what uniquely characterize entities as distinct individuals. Of course, Taylor is being facetious here, his point being that it is an erroneous metaphysical supposition to think that (by analogy) souls uniquely characterize us as separate and distinct human beings.

In contrast to Taylor's negative views on the existence of souls (minds, transcendental selves), Roderick Chisholm in his essay tries to show how philosophers have been mistaken in reaching such negative views vis-à-vis the apprehension of the self (or soul). Hume's classic bundle-theory, of course, claimed that the self is not observable, and that there is no such mental substance as a soul or self. Chisholm points out that Hume's view is inconsistent with his stated findings: namely, "I never can catch *myself* at any time without a perception, and never can observe anything but the perception." Moreover, to restate the theory to avoid the self-defeating findings of Hume to read "Nothing but perceptions are found" (by whom?) is too rash empirically. Chisholm writes:

> The fact that a man finds a certain proposition p to be true does not warrant a subjectless report to the effect that p is true . . . But the fact that he fails to find a certain proposition q to be true does not similarly warrant any subjectless report about q. For one's failure to find that q is true entails nothing about the truth of q. The fact that a man fails to find that q is true entitles him to say only that *he*, at least, does not find that q is true. And this would not be a subjectless report.

Chisholm goes on to suggest that the self or soul is transparent. To know that I perceive myself to be thinking is not necessarily to realize that I perceive a proper part of myself. For instance, in the locution "I feel depressed" (and *not* "I have a depressed feeling"), "being depressed" is not a predicate of the feeling but rather "feeling depressed" is a predicate of the man. In short, Chisholm argues that in being aware of ourselves as experiencing, we are *ipso facto* aware of the self or person as being affected in a certain way: ". . . the items within the bundle are nothing but states of the person . . . what ties these items together is the fact that that same self or person apprehends them all."

John Hick in "Biology and the Soul" takes up the religious (more specifically Christian) view of the human person which holds that God creates an individual soul for each person either at conception or at birth or at some time-slice during the gestation process. Such a view suggests that there are certain characteristics of the soul which are not inherited or explained solely in terms of various biological factors.

What qualities does the soul possess? Is the soul merely an unknown metaphysical substratum? What does it mean to speak of the soul as the animating principle of the body? If (as Taylor seems to suggest) the body can be construed as the principle of individualization, what need have we for the soul? In short, Hick asks, is there a content and function for the soul? Are there any innate personal characteristics of the soul not traceable to heredity or environment but only to divine infusion?

To claim that there is a content and function for the soul as traditional conceptions allow, Hick claims, is to speak of the soul as a cluster of psychic factors, the repository of all basic dispositional characteristics of a moral and spiritual sort. Hick rejects such a metaphysical view, arguing that the soul cannot be literally viewed as a metaphysical entity, divinely infused by God. Rather, Hick claims, soul-talk is basically metaphorical. We speak of "saving our souls" or "selling our souls," but here "soul" serves as an indicator of value. Hence, soul-talk is evaluative, not descriptive! "To speak of man as a soul is, then, to speak mythologically, but in a way which is bound up with important practical attitudes and practices. The myth of the soul expresses a faith in the intrinsic value of the human individual as an end in himself."

In 1975, Raymond Moody, a philosopher and psychiatrist, wrote a best-selling book, *Life After Life*, recounting alleged tales of near-death experiences. That book has spawned a veritable industry of books and articles on the topic. Today, many people are claiming to be resuscitated after having been thought or adjudged clinically dead (i.e., having no visual signs of respiration, low blood pressure, dilation of pupils, apnea, coma-like unreceptivity to external stimuli, etc.) only to report after successful resuscitation that they had conscious experiences and intimations of immortality when supposedly dead.

In short, many people are now claiming that there is empirical support for the survival of the disembodied mind, so that it is factually ascertainable that death is but an event in life. Included among the principle components of these near-death experiences are: out-of-body experiences in which there are visual and auditory sensations but typically no gustatory, olfactory, or tactile sensations; feelings of peace and tranquillity seemingly confirming the Socratic view that death is a liberating experience; telepathic meeting with and review under a "Being of Light" which the religious near-death percipients interpret as God; meeting with other "deceased" spirits or "astral bodies"; rejection of the reward/punishment model of salvation traditionally associated with Christianity and Islam; and ability to offer independent corroboration of the alleged veridicality of these experiences apart from their own personal testimony on behalf of the experience itself.

Skeptics have been quick to criticize this unusual phenomenon. Indeed, even many believers in an afterlife concede that there must have been some residual biological activity occurring on the cellular level. Included among the standard criticisms of near-death experiences are: the violation of the medical doctrine of cerebral anoxia; medical misdiagnosis; the traumatic recalling of the birthing process; the release of endorphins or brain chemicals that sedate a person in the time of great crisis, and so forth.

Not surprisingly, there also has been a logical spin-off of near-death experiences into the new-age fad of spiritual channeling, in which certain individuals such as J. Z. Knight (a woman claims to become inhabited by Ramtha, a thirty-five-thousand-year-old warrior) or Jo Ann Karl (who has two alleged body inhabitants, one of whom claims to have been married to St. Peter) claim to be able to will the removal of their own discarnate personalities from their bodies, and to have their bodies occupied and possessed by other disembodied minds who pronounce such tautologies (and a final blasphemy) as "All that is, is;" "The highest recognition that you can make is that I am what I am;" "Your truth is your truth;" and "You are God."

Amid all this parapsychological flotsam and jetsam, the philosophical community was surprised when in 1988 A. J. Ayer of all people (the former logical positivist and author of *Language, Truth, and Logic*) reported having had a near-death experience of sorts. He was suffering from pneumonia, and after he had choked on some salmon, his heart had stopped beating for four minutes. Upon recovery, he reported having seen a bright and painful red light, which he interpreted as the nondivine governor of the universe, whose two ministers in charge of space and possibly those in charge of time were inept. Upon recovery, and after philosophical reflection, Ayer remained an atheist, but less "inflexible" in his attitude toward the possibility of some form of postmortem survival.

Invoking the principle of cerebral anoxia, Ayer believes his heart stopped but his brain received sufficient oxidation, allowing the prolongation of the series of his conscious experiences. He is quite certain that none of this involves any Cartesian spiritual substance surviving biological death, and he rejects the Christian eschatology of the resurrection favored by Donnelly and Davis. Ayer holds out the possibility for a secular version of metempsychosis or rebirth, which is more Buddhist than Hindu, since there is, he believes, no underlying soul or atman. In short, there could be a reincarnation in *this* world, with memory a necessary condition for survival ("Forgetfulness in this context is literally death") and the need for a physical body to sustain those memories. But, like Bernard Williams, Ayer hopes there is no continuation of his mental episodes after his biological death.

Like Ayer, Kai Nielsen is also an atheist, and perhaps even more skeptical about the prospects for immortality. In his essay, Nielsen argues that belief in an afterlife is either incoherent or so blatantly false (however logically possible, such belief is not physically or epistemically possible) that it should be cognitively dismissed. Yet, surprisingly, he seems to think that if there were a theistic God, that God could gather up the scattered atoms and dust of a deceased individual and recreate that now reconstituted person in a postmortem world. Nonetheless, despite his begrudging wink to theistic resurrectionists such as Donnelly and Davis, Nielsen affords no nod to those philosophers (such as Price, and perhaps Clarke) who defend the survival of the person as some sort of disembodied mind or incorporeal entity or mental remnant; and he also critiques the Chisholm-like view that we have some direct awareness of our self-identity as discarnate minds.

Commenting on the woeful state of the commonweal and the excessive amounts of poverty, malnutrition, starvation, and other forms of evil and injustice in our world, Nielsen minimally tolerates some dim hope for a person to embrace a form of Irenaean universalism. However, he wonders if it can be reasonable to hope or wish for such postmortem survival, given its intellectually suspect nature. Yet Nielsen's evidentialism will not grant any right to so hope or wish if it leads to a neglect of the pressing moral, social, and political struggles of the day, for that would result in a "quietism in the face of evil." However, if a person recognizes the tragic dimension of the human situation and resolutely attempts to transform it, consistent with his or her abilities, and simultaneously clings to some religious hope or wish for an ultimate eschatalogical deliverance, then Nielsen seems to think such a posture is not (epistemically) wrong.

If Nielsen is prepared to tolerate some socialist-minded individual devoutedly wishing for immortality, despite his own considerable conceptual and factual reservations on the matter, Grace Jantzen, by contrast, argues in her essay that, for Christians at least, there is no requirement for a doctrine of postmortem life. She believes that persons can lead fulfilling and meaningful ethico-religious lives without any immortality.

Although she does not wish to rule out the possibility of some type of afterlife, Jantzen contends that the realistic boundaries set by biological death or actuarial lifespans can give our various premortem projects some direction and confer a significance on our choices to attempt to fulfill our various mundane tasks. Jantzen is critical of the Kantian view of immortality as a postulate of practical reasoning, claiming it demeans the notion of virtuous living as intrinsically worth-while and renders moral activity a means to the end of happiness. Of course, some proponents of immortality would point out that people often strive to be morally fulfilled, but fail to attain such a satisfactory state in a world where vice is often triumphant, and accordingly argue for the necessity of a postmortem life where the scales of justice will be balanced. Any resultant happiness in the afterlife is not so much a reward as a fulfillment of our moral struggles and aspirations. In such a Dostoyevskean longing for the lamb to rest with the lion, the upshot is "not a desire for happiness in any hedonistic sense, but a desire to see the point, the fruition of all one's efforts." But, again, Jantzen views such dénouement as debasing virtue as its own reward.

Jantzen also remains skeptical about John Hick's universal salvation thesis, especially in light of the inherent tension between the exercise of human freedom and the activity of divine persuasion. She reminds us that further extension of life (in a postmortem world) will not neces-sarily result in moral growth; and asks if God allows many valuable nonhuman things to perish, why should he not allow human beings to pass out of existence upon biological death? Moreover, we should not be so quick to equate eternal life with everlasting life. The former could pertain (in somewhat neo-Wittgensteinian fashion) to this world, so that ethico-religious activities could be intrinsically worthwhile and not be measured by their duration alone.

The final five essays focus on the coherency and rationality of vari-ous forms of postmortem life, specifically the notion of survival of the disembodied mind (Price), the theistic hypothesis of psychophysical resurrection (Donnelly and Davis), and some metaphysical musings on reincarnation (Martin) and mysticism (Clarke).

What if death is not the end of life but rather an event in life? Is it possible to clarify or outline the possible contents of such a postmor-tem mode of existence? H. H. Price is concerned with just this sort of questions, that is, with the issue of the meaningfulness of the survival hypothesis (in which a person is regarded as a disembodied mind), rather than the factual support for such a theory.

Given his Cartesian sympathies, Price views the next world as a world of desire (cf. the Hindu notion of Kama Loka), that is, a world of mental images which are *imagy* and not imaginary. Price's meta-physical topography of the next world is one in which *imaging* replaces sense-perception (providing us with objects about which we could have thoughts, emotions, and so forth), and he posits the epistemic possibil-ity that memories, desires, images, etc. could exist upon the dissolu-tion of our bodily parts: ". . . the 'stuff' or 'material' of such a world would come in the end from one's memories, and the 'form' of it from one's desires. To use another analogy, memory would provide the pigments, and desire would paint the picture." Such a next world, Price contends, need not prove a solipsistic nightmare for an individual discarnate personality, because the next world would presumably have causal laws of a psychological sort (probably Freudian), and could be spoken of as spatial and public, via telepathic apparitions.

With regard to the location-difficulty, Price claims that the next world could provide its own *where*. That is, mental images are in a space of their own, having spatial relations to one another, but not to our own physical space. Hence, passage to the next world is not a movement in space so much as a change of consciousness for a discarnate personality, which, unlike the relation of waking consciousness to dreaming, is irreversible. Price also believes that there could be many next worlds, each populated with like-minded personalities. Indeed, as (a) wish fulfillment world(s), it seems fair to think that our antemortem repressed desires would come to fruition so that we could have the philosophical correlates of heaven and hell. In short, the next world a person *qua* disembodied mind would find oneself in would be the outgrowth of his or her premortem moral character presented in the form of self-ideating, dream-like images.

The reader may be impressed with the creative and vivid depiction of Price's outline of a next world, but doubtless still be left wondering how thoughts, intentions, and sensations can be ontologically rooted to that which has no physical counterpart. How, for instance, can there be sight without an optic nerve? How can there be rational capabilities without an occipital cortex? Is spatio-temporal bodily continuity not a necessary condition of personal identity? If a person is an indissoluble psychophysical unity, then how can I be identical to Price's discarnate personality?

Unlike Price (and his metaphysical ruminations about imagy, incorporeal, ideoplastic next worlds), I try to defend a resurrection model of (in my case, Christian) eschatology, disavowing any extreme dualistic theory that postulates only the survival of a disembodied mind. With Aquinas I would concur that *anima mea non est ego*, so that persons are properly regarded as psychophysical entities. On such a view, any hope for personal postmortem survival rests on the existence of a theistic God capable of performing violation miracles.

The metaphysical contours of the heavenly resurrection world would be such that there is no physical or natural evil either in the world environment itself or in the glorified bodies of its inhabitants. But, the traditional Christian resort to metaphysical libertarianism and personal autonomy to vindicate God from the classic problem of evil (see my remarks on George Wall) needs to be consistently applied to the afterlife, as well. I am speculating that we continue to have free wills even in heaven, where we are not coerced to be good or divinely programed to be virtuous. As a result, it follows that a person could be evicted from heaven. I suggest that a system of divine intentionalism reigns in heaven. That is, an omniscient God knows our innermost thoughts, beliefs, and intentions; and should a person have *perduring* immoral sentiments—albeit no other person could be physically harmed (or victimized) by such a mind-set—that person might be evicted, being no longer fit for the community of saints.

In outlining such a resurrection model of personal survival, I also attempt to respond to some objections leveled against such an eschatology. Taking some liberties with Williams' paper on the tedium of immortality, but respecting the deep thrust of his philosophical critique, I try to show that a heavenly resurrection would need not prove boring and/or unpleasant, at least to genuine lovers of God. I also try to answer the Marxist challenge that avers that reflecting about, believing in, or hoping for survival is immoral inasmuch as it has the direct or indirect effect of diminishing the importance of premortem moral, social, and political reformation, offering instead an illusory eschatological placebo that fosters an indifference to the ills of this world.

I also take issue with the otherwise friendly eschatological views of Richard Swinburne, objecting to his reading of Matthew's account of the parable of the vineyard, which he reads as supporting his contention that action is less important than character, that faith supersedes works. By so favoring a morality of virtue over an ethics of obligation, Swinburne seems to play into the Marxist, Nielsen-type critique, which is avoided on my view where an ethics of virtue is a necessary complement to an ethics of obligation.

Stephen Davis, like Donnelly, also philosophically defends a resurrection model of personal survival. But unlike Donnelly, who favors the process of the theistic God resurrecting some people upon their individual biological deaths, Davis suggests people do not become fully reconstituted until the general resurrection at the second coming. Accordingly, he tries to unpack the concept of the interim state of temporary disembodiment, that somewhat limbic, interregnum state of incorporeality after biological death in which individual souls await the general resurrection when they will become glorified psychophysical entities.

Davis tries to show how during that interim period (which for Price is a permanent state; for Nielsen, incoherent; and for Williams, all too tedious), the soul, however attenuated and incomplete, can still retain its personal identity, along with its inherent beliefs, thoughts, wishes, memories, and so forth. In line with his patristic perspective, Davis contends that God will ultimately reconstitute, resurrect, and glorify our numerically identical bodies, in the process reassembling our very dispersed matter and reuniting those core atoms and particles with our individual souls. The result is a genuine re-creation of the person, and not a mere cloning or replication of a qualitatively similar individual.

Davis attempts to answer the puzzling question, namely, how can I be in a temporary disembodied state where the soul is the presumed guarantor of personal identity, yet not be me in the parousia if my then animated body does not consist of numerically exact physical constituents from my premortem body? He also defends his position against a host of contemporary philosophical objections that suggest insurmountable verificationist problems for the view that personal identity is based on the soul; against those who question the memory criterion of personal identity given the seemingly intractable (and often circular) problems of genuine *vs.* apparent memories; and against those philosophers who suggest that the possibility of divine postmortem multiple replication rules out any unique numerical resurrection of an individual.

From the *Bhagavad Gita* to today's new-agers, many people maintain that persons are essentially spiritual entities who can assume new bodies, much as persons change their clothes, so that most births are rebirths. These defenders of reincarnation try to support their views with an appeal to facts, such as hypnotic former-life regressions or memories of past incarnations, coupled with independent corroboration of these puzzling discoveries. Critics charge that the appealed-to "facts" are more cultural artifacts than significant empirical findings, and suggest the reincarnationists are forced to resort to ad hoc assumptions to rebut human population statistics or evolutionary discoveries, etc.

Into the breach steps Raymond Martin as a minimalist reincarnationist, who is impressed by the philosophical ramifications of analytic philosophy's discussion of fission cases (e.g., brain-bisection, esoteric branching or splitting puzzles) in which individuals are said to divide into two or more qualitatively similar individuals. As a result, Martin defends the bold claim that meaningful personal survival does not require strict numerical personal identity, so that there is no need to search for individually necessary and jointly sufficient conditions under which personal identity over time is preserved.

Martin admits to a circumspect respect for the work of the contemporary psychiatrist Ian Stevenson who has extensively studied reincarnation claims made by young children (normally aged two to eight) who claim to recall previous lives. He focuses on the case of Jasbir, a three-and-a-half-year-old child in India, who claimed to be Sobha Ram who died at age twenty-two (after Jasbir's own birth!). Martin seems to think that Stevenson has satisfactorily answered alternate physicalistic explanations of such puzzling cases as Jasbir's, especially skeptical rejoinders involving fraud, cryptomnesia, paramnesia, and genetic memory. He thinks the skeptics may have a point with their rival hypotheses of extrasensory perception, but Martin suggests, interestingly, that it really does not matter which account is true here. That is, what really matters in disputed questions about survival is what we *value* about these alleged transformations: "disputes over criteria of personal identity are often simply disguised disputes over what matters in survival."

Martin reminds us that our linguistic conventions applied to puzzling identity-cases are not necessary ontological truths. Musing on Sydney Shoemaker's case of a highly technologically developed but polluted society that has invented periodic body replacements with qualitatively identical bodies (so that getting a body replacement is like our periodic teeth-cleaning at the dentist's), Martin recommends that we tolerate the lightness of being, so that questions about "rebirth" are not just metaphysical in nature but also evaluative, and as such, may differ among individuals with varied egocentric interests in survival.

Lastly, John Clarke in his essay contends that although survival hypotheses offer promissory notes of a person's transformation to a better mode of existence, most accounts of immortality offer only partial or incomplete continuation of our antemortem mode of life. Hence the paradox: either we survive in a resurrection world in embodied form (possibly having astral bodies), but a world that is replete with premortem difficulties; or we survive in sparse, disembodied form with the subsequent dissolution of our personal agency.

> In neither case is the problem for which survival has been offered as a solution—the problem of providing a meaningful and happy apotheosis to a supposedly miserable and senseless existence—solved. The first solution merely restates, in a large measure, the problem; the second dissolves, in varying degrees, the being for whom it is supposedly a solution. Is there any *tertium quid*? Can we offer an account of survival which takes care of both prerequisites, which allows for *persons*, not shadows or memories, to survive, and which makes such survival worthwhile?

Clarke outlines (religious and nonreligious) mystical schemata to allow for both personal survival and a rational apotheosis. Such a mystical experience involves the removal of a sense of alienation from our environment, the development of a sense of total harmony and tranquillity, loss of multiplicity in space and time, and loss of desires and regrets. But isn't this detailed, tranquil, mystical state purchased at the cost of the lessening or loss of the self? However similar the alleged mystical experience, and despite the diversity of interpretation (whether in nature mystics like Tennyson, or nondiscursive Buddhist contemplatives, or religious mystics like Plotinus), isn't this *paradisio* without me?

In response, Clarke claims that such mystical, introvertive experiences (whether of God, Brahmin, Nirvana, etc.) need not involve any negation of self (albeit in having such experiences one is detaching oneself from ordinary states of consciousness, i.e., sensations, thoughts, images, etc.). He seems to think that it is possible to attain a sense of the oneness of all things, while simultaneously retaining personal identity.

I hope this introductory essay will assist undergraduates in identifying the various themes and issues under consideration, so that they might begin the necessary work of critical reflection on the contributors' essays. More seasoned scholars can pass, no doubt, right on to the ensuing twenty essays. Hopefully, all who personally and critically engage themselves with the various essays will come away with a greater appreciation and understanding of some basic philosophical issues inherent in the metaphysics of thanatology.

Is death an evil? Is it rational to fear death? Can a deceased person be harmed or benefited? Can a person survive biological death? Can a meaningful and coherent eschatology be philosophically formulated? Ideally, these and assorted questions should lead to a greater engagement with and contemplation of our impending mortality and (possibly) some coherent philosophical speculation on eschatological issues that suggest that death's sting, however grave, may not be ultimately victorious.

NOTES

1. (Indianapolis: Hackett, 1977), p. 12.

2. The reader might note that Edwards, Slote, Rorty, Rosenbaum, Feldman, Williams, Taylor, Ayer, and Nielsen—along with Nagel—all maintain that death marks the irreversible end of human life so that there is no form of personal postmortem survival.

3. Cf. Peter Geach, *God and the Soul* (London: Routledge & Kegan Paul, 1969), pp. 17–29.

4. Cf. James Van Evra, "On Death as a Limit," *Analysis*, 31 (1971), 170–76.

5. Elsewhere, Edwards draws some important distinctions between the terms "deadness," the "death-moment," "death-producing events," and "dy-

ing." *Deadness* involves the total, irreversible annihilation of all life-processes (perhaps Heidegger's "measureless impossibility of existence") which takes place at a certain time on a certain date—the *death-moment*. *Death-producing events* are those states of affairs which causally bring about a person's *deadness*, the beginning and end of which is the phase of life called *dying*. Existentialists who speak of death as the "crown and culmination of human life" are, given Edwards' lexicon, not speaking intelligibly if speaking of *deadness* or the *death-moment*, although their claims are intelligible (albeit usually false) if referring to a person's *dying* or *death-producing events*. See Edwards' "Heidegger and Death as 'Possibility,'" 84 *Mind*, (1975), 562.

6. In *Life and Death: A Reader in Moral Problems*, ed. Louis P. Pojman (Boston: Jones & Bartlett, 1993), p. 150.

7. *The Tragic Sense of Life* (London: Fontana, 1921), p. 60.

1

Death

Thomas Nagel
New York University

The syllogism he had learnt from Kiesewetter's logic: "Caius
is a man, men are mortal, therefore Caius is mortal," had
always seemed to him correct as applied to Caius, but certainly not as applied to himself . . . What did Caius know
of the smell of that striped leather ball Vanya had been so
fond of?

TOLSTOY, *The Death of Ivan Ilyich*

IF, AS MANY PEOPLE BELIEVE, death is the unequivocal and permanent
end of our existence, the question arises whether it is a bad thing to
die. There is conspicuous disagreement about the matter: some people
think death is dreadful; others have no objection to death *per se*,
though they hope their own will be neither premature nor painful.
Those in the former category tend to think that those in the latter
are blind to the obvious, while the latter suppose the former to be prey
to some sort of confusion. On the one hand it can be said that life is
all one has, and the loss of it is the greatest loss one can sustain. On
the other hand it may be objected that death deprives this supposed
loss of its subject, and that if one realizes that death is not an unimaginable condition of the persisting person, but a mere blank, one will see
that it can have no value whatever, positive or negative.

Since I want to leave aside the question whether we are, or might
be, immortal in some form, I shall simply use the word "death" and
its cognates in this discussion to mean *permanent* death, unsupple-
mented by any form of conscious survival. I wish to consider whether
death is in itself an evil; and how great an evil, and of what kind, it

Reprinted from *Moral Problems*, ed. James Rachels (New York: Harper &
Row, 1971), pp. 361–70; by permission of the author and the original publisher,
the Editor of *Noûs*, 4 (1970), 73–80.

might be. This question should be of interest even to those who believe that we do not die permanently, for one's attitude toward immortality must depend in part on one's attitude toward death.

Clearly if death is an evil at all, it cannot be because of its positive features, but only because of what it deprives us of. I shall try to deal with the difficulties surrounding the natural view that death is an evil because it brings to an end all the goods that life contains.[1] An account of these goods need not occupy us here, except to observe that some of them, like perception, desire, activity, and thought, are so general as to be constitutive of human life. They are widely regarded as formidable benefits in themselves, despite the fact that they are conditions of misery as well as of happiness, and that a sufficient quantity of more particular evils can perhaps outweigh them. That is what is meant, I think, by the allegation that it is good simply to be alive, even if one is undergoing terrible experiences. The situation is roughly this: There are elements which, if added to one's experience, make life better; there are other elements which, if added to one's experience, make life worse. But what remains when these are set aside is not merely *neutral*: it is emphatically positive. Therefore life is worth living even when the bad elements of experience are plentiful, and the good ones too meager to outweigh the bad ones on their own. The additional positive weight is supplied by experience itself, rather than by any of its contents.

I shall not discuss the value that one person's life or death may have for others, or its objective value, but only the value it has for the person who is its subject. That seems to me the primary case, and the case which presents the greatest difficulties. Let me add only two observations. First, the value of life and its contents does not attach to mere organic survival: almost everyone would be indifferent (other things equal) between immediate death and immediate coma followed by death twenty years later without reawakening. And second, like most goods, this can be multiplied by time: more is better than less. The added quantities need not be temporarily continuous (though continuity has its social advantages). People are attracted to the possibility of long-term suspended animation or freezing, followed by the resumption of conscious life, because they can regard it from within simply as a *continuation* of their present life. If these techniques are ever perfected, what from outside appeared as a dormant interval of three hundred years could be experienced by the subject as nothing more than a sharp discontinuity in the character of his experiences. I do not deny, of course, that this has its own disadvantages. Family and friends may have died in the meantime; the language may have changed; the comforts of social, geographical, and cultural familiarity would be lacking. Nevertheless these inconveniences would not obliterate the basic advantage of continued, though discontinuous, existence.

If we turn from what is good about life to what is bad about death, the case is completely different. Essentially, though there may be problems about their specification, what we find desirable in life are certain states, conditions, or types of activity. It is *being* alive, *doing* certain things, having certain experiences, that we consider good. But if death is an evil, it is the *loss of life*, rather than the state of being dead, or nonexistent, or unconscious, that is objectionable.[2] This asymmetry is important. If it is good to be alive, that advantage can be attributed to a person at each point of his life. It is a good of which Bach had more than Schubert, simply because he lived longer. Death, however, is not an evil of which Shakespeare has so far received a larger portion than Proust. If death is a disadvantage, it is not easy to say when a man suffers it.

There are two other indications that we do not object to death merely because it involves long periods of nonexistence. First, as has been mentioned, most of us would not regard the *temporary* suspension of life, even for substantial intervals, as in itself a misfortune. If it develops that people can be frozen without reduction of the conscious lifespan, it will be inappropriate to pity those who are temporarily out of circulation. Second, none of us existed before we were born (or conceived), but few regard that as a misfortune. I shall have more to say about this later.

The point that death is not regarded as an unfortunate *state* enables us to refute a curious but very common suggestion about the origin of the fear of death. It is often said that those who object to death have made the mistake of trying to imagine what it is like to *be* dead. It is alleged that the failure to realize that this task is logically impossible (for the banal reason that there is nothing to imagine) leads to the conviction that death is a mysterious and therefore terrifying prospective *state*. But this diagnosis is evidently false, for it is just as impossible to imagine being totally unconscious as to imagine being dead (though it is easy enough to imagine oneself, from the outside, in either of those conditions). Yet people who are averse to death are not usually averse to unconsciousness (so long as it does not entail a substantial cut in the total duration of waking life).

If we are to make sense of the view that to die is bad, it must be on the ground that life is a good and death is the corresponding deprivation or loss, bad not because of any positive features but because of the desirability of what it removes. We must now turn to the serious difficulties which this hypothesis raises, difficulties about loss and privation in general, and about death in particular.

Essentially, there are three types of problem. First, doubt may be raised whether *anything* can be bad for a man without being positively unpleasant to him: specifically, it may be doubted that there are any evils which consist merely in the deprivation or absence of possible goods, and which do not depend on someone's *minding* that deprivation. Second, there are special difficulties, in the case of death, about how the supposed misfortune is to be assigned to a subject at all. There is doubt both as to *who* its subject is, and as to *when* he undergoes it. So long as a person exists, he has not yet died, and once he has died, he no longer exists; so there seems to be no time when death, if it is a misfortune, can be ascribed to its unfortunate subject. The third type of difficulty concerns the asymmetry, mentioned above, between our attitudes to posthumous and prenatal nonexistence. How can the former be bad if the latter is not?

It should be recognized that if these are valid objections to counting death as an evil, they will apply to many other supposed evils as well. The first type of objection is expressed in general form by the common remark that what you don't know can't hurt you. It means that even if a man is betrayed by his friends, ridiculed behind his back, and despised by people who treat him politely to his face, none of it can be counted as a misfortune for him so long as he does not suffer as a result. It means that a man is not injured if his wishes are ignored by the executor of his will, or if, after death, the belief becomes current that all the literary works on which his fame rests were really written by his brother, who died in Mexico at the age of 28. It seems to me worth asking what assumptions about good and evil lead to these drastic restrictions.

All the questions have something to do with time. There certainly are goods and evils of a simple kind (including some pleasures and pains) which a person possesses at a given time simply in virtue of his condition at that time. But this is not true of all the things we regard as good or bad for a man. Often we need to know his history to tell whether something is a misfortune or not; this applies to ills like deterioration, deprivation, and damage. Sometimes his experimental *state* is relatively unimportant—as in the case of a man who wastes his life in the cheerful pursuit of a method of communicating with asparagus plants. Someone who holds that all goods and evils must be temporarily assignable states of the person may of course try to bring difficult cases into line by pointing to the pleasure or pain that more complicated goods and evils cause. Loss, betrayal, deception, and ridicule are on this view bad because people suffer when they learn of them. But it should be asked how our ideas of human value would have to be constituted to accommodate these cases directly instead. One advantage of such an account might be that it would enable us to explain *why* the discovery of these misfortunes causes suffering—in a way that makes it reasonable. For the natural view is that the discovery of betrayal makes us unhappy because it is bad to be betrayed—not that betrayal is bad because its discovery makes us unhappy.

It therefore seems to me worth exploring the position that most good and ill fortune has as its subject a person identified by his history and his possibilities, rather than merely by his categorical state of the moment—and that while this subject can be exactly located in a sequence of places and times, the same is not necessarily true of the goods and ills that befall him.[3]

These ideas can be illustrated by an example of deprivation whose severity approaches that of death. Suppose an intelligent person receives a brain injury that reduces him to the mental condition of a contented infant, and that such desires as remain in him can be satisfied by a custodian, so that he is free from care. Such a development would be widely regarded as a severe misfortune, not only for his friends and relations, or for society, but also, and primarily, for the person himself. This does not mean that a contented infant is unfortunate. The intelligent adult who has been *reduced* to this condition is the subject of the misfortune. He is the one we pity, though of course he does not mind his condition—there is some doubt, in fact, whether he can be said to exist any longer.

The view that such a man has suffered a misfortune is open to the same objections which have been raised in regard to death. He does not mind his condition. It is in fact the same condition he was in at the age of three months, except that he is bigger. If we did not pity him then, why pity him now; in any case, who is there to pity? The intelligent adult has disappeared, and for a creature like the one before us, happiness consists in a full stomach and a dry diaper.

If these objections are invalid, it must be because they rest on a mistaken assumption about the temporal relation between the subject of a misfortune and the circumstances which constitute it. If, instead of concentrating exclusively on the oversized baby before us, we consider the person he was, and the person he *could* be now, then his reduction to this state and the cancellation of his natural adult development constitute a perfectly intelligible catastrophe.

This case should convince us that it is arbitrary to restrict the goods and evils that can befall a man to nonrelational properties ascribable to him at particular times. As it stands, that restriction excludes not only such cases of gross degeneration, but also a good deal of what is important about success and failure, and other features of a life that have the character of processes. I believe that we can go further, however. There are goods and evils which are irreducibly relational; they are features of the relations between a person, with spatial and temporal boundaries of the usual sort, and circumstances which may not coincide with him either in space or in time. A man's life includes much that does not take place within the boundaries of his body and his mind, and what happens to him can include much that does not take place within the boundaries of his life. These boundaries are commonly crossed by the misfortunes of being deceived, or despised, or betrayed. (If this is correct, there is a simple account of what is wrong with breaking a deathbed promise. It is an injury to the dead man. For certain purposes it is possible to regard time as just another type of distance.) The case of mental degeneration shows us an evil that depends on a contrast between the reality and the possible alternatives. A man is the subject of good and evil as much because he has hopes ˙ which may or may not be fulfilled, or possibilities which may or may not be realized, as because of his capacity to suffer and enjoy. If death is an evil, it must be accounted for in these terms, and the impossibility of locating it within life should not trouble us.

When a man dies we are left with his corpse, and while a corpse can suffer the kind of mishap that may occur to an article of furniture, it is not a suitable object for pity. The man, however, is. He has lost his life, and if he had not died, he would have continued to live it, and to possess whatever good there is in living. If we apply to death the account suggested for the case of dementia, we shall say that although the spatial and temporal locations of the individual who suffered the loss are clear enough, the misfortune itself cannot be so easily located. One must be content just to state that his life is over and there will never be any more of it. The *fact*, rather than his past or present condition, constitutes his misfortune, if it is one. Nevertheless if there is a loss, someone must suffer it, and *he* must have existence and specific spatial and temporal location even if the loss itself does not. The fact that Beethoven had no children may have been a cause of regret to him, or a sad thing for the world, but it cannot be described as a misfortune for the children that he never had. All of us, I believe, are fortunate to have been born. But unless good and ill can be assigned to an embryo, or even to an unconnected pair of gametes, it cannot be said that not to be born is a misfortune. (That is a factor to be considered in deciding whether abortion and contraception are akin to murder.)

This approach also provides a solution to the problem of temporal asymmetry, pointed out by Lucretius. He observed that no one finds it disturbing to contemplate the eternity preceding his own birth, and he took this to show that it must be irrational to fear death, since death is simply the mirror image of the prior abyss. That is not true, however, and the difference between the two explains why it is reasonable to regard them differently. It is true that both the time before a man's birth and the time after his death are times when he does not exist. But the time after his death is time of which his death deprives him. It is time in which, had he not died then, he would be alive. Therefore any death entails the loss of *some* life that its victim would have led had he not died at that or any earlier point. We know perfectly well what it would be for him to have had it instead of losing it, and there is no difficulty in identifying the loser.

But we cannot say that the time prior to a man's birth is time in which he would have lived had he been born not then but earlier. For aside from the brief margin permitted by premature labor, he *could* not have been born earlier: anyone born substantially earlier than he was would have been someone else. Therefore the time prior to his birth is not time in which his subsequent birth prevents him from living. His birth, when it occurs, does not entail the loss to him of any life whatever.

The direction of time is crucial in assigning possibilities to people or other individuals. Distinct possible lives of a single person can diverge from a common beginning, but they cannot converge to a common conclusion from diverse beginnings. (The latter would represent not a set of different possible lives of one individual, but a set of distinct possible individuals, whose lives have identical conclusions.) Given an identifiable individual, countless possibilities for his continued existence are imaginable, and we can clearly conceive of what it would be for him to go on existing indefinitely. However inevitable it is that this will not come about, its possibility is still that of the continuation of a good for him, if life is the good we take it to be.[4]

We are left, therefore, with the question whether the nonrealization of this possibility is in every case a misfortune, or whether it depends on what can naturally be hoped for. This seems to me the most serious difficulty with the view that death is always an evil. Even if we can dispose of the objections against admitting misfortune that is not experienced, or cannot be assigned to a definite time in the person's life, we still have to set some limits on *how* possible a possibility must be for its nonrealization to be a misfortune (or good fortune, should the possibility be a bad one). The death of Keats at 24 is generally regarded as tragic; that of Tolstoy at 82 is not. Although they will both be dead forever, Keats's death deprived him of many years of life which were allowed to Tolstoy; so in a clear sense Keats's loss was greater (though not in the sense standardly employed in mathematical comparison between infinite quantities). However, this does not prove that Tolstoy's loss was insignificant. Perhaps we record an objection only to evils which are gratuitously added to the inevitable; the fact that it is worse to die at 24 than at 82 does not imply that is not a terrible thing to die at 82, or even at 806. The question is whether we can regard as a misfortune any limitation, like mortality, that is normal to the species. Blindness or near-blindness is not a misfortune for a mole; nor would it be for a man, if that were the natural condition of the human race.

The trouble is that life familiarizes us with the goods of which death deprives us. We are already able to appreciate them, as a mole is not able to appreciate vision. If we put aside doubts about their status as goods and grant that their quantity is in part a function of their duration, the question remains whether death, no matter when it occurs, can be said to deprive its victim of what is in the relevant sense a possible continuation of life.

The situation is an ambiguous one. Observed from without, human beings obviously have a natural lifespan and cannot live much longer than a hundred years. A man's sense of his own experience, on the other hand, does not embody this idea of a natural limit. His existence defines for him an essentially open-ended possible future, containing the usual mixture of goods and evils that he has found so tolerable in the past. Having been gratuitously introduced to the world by a collection of natural, historical, and social accidents, he finds himself the subject of a *life*, with an indeterminate and not essentially limited future. Viewed in this way, death, no matter how inevitable, is an abrupt cancellation of indefinitely extensive possible goods. Normality seems to have nothing to do with it, for the fact that we will all inevitably die in a few score years cannot by itself imply that it would not be good to live longer. Suppose that we were all inevitably going to die in *agony*—physical agony lasting six months. Would inevitability make *that* prospect any less unpleasant? And why should it be different for a deprivation? If the normal lifespan were a thousand years, death at 80 would be a tragedy. As things are, it may just be a more widespread tragedy. If there is no limit to the amount of life that it would be good to have, then it may be that a bad end is in store for us all.

NOTES

1. As we shall see, this does not mean that it brings to an end all the goods that a man can possess.
2. It is sometimes suggested that what we really mind is the process of *dying*. But I should not really object to dying if it were not followed by death.
3. It is certainly not true in general of the things that can be said of him. For example, Abraham Lincoln was taller than Louis XIV. But when?

4. I confess to being troubled by the above argument, on the ground that it is too sophisticated to explain the simple difference between our attitudes to prenatal and posthumous nonexistence. For this reason I suspect that something essential is omitted from the account of the badness of death by an analysis which treats it as a deprivation of possibilities. My suspicion is supported by the following suggestion of Robert Nozick. We could imagine discovering that people developed from individual spores that had existed indefinitely far in advance of their birth. In this fantasy, birth never occurs naturally more than 100 years before the permanent end of the spore's existence. But then we discover a way to trigger the premature hatching of these spores, and people are born who have thousands of years of active life before them. Given such a situation, it would be possible to imagine *oneself* having come into existence thousands of years previously. If we put aside the question whether this would really be the same person, even given the identity of the spore, then the consequence appears to be that a person's birth at a given time *could* deprive him of many earlier years of possible life. Now while it would be cause for regret that one had been deprived of all those possible years of life by being born too late, the feeling would differ from that which many people have about death. I conclude that something about the future prospect of permanent nothingness is not captured by the analysis in terms of denied possibilities. If so, then Lucretius' argument still awaits an answer.

2

On Death and Human Existence

JAMES M. CAMERON
University of Toronto

THE TOPIC OF DEATH, now fashionable and much discussed, raises
questions in almost every field of thought. Death has always been
thought hateful, or almost always hateful, and enigmatic. In the Christian and Jewish traditions death has always been terrible, something
that reveals the distance between God and man and man's dereliction;
and it is therefore thought to be something that in some obscure sense
ought not to happen. The primitive account of the passion in Mark
and Matthew—characteristically and no doubt deliberately omitted by
Luke—records the great cry of agony taken from Psalm 22: "My God,
my God, why hast thou forsaken me?" In the same psalm we find: "I
am poured out like water, and all my bones are out of joint; my heart
is like wax, it is melted within my breast . . . and my tongue cleaves
to my jaws; thou dost lay me in the dust of death." Here is no attempt
to prettify death or to make the process of dying acceptable. Death
is intolerable.

Of course, there are other biblical ways of looking at death. In (and
out of) the Bible we are given the picture of the just man full of years
and honour who dies surrounded by his children and his children's
children. This is a fortunate death, and if to this we add the element
contributed by Christianity, namely, the reception of the eucharist (vi-
aticum, journey money, analogous to the placing of a coin in the dead
man's mouth to pay Charon's ferry charges), and the anointing (formerly) of those parts of the body that have so often taken us away
from God, and the sacramental remission of sin through confession
and absolution, we understand how this can properly be called "a

Reprinted by permission from *New Blackfriars*, 57 (1976), 536–48.

happy death." But death (and there can be no guarantee that even the death of the just will be "happy" in this sense) remains terrible and the prospect of dying repugnant. It is true that one element in our tradition is represented by the oracular saying: Those whom the gods love die young. But presumably this is because the young do not endure the long process of decay and the pain and the disappointment that are inseparably a part of a long life.

Death is not only a horror. It may often seem a piece of confusion. This comes out in the wonderful description of Falstaff's death in *Henry V.* II. iii:

> *Pistol.* Boy, bristle thy courage up; for Falstaff is dead. And we must earn therefore.
> *Bardolph.* Would I were with him, wheresome'er he is, either in heaven or in hell!
> *Hostess.* Nay, sure, he's not in hell! He's in Arthur's bosom, if ever man went to Arthur's bosom. 'A made a finer end, and went away an it had been any christom child. 'A parted ev'n just between twelve and one, ev'n at the turning o' th'tide. For after I saw him fumble with the sheets, and play with flowers, and smile upon his finger's end, I knew there was but one way; for his nose was as sharp as a pen, and 'a babbled of green fields. "How now, Sir John?" quoth I. "What man! be o'good cheer." So 'a cried out "God, God, God!" three or four times. Now I, to comfort him, bid him 'a should not think of God; I hoped there was no need to trouble himself with any such thoughts yet. So 'a bade me lay more clothes on his feet. I put my hand into the bed and felt them, and they were as cold as any stone. Then I felt his knees, and so upward and upward, and all was as cold as any stone.
> *Nym.* They say he cried out of sack.
> *Hostess.* Ay, that 'a did.
> *Bardolph.* And of women.
> *Hostess.* Nay, that 'a did not.
> *Boy.* Yes, that 'a did, and said they were devils incarnate.
> *Hostess.* 'A could never abide carnation; 'twas a colour he never liked.
> *Boy.* 'A said once the devil would have him about women.
> *Hostess.* 'A did in some sort, indeed, handle women; but then he was rheumatic, and talked of the whore of Babylon.

The separate threads of life are not here tied together. The end of the great project of life is not rounded, satisfying, and complete. It is a piece of untidiness. Falstaff's death is closer to the actual world than

> Nothing is here for tears, nothing to wail
> Or knock the breast no weakness, no contempt,
> Dispraise or blame, nothing but well and fair,
> And what may quiet us in a death so noble.

The king has broken Falstaff's heart and the great ruin of a man, this compound of sensuality and fantasy, this sophistical dialectician, this parasite on the social body, spittle of diseases, lord of misrule, lies playing with the sheets, looking at his fingers, crying out for sack and for women and for God, fumbling after the Twenty-Third Psalm: "The Lord is my shepherd, I shall not want, / He makes me lie down in green pastures." Today we may think that in some ways even his untidy death is fortunate. He is in his own bed; he has one person with him who loves him in a kind of way, his old bawd, Mistress Quickly; and he calls on God and vomits up his sins and dies with the words of the psalmist in his mouth. We may compare this with a characteristic death of our own time: a man or woman in a hospital bed, drugged into insensibility, without friends present, with a family perhaps in the hospital waiting room wondering when the end will release them; or with what is today called by many a fortunate death—a sudden and unforseen death by stroke or heart failure. How nice for him! we hear people say.

There is another kind of death, perhaps hard to achieve today, what we may call the noble death: Doctor Johnson's death is a case in point, and an interesting one. All his life Johnson had a morbid fear of death; he was just the kind of man doctors today might think ought not to be told about his condition. But when he entered what he thought was probably his last illness he asked his physician for a "direct answer" as to whether or not he was dying. "The Doctor having first asked him if he could bear the whole truth, which way soever it might lead, and being answered that he could, declared that, in his opinion, he could not recover without a miracle. 'Then [said Johnson]; I will take no more physick, not even my opiates; for I have prayed that I may render up my soul to God unclouded.'"

This noble death is in fact the death of a Christian. But the determination to meet death with full consciousness of what is happening, in the presence of friends and family, enemies forgiven, final dispositions made—this is not confined to Christians or to religious believers. Such were noble deaths in antiquity (the pious man freed his slaves)—not so noble as a death in battle but honorable all the same. But even the most tranquil of such deaths has about it the trace of a final combat, a struggle with the grisly king. I am not suggesting that statistical analysis, if it were possible one could be made, would show that this was the *average* way of meeting death in some periods. Many deaths are sudden and unforeseen, many of the dying are comatose before they know they are dying—these things are always true. But so long as such an ideal style of dying was operative it was hard to think it a good thing that a man should be cheated of his death or lied to about it, or left alone with doctors and nurses, these last uncertain about their functions: even now, beginning to conjecture that society may require of them that they be public executioners rather than witnesses to a final solemn act, and consolers of the dying.

When death is faced and valued in the Johnsonian way there is no pretence about the finality of death, about its being the common human lot, about the pangs of death, and about the physical consequences of death. The man we can point to and embrace will fall into decay and the skeleton will show itself; the man has gone. Corpses stink and should be buried quickly. Except sometimes in the case of kings and other notables, dead bodies were not in Christian society stuffed and painted in a stupid parody of life; and the ancient Egyptian habit of embalming did not rest upon sentiment or aesthetic considerations; it was connected with a theory of the afterlife and could be given a rationale. How men thought in the sixteenth and seventeenth centuries, even down to the nineteenth century, is reflected in the Anglican Book of Common Prayer, a book that nourished Johnson's piety and formed the sensibility of the English until the day before yesterday. The Book is not mealy-mouthed about death (or about sex for that matter: marriage is quite properly called "a remedy for fornication," an expression bowdlerized out in the unfortunate 1928 revision). In the litany men pray to be delivered from "sudden death," the fate so much desired by modern men; and we also find in the litany: "In all time of our tribulation: in all time of our wealth; in the hour of death, and in the day of judgment, *Good Lord deliver us.*" In the Burial service we find: "Man that is born of woman hath but a short time to live, and is full of misery. He cometh up, and is cut down, like a flower: he fleeth as it were a shadow, and never continueth in one stay. . . . O holy and merciful Saviour, thou most worthy judge eternal, suffer us not, at our last hour, to fall from thee." Catholics have always had a daily reminder of their mortality in the Hail Mary: "now, and at the hour of our death."

Why should death, the common lot, have to be something that poses a problem, so that we have to be reconciled to it, if we can, or go to it in anger ("Rage, rage against the dying of the light," as a well-known poem by Dylan Thomas puts it)? In the first place, it may be connected with what is perceived as the duality of our existence. This seems to be thought prior to all philosophizing and quite without reference to any religious belief; our duality is felt as agonizing, tormenting, self-dividing; we have the idea that the mind has as it were a crystalline structure whereas the body is warm, thick, indistinct, mutable, fragile, perishable. Each grips the other; and the grip is loosened by the ills of the body and the mind and broken at death. Our duality is a torment when we look at sexuality as well. We are conceived, as are all the mammals, *inter faeces et urinam*—"Love has pitched his mansion in / The place of excrement," as Crazy Jane said to the Bishop in Yeats's poem. Hence the wild swinging between Manichaean and Romantic views of sexuality, from "sex is dirty" to "sex is divine." But in relation to our entire fate, to the tissue of life as it is lived forward in time, the contrast seems to lie between our urgent animal nature which is so plainly tied to change and to the imperatives of appetite, is so subject to pain and weariness, and our ability to transcend space and time, to think eternal thoughts (Pythagoras), to comprehend the world of nature, to survey the fortunes of mankind in the discipline of history, to consider what is good and what evil for man, and to rise in thought to the existence of the one who is alone and beyond us, and yet always present, the one who is God.

To interject a philosophical consideration: an absolute dualism is not thinkable. To put it crudely but accurately and effectively, I see with my eyes, it isn't that I, a mind, peer through my eyes, it isn't that my eyes see and report to the mind. My identity is connected with my bodily persistence through time. I am now in Minneapolis, now in Toronto. *I* don't go to Minneapolis and take my body with me. Newman once put it well in a sermon. "God graciously called Himself *the God of Abraham*. He did not say the God of Abraham's *soul*, but simply of *Abraham*. He blest Abraham, and He gave him eternal life; not to his soul only without his body, but to Abraham as one man."

Dualism is not thinkable to the end; but there are genuine dualities within the one man. Some of these have been given a number of classic descriptions from Saint Paul to Freud; and to speak of dualities seems irresistible, perhaps because it is so familiar. The described dualities do not only rest upon the obvious duality of a being with an animal nature and an intellectual, symbol-framing and -using nature. Take, for example, one of the best-attested features of all intimate personal relations. I hate and I love, says the pagan poet. I hate *because* I love. The one with whom I wish to merge my existence and who provokes in me the impulses of generosity and self-sacrifice is also the one who menaces my existence, my independence, *through* my love. The things I really want to do are the very things I find I don't do; and the things I find myself doing are the very things I loathe. Thus the Apostle Paul. Such inner conflicts are plainly not all straightforwardly spirit/flesh, intellect/appetite conflicts. The division between "passion" and "reason" is from Plato down to Milton thought to be the root of the difficulty and seems to carry with it the implication that our troubles come from our being pure spirits unfortunately (and contingently) connected with wayward bodies.

Oh wearisome condition of humanity!
Born under one Law, to another bound:
Vainely begot, and yet forbidden vanity;
Created sicke, commanded to be sound:
What meaneth Nature by these diverse Lawes?
Passion and Reason, self-division cause . . .

Fulke Greville's lines represent one side of our tradition, and on the whole the predominant one. We might call it the Platonic tradition, represented by Plato himself and the neo-Platonists, by much Christian theology influenced by this tradition, and by Descartes and the empiricists. The central idea is what I have called absolute dualism, that man is essentially two things: a body, perishable and subject to decay; and a soul, spiritual, immortal, the essential man, the man in man, as Plato puts it. The death of John Smith, then, is the death of John Smith's body, not the death of John Smith; and with the death of his body John Smith is at last free to move, as all he essentially is, into the celestial regions. Historically, this is how many men, perhaps most, have thought; dualism has in its favour a striking consensus. It profoundly affects the Christian tradition, despite the authority of the Old Testament and of Aquinas. As the English Penny Catechism puts it, or used to put it: "Of which ought I to take most care, my body or my soul? *Answer.* My soul, because my soul will never die." On this view, the idea of resurrection is accidentally, not essentially, connected with the Christian hope. Resurrection appears as kind of extra, an uncovenanted piece of good fortune. Everything would still have been absolutely splendid without it, even if things are still better with it. And thought about in this way the "I await the resurrection of the dead" at the end of the Nicene Creed seems to lack weight and credibility; even, perhaps, it seems a bit speculative and therefore a piece of mythology to be dispensed with.

But it seemed quite certain to the Apostle Paul that if Christ is not risen then we shall not rise, and then we are of all men most miserable (1 Cor 15:12–19). Paul doesn't say: O well, never mind; after all, we're immortal, so it doesn't really matter about a miraculously renewed personal existence.

Scholars seem to agree that in Judaism before the Christian era the notion of the survival of death is at first scarcely there, develops late, and in the Judaism of the Maccabean period and later appears among some Jews as a belief in the resurrection. In the New Testament sectarian differences within Judaism are connected with the belief or disbelief in the resurrection. (Incidentally, most of the Old Testament record shows that a vigorous religion, with habits of deep personal piety, can flourish without much explicit commitment to a belief in the individual survival of death. The survival of Israel is what people seem to care about. There seem to be traces of a belief in a kind of sad survival—the survival of man as a ghostly being. This isn't thought to be a good thing, any more than it was by the Greeks.) For the Greeks (of course, not all, for there were the Pythagoreans and the adherents of the Orphic cults who had more crisply formulated views on survival) Hades was a place "where the dead live on without their wits as disembodied ghosts"; and Achilles said to Odysseus, when he was summoned from the underworld, that he would rather be a poor labourer on earth than King among the dead (*Odyssey*, Book 11). Survival as such is not a cheerful hypothesis. The epitaphs in the Greek Anthology are not filled with the spirit of hope. But the doctrine of Plato survived, partly because his arguments (*Phaedo* and *Republic*) seemed cogent, partly because the belief in immortality was connected with powerful scientific doctrines about the nature of the world, e.g., the Pythagorean view that in some way numbers constitute reality.

As I have said, there is a striking consensus about the truth of dualism and Christians have never been unaffected by this consensus. But it can't be doubted that on the whole the place given within the biblical tradition to bodily life and to physical reality is quite incompatible with Platonic (or Cartesian) dualism. The Old Testament hope is for a restoration of the physical and social life of Israel, within whatever situation of misery the prophet finds himself; it is not a hope for a timeless spiritual existence in a transcendent realm. And what is in the Old Testament a hope for Israel (though here and there a hope for mankind) becomes in the New Testament a hope for all men, individually and socially, and even for the physical universe. Nothing is more striking in the early centuries of Christianity than the way in which men who are by culture and disposition "Greek" nevertheless in the end are compelled to witness against all Gnostic tendencies and in particular against the various christological heresies that deny the full physical and human reality of Jesus. The Fourth Gospel is in many ways influenced by Greek thought, that is, by the thought of Hellenised Judaism; but it is also by far the most "physical" of the gospels. And in First John the theme is repeated: "That which was from the beginning, which we have *heard*, which we have *seen with our eyes*, which we have *looked upon* and *touched with our hands* . . ." The Hebrew doctrine of creation, the insistence in the early conciliar definitions on the full humanity of Christ, these things have always controlled our fundamental statements of faith and our fundamental responses to the world of nature, despite all the powerful tendencies in our tradition to run off into a kind of Gnosticism. I say "fundamental" advisedly; for I think if we examine the life of devotion and attitudes to life of the senses in the general Christian tradition we shall find that heretical attitudes cluster round all those questions that have to do with the relations between soul and body. As Karl Rahner[1] has shown there is a kind of implicit Docetism in much popular preaching and devotion, just as in the Protestant tradition there is a great deal of implicit Adoptionism. Of course, this isn't to accuse either party of formal heresy. It is simply the case that the balance which is safeguarded by the dogmatic formulas of the great Councils is hard to achieve in practice, just because it involves holding with tenacity to two predicates the conjunction of which is ordinarily absurd.

The analysis of human nature I am trying to stress, with a view to seeing its implications for our thinking about death, is on the whole reflected in our ordinary discourse. The answer to the question: Where does John do most of his intellectual work? is surely: In his study. Where in his study does his intellectual work go on? is either answered—if at all, for it is a very strange question—with a reference to where John is, spatially, e.g., seated at his desk, or dismissed as a nonsense question. "In his head" is not an *alternative* way of answering the question (as in "bed" would be); the force of "in his head" comes from its contrast with such an expression as "on paper". Of course, I don't *do* anything in my head in the way that I bake bread in the oven. (It may be true—no doubt it *is* true—that things happen inside my head when I think; but I am not acquainted with these things and need know nothing about them to think effectively, just as I learn to walk the tightrope without knowing anything about the functions of the middle ear in enabling me to balance myself.) The sense, then, in which men *have* bodies is not a sense which excludes the possibility that a man *is* a body of a certain kind with certain characteristic activities and capacities. Talk about the soul is not talk about a human life which exists side by side with the life of the body; it seems that apart from the body there is no human life, for what would a human life be without sensation and memory, physical movement, all that makes up the substance of our life and underlies all the concepts embodied in our language? We sometimes have the idea that we can imagine how it would be to die and then float above our body and look at it—indeed, some people claim to have done this—just as we can imagine talking beasts in the Beatrix Potter stories or in *Alice*. But we smuggle into our descriptions concepts that would have no purchase except for creatures that occupied space, had eyes and organs of touch, etc.

I won't go into all the philosophical issues connected with these problems. Aquinas, following Aristotle (or what he takes the sense of Aristotle to be), thinks the soul is the "form" of the body. This raises for him a startling problem when he comes to consider the question of the survival of the "separated" soul; for what is a form without its matter . . . ? In discussing the possibility of the survival of the separated soul Aquinas (*qua* philosopher) strikes me as being like a cat on hot bricks, in part because his own analysis doesn't seem to leave room for the soul as a separate and subsistent *entity*; certainly the separated soul seems not to be a substance and it seems therefore that it can have knowledge of itself only through God's action in, as it were, constituting it as a quasi-substance. I sometimes think that what Aquinas has to say is that the survival of the separated soul means that God keeps that man in mind after he is dead. Two things seem to stand in the way of our thinking that, though perhaps they don't. (After all, what limits could be set to the consequences of God's having a man in mind after he is dead . . . ?) First, there is the condemnation as heretical of John XXII's teaching that the just don't enjoy the beatific vision until after the general resurrection; and secondly, the primitive and constant practice of praying for the dead.

At any rate, *anima mea non est ego* (I am not my soul), says Aquinas, commenting on the passage in First Corinthians about the resurrection. My soul's survival is not *my* survival; only *I* survive if in some sense I am recreated as a living body. This is a very difficult idea, a mystery if there ever was one; and if one reads 1 Corinthians 15:35–56 one finds that Paul is reduced to a kind of spluttering wonderment, a vain attempt to say what can't be said. This is why the kinds of questions theologians used to raise (they seem to have stopped doing this, or perhaps I just haven't come across instances), such as, At what age shall we be resurrected? If a man has lost a leg will he get it back? Shall we be able to walk through doors?, have a kind of indecent inappropriateness, as do, for example, nice and intricate questions about the mode of our Lord's presence in the eucharist. (Don John Chapman once said of some of these that they were "merely nasty.") Such speculations belong to what really is mythical, the picture of the resurrection as crowds of people climbing out of their graves, shooting up like torpedoes from the bottom of the sea, flying up into the clouds. For even if such pictures are in a way inevitably constructed, they have to be treated in a spirit of irony. What is interesting about the resurrection is not physical or quasi-physical survival—for any spiritualist seance can offer, no doubt fraudulently, the same assurance through its ectoplasmic figures—but *human* survival. As to what this will mean for us, "it does not yet appear what we shall be, but we know that when he appears we shall be like him, for we shall see him as he is" (1 Jn 3:2).

Now, if man is a unity two things seem to follow. First, certain attitudes to human beings, attitudes that suggest we are concerned essentially only with spirits and accidentally—perhaps inconveniently—with bodies are ruled out. This makes Christianity a very queer religion by world standards. Most world religions are much more *spiritual* than Christianity, which to them must seem very materialistic. And there are many grossly heretical offshoots of Christianity—Mary Baker Eddy's Christian Science is the most familiar in North America—that indict Christianity for its materialism, in that Christians hold it to be a real fact about the world that there is matter and that organic beings suffer pain. Again, "new moralists" of various kinds offer certain high-minded doctrines of a Gnostic kind, doctrines that avoid the truth that it is because men are bodies of a certain kind that there can be moral absolutes about human actions, e.g., it is always wrong deliberately to lie with the wife or husband of another or to slit the throat of, napalm, shoot, or suffocate an innocent human being, no matter how grand the purposes in the mind of the offender may be. Many of our contemporaries don't understand this at all. This comes out in the discussion of abortion. That a foetus is, and recognisably is, from very early on (everyone by now has seen the photographs) human, doesn't seem to many a ground for having a rule against killing a foetus. What matter are "values," "the development of personality" and other airy concepts. By a similar corruption of the mind we slaughter innocent people in war and justify it in terms of "western values," "democracy," and what have you. It isn't accidental that in the gospels the *corporal* works of mercy are the types of what Christ wants us to do. The very imagery used to convey our longing for God comes from our bodily life, and from that part of our life we share with the other animals: we hunger and thirst, we melt inwardly, our bowels are moved. "As the driven hart pants after the streams of water, so longs my soul for you, O God" (Ps 42:1).

It seems then to follow that death, even with the Christian hope of resurrection, is more terrible than we are commonly prepared to admit. It *is* the end of John or Mary, and apart from the Christian hope it would be a dark fact of human existence. It is therefore quite un-Christian in spirit to be too jolly about death. Some of our modern locutions—"passed away," "passed on," "passed to the higher life," all the language that goes with the modern undertaking industry and the death-denying forms taken by modern graveyards (Forest Lawn)—are quite contrary to the Christian tradition. I understand the theological reasoning behind the abandonment of the black vestments and the old form of the requiem mass, but I must confess I am suspicious about the atmosphere out of which it comes and which it seems to encourage. If I thought the liturgical change testified to a more lively faith in the resurrection I should be happy.

Death, then, is dark and—setting aside the Christian hope—tragic, at any rate in the case of mature persons. This is one way of saying that it is a serious business both for the dying man and for the living who have to do with him. It is a feeling for this that has prompted much recent concern about and discussion of our current attitudes to death and to the practices of undertakers and doctors.

There is a growing revulsion from the undignified—and expensive—practices of the undertaking industry, with the mendacity and false sentiment that batten on the days of mourning for the dead person. Again, the whole setting of death (as of birth) has changed. Now we (in the opulent "western" societies) are often born in hospitals and die in them, whereas formerly we were born where we were conceived and died where we were born, that is, at home, in bed. Men are beginning to see this change as a loss, in part because in the hospital setting death is a clinical rather than a human event, in part because the duties of the physician begin to blend imperceptively with the duties of the public executioner wherever it is thought a possible duty to ease the dying out of existence. In general, it doesn't seem to be the function of nurses and physicians—perhaps it can't be their function—to reconcile the dying to their condition or to provide purgation and consolation for the bereaved family and friends. Again, changes in medical technology and the growth in the demand for spare parts of the human body have raised new questions about when a man is to be judged dead; and whether or not there is a distinction, from the standpoint of morality, between letting a man die without inflicting on him a lot of useless plumbing and actually administering a lethal dose of a drug. (The distinction is intuitively clear but holding on to one's clarity in the face of ingenious arguments for euthanasia demands some fairly hard thinking about the topic of intention.) Again, the common and, by many, approved practice of abortion has got people worried about killing, and what kinds of killing count as homicide and what kinds of homicide count as murder. Finally, our time has seen death in bizarre forms: death coming from the sky onto the cities of Hiroshima and Nagasaki and Coventry and Dresden and on terrified and uncomprehending peasants in Indo-China; and death coming to Jews, gipsies, Slavs, in the gas-chambers of the Third Reich and death coming to millions of people in the Soviet Union through starvation and cold in the Arctic and in central Asia.

If men have been inclined to think that God is dead, this has not been on account of the vapouring of theologians in fashionable divinity schools but because the skies were indifferent above Auschwitz and Treblinka. Death on such a scale, and out of such inadequate motives without regard to guilt or innocence, age or sex, seems without sense and without consolation; perhaps only in *King Lear* has the poet ever contemplated happenings so bleak and so absurd. Slaughter attributable to ignorance and fanaticism has been a constant feature of human history, at least since the rise of the first civilizations. What is uncanny about the deaths I am talking about is that they are not the work of such men, but the work of petty clerks, no doubt respectable family men quite without a share in the frenzies of Hitler and Himler, and of nice boys flying the B-52s who rain death on people they have never seen and about whose human reality they are ignorant. We ought not to think of all this as lying behind us. The spirit that lay behind the death camps and the mass bombing lives in the public cult, in the arts of sadism and voyeurism. A profound contempt for copulation, suffering and death has bubbled up in the midst of our culture and has shaken all our minds. It is now difficult to be consistent. The opponent of capital punishment and the critic of American foreign policy in Indo-China may ask for abortion on demand or depict Genet or the Marquis de Sade as a moral pioneer. The opponent of abortion—he who is pro-life!—may look on the possibility of nuclear war with calm of mind; for is not the West justified in taking all measures against the Satanic enemies of God and man?

A difficulty that stands in the way of our looking steadily at the phenomenon of death is that curiously death is in the opulent societies not very visible. In the nineteenth century deaths by tuberculosis and pneumonia were commonplace; these diseases were killers at all ages. Children died frequently (the Victorian novel is realistic in making much of the deaths of children). Women often died in childbirth. Now we have the impression that death is something that can be postponed almost indefinitely through surgery and the use of antibiotics. To adopt Newman's terminology, our assent to the proposition that all men are mortal tends to be notional rather than real. Deaths in war and from natural catastrophes are witnessed on the television screen and have the unreality that belongs to the medium, sandwiched as they are between commercials for deodorants, dog food, instant coffee, and pills to stop men and women from getting old.

But death doesn't go away, neither as *my* death nor as the common fate of all men. I have tried to show that even on Christian premises death is terrible, the splitting of our substantial unity, the end of our human existence; it is something enormously tragic apart from the Christian hope in resurrection, the restoration of *human* existence in a way that is the hidden work of God's providence. To say this is to invite smiles or consternation even among believers, perhaps accompanied by cries of demythologise! demythologise! There are even some "radical" Christians, or so I'm told, who want to get rid of the whole notion of personal survival. If this is a sign that they are discontented with the still influential crypto-Platonism, then I think that this could, as is so often the case with heresies, be a sign of the failings of the orthodox. If we are to be the leaven of our society in this matter of death, we have to think seriously about the place of death in our culture. More important, it seems that we have a duty to make our distinctive faith more obvious, not to be afraid of the spirit of the age as it is represented by the undertaking industry, the hospitals and the doctors, by the high-minded Gnosticism of the fashionable sects, by all those who have power over our lives and over the style in which we shall be allowed to die. If Christians were as distinctive in their attitudes to death—repudiating, for example, the practice of embalming the dead— as are Orthodox Jews, western society would become healthier and saner.

NOTE

1. "Current Problems in Christology," *Theological Investigations I* (London, 1961), pp. 149–200.

3

Existentialism and Death: A Survey of Some Confusions and Absurdities

PAUL EDWARDS

New School for Social Research

THIS PAPER is not meant to be an exhaustive discussion of existentialist pronouncements about death. Some, like the curious notion that life is "essentially being toward death," are not dealt with at all, and others, like the view that an "authentic" mode of life is possible only for a person who "resolutely confronts death," are no more than mentioned in passing. My aim has been to cover those existentialist doctrines which are tied, in one form or another, to confused ways of thinking about death common among people in general and which occur independent of the efforts of the existentialists.[1]

DEATH AS SLEEP IN THE GRAVE

Most human beings, whether they are religious believers or not, appear *at times* to have great difficulty in regarding death as truly and really the *absence* of life. In some contexts they do treat death in this way, but at other times they think of it as a restful or gloomy or undesirable *continuation* of life. There is a very common tendency to think of a dead person as sleeping an extremely deep sleep in his grave—so deep that he will never again wake up. A famous Italian conductor was once

Reprinted by permission from *Philosophy, Science, and Method,* edd. S. Morgenbesser, P. Suppes, M. White (New York: St. Martin's Press, 1969), pp. 473-505.

greatly upset by the way the musicians of the New York Philharmonic were playing the movement of a Brahms symphony at a rehearsal. "If Brahms were alive," he finally exclaimed in exasperation, "he would be turning in his grave." When this story is told, it usually takes some time before people see the absurdity of the conductor's remark. If Brahms were alive he presumably would find better things to do than lie in a grave.[2] However, to a person vaguely thinking of Brahms as sleeping in his grave, the conductor's remark will not seem absurd.

People do not have this difficulty in the case of other absences. If a whisky bottle is empty, nobody is likely to maintain that it is filled with an ethereal liquid; and if one comes across a blank canvas, one is not tempted to describe it as an exceptionally abstract painting. Yet, this is precisely how we frequently think of death. We then refer to it more or less seriously as "the rest which may not be unwelcome after weariness has been increasing in old age" (Bertrand Russell), as "quiet consummation" (Shakespeare), or perhaps as "the cool night" which follows the hot and busy day (Heine). We also think of it as a place to which we "pass on" or depart (at the end of our "journey"), as "the harbor to which sooner or later we must head and which we can never refuse to enter" (Seneca), as "the undiscover'd country from whose bourn no traveller returns" (Shakespeare); and we tend to regard this place as dark and perhaps even terrifying, as "eternal night" (Swinburne), "a beach of darkness . . . where there'll be time enough to sleep" (A. E. Housman), the "engulfing impenetrable dark" (H. L. Mencken). It is not uncommon to speak of this place as the same one which we left when we were born. Schopenhauer speaks of birth as the "awakening out of the night of unconsciousness"[3] and he wavers between regarding our return to this state of unconsciousness as something to be welcomed and something to be dreaded. On the one hand he writes that the "heart of man rebels" against having to return to nonexistence; on the other he claims to be speaking for suffering mankind who would much rather have been "left in the peace of the all-sufficient nothing" where their days were not spent in pain or misery (op. cit., p. 389). Darrow, who shared the latter of these sentiments, spoke of life as "an unpleasant interruption of nothingness." "Not to be born is the most to be desired," in the words of Sophocles, "but having seen the light, the next best thing is to go whence one came as soon as may be." Pliny, who ridicules any belief in survival as the logically baseless "fancy" of human vanity, accuses the believers of robbing mankind of "future tranquillity." "What repose," he exclaims, "are the generations ever to have" if they cannot be "from the last day onward in the same state as they were before their first day?" Seneca, too, thought it fortunate that a person could always, by a voluntary act, "escape into safety." Advocating suicide in certain situations, he asks, "Do you like life? Then live on. Do you dislike it? Then you are free to return to the place you came from." At death, Seneca writes in another place, "you are brought back to your source." A lamp, he also observes, is no "worse off when it is extinguished than before it was lighted," and in the same way "we mortals are also lighted and extinguished; the period of suffering comes in between, on either side there is a deep peace." But not all writers who regard death as a "homecoming" think of the place to which we return as a restful abode. Thus James Baldwin, the novelist, admonishes us to negotiate the "passage" of life as nobly as possible—in this way we will obtain "a small beacon in that terrifying darkness from which we came and to which we shall return."

This tendency to think of death as a shadowy and, especially, a very painful and undesirable form of existence is reinforced by the way in which we place death at or near one end of the scale of our punishments and illnesses. Just as two years of imprisonment are more undesirable than one year and life imprisonment is worse than either, being sentenced to death is regarded by most people as a worse fate yet; and even those who consider life imprisonment worse than death regard the latter as very undesirable—at least as undesirable as, say, imprisonment for ten years. Again, just as we regard a chronic illness involving some pain as worse than a merely temporary ailment involving the same degree of pain, so we regard a mortal illness, because it is mortal, as worse than either; and although many people would regard some chronic (non-fatal) illnesses as "objectively" worse than death, almost everybody treats mortal illneses as (necessarily) very undesirable, even if the amount of pain involved is relatively slight. Since languishing in jail and suffering a painful illness are states or processes of living organisms, it becomes tempting to regard death as another, very undesirable, state of a living organism. We see, in the words of P. L. Landsberg, a philosopher writing in the phenomenological tradition, that "death . . . must exceed all experiences of illness, suffering or old age."[4]

Another line of reflection that may lead to a similar conclusion is suggested by Landsberg in the course of discussing the "community" that two people may form—a husband and wife, for example, who not only love each other but who have braved many a storm together. If one of them dies, this "community," this "we," is destroyed. The surviving person experiences then a "bitter cold." In feeling the death of the "we," he is led into an "experiential knowledge" of his own mortality. "My community with this person," writes Landsberg, "seemed shattered, but the community was to some degree myself; and to this degree I experienced death in the very core of my own existence" (op. cit., pp. 14–16). It is tempting to proceed to the conclusion (though Landsberg in fact does not explicitly go that far) that one's own death is a more extreme instance of the same kind of thing: even more bitter and cold than the bitter cold which the survivor experiences upon the death of the "we."

Fear, Anxiety, and Death

This common human tendency to regard death not as just the absence of life but as existence in a dark, impenetrable abode has been enshrined into a philosophical doctrine by the Christian existentialist, the late Professor Paul Tillich, in his "ontology" of Non-Being or Nothingness. Tillich's doctrine is introduced in connection with his distinction between fear and anxiety (it should be noted that although Tillich's use of these expressions is in harmony with that of other existentialists, it is significantly different from their use by most professional psychologists and psychiatrists). In fear, writes Tillich, we are always facing a definite object: It may be physical pain, the loss of a friend, the rejection by a person or a group or any number of other things, but in each case it is something "that can be faced, analyzed, attacked, endured," and met by courage.[5] In anxiety, on the other hand, the object, if it can be called an object, is "ultimate nonbeing;" the "threat" here is due not to something specific like physical pain but to nothingness. Unlike fear, anxiety cannot be met by courage and it is almost unendurable. "It is impossible for a finite being," in Tillich's words, "to stand naked anxiety for more than a flash of time. People who have experienced these moments, as for instance some mystics in their visions of the 'night of the soul,' . . . have told of the unimaginable horror of it" (CB, p. 39). Although fear and anxiety must not be confused with one another, they are closely related. Among other things, there is an element of anxiety in every fear and it is this element of anxiety which gives the fear its "sting."

Tillich applied his distinction between fear and anxiety to the "outstanding example," namely, the fear of death. There are two elements in this fear—fear proper which has an object like an accident or a mortal illness and anxiety whose "object is the absolutely unknown 'after-death,' the nonbeing which remains nonbeing even if it is filled with images of our present experience" (CB, p. 38). Tillich is very concerned that his use of the word "unknown" should not be misunderstood. It is not any unknown but the *absolutely* unknown that one faces in this "basic anxiety" of one's "ultimate nonbeing." There are "innumerable realms of the unknown" that are faced with fear but without any anxiety. Here Tillich probably has in mind the kind of thing that happens when a person is afraid of a new job in which he has to perform unfamiliar tasks or when an explorer is approaching territory about which no reports are extant. These unknowns are not in principle unknowable. The situation is altogether different in the case of the unknown "which is met with in anxiety." It is an "unknown of a special type," which "by its very nature cannot be known, because it is nonbeing" (CB, p. 37). Elsewhere, in discussing man's finitude, Tillich observes that since man is "created out of nothing," he must "return to nothing." Very much like Seneca and Pliny, he tells us that nonbeing "appears as the 'not yet' of being and also as the 'no more' of being." Like all other finite entities, human beings, while alive, are "in process of coming from and going toward nonbeing."[6] Somebody who accepts this account would presumably hold that while Shakespeare was not far wrong when he spoke of our ultimate nonbeing as the "undiscover'd country from whose bourn no traveller returns," it would have been more accurate to speak of an "undiscoverable country." Mencken was closer to the truth (as Tillich sees it) when he spoke of our death as the "impenetrable dark" that must eventually engulf us. Tillich himself indeed uses practically the same words in one place: "We come from the darkness of the 'not yet,'" he writes, "and rush ahead towards the darkness of the 'no more.'" Our "unavoidable end' is "impenetrable darkness."[7]

THE SEARCH FOR THE "ONTOLOGICAL CHARACTER" OF DEATH

Perhaps it would not be inappropriate to label Tillich an "agnostic ontologist." He is an ontologist in the sense that he regards death as not merely the absence of life but as *state* toward which all human beings inevitably "rush;" and he is an agnostic in that he regards death as an unknowable state. Other existentialists, who share Tillich's view that death is a state, do not agree with him that it is *entirely* unknowable. Prominent among those who believe that human beings can, by suitable "existential" or "dialectical" techniques, achieve *some* knowledge about the nature of death are Professor John Macquarrie, the eminent Protestant theologian, co-translator of Heidegger's *Sein und Zeit,* and author of numerous influential works,[8] and the Spanish philosopher, Professor José Ferrater Mora, renowned for his monumental *Diccionario de Filosofía,* and author of *Being and Death,*[9] a work expounding a "general ontology" in which an attempt is made to "integrate" the achievements of the existentialists with the insights of the naturalists. Neither Professor Macquarrie nor Professor Mora would deny that there are grave difficulties in the way of discovering what death is, but they appear to believe that these difficulties may, to a certain extent, be overcome. We definitely need not, in Mora's words, "resign ourselves to saying nothing about death" (BD, p. 177).

Both Macquarrie and Mora engage very actively in what we may call "the ontological quest" or the search for the "ontological character" of death. To explain what this quest is, or rather what these (and various other) writers believe themselves to be doing, let us first note certain explicit disclaimers on their part. Following Heidegger, both Macquarrie and Mora regard death as more than a mere "natural happening"—as something more than could in principle be explored by the use of scientific methods. Thus, in asking the question "What is death?" or "What is the nature of death?" these philosophers are emphatic and they are not asking the kind of question that a physiologist would ask when he inquires into the nature of death. The ontologists are also not concerned with the traditional religious question of whether human beings live on after the death of their bodies. Nor are they concerned with such "metaphysical" questions as "how and why death came into the world." Heidegger and the various ontologists writing under his influence do not dismiss this last question or the question concerning survival as meaningless, but they insist that their ontological quest is more fundamental and ought to be dealt with first. Both the religious and the metaphysical question, in Macquarrie's words, presuppose "an ontological understanding of death" (ET, p. 117). We cannot hope to answer or even understand such questions until we have "clarified" the ontological nature of death (ibid.), until "the character of death . . . has been fully explored" (SCE, p. 50). These questions can be intelligently approached only after we have "grasped the existential phenomenon of death" (ibid.).

All of this tells us what the ontological quest is not. We can, I think, see what the ontological quest is or what it is supposed to be by first mentioning certain "difficulties" which our ontological explorers freely acknowledge. We cannot find out what death is by any straightforward employment of experience or of the "phenomenological method." "Death," writes Macquarrie,

> is to be investigated by the same method of phenomenological analysis that Heidegger employs in the rest of the existential analytic, [but] there are clearly difficulties here that do not attend any of the other phenomena analyzed. Understanding, moods, speech, anxiety, concern, solicitude—these are all phenomena of existence that undoubtedly go to constitute our daily living. We know them from experience and from continuous participation in them. . . . All this is possible because our

experience of these matters is a "living through" them so that we are then able to reflect upon them and describe them [SCE, p. 51].

Unfortunately death is not like anxiety, concern, or solicitude: The dead person, since he is no longer alive, does not experience his death and hence the phenomenological method cannot be employed by him to study his death. In Professor Macquarrie's words, "Anyone who undergoes death seems by that very fact to be robbed of any possibility of understanding and analyzing what it was to undergo death" (ibid). The dead man's "being is no longer lit up to himself in the only way that would seem to make anything like an existential analysis possible, and so it appears that he cannot by any means understand what the undergoing of death may be like" (ibid).

Macquarrie does not abandon the search after these admissions. He attempts to get at the nature of death by a consideration of various "analogies" and by reflections about the death of others. Although he is very emphatic that the usefulness of these inquiries is limited, Macquarrie believes that they lead to a "preliminary understanding" of the nature of death. Perhaps, he asks, it is possible to compare death "to the ripeness of a fruit, which is not something added to the fruit in its immaturity, but means the fruit itself in a specific way of being" (ET, p. 118). This analogy, unfortunately, breaks down at the crucial point. For, "whereas ripeness is the fulfillment of the fruit, the end may come for man when he is still immature or it may delay until he is broken down and exhausted with his fulfillment long past" (ibid.). Although this analogy breaks down (and the same is true of others which I have not reproduced), Macquarrie believes that such considerations yield a "positive result." It becomes clear that "death belongs to my possible ways of being—though in a unique kind of way, since it is the possibility of ceasing to be. It is already a possibility present in existing . . . it shares a fundamental character of existence, and as a present possibility it is disclosed to me and can be analyzed" (ibid.).

"May information be obtained from considering the death of others?" (ET, p. 117). We cannot phenomenologically study our own death since we shall not be able to do any studying when we are dead, but perhaps we can get at the ontological character of death by paying careful attention to what happens when others die while we are yet alive to witness *their* deaths. As we mentioned previously, Macquarrie does not believe that such an inquiry is entirely fruitless, but at the same time he admits that it does not yield anything like a full answer to his original question. However, in the course of this admission he makes some very revealing remarks. He points out that when we study the death of others our phenomenological exploration is really confined to the mental states of the survivors. Our "vicarious experience" of the death of others cannot be adequate for "grasping death as an existential phenomenon" (SCE, p. 52). "The death of others is experienced as the loss sustained by those who remain behind, and not as *the loss of being which the deceased himself has sustained*" (ET, p. 118; my italics). Nor is this the only trouble. For, in addition to the fact that what we experience is *our* loss and not the loss sustained by the dead person, the latter cannot communicate to us about the loss he has sustained. He cannot "any longer communicate with us to describe that loss of being" (ibid.).

I think that we can now rephrase the ontological question as Professor Macquarrie conceives it in the following ways:

What is death like as it is to the dead?

What is the nature of the loss sustained not by the survivor but by the deceased?

How does the loss of being sustained by the dead person feel to him (not to us) or, since he feels nothing any more, how would it feel to him if he could feel it?

These questions may sound slightly mad, but they are a precise formulation of the ontological quest as conceived by Professor Macquarrie and, in varying degrees, by a number of other existentialist explorers as well.

Before leaving Macquarrie, we should note that in his opinion the study of the death of others yields an important positive result. "One positive character of death" has been ascertained: "Death is always my own since it cannot be experienced vicariously . . . it is untransferable and isolates the individual. He must die himself alone" (ET, p. 118). There are innumerable ways in which one person can represent another, "but nothing of the kind is possible in the case of death . . . no one can die for another, in the sense of taking the other's dying away from him and performing his death for him" (SCE, p. 52). This result may be "combined" with the one achieved in the course of the analogical inquiries mentioned earlier. Together, these results amount to "a preliminary understanding of death as an existential phenomenon." This preliminary understanding may be expressed by saying that "death appears as my own present untransferable possibility of being no longer in the world" (ET, p. 118). In other words, "death belongs to man's possibility—it is, indeed, his most intimate and isolated possibility, always his own" (ET, p. 119).

Like Professor Macquarrie, Professor Mora is much perturbed by the difficulties in the way of a phenomenological exploration of the nature of death. Although, he writes, "we know that there is such a thing or such an event as death, that death is inevitable, that we all must die, and so on, we still do not realize in full measure what death is and what it means until we somehow 'experience' death" (BD, pp. 175–76). But just such an experience seems to be excluded by the very nature of death.

> We can "see" that people die; we can think of our own death as an event which will take place sooner or later, but we do not seem to be able to experience death in the same way as we do other "events" such as pleasure, pain, good health, illness, senility. All we can "see" of death is its "residue," for example, a corpse . . . [ibid.].

It should be noted that a dead person is here automatically regarded as more than a corpse, and it is of course this more which Professor Mora is trying to explore.

Mora agrees with Macquarrie that we cannot get a clear view of the nature of death, but he maintains that we can at least get some kind of glimpse. Although we cannot ever attain a "direct and complete grasp of the nature of death" (p. 178), our experience furnishes us with data that may serve as the basis for "drawing some inferences" (ibid.). Mora's object is to get at the *inside of death* and he thinks that he can, to some slight extent, attain this goal by studying the attitudes which people display toward death. "A description and analysis of some typical attitudes regarding death can cast some light on our subject" (pp. 192–193). It is true that in studying these attitudes we do not experience our death "exactly in the same sense in which we can experience love, friendship, sorrow, and so on" (p. 192), but in our investigation of attitudes toward death "we can place ourselves, so to speak, in front of it (or its possibility)."[10] Professor Mora then surveys different attitudes displayed by people on the point of dying—those who faced a firing squad but were reprieved at the last moment and others who appeared to be drowning but were rescued before it was too late. After enumerating the different kinds of feelings and thoughts that may be going on in people "immediately preceding impending death," Professor Mora does not hide his disappointment and concedes that the value of such a survey is severely limited as far as the purpose of his ontological inquiry is concerned. It must be granted that in attending to our and other people's attitudes, we "see our death" only "somehow from the outside" (p. 194). This is not as much as one could wish, but it is considerably more than nothing—"'somehow from the outside' is not the same as 'completely from the outside.' In some respects we are looking at our death (or its possibility) *from the inside*;

otherwise we could not even take 'an attitude' in front of our death or its possibility" (p. 194; my italics).

Like Macquarrie, Mora pays much attention to the death of others, but he is a little more sanguine in his confidence that such a study can get us to the inside of death. In the absence of a "direct and complete grasp," we can at least "use analogy and conceive of our death in terms of another's death" (p. 192). Professor Mora recounts three personal experiences which "are to be taken as examples of another's death. They cover 'cases' which, as happens in legal matters, can be considered 'precedents'" (p. 178). We shall here confine ourselves to the two which Mora himself regards as his more hopeful cases. In one of them he witnessed the sudden death of a man killed by a bullet in the course of a battle. Professor Mora had not known this man at all and although he felt the death of this man to be symbolic of "the universal and overwhelming presence of death," he experienced neither grief nor anguish. What happened was a "mere fact," something merely objective, "outside there" (p. 183). The second case deals with Professor Mora's maternal grandmother. Here the person who died was not a stranger but on the contrary was somebody whom Professor Mora had known exceedingly well and with whom he had formed "a community of participation" somewhat along the lines described by Landsberg. If the death of a given person is, in relation to a survivor, a "purely external event" then, Professor Mora believes, the survivor would not be justified in claiming that he had experienced the person's death "in the sense of *somehow* sharing it." The death of his grandmother, however, was not experienced by Professor Mora as a merely external event. In such a case "we are not merely 'watching' someone die but we are, or are also, 'sharing' his death—at least to the degree in which we had 'shared things in common.'" However, we must not allow ourselves to be carried away and claim too much. Even when the death is not a merely external event, one only "somehow" shares the deceased's death—"to conclude . . . that we are *actually* 'sharing' another's death," even when the person was terribly close to us, "would be to go too far" (p. 179; my italics). When all is said and done, Professor Mora concludes, "I knew little about the relation between my grandmother and *her* death, and still less about the relation between the man shot down in battle and *his* death" (p. 185; Mora's italics).

DEATH IS NOT A STATE

What is a person who has preserved his sanity to say to all this, more especially to the search for the ontological character of death, the "inside nature" of death as it is to the dead, the nature of the loss sustained not by the survivors but by the deceased, death not as it is observable when we see a dead body, but as it is "undergone" by the dead person? Perhaps the best way to call attention to the ludicrous confusion underlying all such ontological searches is to relate the following conversation between two German pessimists.[11] "It is much better to be dead than to be alive," said the first. "You are right," remarked the second, "but it is still better not to have been born in the first place." "That," replied the first, "is very true, but alas how few are those who achieve such a happy state." Since he regards death as a loss and not as a gain, we may, in this context at least, regard Professor Macquarrie as an optimist and we may imagine an optimist who shares his ontological views reasoning in the following way: "A man who loses both his arms sustains a greater loss than one who loses one arm only, and a man who loses his eyes and his arms sustains a still greater loss. A yet greater loss is sustained by him who loses his life. Even he, however, is not quite as badly off as the man who failed to be born in the first place. The lot of the latter is the worst of all. It is very fortunate that there are not too many who find themselves in this dreadful condition." To diagnose as clearly as possible the absurdity in the procedures of the German pessimists as well as the Macquarrian optimist let us first, following Benn and Peters,[12] distinguish between the "actions" a person performs and the "passions" he experiences or undergoes. An action is anything a person does—for example, singing a song, giving a lecture, assaulting an enemy, resigning a position. A "passion," in the broad sense in which Benn and Peters use the word, is anything that *happens* to a man—a toothache, the tortures he endures, the pleasures he experiences when drinking a glass of orange juice after a game of tennis, the feelings of constrictions he has when gagged or confined to a prison cell. No doubt this distinction is far from sharp, but it is one which all of us make in certain situations. Now, Macquarrie, Tillich, Mora, and most of the poets and philosophers mentioned in the opening section of this article recognize that the death of an individual is not an action, but they mistakenly believe or imply that it is some kind of passion, though a very special and extremely passive type of passion. In fact, however, neither death nor our nonexistence before we were born is a passion any more than it is an action. If we introduce the word "state" to mean any action or passion, then we can express our point by saying that, while feeling the coolness of the night, reaching the last stop of a journey, arriving in a strange country from which one will never return, sleep, and rest, sustaining losses (no matter how serious), undergoing pain and torture, feeling isolated and all alone and even finding oneself surrounded by impenetrable darkness are states or experiences of living human be-ings; death is not a state. At times, indeed, the ontological explorers themselves realize this, for example when they complain about the difficulties of a phenomenological investigation of death. At other times, however, they seriously believe that death is a state, a dark and wholly or largely inaccessible one, to be sure, but a state nevertheless. Without such an assumption they would have to admit that death is simply the absence of life and there would be nothing to explore. It should be added that these strictures do not apply to those who, when asking such questions as "What is death?" or "What are we like after death?" thereby raise the issue of survival. However, the existential ontologists whose explorations we are discussing either do not believe in survival or else explicitly stress that their ontological questions are not questions about whether we survive the death of our bodies.

The linguistic form of the sentences which we use to assert that a person is dead is similar to the sentences which are used to ascribe states to individuals. This similarity makes it tempting to suppose that the former sentences are also used to make state-ascriptions, but a little reflection is sufficient to show that the kind of analysis which will work for state-ascriptions does not make any sense in the case of statements asserting that somebody is dead. Let us briefly look at the following three statements:

(1) A is performing in *Don Giovanni* at the moment.

(2) Tomorrow A will be in one of his gloomy moods.

(3) A year from now A will be dead.

If we go by linguistic appearances alone, we are inclined to say that (3) no less than (1) and (2) are about A, and it is also tempting to believe that in each case we are attributing or ascribing a certain state or experience to A—in (1) an active state, in (2) one that is fairly passive, and in (3) an extremely passive one. In a sense no doubt all three statements are about A—in the sense that we are asserting some fact about A rather than about other people—B, C, etc. In another sense, however, (1) and (2) are about A while (3) is not. In (1) and (2) we *are* ascribing states to A, and we presuppose that A is or will be alive at the times in question. In (3) on the other hand we are not ascribing an extremely passive state to A: We are denying what is presupposed in all state-ascriptions. (1) can be expanded into "A is alive and is performing in *Don Giovanni* now"; (2) into "A will be alive tomorrow and will be in a gloomy state"; but (3) *cannot* be expanded into "A will be alive one year from now but he will then be in the

extremely passive state of deadness." Yet those engaged in the ontological quest treat (3) as if this were the proper analysis.

The Madness of the Ontological Quest

Once death is treated as a state, it is very natural to reach Tillich's
conclusion that it is something absolutely unknowable. It is then quite
natural to reason along the following lines: I am now alive; I am not
yet dead; hence I cannot now know from personal experience what
the state of being dead is like. But this state is different from other
unknowns. It is a very special unknown. Africa is also unknown to
me, but others who have been there can tell me about it when they
return. Again, I have never been skating, but other people can tell me
what it feels like to glide across a frozen lake. Nobody, on the other
hand, can tell me what death is like. For one thing, nobody can come
back from the dead to tell me; but, furthermore, even if somebody did
come back, this would not help, since while he was dead he would
have had no experiences and could not attend to his own state of
deadness. The conclusion thus seems inescapable that, as Tillich so
happily put it, death "is the unknown which by its very nature cannot
be known."

In arguing that death is a totally unknowable state, Tillich dimly
perceived something which ontologists like Macquarrie and Mora obscure when they assert that they have *some little* knowledge of the
nature of death. Tillich dimly perceived that it is *logically* impossible
to attain the object of the ontological quest. The ontologists write
in such a way as to suggest that they are trying to determine the
characteristics of a peculiarly elusive state, but a little reflection makes
it clear beyond any question that what we have here is a series of
self-contradictory expressions and not any kind of state, elusive or
otherwise. To an uncritical reader it may appear—and the remarks
of writers like Macquarrie and Mora are specially apt to foster this
impression—that the object of the ontological quest is a state which
cannot *in fact* be examined by human beings because the only subjects
competent to examine it are chronically absent when they are needed
for the examination. It may thus be thought that the relation of human
beings to the object of the ontological search is like their relation to
some territory which is so extremely hot or so extremely cold that
anybody wishing to explore it is annihilated before he can get to his
destination. In fact, however, the situation is altogether different. The
ontologists are wondering what death would feel like to the dead if
they could attend to their deadness, but part of what is meant by saying

that a person is dead is that he no longer has feelings or experiences. The ontological search thus amounts to the questions "How does it feel to be in a state in which one no longer has any feelings?" or "What kind of an experience does a person have who no longer has any experiences?" These questions are not one whit more sensible than such absurd questions as "How long is the fourth side of that triangle?" asked by somebody who is pointing to a perfectly ordinary triangle or "In which country is the father of this orphan living now?" where the questioner is not referring to any foster father or to any habitat in the next world. The ontological questions do not become any less grotesque by being expressed hypothetically. "How *would* Hume's death feel to him if he could attend to it? is not any less ludicrously absurd than "How *does* Hume's death appear to him?" or "How *does* (the dead) Hume feel about his death?" Once again the reader should be reminded that the ontological explorers have ruled out questions about survival as irrelevant to their problem.

In a decision in which he enjoined the American Nazi Party from holding parades within two miles of Jewish houses of worship, a Chicago judge observed that he would similarly issue an injunction against a group of nudists if they wished to parade in their native attire outside a Presbyterian church. Puzzled by the nature of native attires, an ontologist might now engage in the following investigation: To wear one's native attire is to wear very peculiar clothes. What kind of clothes is a person wearing who is wearing his native attire? There are serious difficulties in the employment of the phenomenological method in this case. When a man is wearing a hat or a woman wearing a skirt and blouse we can perceive the clothes they are wearing. However, when we look at somebody who is wearing his native attire we cannot perceive any clothes. If we could perceive clothes on the person, he would not be wearing his native attire. At this stage a Tillichian ontologist would maintain that we must reach an agnostic conclusion—native attires consist of unknowable clothes—while somebody following Macquarrie and Mora would try to attain a "little knowledge" perhaps by a careful study of the clothes which the nudists wear when they are not wearing their native attire or by studying people who are in the process of changing from their work clothes into their native attire. Perhaps analogies might yield helpful clues—perhaps we should study oranges and apples and bananas after they have been peeled or perhaps an examination of trees, denuded of their foliage, may yield at least a preliminary understanding. The ontological investigation of the nature of death is just as ludicrous as the ontological inquiry into the nature of native attires. To every move in the latter investigation there corresponds a move occurring in the writings of the ontological explorers of death.

There is a familiar story about the boy who, before his first date, was advised by his father to discuss three subjects—love, family, and philosophy. Following his father's advice and taking up love, he first asked the girl, "Do you love noodles?" to which the answer was "no." Remembering that he should next discuss the topic of family, he asked his date whether she had a brother. The answer again was "no." This left only the subject of philosophy and the boy now asked his final question: "If you had a brother, would he love noodles?" I think it would be generally agreed that this last question is absurd, but the ontological question about death is considerably more absurd. Although it would in almost any normal circumstances be utterly pointless to inquire whether a hypothetical brother loves noodles, the question is not self-contradictory: We can describe what it would be like for a girl who in fact has no brother to have a brother and what it would be like for such a person to love or not to love noodles. We might even possess some evidence supporting the claim that a given person's brother would (or would not) love noodles. The ontological question about death, on the other hand, is self-contradictory. The question "How would Hume feel about his death if he could attend to it?" is not merely pointless, but the very meaning of the constituent terms makes it *logically* impossible to obtain an answer. Hume (or anybody else) *cannot both be dead and attend to his deadness*: If he is dead, then he can do no attending of any kind; if he can attend to anything, he is not dead and hence cannot attend to his deadness. While we can describe what it would be like for a girl to have a brother who would (or would not) love noodles, we cannot describe what it would be like for Hume (or anybody) to experience his deadness.

Arleen Beberman, an existentialist explorer from New Haven, Connecticut, finds the ontological quest beyond her capacities. "If we think or imagine what it would be like to be dead," she remarks, "we surreptitiously introduce scenes of life and living people"[13] and thus fail to reach our objective. On the other hand, "if we do experience death," we cannot "report back from the encounter" (op. cit., pp. 18 and 22) and hence our efforts are once again defeated. Miss Beberman decides that she will not aim at anything so ambitious as a "phenomenology of death." "Such a goal," she writes, "is beyond my present intent since the method of coming to that goal requires utmost rigor, boundless creativity, and plenty of time. I lay claim to none of these" (pp. 18–19). In view of her limitations Miss Beberman concludes that her efforts will be merely "episodically phenomenological." Modesty is a most becoming human trait, but here it is out of place. In the present context even the most "creative" phenomenologist, with limitless time on his hands, could not do any better just as a person with perfect vision could not ever detect the clothes which make up a native attire and just as an observer with the most sensitive and highly developed sense of hearing could not discover the language in which somebody is silent.

Death is not a state and once this is clearly seen there is no temptation to engage in an ontological quest and equally no temptation to regard death as unknowable. Death is the absence of life and consciousness; and while in this or that instance it may of course be unknown whether a certain man is really dead (e.g., whether a Nazi leader was killed during the last days of the war or whether he is hiding in South America after undergoing plastic surgery), this is not something that is in principle undiscoverable. Nor do people, in spite of the general tendency to think of the dead as continuing in a dark abode, have in practice the slightest difficulty understanding what is meant by the assertion that somebody is dead. They understand such statements just as readily as they understand statements asserting that a certain person was not yet born at a certain time or that somebody failed to show up at a certain place or that he was silent or that a certain individual wore no clothes.

Something should perhaps be said at this stage about the widespread belief that death is unthinkable and unimaginable. In his discussion of *Grenzsituationen,* Jaspers remarks: "Death is something unimaginable, really something unthinkable. What we imagine and think of in this connection are merely negations, merely associated phenomena [*Nebenerscheinungen*] and never positivities."[14]

Jaspers is surely right in maintaining that when one thinks of such associated phenomena as funerals or the mourning of the bereaved survivors, one is not thinking of death itself, i.e., of the death of the person who died. However, if life and consciousness are in the present context taken to be "positivities," then, in thinking of death, one would *have* to think of a "negativity." If thinking of President Kennedy's life is thinking of a positivity, then thinking of his death is thinking of the termination of his life—of the absence, the nonoccurrence ever again of any actions or passions that would be part of his biography. But this is apparently not enough for Jaspers and others who are under the impression that death is a state. They presumably require that a person, in order to think of death, should be thinking of a dark presence and not merely of the termination of life and consciousness; and, since unfortunately there is no such presence (or else it is impenetrably dark), one will conclude that death itself, as distinct from side-phenomena and negativities, is altogether unthinkable."[15]

THE PSEUDO-EMPIRICAL PROCEDURES
OF THE ONTOLOGICAL EXPLORERS

The full ludicrousness of the ontological search is hidden from the explorers (and presumably also from their less critical readers) by the employment of certain highly misleading strategies. The first of these to which attention should here be called is the frequent use of quasi-inductive techniques and language and the related claim, made by some ontologists, that although the nature of death must remain *largely* unknown, a certain amount of understanding has in fact been achieved by their methods. These strategies suggest that the ontologists are engaged in a quest that is not in principle different from the investigations of a scientist, however much more difficult it may be because of the peculiar nature of the subject matter.

In this connection it is worthwhile to engage in a rather full examination of the ontological "investigations" carried out by Professor Mora. It will be recalled that, according to Professor Mora, we can "somehow" get on the inside of death by studying the various attitudes which people display toward death and that we can gain a little knowledge of what death is in those cases in which there had been a community between us and the dead. Professor Mora believes that in the latter kind of case the survivor, to some extent, shares the dead person's death and that as a consequence he obtains a little knowledge of what this death is like on the inside. If a survivor and a dead person did not form a community, the death in question is merely an "external" event, but where there was a community, the death becomes more than a merely external event. It seems clear that Professor Mora is misled here by the pictures associated with the words "external" and "internal." No matter how much a person may be shaken by a given death, he cannot get at it from the inside any more than a survivor who is altogether indifferent. He does not get inside the dead person's death—not even a tiny bit—not because he lacks some special gift of empathy which other human beings possess or might conceivably possess but because *there is nothing to get into*: There is nothing to get into since death is not a state or condition "of the deceased" and since, if it were a state, it would not be one to which anybody, the dead person or any survivor, could conceivably attend.

The word "share" is commonly used in a number of different senses.

For example we say that two people share a certain object, like a house or a car or a restaurant, if both of them legally own it. Again, we say that people share the same outlook or convictions—e.g., when both of them are socialists or absolute idealists or admirers of Heidegger. Here what we mean is that the two people have similar views or similar attitudes. When Professor Mora claims that on certain occasions one human being can (to some extent or somehow) share the death of another, he evidently has neither of these ordinary senses in mind. In all likelihood he is thinking of the sense in which we say of a person that he shares the grief or the suffering of somebody else if he is so sympathetic that, upon observing the other person's grief or suffering, he experiences a kind of duplication of these in himself. In general, when we use the word "share" in this last sense, we mean more than that the two people have similar feelings: We mean that the first person is so attached to the second that the feelings of the second immediately lead to similar feelings in him. A little reflection makes it quite clear that "share" can no longer be intelligibly used in this sense when a survivor is said to share the death of somebody else. For no matter what the survivor feels, he is not reproducing death in himself. One cannot be significantly said to "share" in this sense unless there is something to share—something like grief or pain—and death does not qualify as such a something. Of course, a person may in this sense share somebody else's *dying*—he may experience in himself the anguish or the serenity or whatever emotions the dying person feels; but this is totally beside the point since what the ontologist is out to explore is death and not dying.

A study of the attitudes of people toward death, whatever its intrinsic interest, does not help the ontological quest along any more than a consideration of bereavements which are classified as more than merely external events. In both cases Professor Mora seems to think that the psychological data available to us (in one case the feeling of the survivor, in the other the attitudes of the people who are thinking about their death) are related to death itself somewhat like the reflections or images of an object (in a lake or a mirror or on a photographic plate) are related to the objects whose reflections they are. However, it is not and cannot be so. Any opinion to the contrary is bound to be the product of confusion. Mora's main confusion consists in an amalgamation of two questions which are logically quite distinct. The first is the psychological question "How do people face death?" The second is the ontological question "What is death like from the inside?" or "What is deadness as it is to those who died?" Mora manages to confound these questions by an ambiguous use of the phrase "experience of death." Neither of Mora's uses can be regarded as an ordinary sense,[16] but it is easy to track down the ambiguity involved. In one context Mora refers to that experience, if such a thing were possible, which the dead person would have if he attended to his deadness. In the other sense he simply refers to the feelings and attitudes of people who contemplate their impending death. Let us call the former the "ontological" and the latter the "attitudinal" sense. Professor Mora himself in one place realizes that he is using the word "experience" in this ambiguous fashion when he concedes that "no doubt an 'attitude' is not exactly the same as an experience" (BD, pp. 193–194). This does not, however, prevent him from proceeding as if no such ambiguity existed. He argues that since people do experience death in the attitudinal sense they therefore have *some little* experience of death in the ontological sense as well. But this is a gross non sequitur and a most confusing amalgamation of two issues. To the question "Do people have experience of their death in the attitudinal sense?" the answer is clearly a ringing "yes," while to the question "Do people have experience of their death in the ontological sense?" the answer is an equally ringing "no." Professor Mora apparently thinks that by amalgamating the two questions we can reach a happy compromise and answer *the* question (suggesting that this is still just the original ontological problem) with a hesitating and soft-spoken "yes." We do not, using his favorite image, ever obtain a full inside knowledge, but equally the knowledge we have is not "wholly from the outside." Using this language, we may express the real situation by saying that if by "the nature of death" one is referring to nothing more than the ways in which people feel and think about their death, then human beings have a very good knowledge of death from the inside, while if by "nature of death" is intended what the ontologists originally set out to explore, then we do not have *even a tiny bit of inside knowledge*—or at any rate this in no way follows from our inside knowledge of death in the other sense. Mora insists that when a person thinks about his attitude he does in a sense stand "in front" of it. This is not an unnatural way of speaking, but the "in-frontness" here involved is not the in-frontness required by the ontologist. The in-frontness required by the ontologist is the kind which occurs when human beings look at a mountain or when they attend to their own feelings. In this sense, when a person attends to his attitude toward death, he is "in front" not of death but of his own feelings and thoughts about death.

Professor Mora maintains that he possesses some "little" knowledge concerning the relation between his grandmother and her death, but he nowhere tells us what this little knowledge consists of. This is not surprising for the simple reason that Professor Mora has no such knowledge and can have none. If anybody thinks otherwise this can only be due to the failure to recognize an ambiguity similar to the one described in the preceding paragraph. It should be noted that Mora does not adduce the fact that he could not achieve more than a little knowledge about the relation between his grandmother and her death as peculiar and exceptional. In other words, it is not just Professor Mora who possesses no more than a little knowledge in such a case, but all human beings are similarly handicapped and inevitably so, no matter how well they may have known the deceased, no matter how close they may have been to him or her throughout life and throughout the last days. Human beings do not even, in their own cases, have any greater access to the relation in question. The reason for this is not, as Professor Mora's language suggests, some kind of empirical limitation like that of a thief who cannot get into an apartment he wishes to rob because he finds it impossible to break through the lock. The reason is the senselessness of the expression "X's relation to his death" as this is used by the ontologist in the course of his quest. This senselessness is obscured by the fact that the expression "X's relation to his death" also has a rather clear meaning in *other* contexts. In nonontological contexts the question "What is X's relation to his death?" would be naturally interpreted to be a means of asking for information about X's attitude toward his death. Here, while we may in this or that case be very ignorant about the person's attitude, we can frequently have a *great deal* if not indeed complete knowledge; and certainly the person himself very often has more than merely a little knowledge. In this sense it seems to me that Professor Mora, having known his grandmother very well and having spent much time with her while she was dying, probably had more than a little knowledge of her relation to her death. Or if *he* did not, the ignorance is not something that is universal and inescapable. However, none of this is of any aid to the ontologist. For what the ontologist is concerned with is not how people feel about their death while they are alive but what death is, i.e., what it is to the dead, what the loss is that the deceased has sustained—not how the deceased felt prior to sustaining the loss. And if the question is taken in this ontological way, Professor Mora has not little but no knowledge whatsoever of the relation between his grandmother and her death. One would know somebody else's relation to his death when the question is asked in the spirit of the ontologist only if one were that other dead person and could then attend to that person's deadness. This, however, is a *logical* impossibility even if it were not a logical impossibility to be somebody else. It is, as we pointed out in the last section, a logical impossibility because if one is dead one cannot do any attending. Not only can Professor Mora have no knowledge about the relation between his grandmother and her death, but in the ontological sense even his grandmother herself can have no such knowledge.

It is important to realize not that Professor Mora's empirical arguments do not "happen" to be invalid, but that they are bound to fail. What is most objectionable about them is not their detailed defects but their very production in the spirit that empirical arguments of some kind might conceivably provide clues to the nature of the object of the ontological search. Much the same applies to "analogies" like that between the ripeness of a fruit on the one hand and death on the other which Macquarrie (and Heidegger) reject but whose very consideration suggests that we have here an inquiry that might conceivably be carried on by means of analogical "indications." Macquarrie and Heidegger are right in rejecting such comparisons, but they give the wrong reasons. In the case of the analogy between the fruit and death, Macquarrie and Heidegger complain that the analogy breaks down because the ripeness of the fruit is "the fulfillment of the fruit," but the end for a man may come when he is still immature or long after he has passed the peak of his powers. Let us suppose, however, that all human beings were to die precisely at the moment of their greatest fulfillment, neither too young nor too old, i.e., when their powers are at their peak. Let us suppose for example that Mozart had not died at the age of thirty-four but that he had lived on until he was sixty-five when his powers finally began to decline, and that Winston Churchill had not lived on into a state of near-senility but that he had died shortly after the successful conclusion of the war against the Nazis. Even if this sort of thing happened universally, the analogy would break down for the simple reason that the fulfillment or maturity of the fruit is a state of the fruit while the death of a man is not one of his states—mature, immature, or any other kind. It is conceivable that a certain kind of person, like Bardone in Rossellini's *Il General Della Rovere,* would experience the greatest moments of fulfillment in the course of sacrificing himself for somebody else or for a cause; but these experiences would still be states of his living organism. In such a case one may, using language loosely, say that the person's death was his greatest fulfillment. However, if one is talking sense, one is really referring to what the person did or experienced while he was dying or going to his death. It is important to bring out the proper reasons for dismissing the above and other analogies since the reason given by Macquarrie and Heidegger suggests that if only human lives were different in certain ways some of these analogies would work. Analogies in which death is compared with a state cannot work, but of course there is not the slightest need to introduce any of them in order to discover what death is. As already pointed out we know quite well what death is and we no more need "analogical clues" in the present case than we need them in order to understand the nature of silence or of native attires.

THE SHIFT FROM THE ONTOLOGICAL PROBLEM
TO OTHER QUESTIONS

In both of his discussions of the ontology of death, Professor Macquarrie reaches a stage at which he claims to have achieved "a preliminary understanding" of death. This "preliminary understanding" consists in the conclusion that death "is man's untransferable possibility of being no longer in the world." I now wish to call attention to the following features of his procedure: first, whatever one may think of the assertions to which Professor Macquarrie refers as "preliminary understanding"—whether they are meaningful or not, true or not, important or not—they do not constitute any kind of relevant answer to his original question. They are in this sense not even a "preliminary" understanding. They tell us nothing about the ontological character of death—the nature of the loss sustained by the deceased, the nature of death as undergone by the dead. The statement that a person cannot transfer his death to somebody else no more tells us anything about the *content* of death than the statement that one human being cannot transfer his native attire to another tells us what native attires are. Or, to use a different illustration, in pointing out that nobody can eat or digest my food for me or that nobody can do my sleeping or resting for me, one does not explain what eating, digesting, sleeping, or resting consist in. Secondly, in the remainder of his discussions Professor Macquarrie confines himself *exclusively* to nonontological issues— chiefly to the psychological questions "How do people in fact think and feel about death?" and "Do they face it honestly or do they try to evade it and, if so, how?" and to what we may call "moral" or "practical" questions like "How ought a person to act in view of his inevitable death?" Practically the entire discussion in both books after reaching the "preliminary understanding" is devoted to an advocacy of the "authentic" attitude toward death (in which one "resolutely anticipates" one's "capital possibility" and even finds "joy in this mode of life" [SCE, p. 55]) and to an analysis and condemnation of the inauthentic approach of those who are in a "fallen" state and who "cover up" for themselves the "present possibility of death" (ibid.). Professor Macquarrie began by telling us that he is out to discover "what the undergoing of death may be like," what death is for the person who has been robbed of his being, and he rightly points out that the phenomenological method encounters difficulties here. Before long these difficulties are overcome by investigating not death but our present feelings about death. This transition is effected with the greatest ease. "Existence," we are told, "is dying, and death is present to us and, *in a way,* accessible to us" (op. cit., p. 52; my italics). And again "death is, . . . *in a sense,* already in the present. It is already accessible, as thrown possibility, to the investigation of the existential analytic" (op. cit., p. 55; my italics). Any consistent ontologist ought surely to protest that Professor Macquarrie simply abandons ontology for introspective psychology here. What is "present" and "accessible" is not death but thoughts about death and no amount of qualifications ("in a way," "in a sense," and many more I have not reproduced) can undo the difference. What becomes accessible to phenomenological study or to the existential analytic had always been accessible, and what had not been accessible (the state of deadness as distinct from thoughts about death) is no more accessible after the shift than it had been before. Macquarrie first ruled out the study of the death of others on the ground that although it "might teach us much . . . about psychological reactions in the face of death," it "can never disclose death as an existential phenomenon," but he ends up studying precisely such psychological reactions.

It should be emphasized that Professor Macquarrie is by no means alone in shifting from ontological to psychological and practical issues, and it should also be noted that these psychological and practical questions are not usually senseless. The failure to detect the shift and the intelligibility of the questions to which the ontologists transfer their attention are perhaps as much responsible for their not perceiving the ludicrousness of the initial ontological quest as the use of such quasi-inductive techniques as we described in the last section. In Macquarrie's case the main mechanism of the shift is an ambiguity in the word "existential" as it is used in such expressions as "existential character" or "existential phenomenon." All existentialists are agreed that death is more than a biological phenomenon; and to this "more" they refer as the "existential character" or the "existential aspect" of death. However, different existentialists and sometimes the same existentialists at different times have different things in mind when they speak of this "more." Sometimes when we are told that the existential character of death must escape the biologist, what is meant is indeed the "ontological character" of death—the object of what we have been calling the ontological quest; but at other times, when the limitations of the public methods of biology are stressed, the writers refer to the inner[17] feelings of anguish, horror, serenity, or whatever people experience when they think about their death. Since the word "existential" is used in both of these ways, Professor Macquarrie can maintain that all his answers are answers to questions about the existential character of death and anybody who is not attentive to the ambiguity just described would not notice the shift that has taken place.

In Mora's case the mechanism of the main shift is an ambiguity in the word "understand." Professor Mora sets out to "understand" death and originally this means finding out what death is on the inside in the ontological sense. But he is also concerned with the question "Does death ever (and perhaps always) have meaning or is it always or at least sometimes an absurd happening?" To this latter question Professor Mora proposes the answer that "human death is never completely meaningful, nor is it entirely meaningless—it is meaningful and meaningless in varying degrees" (BD, p. 186). I do not profess to understand what he means either by this question or by his answer, but this does not affect the possibility of tracking down his shift. It seems quite clear that when we say about something, x, that we know what it means, it is permissible to express this by saying that we understand x, whether x is a word, a phenomenon, or a theory. It is thus quite natural for Professor Mora to believe that he has answered his original ontological question after concluding that death is always meaningful in varying degrees and that this meaning can be ascertained. Whatever the merits of these last contentions may be, they do not constitute any kind of answer to his original question—they do not make death "comprehensible" or "understood" in the sense in which these words must be used when they express the ontological problem.

THE CLAIM THAT DEATH IS MORE THAN A "NATURAL" PHENOMENON

All existentialists agree that death is more than a natural phenomenon and that some nonscientific technique (variously called the "phenomenological method" or the "existential analytic") is required for the study of its nonnatural aspects. This conviction is shared by existentialists who actively pursue the ontological quest and by those who only occasionally show some slight inclinations in that direction without ever setting out on a full-fledged expedition. Professor John Wild, who belongs to the latter group, offers the following considerations in support of the view that death is not merely a natural phenomenon:

> The existentialist thinkers have performed an important service in recalling our attention to the actual phenomenon of personal death. They have shown with great cogency and clarity that this is something more than the objective biological stoppage which can be observed from the outside. The limited methods of science can shed no light on this inner

existential phenomenon which is open only to philosophical description and analysis.[18]

The existentialist contributions to the phenomenology of death are also of major importance. They have certainly shown the incapacity of naturalistic and pan-objectivistic interpretations to account for the more important existential phases of this mysterious and long-neglected phenomenon. In this sense, death is not something universal. It concerns me as an individual. It is not a replaceable, interchangeable function, but something I must face by myself alone. It is not an event that I will observe in the future, but something that I must either evade or face authentically here and now.[19]

There is a great deal that is objectionable in all this. With the claims that death is a "mysterious" phenomenon and that I *must* face death "by myself alone" I shall deal in later sections. Right now, however, it is necessary to observe that although some of Professor Wild's remarks are true, they do not in any way imply his main conclusion about the existence of aspects of death which cannot be studied by the "limited methods of science." To begin with, Professor Wild is quite right in calling attention to the difference between what one may call the statistical and the personal perspectives. It surely cannot be denied that a person's state of mind is very different when he gives his assent to the proposition that all men are mortal from what it is when he realizes that he himself is one of those who will inevitably die. Although this is certainly not something that existentialists have discovered, people do perhaps on occasions forget it and it may well be salutary to be reminded of it from time to time. To this, however, it must be added that the differences are not peculiar to the subject of death. It is exactly the same with thousands of other things—e.g., suffering imprisonment unjustly or contracting a chronic and painful disease. The state of mind of a person who reads in a book that 10 per cent of all people condemned to prison sentences are in fact innocent is very likely to be significantly different from what it would be if he became one of those convicted for a crime he did not commit; and the state of mind of somebody who reads about what patients suffering from chronic arthritis go through is likely to be very different from what it would be if he himself became such a sufferer. Convictions, just and unjust, are phenomena that can be studied by the methods of science and so can the feelings of those convicted; and the same is true of arthritis and the states of mind of those suffering from this disease. It is not easy to see why the admission that there is a genuine difference between the personal and the statistical viewpoints should imply that either the subject in question (be it arthritis, convictions, or death) or the mental states which make up the personal viewpoint fall outside the scope of scientific inquiry.

Professor Wild, like other existentialists, has a tendency to define "science" in a misleadingly narrow way. It may be granted that death is "something more than the objective biological stoppage which can be observed from the outside." Death is also the termination of consciousness. However, for this insight it is not necessary to appeal to phenomenology or to the existential analytic. Professor Wild no doubt in this context also thinks of *dying;* and again it may be granted that the biologist, in studying the physiological processes that go on in a dying organism, does not thereby study the experiences of the individual which, from the human point of view, are usually the most poignant aspect of the situation. Again, however, from this it does not follow that science cannot study these inner experiences; and in fact Feifel and other contemporary psychologists[20] have amassed a good deal of interesting material which is not one whit less scientific than the work of other psychologists who rely on the introspective reports of their subjects. Some of Heidegger's own most interesting comments about human attitudes toward death, which carry the wholehearted endorsement of Professors Macquarrie and Wild, would, if true, be part of this branch of scientific psychology.

Somebody might admit all of this but maintain that science cannot tackle the practical and moral issues about death—how human beings *ought* to face it and conduct their lives in the light of their inevitable doom. This may be admitted, although it is an exaggeration to say that scientific information can *never* have *any* bearing on such moral questions. It may be conceded that science cannot answer these questions without, however, conceding that there are some nonnatural features of death which require investigation by the "existential analytic." There are many other practical questions which also cannot be answered (simply) by using scientific techniques. If a man is contemplating marriage and the question before him is which of two women he should choose, or, to take a less momentous example, if a person asks himself which tie he should wear with his new blue shirt, science too does not provide the answers. However, it does not follow from any of these admissions that the choice of a wife or of a tie are phenomena with aspects that can be investigated only by some nonscientific technique.

DYING ISOLATED AND ALONE

One of the most pervasive confusions in the writings of the existentialists is their failure to distinguish between death and dying.[21] The existentialists themselves on occasions endorse this distinction in a *general* way. Thus both Macquarrie and Mora quote, with apparent approval, Wittgenstein's dictum that "death is not an event of life"[22]—at any rate if they think that Wittgenstein was wrong they nowhere give us their reasons. Such admissions in general terms do not, however, prevent these writers from constantly confounding death and dying in discussions of specific topics. Unlike death, dying *is* a process or, in our use of the word, a state or succession of states, and many of the existentialist pronouncements cease to be senseless when they are interpreted as statements about dying. Thus it is not nonsense to maintain that a person finds his greatest fulfillment in dying, although cases of this sort are certainly very rare. It is not nonsense, but frequently true, that a person while dying is *undergoing* a great deal of suffering. Again, if we have in mind the anguish or the other feelings experienced by a person who knows that he is dying, then it is conceivable that others may share his dying in the same sense in which one sympathetic human being may share the emotions of other human beings. Or, to take one of Tillich's favorite statements, it is indeed absurd to maintain that a person finds himself, after death, engulfed by an impenetrable darkness, but similar remarks about dying are not only not absurd but may well be true. Thus a German physician, Johannes Lange, who studied patients dying very gradually of degenerative diseases, reports that as their life was slowly ebbing away, they felt that they became more and more surrounded by darkness.[23] In our ordinary thinking we also frequently fail to keep death and dying clearly apart, and this is one reason why the full ludicrousness of the ontological quest is not always noticed. When the existentialists mean death (and I am here referring to situations in which they must mean death if they are to do ontology), many an innocent reader tacitly substitutes "dying" and the resulting statements, though frequently false, are no longer senseless.[24]

The confusion between death and dying is unquestionably one of the factors responsible for the extremely misleading assertions, endlessly repeated by all existentialists, that all of us must die isolated and alone. "No one can die my death for me," writes Professor Wild; "this thing at least I *must do alone*" (op. cit., p. 82; my italics). Death, he later remarks, "is an actual act to be lived through by an individual *alone*" (p. 83; my italics). Again, in a passage quoted previously, we are told that death is "something I must face by myself alone" (p. 239; my italics). Professor Macquarrie expresses this doctrine of what we may call "the privacy of death" by declaring that death "*isolates* the individual. He must die himself *alone*" (ET, p. 118; my italics). In a similar vein, though not using the word "alone," Professor William Barrett writes: "Death is not a public fact occurring out there in the world; it is something that happens within my own existence."[25] When these writers maintain that human beings die isolated and alone (and this of course is asserted not of some but of all human beings), they presumably wish to claim more than merely that all human beings eventually die. They give the impression and they themselves undoubtedly believe that they are not merely redescribing the latter familiar fact. However, if "alone" is used in any sense in which "all human beings die alone" asserts more than that they all eventually die, it is quite clearly false. In one natural sense of this expression, somebody dies alone if he is physically isolated as in the case of a man who gets lost on an Arctic expedition and freezes or starves to death before the rescuers arrive. There is another sense in which one may quite naturally speak of somebody as dying alone or in solitude, although the person need not be physically isolated like the man lost in the Arctic. What we then mean is that, while dying, the person is psychologically or emotionally isolated—he does not greatly care about anybody else and nobody else cares much about him. It is in this latter sense that Ivan Ilyich in Tolstoy's moving story dies alone although he has a dutiful wife and daughter. Now, it is clear beyond any doubt that, while some people die alone in one and some in both of these senses, others do not die alone in either sense. Winston Churchill, Louis XIV, and David Hume, to cite some familiar cases, did not die alone in either of these senses.

The existentialists suggest that there is a third sense in which "dying alone" means more than just "dying" and in which all human beings necessarily die alone. It is easy to show that there is no such further sense and that the only sense in which it is true that all human beings necessarily die alone is one in which "dying alone" is logically equivalent to "dying." As the existentialists use "alone" (or rather as it must be interpreted if their statement is not to be plainly false), it is *logically inconceivable* for a person not to die alone. Let us suppose that a human being is not dying in either physical or emotional isolation but is, on the contrary, experiencing the greatest and deepest love and happiness of his entire life during his last days.[26] As the existentialists use "alone" in the present context, such a person would still have to be described as dying alone for the simple reason that he is dying. If "alone" had some additional content, then it would be possible to describe what it would be like for a person to die without dying alone; but as the existentialists use these words, such a description is not possible. The existentialists *seem* to be saying something novel and of interest here and they also *seem* to be saying something that is plainly true. However, the upshot of our discussion is that if their statement is interpreted in such a way that it says something interesting, then it is clearly false; while if it is interpreted so as to make it true, it becomes

nothing more than a rhetorical way of asserting the exceedingly familiar fact that everybody dies some day.

Much the same comment is applicable to the other formulation that
is commonly given to what we called the doctrine of the privacy of
death. We are told that nobody can get another human being to die for
him, to act as his substitute or representative in the matter of death;
and this is put forward as a statement asserting more than the familiar
fact that everybody eventually dies. However, the key expressions in
these formulations are ambiguous: When used in one sense, the statement to the effect that nobody can die somebody else's death is not
platitudinous and goes beyond the assertion that everybody eventually
dies, but in this sense it is false; when used in another sense the statement is true, but then it becomes a platitude simply reasserting that
everybody dies some day. There is a perfectly natural sense in which
people can get others to die as their substitutes. During the French
Revolution the authorities in Paris would occasionally allow a man
who had been sentenced to death to leave his prison in order to attend
to urgent business provided that somebody else took his place as a
kind of human bail. If the person sentenced to death did not return by
a given time, the man substituting for him would be guillotined in his
place. Heidegger and his followers point out that in such a case the
evil day is postponed and not ultimately avoided: The person who
absconded will some day die and then he will not be able to have
somebody else die in his place. In Heidegger's own words: "No one
can die for another. He may give his life for another, but that does not
in the slightest deliver the other from his own death."[27] To keep these
two senses apart, let us insert the adjective "ultimately" whenever we
use the expressions in the sense in which it is clearly true that nobody
can get somebody else to die as his substitute or representative. Now,
it seems clear that what prevents a person from *ultimately* getting a
substitute is simply the fact that he will eventually die. It is part of the
meaning of "he will die" that he cannot ultimately get a substitute. It
is not one fact that all human beings eventually die and a further fact
that they cannot ultimately get a substitute for their death: These are
two different ways of referring to *the same fact*. Suppose there were
a tremendously powerful tyrant who has for many years been in the
habit of getting other people to do the most varied things in his place.
Whenever an unpleasant task comes up—e.g., to meet a foreign digni-
tary, to attend the opening of a boring play, or to receive an honorary
degree—he sends somebody else. When he is challenged to a duel, he
sends a substitute, and when he wishes to get rid of dangerous opponents, he sends other people to do the killing for him. After many
years of this, he comes to believe that he can also (in our second sense,

i.e., "ultimately") get somebody else to die for him. How would we, if this were possible, convince the tyrant that he was mistaken? In effect he believes that he will never die and to show him that here he cannot ultimately get a substitute we would have to convince him that, like all others, he will eventually die: We do not have to convince him first that he will eventually die and then, separately, that he cannot ultimately get a substitute in the matter of dying.

To the above criticisms of the doctrine of the privacy of death, it may be replied that although not everybody is necessarily alone while dying, *in death* this is the fate of all human beings; and this contention will appear plausible to all, whether they are ordinary people or philosophers engaged in the ontological quest, who are under the influence of the notion that the dead person is sleeping in the grave or that he somehow continues to exist in a dark abode. The man who is lying in his coffin is there all alone and his loneliness would not be remedied even if we put a few corpses or perhaps a few living people into the same coffin since he would not be able to converse with them. Somebody under the sway of this picture might exclaim that the dead are in fact more alone than any living person can be. For, unlike the living they cannot obtain any of the relief that comes from talking about one's losses. The dead cannot talk to the living or to their fellow dead or even to themselves. Their loneliness is thus seen to be truly staggering! Once this is spelled out in full, the absurdity becomes quite obvious; while it is *false* to assert that everybody dies alone in any sense in which this asserts more than that any people eventually die, it is *senseless* to say about anybody that he is alone in his death. To be alone, one has to be alive, and the dead are neither alone nor not alone for the same reason that Julius Caesar is neither an even nor an odd number and that feelings of anger are neither blue nor red. As for Professor Barrett's statement that death is not a "public event," it is appropriate to remark that unless death is taken as the inner state of the deceased in which he has the experience of having no experiences—and we saw that there were "difficulties" in conceiving death in this way—death *is* a public event, though not one which the dead person can witness. What is not or not exclusively a public event is dying, or more specifically the experiences of the dying person; but these, it should be added, are no more private than other feelings and thoughts.

THE "MYSTERY" OF DEATH

Almost as frequently as they assert that each person must die his death alone, the existentialists make remarks to the effect that death is something mysterious. They do not merely mean that this or that man's death is a mystery but that all deaths anywhere, at all times, and under all imaginable circumstances are, and are necessarily, mysterious. Thus Professor Wild, in a passage quoted previously, speaks of "this mysterious and long-neglected phenomenon" (op. cit., p. 238) and earlier in the same work he observed that "harsh, mysterious, and inexorable, death places all else in question and reveals the uncanny strangeness of the world" (p. 84). In several places Wild also asserts that death is "opaque to theoretical analysis" (p. 82) or "opaque to understanding" (p. 81). Professor Tillich, needless to say, since he regards death as the "end . . . with its impenetrable darkness," concurs in this opinion and adds that time too is a mystery.[28] Professor Macquarrie complains that people who treat death as an impersonal phenomenon are thereby taking the "mystery and imminent threat" out of it (ET, p. 121). The remarks about the mysterious nature of death just quoted are rather cryptic, but there is a much fuller statement in a recent work by an English writer who, while not calling himself an existentialist, expresses great sympathy for the movement. In his *Existentialism—For and Against,* Paul Roubiczek praises the existentialists for offering valuable correctives of errors associated with positivism and the thinkers of the Enlightenment. "The mystery of death," he writes, "even more than that of birth, is bound to invalidate all the false convictions which survive from the Age of Reason." To this he adds:

> Purely rational thought, though it can explain the causes of death in scientific terms, can never account for the fact that we can die at any moment and are beings who, in any case, must die sooner or later. The length of our lives seems to be fixed in a purely arbitrary way which, being inexplicable, defeats the power of reason [p. 113].

Perhaps none of the existentialist theses about death strikes a more responsive chord in ordinary readers than this claim that death is mysterious; and it is echoed in countless statements found among poets, novelists, orators, religious writers, and even psychologists.[29] The feelings of helplessness and horror which death inspires in most people seem to lead very naturally to the remark that death is a mystery or to other remarks along the same lines. It is probably sacrilege of the most damnable kind to subject such statements to a critical examination, but those who prefer clear thinking to nebulous rhetoric will not wish to shirk this task.

Of the various senses in which the word "mystery" has been used, either in ordinary life or by philosophers and theologians, there seem to be only two in which the statement that death is a mystery could make any sense. We refer to something as a mystery in one of these senses if we do not know its cause or if we are ignorant of certain of its features. It is in this sense that various diseases are mysteries even at the present time and it is in this sense that somebody, accustomed to the beautifully simple arrangement of streets and avenues in midtown Manhattan, is liable to find parts of Brooklyn or the North Side of Chicago baffling mysteries. Although this or that death may well be mysterious in this first sense, it cannot be reasonably maintained that the same is true of every death: We frequently do know the causes of death as well as the surrounding circumstances. In any event, as Mr. Roubiczek remarks quite explicitly, this is not the sense in which he or the existentialists declare death to be a mystery.

In the other sense we say of something that it is a mystery if it conflicts, or at least if it appears to conflict, with some proposition that is neither well established nor extremely probable nor at least fervently adhered to. Let us suppose that a man whom we thought happy and exceptionally stable suddenly suffers a psychotic breakdown or that he commits suicide. We would be inclined to describe his breakdown or his suicide as mysterious. By this we would mean that they cannot be reconciled with the proposition, apparently based on very strong evidence, that he was happy and stable. It is in this sense that believers in an all-powerful and all-good God frequently use the word "mystery," when they concede that evil or at least certain forms of evil found in the world are a mystery. Now, if somebody believes in such a God and it he regards death as something evil and as the kind of evil which an all-powerful and all-good God might have been expected to prevent, then *his* statement that death is a mystery makes perfectly good sense. One may think that he is irrational in not abandoning his belief in an all-powerful and all-good God in view of the facts of evil that cannot be reconciled with such a belief, but that is another matter with which we are not here concerned. What does concern us here is that it is *not open* to those existentialists who are not believers in such a God to regard death as a mystery in the sense under discussion. And to this it should be added that, as far as one can judge from their writings, those existentialists who are believers in an all-powerful and all-good God do not mean this either. Although they may in fact be perplexed by the problem of evil, they are not discussing this problem in any of its forms and shapes when they describe death as a mystery.

I may of course be mistaken in thinking that the two senses just discussed are the only ones in which the word "mystery" can be understood if the declaration that death is a mystery is to make any sense. If I am mistaken, I hope than an existential ontologist will come forward and tell us what other sense there is in which death can be intelligibly characterized as a mystery. If, however, I am right and the above two senses are the only ones to be considered in this context, we may reach the following conclusion: It is meaningful but false to maintain that death is always a mystery in the first sense; religious believers could say something sensible by calling death a mystery in the second sense, but the existentialists are not, and many of them cannot be, using "mystery" in this sense.

We can perhaps obtain some understanding of what these writers are doing by comparing their statements about the mystery of death with what I have elsewhere called the "quasi-theological why."[30] People who do not or who no longer believe in God nevertheless quite frequently ask such apparent questions as "Why do I have to suffer so much?" or "Why is it that, although I try so hard and mean so well, happiness in the end always eludes me?" As asked by somebody who believes in a just and good God, these are genuine questions, asking how the initial theological assumption can be reconciled with the injustice and suffering experienced by the questioner. However, when an unbeliever uses such language, we no longer have anything that can be treated as a genuine question. What we have before us are *complaints* about the nature of the universe, expressions of disappointment and perhaps despair that the operations of the world are not in accordance with the individual's moral demands. Similarly, when somebody like Mr. Roubiczek speaks of death as a mystery and excludes from the start as irrelevant any information that science might provide, he may well be using the word "mystery" in a quasi-theological way. He does not seem to be raising a question but to be complaining about the "absurdity" of death: He seems to be complaining that death occurs at all and, furthermore, that there is no correspondence between the length of a human life and the moral caliber of the particular human being.

It is a pity that Mr. Roubiczek does not identify the thinkers of the Age of Reason whose "false convictions" he wishes to demolish. It is more than doubtful that philosophers like Hume or Diderot would ever have wished to dispute the assertion that death is a contingent fact or that the lack of any correspondence between the length of a human life and the moral qualities of the person in question is a feature of the world which cannot be further explained. What they would probably have added to these admissions is that one is not advancing the understanding of anything by referring to such contingent facts as "mysteries."

CONCLUSIONS

It may be helpful to bring together the main conclusions reached in this article:

1. There is a real difference between what we called the "statistical" and the "personal" perspectives. This, however, is not peculiar to the subject of death; and the feelings and thoughts which constitute the personal perspective can be made the object of scientific inquiry no less than other psychological phenomena.

2. Death is the absence of life and is no more inconceivable than other absences—e.g., the absence of sound or of clothes. Not only is death not inconceivable, but in fact people conceive of it constantly and without the slightest difficulty.

3. Although this or that death may be a mystery, it is not true that all deaths are necessarily mysterious—at any rate the only people who could justly make such a claim are believers in an all-powerful and all-good God provided they also regard death as an evil which such a God might have been expected to prevent.

4. The doctrine of the privacy of death, whether it is expressed by the statement that everybody dies isolated and alone or by the statement that in the matter of death one cannot have a representative, is either false or platitudinous, asserting no more than that everybody eventually dies.

5. The writings of the existentialists are pervaded by a confusion of death with dying. Many of their pronouncements which are absurd when interpreted as statements about death cease to be absurd when treated as statements about dying.

6. It is claimed by many existentialists that *their* question "What is death?" is distinct from scientific questions about the nature of death, from religious questions about survival, and from such metaphysical questions as "Why does death occur at all?" Their question is said to be concerned with the "ontological character" of death. However, we found that when they discuss the "ontological character" of death, the existentialists do one of two things: They either address themselves to certain psychological and practical issues, in which case the use of the word "ontological" is highly misleading, or else they engage in what we called the "ontological quest," which amounts to asking "What does death feel like to the dead?" and this turned out to be a grotesque pseudo-inquiry. It would perhaps be claiming too much to say that there is no genuine ontological question here, but if there is one, this has yet to be demonstrated.

NOTES

1. I wish to thank my friends Martin Lean, Donald Levy, Margaret Miner, Mary Mothersill, and Elmer Sprague for reading an earlier version of this manuscript and for making helpful suggestions.

2. The only person known to me who habitually slept in his coffin was "Lord" Timothy Dexter, an illiterate Yankee trader who made a fortune during the Revolutionary War and who subsequently settled in Newburyport, Massachusetts. There he built a Hall of Fame containing statues of Napoleon, Benjamin Franklin, George Washington, George III, and himself as well as a mausoleum with an enormous coffin painted white and green. To enjoy the coffin while he was still alive, Dexter had a couch put into it and not infrequently he took his nap on the couch. Brahms was an eccentric man, but it was not his habit to sleep in a coffin.

3. *The World as Will and Idea,* III 382.

4. *The Experience of Death,* p. 13.

5. *The Courage to Be* (referred to as CB), p. 36.

6. *Systematic Theology,* I 188–89.

7. "The Eternal Now, in H. Feifel (ed.), *The Meaning of Death,* pp. 303–31.

8. Macquarrie's discussions of death are contained in his *An Existentialist Theology* (abbreviated as ET) and *Studies in Christian Existentialism* (abbreviated as SCE).

9. Referred to as BD.

10. There is a constant shift in Mora's discussion from talk about death to talk about the possibility of death. I am ignoring this here because experiences of the "possibility of death" have nothing to do with the original ontological aim which, in Professor Mora's words, is "to scrutinize in detail the nature of human death" (p. 170). In a later section of this article I shall provide a detailed account of the chronic shifts of existentialists from ontological issues to psychological and moral questions.

11. Adapted from Bertrand Russell's *Portraits from Memory,* p. 147.

12. *Social Principles and the Democratic State,* p. 200. Needless to say, Benn and Peters are not the first to make this distinction. It is already found in Aristotle and Descartes.

13. "Death and My Life," *The Review of Metaphysics,* 1963, p. 22.

14. *Psychologie der Weltanschauungen,* p. 261.

15. For a discussion of the peculiar arguments in support of the claim that although the death of others is conceivable and imaginable, one's own death is not, see my article "My Death," *The Encyclopedia of Philosophy,* V, 416–19.

16. The only ordinary sense known to me in which we ever say of somebody that he "experiences death" occurs in connection with people, like doctors, nurses, and coroners, who frequently observe dead bodies (and dying patients). By saying that these people "experience death" we mean that they habitually observe human beings as they are dying and their dead bodies shortly after death has taken place.

17. The word "inner" is used ambiguously in much the same way as "existential." Biology, we are told, cannot explore the "inner" nature of death; and sometimes this means the inner nature as it would appear to the deceased if he could attend to it while at other times it just refers to attitudes toward death on the part of the living.

18. *The Challenge of Existentialism*, p. 218.

19. Op. cit., pp. 238–39.

20. See H. Feifel, "Death—Relevant Variable in Psychology," in R. May (ed.), *Existential Psychology*; the same author's "Death" in N. L. Farberow (ed.), Taboo Topics; and the contributions by C. W. Wahl, N. H. Nagy, R. Kastenbaum, H. Feifel, A. A. Hutschnecker, G. J. Aronson, and E. S. Shneidman and N. L. Farberow to H. Feifel (ed.), *The Meaning of Death*. Feifel's own contribution to the last volume contains a valuable bibliography.

21. One notable exception is Jaspers, who is hardly ever guilty of this confusion and who in fact makes a clear distinction between them on several occasions. Thus he writes: "Death cannot be an experience. Whoever has an experience is still alive" (*General Psychopathology*, p. 477). Again: "Every report on dying persons refers to their attitude to death, not to death itself" (p. 478).

22. The full text is as follows: "Death is not an event of life—death is not lived through" (*Tractatus Logico-Philosophicus*, 6.4311).

23. Quoted by Jaspers in his *General Psychopathology*, p. 478.

24. In one place Macquarrie remarks (SCE, p. 237) that although a "sinless" person cannot avoid death any more than one who is "fallen" or living inauthentically, their deaths are significantly different—"the end of the 'sinless' person would be somehow different from death as we ordinarily know it." Macquarrie, it should be emphasized, is not in any way referring to some differences in the afterlife; but, if so, what he says can make sense only if he means "dying" and not "death." In the absence of an afterlife, the deaths of the sinless and the sinful man are not "somehow" different. When they are dead, neither of them is alive and neither can take any satisfaction in anything or suffer any regrets about a previous inauthentic existence.

25. *What Is Existentialism?* p. 63.

26. Cases of this sort are found both in literature and in real life. Thus Hume, while close to death, wrote referring to the days of his final illness: "Were I to name the period of my life which I should most choose to pass over again, I might be tempted to point to this later period." Matthias Clausen, in Gerhardt Hauptmann's magnificent play *Vor Sonnenuntergang*, is experiencing his greatest love and his deepest feelings during his last months. Many other such examples could be cited.

27. *Sein und Zeit*, p. 240.

28. "We speak of time in three ways or modes: the past, present and future. Every child is aware of them, but no wise man has ever penetrated their mystery. . . . The mystery of the future and the mystery of the past are united in the mystery of the present. . . . The mystery is that we *have* a present; and even more, that we have *our* future. Also because we anticipate in the present; and that we have *our* past; also because we remember it in the present. The present, our future and our past are ours" ("The Eternal Now," op. cit., pp. 31–36, 37). One cannot help wondering what is troubling Tillich: Under what circumstances would time no longer be a mystery? Unless Tillich can

answer this question, it is not easy to see what is meant by saying that time is a mystery.

29. Herman Feifel, the psychologist, who seems otherwise a sensible man and not given to nebulous pronouncements, cannot refrain from speaking of death as "the eternal mystery" ("Death—Relevant Variable in Psychology," in Rollo May [ed.], *Existential Psychology,* p. 61).

30. See my article "Why?" *The Encyclopedia of Philosophy,* VIII 296–302.

4

Existentialism and the
Fear of Dying

MICHAEL A. SLOTE

University of Maryland

IN THIS PAPER I shall present a fairly systematic "existentialist" view of human anxiety about death and human responses to that anxiety, based on the work of Pascal, Kierkegaard, Heidegger, and Sartre. My main purpose is constructive, rather than exegetical. What seems to me most distinctive and important about the work of these existentialist authors is their approach to the fear of dying—or at least the relevance of what they say to that subject, for sometimes, when they deal with other topics, what they say can (I shall attempt to show) be used to illuminate the nature of human responses to the fear of death. But I think that much of what these authors say about the fear of dying is inchoate, confusing, or incomplete, and requires supplementation, clarification, and systematization of the kind I shall be attempting to provide here.[1]

I

Perhaps the central locus of discussion, by an Existentialist, of human attitudes toward and responses to death is the section of Kierkegaard's *Concluding Unscientific Postscript* called "The Task of Becoming Subjective." According to Kierkegaard, becoming subjective is "the most difficult of all tasks in fact, precisely because every human being has a strong natural bent and passion to become something more and dif-

Reprinted by permission from *American Philosophical Quarterly*, 12 (1975), 17–28.

ferent."[2] But what is it to be subjective or to be objective, and why is the former so difficult and the latter so tempting? Part of Kierkegaard's explanation involves him in a contrast between the subjective and objective acceptance of Christianity. But Kierkegaard also applies the subjective/objective distinction to attitudes toward life and death generally. And what unites Kierkegaard in the "Becoming Subjective" section of the *Postscript* with such non-religious Existentialists as Heidegger and Sartre is the fact that he has something to say about human attitudes toward life and death that presupposes no particular form of religiosity and that has not, I think, been said by anyone outside the existentialist tradition. And it is this aspect of Kierkegaard's work that I shall be examining.

According to Kierkegaard, to have an objective attitude toward one's life is to have the kind of attitude toward one's life encouraged by an Hegelian view of the world. On such a view, one is part of a larger "world-historical" process of the self-realization of Reason or Spirit, and one's life takes on significance if one plays a role, however minor, in that world-historical process. One does not have to be an Hegelian to think in this kind of way. One can be thinking in a similar way if, as a scientist or philosopher, e.g., one devotes oneself to one's field in the belief or hope that one's life gains significance through one's contribution to something "bigger."

Kierkegaard says that people with such an attitude have an objective attitude toward their lives; and he wants each of us to dare to become subjective and renounce this "loftily pretentious and yet delusive intercourse" with the world-historical.[3] Those who live objectively are, according to Kierkegaard, under a delusion or illusion, and if so, then surely he has a real argument in favor of being subjective. For Kierkegaard, at least part of the illusion is, I think, the belief that by living objectively, one's dividend, what (good) one gets from life, is greater.[4] In the first place, even if a certain word-historical process of development is a great good, it is a good that is divided up among those participating in that development into many parts, none of which, presumably, is large in relation to the whole, and so perhaps the good to be derived from participating in that development will be less than the good to be gained by living subjectively. But Kierkegaard then seems to question whether indeed there is *any* good to be gained from living for some world-historical process, since one who does so may not be around when it comes to fruition. But it is not clear that the good of such a process of development must all come at the end of that development, so I think Kierkegaard has still not given us any very strong reason for believing that one who lives objectively is under some kind of illusion that his life is better.

However, in the *Postscript* Kierkegaard attempts to tie up his discussion of living objectively, i.e., of living for the world-historical, with certain illusory "objective" attitudes toward death. One who lives world-historically will sometimes say: "What does it matter whether I die or not; the work is what is important, and others will be able to carry it forward." But this is to think of one's death as nothing special, as just one death among others, as a "something in general." And Kierkegaard seems to believe that one who thinks this way is under an illusion, the illusion that his own death has no more significance *for him* than the death of (random) others, or, to put it slightly differently, that he *should be* no more concerned about his own death than about that of others. However, various Stoic philosophers would, I think, tend to argue that it is Kierkegaard's belief that one should be especially concerned about one's own death that is an illusion, an illusion born of irrational self-centeredness. So it is not obvious that Kierkegaard is correct about the illusory nature of objective living, or about the advisability of living subjectively. In any case, the attitude of people who live for the world-historical toward their own death is of some interest: they are, at least at some level, not as afraid of dying as they might be or as some people are. And I think there are interesting implications to be drawn from this fact that have some of the spirit of what Kierkegaard says in the *Postscript*.

II

Those who live world-historically for some enterprise like science or philosophy seem not to be very anxious about dying. And I would like to suggest, what Kierkegaard never actually says, that we may be able to *explain* the tendency to live for the world-historical as resulting from our characteristically human fear of dying. For no one wants to live in fear, and since one who lives objectively, for the world-historical, does not feel the fear of dying that some of us do, there is reason and motive for people who have experienced anxiety or fear at the prospect of dying to (try to) adopt an objective existence, including an objective attitude toward their own deaths. But what are the psychological mechanisms by which living world-historically assuages someone's fear of death? Here I can only suggest, not establish, an answer, and what I shall say is intended as exploratory and somewhat speculative.

Consider the claim that people who live for the world-historical sometimes make that they will *be or become immortal through their works*, or that they will *live on through their works*. Why do people ever say such things; if what they are saying is just metaphorical, why do they use *that* metaphor and why do they seem to take the metaphor seriously?[5] It seems to me that such claims of immortality or living on are not (if there is no afterlife along traditional religious lines) literally true. It is not even literally true to say that part of one lives on in one's works, for books, e.g., are not literally parts of those who write them. Moreover, even if there is a traditional religious type of afterlife, one presumably does not live on *through one's works.*[6]

When we say that we shall live on or be immortal through our writings, e.g., I think we sometimes make that claim in a serious spirit. We are not just joking or deliberately speaking loosely. But when someone points out that what we are saying is not literally true, I think that most of us are willing to admit that what we have said is not literally true. How is this possible? It is my conjecture that someone who says he will live on, at least unconsciously believes that what he has said is (literally) true. Part of the evidence for the *unconsciousness* of the belief, if it exists, is the fact that when someone brings it to our attention that it cannot literally be true, we are ready, at least on a conscious level, to admit that this is so. What (further) supports the idea that the belief exists on some unconscious level is the fact that we at first express it in a serious vein and are not fully conscious that what we are saying is not literally true. We have to be reminded that what we have said is not literally true, and in this respect are not like someone who says that a certain person has a heart of gold. In the latter case, one is quite clear in one's mind *ab initio* that what one is saying is not the literal truth. One is, I think, often less clear, and in some sense more confused, about the literal falsehood of what one says when one says that one will live on in one's works. And this unclarity or confusion, as compared with the "heart of gold" case, is some evidence that one who speaks of living on in his works unconsciously believes that he will do so, inasmuch as the existence of such an unconscious belief is one very obvious possible explanation of that unclarity or confusion.[7] But what lends the greatest support to the view that such an unconscious belief exists in those who live world-historically and say they will live on in their works is the generally accepted fact that human beings naturally tend to fear dying. It is to be expected that men will try to avoid that fear and repress it, if possible. One way of doing this would be to convince oneself that one was immortal through one's works, so that death was not really or fully the end of one's existence. It would be hard to convince oneself of such a claim on a conscious level, just because of its literal falseness. But such belief in one's immortality could perhaps survive on an unconscious level where it would be less subject to rational scrutiny, and perhaps be capable of counteracting one's fear of death. The unconscious delusion of one's immortality (or living on) through one's works can, if we adopt Freudian terminology, be thought of as an unconscious defense mechanism of the ego that protects us from conscious fear about death by repressing that fear and counterbalancing it in such a way that it for the most part remains unconscious.[8] And this would explain why people who live for the world-historical are not consciously afraid of dying much of the time, and, in effect, why people so often live for the world-historical.[9]

Let me carry my speculation further. At one point in the *Postscript* (p. 274), Kierkegaard says that to live for the world-historical is to forget that one exists. This curious claim is, I think, more plausible or forceful than it may seem at first. Consider a person who lives objectively and unconsciously believes that he will live on through his books. Such a belief is not just false, but necessarily false, since it involves both the idea that one is alive and the idea that the existence of certain works like books is sufficient for one's continued existence; and nothing whose continued existence is entailed by the existence of such works can be *alive*. Moreover, the belief that one's books' existence is sufficient for one's continued existence seems to involve the idea that one has roughly the same kind of being as a book or series of books. So I think there is something to the idea that one who lives objectively somehow thinks of himself as not existing as a person, and as not being alive. But he presumably does not think this on a conscious level, for much the same reason that one does not on a conscious level think that one is going to live on through one's works. On the other hand, the *unconscious* delusion that one is not alive (or is of the same kind as a series of books) would seem capable of counteracting and allaying anxiety about dying just as easily as the unconscious belief that one is immortal through one's works does so. If one is going to live on in books, one is not going to lose one's life and there is nothing to fear from death, so that fears about dying may be prevented from becoming conscious by being allayed on an unconscious level. Similarly, if one is not really alive, or is of the same "stuff" as books, then one also has nothing to fear from dying; and one's ceasing to be, if it occurs, will be no more tragic than the ceasing to be of a book.[10] So if one believes this kind of thing on an unconscious level, it is again not hard to see how one's fear of death may be allayed and kept unconscious.[11] Thus it would seem that people so often live for the world-historical because such living involves unconscious beliefs (delusions) that help them, more or less successfully, to avoid conscious fears about dying.[12]

According to Kierkegaard, however, not only does one who lives for the world-historical forget that he exists, but such a person at least to some extent ceases to exist as a person, ceases to live.[13] For if we use our lives as a means to the existence of certain works and/or to be mentioned in some paragraph or footnote of some authoritative history of our field of endeavor, then we are valuing our lives no more than we value the existence of certain works or our being mentioned in paragraphs or footnotes. And when we unconsciously think of ourselves as immortal through our works, we are in effect thinking that what we lose when we die cannot be that important or valuable. And to do and think in this way is to put a low value on one's living. But if one places a low value on actual living, one will not take full advantage of one's life (living) and that is a bit like already being dead, or not alive. So I think there really is something to Kierkegaard's claim that to live world-historically is to some extent to cease to exist as a person, to cease to be alive. The claim constitutes, not literal truth, but a forceful and penetrating metaphor.

It is well known that the fear of dying is a prime source of much of human religiosity. Belief in an afterlife of the traditional religious sort is one way that men can assuage their anxiety about dying. What is perhaps not so well known is how the fear of dying can give rise to (and explain) certain attitudes and activities of people who are not in any ordinary way religious, and perhaps also certain attitudes and activities of religious people that are not generally associated with religion. What I have tried to show here is that there are in Kierkegaard's *Concluding Unscientific Postscript* insights about our attitudes toward life and death that can be used to help us understand how certain nonreligious aspects of human life result from the fear of dying.

In doing so, I have assumed that people who live objectively and say that they are not terribly anxious about dying are nonetheless afraid of dying at some level. And this may seem high-handed. However, I am inclined to think that in general people living world-historically (who do not believe in some traditional religious type of life after death) continue to be subject to a certain welling-up of death anxiety that can overtake them in the midst of their daily lives.[14] Despite my own tendencies toward the world-historical, I have often experienced this sudden welling-up of death anxiety, and I think that the fact that this phenomenon is widespread among non-religious world-historical people (and indeed among people in general) is evidence that fear of dying never entirely ceases to exist in (such) people, but always continues to exist at least on an unconscious plane. For it is easier to imagine such a sudden welling-up of fear as the "return of the repressed" and as indicating a certain inefficiency of one's repressive mechanisms than to think of it as resulting from the sudden regeneration of death fears within one. What could plausibly explain such a sudden rebirth of death anxiety *in medias res?* Moreover, the earlier-mentioned fact that world-historical people (people who live for the world-historical) sometimes seriously say that they will be immortal through their works, without being clear in their own minds that this is just a metaphor, is, as I have already argued, evidence that such people unconsciously believe that they are immortal through their works (or that they are not alive). But why should they have such unconscious beliefs, except as part of a mechanism to relieve and keep repressed their fear of dying? So even such seemingly innocuous locutions as that we shall be immortal through our works indicate the existence of death fears even on the part of people who live for the world-historical and claim not to be afraid of dying. Let us now turn to Pascal's *Pensées* to see how the fear of dying affects other aspects of human life.

III

There is a famous long passage in the *Pensées* where Pascal talks about diversion, its role in human life, and its sources. Men "cannot stay quietly in their own chamber" alone and meditating, for any length of time.[15] We need or think we need diversion and activity and cannot be happy without diverting ourselves from ourselves because of the "natural poverty" of our feeble and mortal condition, so miserable that nothing can comfort us when we think of it closely."[16] Now, Pascal does not go on to decry the vanity of human diversion and claim that life would be less vain if we thought more about ourselves and our mortality. He is not arguing for the vanity of worldly human concerns in the timeworn manner of Ecclesiastes. He has an entirely new perspective on where the vanity of human life really lies. The vanity of our lives consists, for Pascal, in the fact that when we divert ourselves (from ourselves), we typically deceive ourselves about our motives for behaving as we do.[17] For example, a man who gambles often convinces himself that obtaining the money he is gambling for would make him happy (at least for a while). He focuses on the getting of the money and forgets that his real or main purpose is to divert himself. Thus if he were offered the money on condition that he not gamble, he would be (at least temporarily) unhappy, because he seeks diversion. On the other hand, if he were offered the diversion, say, of playing cards without being able to gamble for money, he would also be unhappy. For it is not just diversion he seeks; he must also have some imagined goal which he focuses on in such a way that he does not see that diversion is his real or main goal. Pascal does not, however, explain why men cannot simply seek diversion without fooling themselves about their goal. But an explanation can be given along lines that Pascal might have approved. Imagine that we divert ourselves in order not to have to think of ourselves, and also realize that this is so. Shall we not *ipso facto* be thrust back into that very awareness of self which we sought to avoid through diversion? To realize that one wants not to think of oneself because it is unpleasant to dwell on one's feeble and mortal condition is *ipso facto* to be thinking of oneself and opening oneself up to the very unpleasantness one wishes to avoid. And if those who want to avoid thinking of themselves must remain ignorant of that fact if they are to succeed in not thinking of themselves, how better to accomplish this than by focusing on something outside themselves and thinking of it as their goal?

This explanation of human striving and activity applies not just to gambling, but, as Pascal says, to the waging of campaigns in love or in war and to many other human activities. Many of us fool ourselves about our motives much of the time when engaged in such activities. One objection to this analysis, however, would be that to explain so much human activity in terms of the fear of, or desire not to be, thinking of oneself is to offer a gratuitous explanation of our behavior. Why not just say that as animals we have an instinctive desire for certain activities which typically involve a lack of self-consciousness and which are called "diversions?" But the instinct theory of the origin of our diversions has, as it stands, no obvious way of explaining the self-deception Pascal points out. If we simply have an instinct for certain activities, activities that in fact tend to divert us from ourselves, why do some of us much of the time and many of us some of the time deceive ourselves into thinking that it is winning a certain victory or honor or woman that is our main goal, when it is the diverting activity leading up to that winning that is our main goal? On the theory that we do not like thinking about ourselves, however, the fact of self-deception can be explained along the above lines; so the assumption of a desire not to think of oneself is not gratuitous.

Furthermore, there is good independent evidence that people do not like to think about themselves. There is, for example, an experience that I have sometimes had, and that I think the reader will probably also have had; in the middle of thinking about something else I have all of a sudden thought to myself: "All this is being done by *me* and all these people are talking about *me*." I hope this description will suffice to convey the kind of experience I have in mind. What is interesting, but also perplexing and distressing to me, are the following facts. When I have this experience of myself, there seems to me to be something precious about it; and I think: "This is the moment when I am most alive; it is very good to have this experience." (There is, after all, a long tradition in which self-consciousness is a great, or the greatest, good.) I usually also think that though I am at that moment too busy to prolong the self-consciousness, I shall definitely set aside a good deal of time in the future to take full advantage of this kind of experience of self-awareness. But somehow that never happens. And when I am again momentarily self-conscious in the way I have been describing, I again put off a long bout of such self-consciousness to the future, despite my typical accompanying conviction that the experience of being self-conscious is a wonderful one that I really should and shall take greater advantage of. All this needs explaining, and the obvious explanation, I think, is that I really do not like the experience of self-consciousness, as Pascal suggests.

But why, in the end, should we not want to think about ourselves? Pascal suggests that the reason is that thinking about ourselves makes us think of our feeble and mortal condition. He also says about man: "to be happy, he would have to make himself immortal; but, not being able to do so, it has occurred to him to prevent himself from thinking of death."[18] Presumably, then, Pascal thinks that there is a connection between thinking about oneself and thinking unpleasant thoughts about one's death; and this seems to me to be quite plausible. For at least while we are absorbed in things outside us, we do not think of ourselves, or thus, it would seem, of our death; whereas if and when one does think about oneself, one might very easily think about one's death. It would seem, then, that the explanation of our diverting ourselves from (thinking about) ourselves is that this at least to some degree enables us to avoid thinking anxiously about our mortality. And so we have now clarified two general areas or aspects of human life in terms of the fear of dying. Let us turn next to Heidegger.

IV

Men's attitudes toward death are a major theme in Heidegger's *Being and Time*.[19] For Heidegger, in everyday life we exist in a mode that Heidegger calls the "they" *(das Man)*. Heidegger characterizes this mode of existence as inauthentic, at least in part because in it, one is forgetful of the fact that death is one's ownmost possibility and cannot be outstripped. By this he means something close to the Kierkegaardian idea that one's own death has greater significance for one than does the death of others. Heidegger says that such a mode of existence is tempting because it tranquilizes one's anxiety in the face of death.[20]

So it would seem that Heidegger can be thought of as providing a psychological explanation of certain aspects of human life, which he calls collectively "(being lost in) the 'they,'" and thus that Heidegger is doing something similar to what we have seen Kierkegaard doing in the *Postscript* and Pascal doing in the *Pensées*.[21]

According to Heidegger, one important aspect of our average everyday lostness in the "they" is its typical modes of discourse, chatter, and idle talk, and the busy-body curiosity that characterizes such discourse. Heidegger points out that when people are idly and curiously talking about whether John and Mary will get divorced, the actual event, the divorce, if it occurs, actually disappoints the idle talkers; for then they are no longer able to conjecture about and be in on the thing in advance. The curiosity of everyday idle talk is concerned with the very latest thing(s), with novelty; and what interests in anticipation may be "old hat" or out of date when it occurs. Horse races and even pennant races in baseball seem to me to be good examples of this tendency. We have the keenest interest in who will win, but it is hard to maintain much interest in such races once we know their outcome; there is even a certain disappointment or let-down sometimes when the results of such things finally become known.[22] Heidegger's discussion here seems to have a good deal in common with what Pascal says about diversion, for one way of diverting ourselves from ourselves would be to be constantly curious about the latest things. But why not be interested in things that are not new and be diverted by them? The answer here—though it is not one that Heidegger actually gives— seems to me to lie precisely in the desire not to think of oneself that Pascal lays such emphasis on. What is newer is less well known, and the more there is to learn about something, the less likely one is to get bored with it or to cease being absorbed in it, and so be thrust back into thoughts about oneself. Furthermore, our earlier discussion of Pascal can help us to explain why we are sometimes let down when a certain event we have (only) conjectured about occurs, even though in advance we thought that "nothing would make us happier" than to know exactly when and how the event would occur. For if our goal is distraction from ourselves through conjecturing, we cannot very well admit this to ourselves without (running a grave risk of) defeating that goal; so we somehow fool ourselves into thinking that what we want is to know for sure about the character of the event we are conjecturing about, as a means to our real goal of diverting ourselves through conjecturing about something or someone outside ourselves; and when we cannot conjecture any more, then of course we are let down.

There may be a further reason why the desire for novelty is so pervasive in human life—though what I shall now be saying is perhaps more speculative than anything else I have to say here. As Heidegger says (p. 217), when one has the desire for novelty, it is as if one's motive were to have known (seen) rather than to know (see); for as soon as one has known (seen) something, one no longer wants to know (see) it. And there seems to be a certain vanity in such a way of dealing with things. Now consider what is implicitly involved in wanting, say, to have seen Rome, but not to see (keep seeing) Rome. There are tours whose advertising has the feeling of: "Come to Europe with us and you will see 8—count 'em, 8—countries in 8 days;" and such advertising and such tours appeal to many people who want to (say that they) have been, e.g., in Rome, but who do not much want to *be* in Rome. When one makes such a tour, one often even wishes the tour were already over so that one (could say that one) had already been to Rome in Italy (and to the other seven countries). The actual touring, with its "inconveniences," is often not desired or enjoyed. But to want the eight days and the trip to be already over with is in a certain sense to want a part of one's life over with in exchange for a being able to say one has been. This desire is in many cases unconscious. Sometimes some of us say, with an air of seriousness, that we wish that a certain trip or period of time were already over. But when confronted with the implications of what we have said, we almost inevitably recoil from what we have said and say that of course we do not *really* want a certain part of our life to be already over, perhaps adding that we were only speaking loosely or jokingly in making our original remark. In that case our desire to have a certain part of our life over with exists, if at all, only on an unconscious level. Evidence that there *is* such an unconscious desire comes from the fact of our original seriousness in saying that we wished a certain trip over with and from the fact that we are by no means clear in our own minds that we do not mean our statement literally, the way a hungry man is, for example, when he says that he could eat a mountain of flapjacks. I think this initial unclarity is best explained by (and thus evidence for) the existence of an unconscious desire to have a certain part of our life over with.[23] And perhaps for the very purpose of keeping this desire out of consciousness, we convince ourselves at least temporarily that we really want to *be* in Rome, or *feel* its living antiquity, etc. But then, after we have spent the tour rushing about, impatient with tarrying in one place too long, we *may,* upon reflection, recognize that we wanted the having seen more than the seeing of the places, like Rome, that we visited.

The logical extension of the wish to have a certain portion of one's life already over with is the wish to have one's whole life over with, and I would like now very tentatively to argue that at some deep level many of us have this latter wish, and so want not to be alive. Part of the reason for thinking so consists in the way we deceive ourselves about the extent of our desires to have portions of our lives over with. We sometimes think: if only it were a week from now so that I knew whether *p*, everything would be all right. But then when the time comes at which everything is supposed to be going to be all right, we soon find another reason for thinking things are not all right and for wishing other parts of our lives over with. I think that the initially implausible assumption that some people unconsciously wish their whole lives over with, wish not to be alive, provides the best explanation of this whole perplexing phenomenon. For if one has the unconscious desire to have one's whole life over with, there will be mechanisms in force to prevent it from becoming conscious. If one were conscious that one wanted *many different parts* of one's life over with *seriatim,* one would be dangerously close to being conscious that one wanted one's *whole life* over with. So it might reasonably be expected that someone with the unconscious wish or desire that his whole life be over with would be (made to be) unaware of the extent to which he wanted particular portions of his life over with before they were lived. Thus I think there is reason to believe that people who deceive themselves in this way unconsciously wish not to be alive.[24]

It will perhaps seem more plausible to hold that such a wish exists if I can show how it is explained by our fear of dying. One way of allaying fear of the loss of something is a kind of denial that one might call the technique of "sour grapes in advance." We can convince ourselves that the thing we may lose is not worth having or that we do not really want it. (This recalls the studies psychologists have done on the resolution of "cognitive dissonance.") An unconscious desire not to be alive might, then, help us to counterbalance or to keep repressed our fear of dying. The existence of such a desire can thus be supported in various ways and fits well into the kind of theory about our attitudes toward death so far proposed. But there is no time to speculate further in its favor.[25]

We argued earlier that if someone thinks of himself as not alive, he will not take full advantage of his life and it will be as if he is not (fully) alive. The same can be said for someone who wants not to be alive. We saw earlier the force of the metaphor that some of us are dead. Since it is as if some of us are dead because of what we have, unconsciously, done to ourselves, there is also force to the metaphor that some of us have killed ourselves. To live for the having seen and known of things is, metaphorically speaking, not to be alive, and to have killed oneself.[26] And one can also say this about those who live for the world-historical. I have a tendency to put myself entirely into my work and to live for something "bigger," philosophy. But sometimes I recoil from such an existence and from myself, and I feel that I have really just thrown my life away, have been personally emptied, through world-historical living. At such a time the metaphor of killing oneself seems particularly compelling.

We have thus far characterized those who live world-historically as assuaging the fear of dying via the *beliefs* that they are immortal and/or that they are not alive. But I think that such people also sometimes unconsciously wish not to be alive in the manner of those who divert themselves with novelties.[27] (Of course, those who live world-historically can be diverting themselves as well, e.g., with busy research or advocacy of causes.) For one thing, as we have already seen, people who live world-historically unconsciously think that they are not alive. And they want to think this, at least unconsciously, as a means to less fear or anxiety. But presumably if one wants to think one is not alive, that is because one wants not to be alive. This kind of inference from what one wants to think to what one wants is surely *usually* in order. Secondly, there is evidence that world-historical people tend to want parts of their lives over with in much the same way that seekers after novelty do. Someone writing a book that is intended to advance some field in the long run will often wish that the next six months of his life were already over so that he could see the book in finished form and have the writing of it over with. If only this were possible, everything would start being all right, he thinks, and he would be ready really to live his life again. Such a person, however, will, in many cases, be fooling himself about the extent to which he wants to "put off living" by missing parts of his life. As soon as there is another book to write, or academic appointment in the offing, he may very well once again want some part of his life already over with. Saying that such a man really wants to live, but only wants to avoid certain tense or burdensome parts of his life, does not really allow us to understand why he so often on such slight pretexts (is writing a book really so unpleasant and tense, considering the rest of the things that can be going on in one's life at the same time?) thinks up reasons for wanting to postpone living by omitting some parts of his life. Just as a man who is always *just about* to take a vacation and really live (it up) for a change, but who never does, can be plausibly suspected of preferring his work to a vacation or to "life" despite his protestations to the contrary, the perplexing behavior of one who lives world-historically and keeps wanting parts of his life over with while remaining unconscious or unaware of the extent to which this is so can, I think, only be made sense of in terms of an unconscious desire not to be alive.[28] Such a desire is strange and perplexing, perhaps, but no more so than the behavior it is supposed to explain.

Heidegger says many more interesting things about the "they." Idle talk and curiosity seem to be interested in anything and everything, though in fact, unbeknown to us, limits have been set on what we are to be interested in. For example, one is not, in the midst of curious talk, supposed to bring up the tragedy of life or the inevitability of death. Anyone who brings up such things is told not to be "morbid." Heidegger suggests that idle talk and curiosity function as a way of keeping us from thinking of our own death. For one thing—if I may borrow again from our discussion of Pascal to supplement what Heidegger is saying here—the illusion of interest in everything is an excellent means for blocking off thought about dying and its consequent anxiety, since if we believed, while we were engaged in idle talk, that we were not supposed to be deeply talking about death, we might very easily be thrust back into the very anxiety that idle talk was supposed to avoid. Moreover, the very self-assurance and harshness with which someone who brings up death in the midst of idle talk is branded as morbid tends to encourage and rationalize our avoidance of the topic of death.

Another device by which everyday living in the "they" keeps us from fears of death is by branding such fears as cowardly. Heidegger, however, thinks that it is more cowardly *not* to face death anxiously. Now there certainly seems to be room for disagreement on this issue. Some of the Stoics seem to have thought that it was irrational, rather than courageous, to be anxious about one's own death because death was a matter of indifference. And this latter philosophy of death may be correct; but it might be interesting at this point to make some educated guesses about the psychology of those who have advocated the "Stoic" view of death. For to my mind there is something strange and suspicious about (holding) the view that one's own death is not an evil. I have already discussed the fact that despite our best repressive mechanisms, the fear of dying sometimes comes upon (some of) us suddenly in the midst of life. When others tell us that it is morbid or cowardly to worry about death, we are given an excuse or motive not to worry about death, and such advice may well help us to get rid of the conscious fear of death at least temporarily. The philosophical view that it is irrational to worry about death because death is a matter of indifference may have a similar function to play in the psychic lives of those who propound it. Philosophers pride themselves on being rational, and by branding the fear of dying as "irrational" they may give themselves a motive for ceasing consciously to worry about death and actually help themselves to get rid of the conscious fear of dying. I am inclined to think, then, that the view that it is irrational, and not courageous, to fear death, because death is no evil, may well be motivated, in many of those who propound it, by the fear of death itself, a fear that they are consequently able to repress, but not to get rid of. If so, then those who are helped to repress their fear of dying by holding a "Stoic" view of death are under an illusion when they claim as rational philosophers to be totally indifferent to death. But it might be better to live under such an illusion without consciously worrying about death than to know that one was not indifferent to death because one *was* consciously afraid of death. In the light of these complexities, it would seem hard to decide between Heidegger, on the one hand, and the Stoics and the "they," on the other, as to whether it is courageous to be (consciously) anxious in the face of dying.

Heidegger suggests yet further ways in which existence in the "they" tranquilizes our anxiety about dying. In the "they" there is an emphasis on keeping busy doing things, as the means to, or sign of, a full and good life. When someone suggests that one might do better to be more reflective and less busy, the response of the "they" is that by keeping busy, one is living "concretely" and avoiding self-defeating and morbid self-consciousness; this encourages the person who hears this to keep busy and not reflect on himself, and thus functions as a means to keeping us from the conscious fear of dying. (Consider, in particular, how the old, who are especially subject to fears of death, are told to keep busy and active.)

Heidegger points out that someone lost in the "they" will *admit* that death is certain and that one (everyone) dies in the end. According to Heidegger, in speaking of what happens to "everyone" or to "one" eventually, we "depersonalize" and "intellectualize" death. In thus depersonalizing death, it is as if the person were saying that death has nothing to do with *him right now,* and this enables him to talk about death without focusing on himself or having that particularly intimate experience of self-awareness described earlier or, thus, having fearful thoughts about death. Also, talk about the inevitability or certainty of death, etc., may be part of a process of "isolation of affect" in which one intellectualizes (about) a certain phenomenon to keep away from (consciousness of) certain related feelings.[29] Heidegger also points out that social scientists often seek to create "typologies" and systematic theories about humanity in the belief that they are thereby penetrating to the deepest level on which one can understand humanity and oneself, but that such intellectual "hustle and bustle" may entirely ignore the question of the significance for men of their own death and death anxiety; such intellectualization, he suggests, may serve to keep one from anxious thoughts about death by convincing one that one has reflected as deeply as it is possible to do. And the very stuffiness and detachment with which some sociologists, psychologists, etc., sometimes declare their desire to plumb the depths of the human spirit is, I would think, some evidence that they have a deeper need to avoid the *feeling* of their own mortality.

An important further point that is due to Kierkegaard rather than to Heidegger is that one can even overintellectualize one's response to a work, like that of Kierkegaard or Heidegger, which attempts to reveal in an "existential" manner the importance of our attitudes toward dying.[30] Spinoza has said that "passive" feelings like fear tend to dissipate when we scrutinize them, and this may well mean that it is difficult at one and the same time both intellectually to focus on and learn the significance of death anxiety and to *feel* that significance. And so there seems to be a real danger that someone who reads the writings of Existentialists will only intellectually understand and agree with what they say, and thus fail to derive all the benefit one could or should get from reading them. Of course, Spinoza's dictum also implies that it is difficult to think intellectually about death anxiety while feeling such anxiety. And one reason why I and others may be so interested in thinking and writing about death anxiety is that such thinking and writing may, in effect, involve an isolation of affect about death.[31]

In discussing Heidegger, we have brought in Kierkegaard and Pascal to help "deepen" his analysis of how death anxiety affects large portions of human life. I would like now to make use of certain ideas of Sartre's (in ways that Sartre undoubtedly would not approve) to point out yet another aspect of human life that can be explained in terms of the fear of dying. (However, I shall not discuss Sartre's own views on death, which in fact run counter to much of what we have to say on that subject.)

V

Being and Nothingness is perhaps most famous for its discussion of what Sartre calls "bad faith," which consists in being or putting oneself under the illusion that one is not free and cannot do other than what one in fact does.[32] For Sartre, one is in bad faith when one says: I have to get up and get to work; I can't stay in bed, I have a family to feed. Bad faith is involved because one does not *have* to get up and go to work.

Some people will immediately object to what Sartre is saying on the grounds that if determinism about human behavior is true and a certain person in fact will not stay in bed, then he is under no illusion when he says that he cannot stay in bed. Since, despite anything Sartre says, it is by no means obvious to me that such determinism is not (approximately) true or that human beings possess free will, I would like now to (re)interpret Sartre's "bad faith" in such a way as to avoid assuming either human indeterminism or human free will.

Someone who says he has to go to work in the morning will sometimes say: "I have no choice in the matter." But I think that he does have a choice, even if a determined and unfree one, and that if he cannot stay at home, that is in part *because* of his (perhaps determined and unfree) choice. Moreover, I think that someone who is reminded of these facts will typically be willing to take back his original claim to have no choice in some matter, will grant that he had been speaking loosely or metaphorically. But it seems to me that such a person will typically not have been clear in his own mind about all this at the time when he originally claimed to have "no choice." And for reasons we have already gone into at length, I think this indicates that the person making such a claim unconsciously believes that he has no choice in a certain matter, even though he really does have a (possibly determined and unfree) choice in that matter and can be brought to conscious awareness of that fact. Such a person is under an illusion about the part he (and his choosing or deciding) plays in certain events or situations, and it is *this kind* of illusion that *I* shall call "bad faith."

Bad faith in this new sense is clearly related to bad faith in Sartre's sense. And, assuming that the new kind of bad faith does exist, it would be good if we could give some sort of explanation of it. Sartre's explanation of bad faith in the old sense will not be of much help to us here, since it assumes not only that human behavior is undetermined but also (implausibly enough) that human beings basically realize (believe) that this is so. My suggestion is that we explain bad faith in my new sense in much the same way that we have been explaining various other phenomena—namely, in terms of the fear of dying. (Indeed, Heidegger hints at this idea in *Being and Time,* p. 239.) I think that we can explain bad faith in terms of the fear of dying, if we suppose that the illusion of bad faith helps to repress such fear and if we borrow one further idea of Sartre's. According to Sartre, someone in bad faith (in his sense) who denies his own freedom is, in effect, thinking of himself as a thing or object, since things and objects are unfree, etc. I would like tentatively to claim that people who unconsciously believe that they have no choice, say, about getting up in the morning are, in effect, thinking of themselves as things or objects,[33] since things and objects really do lack choice. If we make this assumption, we can explain how bad faith in my sense enables one to relieve or repress death fears. For objects cannot die, and so unconsciously thinking of oneself as an object is unconsciously to think that one has nothing to fear from death.[34] (And if one passes away but is a mere object, then that is no more tragic than the passing away of a rock.)

Bad faith in the new sense seems to have much in common with living for the world-historical. In the latter case, one thinks of oneself as not alive; in the former, one thinks of oneself as a mere thing; and one might wonder whether there is much difference here either in the content of these unconscious beliefs or in the way they act on the fear of dying. Furthermore, just as one who lives for the world-historical can aptly be described metaphorically as not alive[35] and as having killed himself, one who lives in bad faith is, metaphorically speaking, a mere thing and not alive, and since he has (unconsciously) done this to himself, he has, metaphorically speaking, turned himself into a thing. And given the fact that the only way a person really can turn himself into a thing is by turning himself into a corpse, it is perhaps metaphorically appropriate to describe someone who is (constantly) in bad faith as having killed himself. Sartre holds that someone who thinks of himself as a mere thing wants (among other things) to *be* a mere thing. And I think we could argue that people in bad faith in my sense sometimes unconsciously want to be things in something like the way we earlier argued that people living for the world-historical want not to be alive. Furthermore, the unconscious desire to be an object would seem capable of countering the fear of dying in much the same way that the unconscious desire not to be alive does so, and so there is this further similarity between living in bad faith and living for the world-historical.

VI

If what has been said here is on the right track, then it would seem that Pascal, Kierkegaard, Heidegger, and Sartre all describe phenomena that pervade our lives and that are best explained in terms of their efficacy in relieving or repressing the fear of dying. Our explanation has made use of a Freudian type of view of repression and of the unconscious. This will certainly make our arguments here suspect in the eyes of some people. I have in effect been "practicing" a kind of "existential psychoanalysis," and though this term is one that was originally used by Sartre in *Being and Nothingness* to describe some of his own procedures, it may well apply more accurately to the kinds of things I have been doing here. For Sartre does not posit an unconscious, but I have followed Freud in doing just that.[36] In any case, I hope that this paper may bring to light an area, or areas, where Existentialism and Psychoanalysis can be mutually enlightening.

Of course, in addition to using psychoanalytic ideas, I have also frequently appealed to my own experience and intuitions, to how things strike me and to the "feel" of certain ideas. Though some things, I trust, will strike readers the way they have struck me, this will no doubt not always be the case; and when it is not, my appeals to how things feel to me, etc., are bound to seem like special pleading. Perhaps I *am* guilty of this, but I do not know how to avoid it in a paper like this where personal experience may be more relevant to seeing certain points than abstract arguments. And perhaps some of the ideas or intuitions I have relied on will seem more palatable to the reader if he "lives with them" and takes the time to see whether they do not, perhaps, make sense in and of his experience of himself and the world. For it is in something like this way that many of the ideas and intuitions of this paper have become acceptable to me.

In this paper, I have pieced together various ideas from Pascal, Heidegger, Sartre, and Kierkegaard, as well as extrapolated beyond what any of them has said, to provide a fairly general picture of how the fear of dying accounts for many aspects of human life. The explanatory "theory" we have presented links together phenomena that the various Existentialists discussed separately, and as such should, given any standard account of scientific method, be more plausible than the accounts of the various Existentialists taken separately. So I hope I have helped to support and fill out the basically existentialist notion that the quality of a (non-religious) man's life greatly depends on his attitude toward his own death. And even if this idea is not particularly prevalent in Sartre, we can use things Sartre says to substantiate it.

Some people will complain that I have only been doing psychology, not philosophy. But it may not be important whether this accusation is true. And I also think that when psychology is general enough and speaks directly to the human condition, it can also count as philosophy. If, as we have argued, the main motive for world-historical (or busily self-distractive) participation in certain enterprises comes from (desire to avoid) the fear of dying, then a good many intellectuals, scientists, and others may be less pure in motive, less selfless, than they are often thought to be.[37] And this fact, if it is one, is surely very relevant to our understanding of the human condition, and so counts in favor of calling what we have been doing philosophy.[38]

NOTES

1. I shall by no means, however, be discussing all the things these authors say on the topic of death.

2. *Concluding Unscientific Postscript* (Princeton, 1960), p. 116.

3. *Ibid.*, p. 133.

4. *Ibid.*, pp. 130ff.

5. Horace in the *Odes* (3, xxx) seems to be an example of someone who takes the metaphor seriously.

6. I think that people who talk of gaining immortality through their children also say what is literally false, and their psychology is, I think, significantly similar to the psychology of those who talk of living on through their books.

7. Kierkegaard hints at the idea that world-historical people believe they live on through their works when he implies (*Postscript*, p. 140) that such people need to be reminded that "in the world-historical process the dead are not recalled to life."

8. For examples of reasoning similar to that just used that appear in the psycho-analytic literature, see, e.g., S. Freud's "Splitting of the Ego in the Defensive Process" (in his *Collected Papers* [London, 1956], 372–75) and Otto Fenichel's *The Psycho-analytic Theory of Neurosis* (New York, 1945), pp. 479–84. For another *philosophical* use of an argument like mine above, see M. Lazerowitz' *The Structure of Metaphysics* (London, 1955), pp. 69ff. and *Studies in Metaphilosophy* (London, 1964), pp. 225ff., 251. I am indebted to Lazerowitz' account for some of the structure of my own analysis.

9. J. P. Sartre (in *Being and Nothingness* [New York, 1956], p. 543) says that "to be dead is to be a prey for the living." And Thomas Nagel (in "Death," Ch. 1) has tentatively claimed that a man can be harmed or unfortunate as a result of things that happen after his death, e.g., if his reputation suffers posthumously. I wonder whether these views are not, perhaps, indicative of some sort of unconscious belief that people live on in their works.

10. The unconscious belief that one is going to live on and the unconscious belief that one is not alive seem to counteract the unconscious belief or fear that one is going to die in contradictory ways, the former with the "message" that we are not really going to lose what we have, the latter with the "message" that we really have nothing to lose. But we have already seen that the unconscious belief that one lives on in books is itself contradictory or necessarily false, so it should not, perhaps, be so surprising that the unconscious uses mutually contradictory means to repress death-fears. On this see Freud's *The Interpretation of Dreams,* ch. 2. For similar use of the (metaphorical?) notion of unconscious "messages," see Otto Fenichel's *Outline of Clinical Psychoanalysis* (New York, 1934), esp. pp. 13, 30, 33, 52, 250, 260, 275f.

11. In "A Lecture on Ethics," *The Philosophical Review,* 74 (1965), 8ff. Ludwig Wittgenstein speaks of the feeling people sometimes have of being safe whatever happens. He claims that such a feeling or belief is nonsensical; but perhaps this occasional feeling is better thought of as the expression of a meaningful, but necessarily or clearly false, unconscious belief that we are safe whatever happens, a belief that counteracts the fear of dying and that is roughly equivalent to the unconscious belief that one is not alive. For one is absolutely safe (from death) if and only if one is not alive.

12. I do not want to claim that everyone dedicated to some "cause," to something "bigger" than himself, is living world-historically. Such dedication may result from altruism or "conviction" and may not involve the world-historical psychology if it is not accompanied by delusions of immortality through one's works or actions, or the view that one's own death is unimportant.

13. *Ibid.,* pp. 118, 175, 271, 273.

14. See Heidegger's *Being and Time* (New York, 1962), pp. 233f.

15. (New York, 1958), p. 39.

16. *Ibid.*

17. *Ibid.,* p. 40.

18. *Ibid.,* p. 49.

19. Our discussion here will be based on sections 27, 35–42 and 47–53 of *Being and Time*.

20. Heidegger uses "fear" only with respect to things in the world. For death "anxiety" is reserved; but this is not necessarily dictated by ordinary usage.

21. Of course, some philosophers will say that by treating Heidegger as an explanatory psychologist, I am treating him as if he were operating on the "ontic" level, whereas Heidegger thinks of himself as operating on an "ontological" level deeper than the "ontic" level on which science, psychology, and most pre-Heideggerian philosophy typically function. However, despite many efforts, I myself have never been able to make satisfactory sense of the ontic/ontological distinction. If the distinction is viable, Heidegger may have a good deal more to say than I shall be giving him credit for; but we can at least credit him with insights on a level with those of a Pascal or a Kierkegaard.

22. Of course, some people constantly dwell on past (sporting) events (and their part in them), but I do not think this is incompatible with the general tendency I am describing.

23. Compare here our earlier argument for the existence, in world-historical people, of an unconscious belief in their immortality through their works.

24. Our earlier argument that we do not like thinking about ourselves can be strengthened along the lines of our present argument for the existence of an unconscious wish not to be alive. Similar self-deception occurs in the two cases.

25. I have posited the wish not to be alive as an unconscious defense mechanism of the ego that responds to (prior) fear of dying. Freud, on the other hand, late in his career posited a basic (id-based) death instinct to account for various phenomena. See *Beyond the Pleasure Principle* (New York, 1950). The two sorts of views are incompatible, and so the explanation given just now in the text may be mistaken. However, there is some reason to prefer it. Our ego-theory of the death wish fits in better with our earlier-discussed theories about the ego's unconscious handling of the fear of dying. Moreover, other things being equal, it is better to treat a phenomenon as a derived phenomenon, within a theory, than to treat it as basic, within that theory. In addition, there is the sheer unintuitiveness of supposing that we have death wishes *ab initio,*

rather than acquiring such (irrational) wishes in the *neurotic* process of repression. Finally, it is by no means clear that a basic death instinct is needed to account for clinical phenomena. On this see Otto Fenichel's "A Critique of the Dead Instinct" in *The Collected Papers of Otto Fenichel,* first series (New York, 1953), pp. 363–72.

26. I think we have some inkling of this metaphorical killing when we speak of "killing time" at moments when we want to have something over with, want a certain (perhaps boring) part of our lives over with. Use of that phrase may be a disguised conscious expression of the unconscious desire not to be alive.

27. Kierkegaard's claim in the *Postscript* (p. 137) that one whose eye is on world-historical things has perhaps found "a highly significant way of . . . killing time" seems to indicate some awareness on his part that world-historical people want not to be alive and have, metaphorically speaking, killed themselves. Whose time, after all, does one kill except one's own? And one's time is one's life. Incidentally, it is natural to say that world-historical people "bury themselves in their work," and this metaphor seems to suggest the very same things that our use of the metaphor of killing time does.

28. Cf. Emerson's remark in his *Journals* (April 13, 1834) that "we are always getting ready to live, but never living."

29. Cf. O. Fenichel's "Outline of Clinical Psychoanalysis," *op. cit.,* pp. 190f., for ideas about "isolation of affect" that are related to some of the things we have said here and earlier in the paper.

30. *Postscript,* pp. 166f.

31. Heidegger also points out that the force of living in the "they" is such as to make people lost in the "they" scoff at his analysis of such lostness. Once one is aware of one's tendencies to cover up certain anxieties, it may be harder to use the mechanisms one has previously used in doing so; so one who wishes at some level to keep covering up his anxiety has a motive to reject Heidegger's analysis and, indeed, our analysis here.

32. See *Being and Nothingness,* Pt. 1.

33. I hope I shall be forgiven for ignoring plants.

34. This recalls the Simon and Garfunkel song that goes: "I am a rock, I am an island; and a rock feels no pain, and an island never cries." The idea that we sometimes want to think of ourselves as things to avoid the pain of life or of facing death is not new or silly. Moreover, even if people in bad faith only think of themselves, unconsciously, as *similar to* mere things, that thought may itself be capable of relieving the fear of death.

35. Kierkegaard says that such a person is also a "walking stick," which suggests the similarity of such a person to someone in bad faith who exists as a mere object.

36. Sartre rejects the unconscious for reasons that seem to me to be interesting, but ultimately unacceptable.

37. This is not to say that such people should stop doing science, etc., with their present motives. They may be happier than they are otherwise likely to be, and may be contributing to the intellectual or practical good of other people. Also see note 12, above.

38. I am indebted to G. Boolos, E. Erwin, B. Jacobs, D. Levin, S. Ogilvy, and M. Wilson for helpful comments on earlier drafts of this paper.

5

Fearing Death

AMÉLIE OKSENBERG RORTY

Mount Holyoke College

MANY HAVE SAID, and I think some have shown, that it is irrational to fear death.[1] The extinction of what is essential to the self—whether it be biological death or the permanent cessation of consciousness—cannot by definition be experienced by oneself as a loss or as a harm.

Many have said, but I think none shown, that one's own death is nevertheless an evil. Death is the privation of life, and life is (generally) a good, or at any rate a precondition for any experience of what is good. But the absence or deprivation of a good is not, just on that account alone, necessarily an evil or a harm. A harm must be a harm-to-someone; but if the dead are by definition extinct, they cannot be harmed by not existing. Yet even if it is not to be feared, the privation of a good may well be regretted, and regretted before it occurs. One can regret that one will not see the outcome of projects that are important to oneself; that one will not see or know one's distant progeny or the progeny of those whom one loves; that one will be deprived of conversations, friendships and books that would have given one joy and understanding and that might have made one's life immeasurably happier than it could be without them; that one will not hear the western wind bring down the small rain. But indeed one might regret—and even fear—that one might sustain such losses while one is alive. In any case, regret is an activity of the living, and not of the dead. While one can regret and sometimes fear that there will be a time when one will not have whatever the goods of life may be, one cannot regret that one will be harmed by not having them after one is dead.

But if it is not rational to fear death, it does not follow that we should try to free ourselves from such fear. For while there may be

Reprinted with permission of Cambridge University Press from *Philosophy*, 58 (1983), 175–88. Copyright © Cambridge University Press, 1983.

many good reasons for not fearing one's own non-existence, there might still also be strong reasons for fearing, as well as for regretting one's own death.[2] I shall argue that it is proper to have irresolvably conflicting attitudes towards one's own death; it is inappropriate to fear death and yet it is also inappropriate not to fear it, or to attempt to cease fearing it. Sometimes, when there are reasons for a course, and reasons against it, it is possible to weigh the strengths of the reasons on both sides, and to form a judgment about what is best, or most reasonable, all things considered. But in this case, the reasons for fearing death are not commensurable with those for not fearing it: no summary weighted judgment is possible. Both views are categorically valid, requiring full assent. The issue is, then, not whether we should or should not cease fearing death, but rather what attitudes to take towards one's irrational but nevertheless functional fears.

Let us be clear about a few minor issues. Our concern is with death and not with dying or horrible ways of dying. Certainly there is nothing amiss in fearing certain sorts of dying, especially if such fears could help prevent one's dying in those ways. If fear of the horrors of dying from lung cancer (as opposed to a sudden massive coronary thrombosis) could be among the necessary causes of a person's taking steps to avoid that sort of death—his ceasing to smoke, changing his job or residence—then there would be good reasons for him to fear that sort of death. Indeed a person might judge that it would be wise for him to acquire that sort of fear, if doing so would lead him to take effective safety measures he is otherwise insufficiently motivated to take.

We should also be clear about what sort of fear is at issue, and what it is we fear, in fearing death. Although we shall later turn to other sorts of fears—generalized anxiety, fear without a specifiable object— we are initially primarily concerned with a state of fear, experienced in a specific harm-avoiding way, fear of . . . rather than fear that . . . Such fears presuppose apprehending an object as dangerous or threatening in such a way that it generates some sort of flight reaction, one that can be checked or overcome, although usually with some difficulty. The specific forms of flight reaction can, as both Freud and Sartre noted, vary greatly. Without necessarily being fully propositional, such fears are intentional. We react to the object only under a certain description, even if we do not have a properly formed propositional belief about the character of the danger or an estimation of its probability.[3]

What then is it we fear when we fear death? Perhaps not all those who do fear it fear the same thing. What a person fears, in fearing death, often reveals what the person takes to be essential and prizeworthy in his life. The hidden content—the details—of a person's fear of death reveals his deepest conception of himself and his life.

1. Some fear death as the permanent loss of (what they take to be) the goods of life. For some, the goods of life are the activities of life: the growth and thriving of their children, the joys of their work and friendships, the development and acceptance of their beliefs and commitments. For others, the good of life is consciousness itself, the awareness of the activities of life. For them, the loss of consciousness is the greatest possible loss, quite independently of the content of experience. But we can lose these goods—the activities of life, or the conscious awareness of these activities—in other ways. This form of the fear of death is then to be classified with the fear of senility, exile, ostracism, friendlessness, the loss of our faculties, debilitating diseases, madness. Death represents the limit of all these diminishings and debilities: it has no special psycho-ontological status except as the irreversible limit that compounds all these fears.

2. Some fear death because it endangers those they cherish, leaving them vulnerable or helpless, their condition in the world worse for lack of a special protection. When a person fears her death will damage her primary concerns she fears the harm done to those concerns, rather than her experiencing such harm. And while in principle someone else might be more efficient, more effective, and certainly more admirable than ourselves in forwarding our projects, it need not be vanity but a perfectly reasonable calculation of probabilities that someone who does not stand in just our relation to our projects is unlikely to give them the same care and devotion that we do. But when we fear the harm that our death might bring, it is the harm that we fear, and not our death, in and of itself. Such harms would also come if we were incapacitated, senile, diseased, imprisoned or exiled.

3. Some fear that the world will go on without their being there to experience it, to comment on it, to understand and explain it, to joke about it, and to attempt to improve it by their own lights, even when they despair of doing so. The drama will continue without their participation and perhaps none the worse for that. What turns such sorrow into fear is the thought that all our efforts to live well, our attentions and dedications were for nothing, that our joys and generosities, pains and stoic resolutions were all in vain. We may fear that the balance of our lives was wrong: the fear is a terror that death shows our significant projects were meaningless, that our lives were idle and pointless, our enterprises arbitrary.

4. In fearing death some fear that their lives will be assessed and judged in ways that they can no longer influence. There it is, all one's life, now taken as a whole and of course found wanting. All possibilities

are closed; one can no longer try to remedy those things which we would have otherwise, cannot make restitution, ask for forgiveness and, above all, we cannot have that last explanatory word that would make it all come out right. But this too is something that might occur during one's life: with senility, aphasia, and other forms of debility and exile.

5. For some the fear of death is an extreme form of the fear of the unknown. Some fears of the unknown are quite specific: fear of the dark, fear of what lies beyond the boundary of the hearth. Animal alertness to danger often closely resembles human terror; when a rabbit or squirrel is strongly attentive to the environment, its senses are maximally alert, its heart beats violently; the creature is all aquiver. For some animals, being alert to the environment just is being alert to predators and to prey. It seems that for them, to live is to be in a state of fear. For some, the fear of death is a heightened awareness of danger, with extreme generalization of stimulus conditions. For them, death is the symbolic representation of the most vulnerable condition, where a person is abandoned without hope, recourse or help.

All these fears of death seem to be fears of the harms that attend not only death but other conditions as well. They are fears of what death brings rather than fears of being dead. But evidently there are some who fear death as such, who fear their non-existence. It is the appropriateness of this fear that I should like to examine: the fear of death as a fear of non-being, rather than the fear of the various harms that attend death.

It seems all too easy to show that at least some fears of death— those that implicitly re-introduce a subject to experience its own non-being—are irrational because they presuppose an incoherent belief. Similarly, it is all too easy to show that if it is rational to fear or regret losses, it is rational to fear or regret the loss of life. But there are other dimensions for the evaluation of the appropriateness of such psychological attitudes as fear, besides that of determining whether the beliefs they presuppose are coherent, valid or at least justifiable by appropriate canons of argument or evidence. It might be appropriate and desirable to have the capacity for and even to develop the disposition to certain fears, knowing that they will sometimes involve rash and inconsidered beliefs and actions. One can evaluate the rationality of maintaining and developing a generalized disposition, independently of evaluating a specific exercise of that disposition. There might be rational grounds for acquiring a disposition whose exercise is admittedly often irrational.

But what could be meant by evaluating the appropriateness of an attitude, if not evaluating the truth or validity of the belief it presupposes? Evaluating the functionality of a psychological attitude is one thing; evaluating its rationality is another. An attitude that is highly functional is not therefore automatically rational; nor is a dysfunctional attitude automatically on that account irrational. Besides being intrinsically interesting, the fear of death is also interesting as an example of the various dimensions on which we evaluate the appropriateness and the propriety of psychological attitudes. We shall see why it might be appropriate and even rational to choose to be capable of the sort of fear that has, as one of its consequences, a susceptibility to the fear of death, even when, in some particular cases, that fear is incoherent.

An analogy should clarify the strategy of my argument. Standardly, pain is undesirable; it is a harm to be feared. Yet our constitutions being what they are, we would not choose—it would not be rational to choose—to be incapable of feeling pain. This is not for any dark or Dostoyevskian reason that pain or suffering brings nobility. Suffering and pain can sometimes ennoble some people; but one had better not count on it. Certainly it would be a high risk gamble to seek suffering for the sake of being ennobled. It is a tragic irony that we are generally not only harmed by whatever causes us pain or suffering, but also harmed by suffering itself, since it intends to engender the further damages of self-pity, hypersensitivity, alienation and misanthropy. Pain is useful for a much simpler and more straightforward reason than the Dostoyevskian one: it is an important signal that damage is being done, a signal to move away from what is damaging. The victims of Hansen's disease suffer many further damages to their bodies because they lack the danger signals that pain brings.

Of course pain does not always contain or reveal its message clearly or unequivocally. It generally signals that something is wrong, without always signalling what is wrong. Some pains have physical reactions built into them: withdrawing the hand from the fire is standardly part of the behaviour of pain-at-being-burnt. But not all signalling pains carry reflex actions with them. It takes experience, intelligence, and a considerable amount of good fortune to read pain signals in the right way. Often pains locate a damaged part of the body; but the source of the damage may be in some other part of the body. And if the cause is some external object, considerable deciphering and even theory may be required for appropriate diagnosis. Nor is the appropriate remedy evident from the pain itself. The element of good fortune in being able to be informed by one's pains is that of having been brought up knowledgeably, acquired an astute lore about the characteristic causes and remedies for various sorts of pains. In any case, it seems clear that without any sentimentality about pain or its ennobling effects (things being what they are, and we being constituted as we presently are), one might well reasonably choose to be capable of pain and pain reactions, to have 'reasonably' sensitive receptors, with 'reasonably' low thresholds. But the safeguarding effects of pain require an aversion to pain, an aversion roughly proportionate to the damage indicated by the severity of the pain. One form that such an aversion can take is fear, especially when fear involves actually beginning to remove oneself from the damaging object, to take motion before one has had time to weigh matters carefully.

It is precisely this precipitous character of basic or fundamental fears that makes them functional in situations that require rapid and relatively undiscriminating global reactions. This suggests that the non-rationality of fear is inextricably interwoven with its functionality.[4] At least some basic fears are expressed in rapid safeguarding action, triggered when something is perceived as dangerous, without its being rationally evaluated in any precise detail. We are set in motion before deliberation takes place. These are fears of clear and present dangers to our well-being, not fears of dawn, or the state of the GNP, potato pancakes, or the song of the nightingale. Some of our basic reactive fears seem constitutionally based; others are acquired, sometimes as part of our socialization in a certain culture, sometimes from individual experience. Even acquired fears can come to have the force of second nature: no particular rational evaluation is necessary to elicit the appropriate reaction. It is enough that the person roughly gauge a situation as potentially dangerous. (Think, for instance, of the quick fearful intake that leads us to brake in order to avoid a collision, even before we determine exactly how probable it is.)

For acquired fears, the question arises: would I undo this fear if I could? Or would I try to ensure that my children and others near or dear also share those fears, reacting to them as I do? It is sometimes rational to choose to be capable of such fears. And in the same way, and for the same reasons, one would choose to be capable of those fears that, among other things, issue in the fear of death. When fearing is the beginning of appropriate safeguarding motion from danger, and when it is the most rapid and efficient motivational assurance of safeguarding behavior in certain sorts of circumstances, then the capacity for fearful reaction is desirable. Though it is not desirable to experience fear, it is desirable to be capable of experiencing it, and to tend to feel it when doing so is the most efficient trigger for moving us out of harm's way.

There are several reasons why such basic fears might be thought undesirable. Though these reasons are distinct, they are psychologically connected. (1) It is part of the very structure of such fears that they lead to relatively unconsidered reactions: they are attitudes whose exercise is in its very nature prone to irrationality because they operate before rational evaluation takes place. (2) The subjective experience of a fearful reaction is, like pain, an unpleasant one to have. If we standardly enjoyed fear or other painful attitudes, they would be highly dysfunctional: our taste for them would lead us to seek out dangerous and harmful situations. (3) Fear is not only a relatively unpleasant attitude; it is also one which, when present, dominates and interrupts other activities. But the insistent character of fear, its unpleasantness, and its precipitous character are all part of its efficacy as a safeguarding motive. If fear were a relatively muted pastel sort of emotion that, like nostalgia, stayed in the background of our attention, it would not be efficacious as a reaction to danger. It is precisely because fear is unpleasant, because it is insistent and disturbing, and because it is often pre-rational in its occurrence and in its effects, that it helps move us out of harm's way. Fear is one of our conservative attitudes, inhospitable to the gambler's calculated evaluations of tolerable risks. Its very essence is a low tolerance for risk, even when the risk is rational. But it is then the very undesirability of the experience of fear that provides the grounds of choosing to be capable of such reactive fears.

We might of course wish we had been constituted in a different way, wish that we had less unsettling and unpleasant sorts of motives or reactions in moving away from danger. We might wish that some of our more considered and rationally evaluative and discriminating motives could move us as rapidly as do fear and other disturbing conditions. What might be rational for us to wish if we were constituted quite differently is, however, a matter for the speculations of science fiction rather than those of philosophic analysis.

Still, there might be considerable leeway within the bounds of our present constitutional structure. Sometime we can acquire traits that are less disturbing and no less efficient than those associated with fear. But when such a trait—say a certain sort of reactive caution—becomes second nature in this way, when it can operate with the rapidity and motor efficiency of fear, then it seems to lose the fine discrimination of weighed and weighted thought. Precisely to the extent that it involves quick reaction before detailed comparative evaluation, precisely to the extent that it begins motion straightaway, such a dispositional motive becomes liable to inappropriate and irrational use. Any capacity whose operations are functionally equivalent to fear—a capacity activated by the rough gauge of a stimulus, one that sets us in motion before fine evaluative discriminations are made—becomes, just by virtue of the rough rapidity of its operations, subject to erroneous exercise. The principle is this: we are better served by being constituted so as to move (even often move) foolishly and mistakenly from mere shadows than we would be by being constituted so as to fail to move the one time that the shadow is that of a hungry lion. Even if death is not an evil, life is, other things being equal, a good. Better a live jumpy fool, than a prematurely dead sage.

But, one might say, what has this to do with fearing *death?* All that has been established is that it is rational to want to be capable of fearing certain sorts of harms. Why should it on that account be rational to fear death? If the extinction of life is not a harm, then why should the sort of damage to ourselves that causes death be feared? Certain sorts of painful and debilitating damages to the body might be feared: the fear of being blinded, or maimed in ways that make one dependent and so also prey to resentment and other similar debilities. But why fear damages that lead to *death?* One reason is that it is by no means always easy in the moment to distinguish debilitating from mortal damages. However incoherent and perhaps even in itself harmful, the fear of death seems more efficient than an indefinite number of particular fears we would have to have: fear of exposure in very low temperatures, fear of dehydration, fear of this and fear of that. Suppose the question arises, why should one fear—why should one wish to be able to fear— to be up on the 200th floor of a skyscraper, to be there exposed to winds of 100 mph when there is no barrier or retaining wall, to be there wearing the slipperiest of shoes, whose bottoms have been covered with grease, to be there on the 200th floor without a parachute? In itself, just as such, that condition is not to be feared. What makes it reasonable to fear going up to the 200th floor of a skyscraper under those conditions is that it would be likely that one would fall off the building, plunging painlessly and perhaps even exhilaratingly to one's death. Without a healthy fear of death, we would have no reason not to go to the top of the skyscraper for the view.

But it might be objected: none of this need presuppose the *fear* of death. Why can't the *recognition* of danger be a sufficient safeguard? That recognition can be as indeterminate and strongly dominant as is necessary for taking efficient safeguarding measures, without having to be a *fearful* recognition. At least since Descartes, we have distinguished cognitive psychological attitudes from straightforwardly motivational ones. Certainly motivational attitudes have a cognitive component: they are directed to ends under certain descriptions, they presuppose a set of values, they can only be exercised with perceptual and categorial discrimination. But on the Cartesian map of psychological functions, cognitive attitudes are in principle motivationally neutral. The same cognitive content can be asserted or denied, can be the subject of desire or of aversion. The presumption is that as one can deny or assert or refrain from judging the truth of any propositional content, so the rational person is able to take favourable or unfavourable attitudes towards any state of affairs, as his best reasoning dictates. On this view, such separation of powers is necessary in order to explain why we need not automatically follow our strongest, most entrenched motives. But if recognizing a mortal danger does not entail taking safeguarding measures, such reactive measures are not *part* of our perception of the recognition of such danger. The view that assures the possibility of opposed propositional attitudes towards the same propositional content requires a set of motivational attitudes that operate independently of cognition and recognition. If recognizing danger doesn't automatically in and of itself generate specific motivational attitudes, something else must be introduced to do that work. Clearly on this view it follows that the recognition of danger cannot *as such* play the same safeguarding functional role that fear and similar motivational attitudes play.

But even theories that do not separate cognitive from motivating attitudes classify certain sorts of fear as functional. To be sure, if the recognition of danger directly motivates, if reacting to danger is built into perceiving danger, then such recognition could be a functional replacement of fear. But motivationally charged recognition of danger seems no less free from the little disturbances of man, no less disturbing and perturbing than fear. Suppose that for safeguarding purposes the recognition of danger were functionally equivalent to fear. The question would arise, how does that recognition work, as the beginning of the motions of running away, removing the hand from the fire, etc. Does it work because the recognition is *felt* in a certain way, felt in the way that fear is felt? Or does it work directly, without the intervention of an emotional state, the cognitive state itself beginning the motion of the muscles? This looks suspiciously like an empirical question about the antecedents of various types of safeguarding behaviour. It looks like a question about whether a person whose glandular functions were damaged without affecting his cognitive functions could in fact take the same safeguarding measures to perceived dangers as one whose glandular system was in functional order.

At this juncture of the argument we can only speculate about what would be the appropriate attitude, on each of the various possible empirical outcomes. (Philosophical questions that lead to an empirical turn signal neither the end nor even the interruption of philosophical analysis.) Suppose that the recognition of danger could directly motivate safeguarding measures, without the intervention of any independent motivational attitude like fear, but that it did so less efficiently and effectively than fear. Suppose that such recognition is more discriminating and less disturbing than fear, that it involves fewer unnecessary safeguarding measures that interrupt ongoing projects. But suppose that affectively uncharged reactions to sudden unpredictable dangers are also slower and less effectively mobilized. Then one might wish to be capable of the fears associated with the danger of death, even though there were less unpleasant ways of safeguarding oneself for standard minor dangers that do not require massive rapid reaction. Oddly and interestingly, a person's choice between the dominant capacities of fear and those of more discriminating and calmer recognitions might vary with the sorts of dangers that he would expect to encounter in the standard difficulties of his ordinary life. If his natural environment has a relatively high frequency of sudden mortal danger, he might sensibly prefer the unsettling follies of irrational fear in order to secure efficient safeguarding measures. But if he lives in a relatively controlled environment, whose dangers are normally foreseeable, then it might be sensible to prefer the functional recognition of danger, even if its safeguarding strategies were slower than those of fear.

It might at this point be objected that I have slid suspiciously among several quite distinct kinds of fear: reflex avoidances, heart-in-the-mouth fearful reactions to situations perceived as dangerous, and generalized global metaphysical anxieties about one's non-being. The structure and function of each of these 'fears' is quite distinctive. On the one hand, it might seem unnecessary to introduce fear as embedded within or presupposed by certain sorts of reflex avoidances. Such behaviour might be adequately explained by reflex action and aversions to pain, without introducing any intentional attitude at all. On the other hand, Epicureans might argue that the propriety of danger-averting behaviour does not affect the impropriety of a generalized metaphysical fear of non-being.

Before turning to metaphysical anxieties, we should consider whether reflex avoidances and aversions to pain and danger should be classified as species of fear. It is important to distinguish reflex actions that presuppose beliefs or perceptions from those that do not. Jerking one's knee when the patella is struck is quite different from blinking at an oncoming object. But there is also a significant difference between blinking one's eyes at an oncoming object and running in fear from a charging lion. While the former involves some perceptual-conceptualization (that there is an object, not a shadow, and that its motion has a certain trajectory), there need be no set of specific beliefs about the character of the object and its effects. One blinks at the drop of eye-medication as well as at a cinder. But some reflex reactions not only presuppose a belief about what is dangerous: they also contain a specific evaluation about the character of that danger. The details of that evaluation determine the desire or aversion that is part of the person's reaction: it fixes the character of the person's reaction. One does not dodge, but runs away from a charging lion; one neither dodges nor runs away from a tornado in Kansas: one gets into the cellar. It is this class of reflex actions that concern us: those which would not have taken just *that* specific form of action without specific beliefs about the *kind* of danger the object presents. Despite the great differences in the range of appropriate reactions and actions, the phenomenologically experienced quality of such avoidances *is* the quality that is normally the quality of fear experiences. While it is not logically necessary that the person who runs from a charging lion experiences what is standardly called fear, it is characteristic that he does; and moreover, his fearful state is characteristically part of the explanation of his reaction. Since such reactive avoidances are experienced as fears, it seems reasonable to classify them as such, especially as the perceptual-conceptualization that is embedded in such reactions, their intentional component ('this is dangerous'), is the intentional component that is ingredient in fear.

It is true that we *could* explain such reactions—not all of them reflex actions and not all of them experienced as fears—by other theoretical constructs: by the instinct for survival, or by specific reactions, some of them learned, to specific stimuli. But these solutions raise the further question: what beliefs and attitudes are presupposed by *those* reactions? Postulating an instinct for survival commits one to a range of theoretical apparatus of instincts, their vicissitudes, their transformations. It is by no means clear that any of the usual advantages of theory construction are gained by replacing *fear* with *instincts to survival*, whose operations are far more questionable and baroque than those of fear. What about simply introducing certain aversions instead of fears? But either aversive behaviour will be functionally equivalent to fear, or it will not be strong enough to do the explanatory work that is required. As a psychological attitude, aversion in itself is not strong enough to explain massive reactive behaviour. Aversion is much more easily controlled and directed, much more selective than the sorts of fears we are discussing. So it is the subclass of aversions that are fearful aversions that are at work. Moreover, we shall either take certain sorts of aversions as primitive—the rock bottom of explanation— or we shall look for some explanation of the selection and direction of our primitive aversions, those that do have an action-component presumptively built into them. Both alternatives lead back to the sorts of fears we have been discussing. Primitive aversions turn out to be not only functionally equivalent to primitive fear, but also to be characteristically phenomenologically indistinguishable from them. Those that direct actions in the appropriate way presuppose the perception of something as dangerous, rather than, say, disgusting or vicious.

We can now turn to the objection that the metaphysical fear of death—*angst* at one's non-being—is entirely different from the functional reflex safeguarding reactions we have been discussing. A metaphysical fear of death is the sort that a person might have when there is no clear and present danger, a fear she might have sitting in her study and looking out of the window and brooding on the nature of things. Certainly anxious metaphysical fear is quite different from the sort of functional fear we have been discussing, and it is this fear that might be thought irrational. It is this sort of gratuitous metaphysical fear, surely, that was the subject of Epicurean attack: it is this sort of fear that brings us to foolish enterprises, engages us in pointless activities about whose importance we deceive ourselves. Epicurus argued that if we could conquer the fear of death—and he surely meant the metaphysical terror of non-being—then a great deal of our lives would be more rational, calmer and happier. Our dreadful gravity towards fame, the endless trouble we take to secure ourselves by amassing worthless goods, our undignified servility to people whom we do not respect—all these indignities are, Epicurus thought, superstitious protections against the dangers that bring death. Surely Epicurus is right in at least this: the ramifications of our fears of death are subtle and far reaching. They stand behind and explain otherwise baffling and bizarre activities, activities that would make sense if they spring from, and are directed by, the mistaken belief that they will protect us from death. (Of course there are many other hypotheses that would also explain these activities, many other beliefs that would rationalize this sort of behaviour. All that is required for our account is that the Epicurean hypothesis be among the plausible ones: we are only considering whether, if Epicurus is right, and the irrational fear of death explains a great deal of futile and troubled human activity, it follows that we can and should give up the irrational fear of death.) Now on the Epicurean account, if we abandon the metaphysical fear of death we need then no longer suffer the smaller fears: we need no longer fear the heat o' the sun, or the furious winter's rages, or even the intimations of mortality. Abandoning the metaphysical fear of death would free us from the particular superstitious and fetishistic fears that are its consequences.

But even if the fear of death leads to much folly, that does not prove that it always leads to folly, or that it only leads to folly. There might be other good reasons to be committed to such folly. Fetishistic fears and superstitious actions might even be beneficial, despite the care they give us and the false beliefs they involve. One might ask: what else would we be doing with our time? If we did not fear death, would there be a more rational measure of how best to engage our interests and spend our time? Consider the inquiries—astronomy, biology, psychology, the range of agricultural and medical sciences—that on an Epicurean account might have begun with the fear of death. It is of course important that they became independent of their origins: but would they have begun at all without pressing needs and the fears that attend them? (Do we indeed have a notion of psychologically experienced biological *need,* without a notion of the distress and fear that accompanies the frustration of what is needful to survival? Needs characteristically motivate by being felt, and felt as discomforts. A creature capable of reflecting on what the need signifies, as a signal of a somatic necessity for survival, implicitly has the idea of its death.)

The anxious metaphysical fears castigated by the Epicureans—the scholar's terror of his non-being or that of the poet contemplating Chamonix or Mt Aetna—are indeed irrational. We have suggested that these fears are by-products of functional fears. From an extension and improvisation of a Kantian argument we can derive other reasons for thinking that irrational attitudes to death are ineradicable. Kant argued that reifying the soul—treating it as a possible object of experience that can be brought into being and go out of being, something that can be caused and that can have causal effects—is an inevitable but inappropriate metaphysical application of certain rational argument forms. He tried to show that the illicit reification of the soul is built into the structure of reflective inferential thinking, built into the structure of certain sorts of arguments. The *structure* of a rational argument form is universal in its application, indiscriminate to variations in content. If Kant is right, a mind capable of certain kinds of causal reasoning cannot restrict the use of such reasoning: though we necessarily and properly apply the categories of substance and cause within experience, we inevitably and also necessarily apply those categories improperly to what falls outside the limits of experience. Reifying the totality of experience, illicitly treating it as if it could itself be a possible object of experience, we ask questions that are appropriate only within experience: when, where and how did it come into being or cease to exist? Similarly we ask these questions about the simple unified soul, the subject of experience reified as what it cannot be: an object of possible experience.[5] These questions are both inevitable and illicit: they are built into the operations of rational inference, and yet are improper and meaningless. If, as Kant thought, reification and the causal and temporal reasoning that accompany it are part of the very structure of thought, then we cannot regionalize or check such thought or the attitudes that are ingredient in it. Of course such reifications and the attitudes that attend them need not be verbally articulated.

The person whose reflections have generated metaphysical terror need not to be a poet or a philosopher: *l'homme moyen sensuel* can awaken to the dark night of the soul at four in the morning. The Kantian argument does not claim that everyone actually harbours metaphysical fear, if they would but admit it or focus on it. His argument only shows that the thought which is the core of metaphysical fear—the thought of experiencing one's own non-being—is implicit in and presupposed by reflective patterns of transcendental thought, which are themselves conditions for the possibility of experience and rational reflection on experience.

But it might be argued that these improvisations on Kantian arguments at best shows the inevitability of certain sorts of inference patterns: they by no means establish that specific *attitudes* must accompany such thinking. Couldn't a rational Martian or rational machine draw metaphysical inferences without suffering *angst?* Indeed they could; and nothing is more likely than that they would. But we are concerned with the reactions of rational human beings, embodied as we are. Just as Kant argued that certain 'naturalistic' human motives—the universal desire for happiness, for instance—supplement and accompany strictly rational moral motives, so one would expect that there would be an equivalent set of naturalistic human attitudes that would accompany metaphysical thinking beyond the limits of experience. (For instance, in the *Critique of Judgment,* Kant treats *awe* as the natural attitude towards the indefinite; and he introduces *respect* as the appropriate attitude towards the categorical imperative. So a Kantian might well analogously introduce *angst* as the natural human attitude towards non-being.)

Is there anything left of the Epicurean view that it is not rational to fear death even though the loss of life is a grief? Certainly everything of the original argument remains: death as such is not to be feared; nothing in that state can bring us harm. Is it then a matter of evaluating the arguments that death is not to be feared, against the arguments that the fear of death is functional, and in any case ineradicable by creatures constituted as we are, with our sorts of bodies and our sorts of rational capacities and structures? Surely not: the two sides of the argument are not commensurable; they cannot be weighed and summarized in such a way as to allow us to determine what is, all things considered, the rational attitude towards death.

Are we then simply left with the unresolvable opposition, a dilemmatic conflict in our attitudes towards death? There is another way of reading the Epicurean position, a way that brings it closer to Stoicism. The person who has, and recognizes that he has, an irresolvable conflict between regarding his fear of death as irrational and yet inevitable and even functional, can still take attitudes *towards* his condition. He can take a certain sort of second-order position towards his fear of death, distancing himself from its irrationality, and minimizing as best he can the damaging effects of such fears. But he could at the same time (and not just alternately in a vacillating way) recognize his fear as a natural fact, a consequence of being constituted in a certain way, having certain sorts of rational capacities. Taking this sort of dissociative attitude towards his irrational fear would not necessarily assuage his fear: but it would mean that he was not simply identical with the fearful person. He might then be able to develop distinctive attitudes towards his functional and his dysfunctional fears, perhaps learning how to modify, or at least modify the effects of, his irrational fears, recognizing that there are limits to his control over them. Recognizing the (natural) inevitability of such fears while also dissociating oneself from them can illuminate a dilemmatic conflict that might otherwise have been merely debilitating.[6]

NOTES

1. E.g., Epicurus and Spinoza.

2. Thomas Nagel, 'Death,' reprinted in James Rachels, *Moral Problems* (New York: Harper & Row, 1978), and above, chap. 1.

3. Cf. Robert Gordon, 'Fear,' *Philosophical Review* (October 1980), and my 'Explaining Emotions', *Journal of Philosophy,* 75 (1978), 150, reprinted in *Explaining Emotions* (Berkeley: University of California, 1980).

4. Cf. Hume, *Enquiry Concerning Human Understanding,* Sec. 4, Part II, 45, and Sec, IX, 85.

5. Kant notoriously did not apply the arguments of the first antinomy to the substantiality of the soul (conceived as a unified object), as he had applied them to the world (conceived as a totality). The reasons for his failure to extend those arguments lie in his ethics: although moral action is performed solely as a duty to what is right, the moral agent should in principle receive benefits from morality. As it seems evident that such benefits do not always accrue in life, Kant postulated an immortal soul to receive them. Despite this lapse, however, it seems clear that the arguments of the necessity *and* the impropriety of certain metaphysical inference patterns should consistently apply to the soul as well as to the world considered as a totality.

6. I am grateful to the participants in an NEH Summer Seminar for their helpful discussions of this paper.

How To Be Dead and Not Care: A Defense of Epicurus

STEPHEN E. ROSENBAUM

Illinois State University

Non fui; fui; non sum; non curo.

Roman epitaph

THE PROSPECT OF DEATH is at best a disquieting annoyance; it is at worst a terrifying mystery. However we react to the prospects of our deaths, we try to suppress our thoughts about death, and live as if our time were endless. Long ago, Epicurus offered a remedy for our attitudes toward our deaths. He apparently argued that since death is neither good nor bad for the person dead and since the fear of that which is not bad for one is groundless, it is unreasonable to fear death; consequently, no one should fear death. If Epicurus were correct in this, we should perhaps try to revise our attitudes toward our deaths. Without regard to what we can do or what we should do about our attitudes, I wish to discuss Epicurus's view that one's death is not bad for one. Since Thomas Nagel's article, "Death," published in 1970,[1] Epicurus's view has come under strong attack from various sources, but has not yet received a sound defense.[2] I undertake to supply that defense.

Before reconstructing Epicurus's argument, it would be well to make explicit certain basic assumptions and certain basic concepts

Reprinted by permission from *American Philosophical Quarterly*, 23, No. 2 (April 1986), 217–25.

involved in the issue to be discussed. First, I suppose that being alive is generally good. Some argue against Epicurus partly on the ground that life is good, and I wish to make clear at the outset that I shall not challenge that supposition. Second, I accept the proposition that when one dies, one ceases to exist, in some important sense. Although this proposition is not completely unproblematic, it is one of the bases for the discussion of Epicurus's doctrine. Those who find death frightful and evil find it so precisely because they consider it, or think it might be, the end of their existence as persons. Epicurus finds death harmless partly because it brings about (or is) nonexistence. The issue between Epicurus and his antagonists is how to view one's death, if it leads to nonexistence. Of course, if one could justifiably believe in life after death, the issue would be different, though if one knew merely that one would continue to exist after one's death, one would not thereby know whether one's death is good, bad, or neither.

It is useful additionally to distinguish three concepts from one another, those of dying, death, and being dead. Attempting a careful explication of the issue raised by Epicurus using only the word "death" would be futile, for the term is ambiguous, being used to mean sometimes dying, sometimes death, and sometimes being dead, as I shall explain those terms. Dying, we must say, is the process whereby one comes to be dead or the process where certain causes operate to bring about one's being dead. As such, dying takes place during, and at or near the end of, one's lifetime, however extensive it may be. The time dying takes may be short or long. The process of dying may be comfortable or uncomfortable. When we say about a person that it took a long time for the person to die, we are commenting about the person's dying. An important truth about dying is that it takes place during a person's lifetime and may thus be experienced. We should distinguish dying from death. Doing so is not perfectly in accord with common usage, but this is insignificant, since common usage is not perfectly unambiguous. When we say, for example, "Her death took a long time," we could substitute the word "dying" for that of "death" with no loss of meaning. Nevertheless, I want to focus on that sense of 'death' in which the word might be used to say, "Though he had a long, fatal illness, his death came unexpectedly." In this context, death is roughly the time at which a person becomes dead, and is different from dying, the process leading to death. Metaphorically, death is the portal between the land of the living and the land of the dead; the bridge over the Styx. Several facts should be noted about death, in this sense. It is not clearly a part of a person's lifetime, although it may be a (very) small part. Also, it is not clear that it takes time or, if so, how much time it takes. It may be a mere moment in time separating being alive from being dead. Distinct from dying or death is being dead. Being dead is the state in which one finds oneself (so to speak) after one dies. Being dead is clearly not part of a person's life, in the normal sense, though we might say that it is part of a person's history. The differences among these concepts may be summarized easily: death comes at the end of a person's dying and at the beginning of a person's being dead. There are two points in making these distinctions. One is that doing so will enable us to understand Epicurus's view about death in the clearest way. The other is that it will enable us to notice ambiguous uses of the term "death" which embody rhetorically, but not logically, persuasive ways of insinuating the falsity of Epicurus's view.

Now we are in a position to formulate Epicurus's argument after reminding ourselves of what he said in his "Letter to Menoeceus."

> Accustom thyself to believe that death is nothing to us, for good and evil imply sentience, and death is the privation of all sentience; . . . Death, therefore, the most awful of evils, is nothing to us, seeing that, when we are, death is not come, and when death is come, we are not. It is nothing, then, either to the living or to the dead, for with the living it is not and the dead exist no longer.[3]

I offer the following reconstruction of Epicurus's argument. In formulating the argument as I do, I attempt to do justice to Epicurus's philosophical insight, caring less for historical accuracy than for verisimilitude. The reconstruction runs as follows:

(A) A state of affairs is bad for person P only if P can experience it at some time.

Therefore, (B) P's being dead is bad for P only if it is a state of affairs that P can experience at some time.

(C) P can experience a state of affairs at some time only if it begins before P's death.

(D) P's being dead is not a state of affairs that begins before P's death.

Therefore, (E) P's being dead is not a state of affairs that P can experience at some time.

THEREFORE, P's being dead is not bad for P.

Before discussing objections to this argument, several comments are in order. First, the conclusion does not entail that P's being dead is not bad for others or that P's being dead is not bad in any way in which something might be bad but not *for* anyone, if there is such a way. So, the argument, if sound, should not inhibit our thinking that a person's being dead is bad in these other ways. Second, the conclusion is not about death or dying, but rather it is about being dead. So it does not rule out a person's dying being bad for the person, as painful experience makes obvious it should not. Neither does it rule out a person's death being bad for the person. There are several reasons why I express the conclusion in this way. It makes Epicurus's argument clearly sensible in a way in which it would not otherwise be. When Epicurus said that "death . . . is nothing to us, seeing that, when we are, death is not come, and when death is come, we are not,"[4] he is most plausibly interpreted as talking about being dead. Taking death to be a sort of tertiary period in one's history, one could construe Epicurus as being concerned about death (in my sense), but I believe that it would be an exceedingly uncharitable way of making him look silly. The term "death" as ordinarily used, is ambiguous, being used sometimes to mean dying, sometimes death, and sometimes being dead, as I have explicated the terms. There is no reason to expect Epicurus thoughtfully to have distinguished these and to have selected the Greek equivalent of "being dead" to express his view.[5] Second, the issue would be much less interesting if it concerned death instead of being dead. What people seem to think bad is not the moment of death itself, but rather the abysmal nonexistence of being dead. That, at any rate, is what they fear, and that fear is what Epicurus wished to extinguish. In addition, I am not sure that a person's death (in my sense) could be bad for a person, since the death of a person may have no temporal duration, being a mere moment in time separating being alive from being dead. Even if death endured a fraction of a second, most rational beings would not be very concerned about it no matter how much agony were believed to be involved. Finally, there are sympathetic proponents of Epicurus's view who take him to be concerned about being dead, not death. Lucretius, for example, understood Epicurus's view about death as a view about being dead.[6] So we have good reason to express the conclusion in the way we do.[7]

It is important, furthermore, to spend some time explaining and commenting on the concept of experience, which plays a crucial role in the argument. Comments about experience should be made in full realization of the woes that can befall one who attempts to look too deeply into Pandora's box. The word "experience" is ambiguous, and it is not possible to review the analysis of the concept briefly, nor is it useful to do so.[8] Nevertheless, some helpful remarks can be made in the context of an argument for (A), that a state of affairs is bad for a person only if the person can experience it at some time.

Suppose that a person P cannot hear and never will hear. Then the egregious performance of a Mozart symphony cannot causally affect P at any time, supposing that what makes the performance bad is merely awful sound, detectable only through normal hearing, and supposing further that the performance does not initiate uncommon causal sequences which can affect the person. It is clear that the person cannot experience the bad performance, auditorily or otherwise. Furthermore, it seems clear that the performance cannot be bad for the person in any way. It cannot affect the person in any way. The reason why it is not bad for him is that he is not able to experience it. The person's being deaf insulates him from auditory experiences which might otherwise be bad for him. Similarly, a person born without a sense of smell cannot be causally affected by, and thus cannot experience, the stench of a smoldering cheroot. The stench cannot be an olfactory negativity for her. We could imagine indefinitely many more such cases.

Since I see nothing eccentric about these cases, I believe that we are entitled to generalize and claim that our judgments about these cases are explained by the principle that if a person cannot experience a state of affairs at some time, then the state of affairs is not bad for the person. Dead persons cannot experience any states of affairs; they are blind, deaf, and generally insentient. So no state of affairs is bad for a dead person. The principle which explains these cases is, moreover, logically equivalent to (A), a state of affairs is bad for a person only if the person can experience it at some time. We may take it that we thus have a positive reason for believing (A).

Now, clearly there are certain suppositions about experience used in this argument. Foremost is the assumption that one experiences a state of affairs only if it can affect one in some way. There is supposed to be a causal element in experience. In this sense of "experience," then, one does not experience a situation merely by believing that the situation has occurred or will occur, or by imagining a certain situation. A person can believe that a state of affairs has occurred or will occur even if the state of affairs has had no causal effects on the person. The event may not have occurred and may never occur. Thus, in the sense of "experience" presupposed here, one does not experience just by believing. Similarly, one does not experience a situation just by imagining it. One might imagine oneself basking lazily on a sunny beach, but that situation is not thereby a situation that one experiences. The apparently required causal connection between the situation and the person is missing.

Notice that I have assumed here only a necessary condition for experiencing a situation, not a sufficient condition. Hence, one might be causally affected by a situation and not experience it. Perhaps awareness of the causal effects is also required. I believe there may be one sense of the term "experience" in which awareness is required, another in which it is not. It is difficult to think that one could perceptually experience something, for example, without being aware of it. However, there is that way of experiencing in which we are said to undergo an experience, of which we need not be aware. If one undergoes (as we say) the experience of being irradiated by low level radioactivity, one might well not be aware of it. It seems to me that one clear requirement of experience, in at least in one clear sense, is that one be causally affected in some way by situations one experiences.

Finally, if a requirement of experiencing a state of affairs is that the state of affairs be able to have causal effects on one, then we can express a positive reason for believing not only premise (A) but also premise (C), that P can experience a state of affairs at some time only if it begins before P's death. Surely a state of affairs can causally affect a person only if the person exists after the state of affairs begins to occur, for effects occur only after their causes. To be sure, a person's dead body can be affected after the person ceases to be, but a person is not identical to its lifeless body. A person exists after a state of affairs begins to occur only if the state of affairs begins before the person's death. Therefore a state of affairs can causally affect a person only if the state of affairs begins before the person's death. So a person can experience a situation only if the situation begins to occur before the person's death. Obviously, this is (C). According to one reasonably clear concept of experience, then, we have reasons to believe basic premises in the argument.

Before considering objections to the Epicurean argument, I want to characterize what I take to be the purpose of Epicurus's argument. I do this because some discussions of the issue seem to have misunderstood entirely what Epicurus was trying to do. Simply, he was trying to show us the truth about being dead so that we might not be excessively troubled about it. His general philosophical aim seems to have been much the same as that of Lucretius, his disciple, to know the truth and thereby achieve *ataraxia*. There is no reason to believe he would have been willing to peddle *ataraxia* by means of rhetorical trickery, not that he may not have done so inadvertently. Indicative of his purpose is a comment in his "letter to Herodotus," in which he discussed metaphysics. He said that ". . . mental tranquility means being released from all . . . troubles and cherishing a continual remembrance of the highest and most important truths."[9] Thus, I believe that Mary Mothersill seriously misunderstood Epicurus when announcing her view that his argument ". . . will hardly bear looking into, but may have been intended as little more than an eristic flourish," and that "Epicurus was not much interested in logic. . . ."[10] Epicurus did have a serious purpose, to establish the truth and thereby gain mental tranquility and show the way to mental tranquility. In fairness to Mothersill, we should admit that there would be more to her comment if Epicurus's argument were to be understood only as he expressed it. There is not much there. Nevertheless, I think that it is uncharitable caviling to dismiss his argument without an attempt to state the argument clearly.

Others have not fully appreciated the revisionistic character of Epicurus's philosophy. Harry Silverstein, for example, sees the matter raised by Epicurus as a sort of contest between the Epicurean view and the common sense view ". . . that a person's death is one of the greatest evils that can befall him."[11] Seeming to believe that the philosopher's task is to bolster the deliverances of common sense against all antagonists, Silverstein is driven to extreme lengths in the effort to undermine Epicurus's view. Epicurus believed, however, that unreflective common sense frequently was a source of bemusement and misery, and he wished to make common sense conform to the results of philosophical reflection. He believed that one of the results was a realization that death is not bad for the person who dies. I do not want to argue for Epicurus's apparent view of philosophy, and I certainly do not wish to dismiss arguments against Epicurus on the ground that they presuppose a distinct view of philosophy. I merely note that the argument is offered in a revisionistic spirit and that those who conjure ways to defend common sense against Epicurus are arguing in a very different context from that of Epicurus. Whether one takes philosophy to be revisionistic or not, perhaps one should approach philosophical arguments from the point of view of possible discovery, not from that of the infrangibility of one's own prereflective inclinations. However this may be, the philosophical issue is whether the argument is sound. To objections against the argument I now turn.

Given the Epicurean argument as I have stated it, there are only three premises one could question. Those are the basic ones, (A), (C), and (D). The others, (B) and (E), are merely logical consequences of (A), (C), and (D). Since (D) is true by definition, we shall consider only (A) and (C), which have, in fact, been attacked by Epicurus's adversaries.

Thomas Nagel argues that what a person does not know may well be bad for the person.[12] Nagel seems thereby to object to premise (A). He gives plausible cases in which something can be bad for a person even if the person is unaware of it. Unknown betrayal by friends and destruction of one's reputation by vile, false rumors of which one is unaware are examples of evils which a person might not consciously experience. Strictly, however, such cases are logically compatible with (A) and hence do not refute (A), since all (A) requires for something to be bad for a person is that the person *can* experience it (perhaps not consciously) at some time, not that he actually experience it consciously.[13] We can grant that what one *does not* consciously experience can hurt one without granting that what one *cannot* experience can hurt one. All (A) requires for an event or state of affairs to be bad for a person, implicitly, is that the person be able to experience at some time, not that the person be aware or conscious of the causal effects at some time.

Nagel tries to deny the conclusion directly by characterizing death as a loss to the person who suffers it, and, taking losses to be bad, concludes that a person's death is bad for the person. He seems relatively unconcerned about the proposition that once a person dies, that person no longer exists, and thus does not and *cannot* experience the loss, a proposition which he accepts.[14] L. S. Sumner is more explicit about the issue and claims that though the person who dies no longer exists ". . . the only condition essential to any loss is *that there should have been a subject who suffered it.*"[15] It is all right, I suppose, to *call* a person's death a loss for the person, but it is clearly not like paradigmatic cases of losses which are bad for persons. Consider the case in which one loses one's business to creditors. One has the business, the creditors get it, and then one does not have it. We may suppose that the loss is bad for the person. Such cases are common. We should note that in such cases the loss is something the person is able to experience after it occurs. Typical losses which are bad for persons seem to instantiate the following principle: A person P loses good g only if there is a time at which P has g and there is a later time at which P does not have g. If P ceases to exist when P dies, then being dead cannot be considered a loss of this typical sort in which losses are bad for persons, for in typical cases P exists after the loss and is able to experience it. If being dead is a loss, it is so insufficiently similar to paradigm cases of loss which are bad for persons that we need special reasons or arguments why treating death as a loss enables us to reject (A). Neither Nagel nor others offer such reasons. Therefore, the argument that death is a loss and is thus bad is not convincing.

Nagel believes further that by treating death as a loss for a person, he has a way of resolving *the symmetry problem,* noted by Lucretius.[16] Considering this problem will help us understand more clearly the problems in holding that death is bad for one. Taking being dead to be nonexistence, Lucretius compared the nonexistence after death to that before conception, and apparently thought that since prenatal nonexistence is not bad for a person (and no one finds it distressing), then posthumous nonexistence is not bad either (though people *do* find it distressing). He seemed to have thought that we should rectify our unjustifiably asymmetrical attitudes toward the two symmetrical states. The argument would be that if being dead (when one is nonexistent) is bad for one, then not having had life before one's conception (when one is also nonexistent) should be bad for one. Since the latter is not bad for one, then the former is not.

Nagel's response to this argument is that ". . . the time after his [a person's] death is time of which his death deprives him. It is time in which, had he not died then, he would be alive. Therefore any death entails the loss of *some* life that its victim would have led had he not died at that or any earlier point."[17] By this, Nagel intends to suggest implicitly that we cannot say something similar about birth, hence, there is an asymmetry, contrary to Lucretius. However, we can say something quite analogous about birth: The time before a person's birth is a time of which his not having been born earlier deprives him. It is a time in which, had he not been born as late as he was, he would be alive. Therefore any delay in being born entails the loss of some life that its beneficiary would have led had he been born earlier. To be clear about the analogy, if life is a good, then, given a living person, if losing life so soon is bad for the person, then not having acquired life earlier should be bad for the person. In either case, one misses out on life. Shall we say that the issue is whether it is worse to have lived and lost than never to have lived at all? No, because it is not true of a living person that that person *never* lived at all. A living person can live longer not only by dying later but also by being born earlier. The issue really is whether it is worse to have lived and lost than not *yet* to have lived. I do not see that it is worse. What makes the symmetry is, in part, the fact that a living person who *was* prenatally nonexistent *was going to live,* just as the living person who *will be* posthumously nonexistent *has lived.* The symmetry is plausible because the analogy between the two relevant states seems quite sound.

Nagel objects to the proposed symmetry by insisting that ". . . we cannot say that the time prior to a man's birth is a time in which he would have lived had he been born not then but earlier. . . . He *could* not have been born earlier: anyone born substantially earlier than he was would have been someone else. Therefore, the time prior to his birth is not time in which his subsequent birth prevents him from living."[18] The reply to this is obvious. If the time at which we are born is *essential* to who we are, to our identity, then the time at which we die should be also. If *we* could not have been born earlier (because if "we" had been, "we" would have been someone else), then *we* could not have died later (and still have been us). Nagel's answer relies on the view that there is an asymmetry between time of birth and time of death, implicitly because time of birth is not essential to us while time of death is. But *this* putative asymmetry is invisible. Thus it cannot be used to argue for the asymmetry between prenatal and posthumous nonexistence. If Lucretius's symmetry thesis is correct, as it seems to be, then there is no reason to think that being dead is any worse than not having been born yet.

A recent objection to the Epicurean argument is that of Harry Silverstein, who, defending common sense, apparently believes that a person can, in some way, experience posthumous states of affairs, thus seeming to reject (C). He apparently argues against (C) by proposing an analogy between spatially distant events and temporally distant (future) events. He believes that the view that spatially distant events exist (but not *here*) and that temporally distant events do not exist ". . . presupposes a conceptual ontological framework which is significantly biased in favor of space, a framework according to which we inhabit an essentially three-dimensional, spatial, universe and which condemns time to a purely ancillary treatment befitting its status as space's poor relation."[19] Wishing for a less biased ontology, Silverstein proposes to treat time on a par with space and to say that just as spatially distant events exist so too do future events. Thus, he has a possible way of negating (C): A person can experience states of affairs or events that begin after that person's death, because such things *exist* atemporally ("during") a person's life.

There is much to say about Silverstein's argument, which is, at points, quite complex. However, I shall be content to make a few points, one of which seems to me quite telling against his argument. Silverstein wishes to show, as he puts it, ". . . that A's death can be the *object* of his grief in the same way that the death of a spatially distant friend can be such an object. . . ."[20] He wants to make this point because he thinks that "where A's 'appropriate feeling' results from his apprehension or consciousness of the event (etc.) in question, what seems important in any case is not the event's being the *cause,* but its being the *object,* of this feeling."[21] To make the point, he feels he must hold a metaphysical view according to which it is possible that future events or states of affairs exist now, atemporally. There are several appropriate comments to be made about Silverstein's view. First, one of his basic assumptions goes without support, that assumption, namely, that an event's being an object of feeling, not a cause, is what is important in saying whether posthumous events are bad for a person. It seems to me that unless this hypothesis receives some support, we are free to reject it, especially since I have already argued that a causal relationship between the event and the person is necessary. Second, he assumes that a person's having, at some time, an actual feeling about an event is necessary for the event to be bad for the person. This assumption, too, is without support. To be sure, it is his interpretation of Epicurus's view that bad is associated with sentience, but it is not the only or the most obvious interpretation. If we say, for example, that one must experience an event consciously for it to be bad for one, it does not follow from what we say that one must have certain feelings about the event, about one's awareness of the event, or about anything. It should be argued that feelings of some sort are involved.

Finally, it is clear that events which have never occurred and will never occur *can,* in some sense, be *objects* of our psychological attitudes. For example, Britons in the early 1940's feared an invasion of Britain by the Nazis. Yet that event never occurred. They dreaded being governed by Hitler, yet that state of affairs did not obtain and never will. Silverstein insists that "the problem of existence constitutes the sole obstacle to the claim that posthumous events, like spatially distant events, can be objects of appropriate feelings and experiences. . . ."[22] But should we say that the event and state of affairs in the previous examples had to exist (and existed) for them to have been objects of fear and dread? We can say so, if we like, but whether we say thus that the Nazi invasion of Britain existed (or exists), atemporally, it is nevertheless an event that Britons never experienced (it is natural to say), because it never occurred. This suggests that something is seriously wrong with Silverstein's objection to premise (C). Very simply, he fails to distinguish the existence of an event or state of affairs from the occurrence of an event or state of affairs. Certainly, there might be no need to make such a distinction for one who takes it that the class of occurring events is identical to the class of existing events. Without such a distinction, one would hold that an event exists if, and only if, it occurs. If Silverstein identifies the classes of events, then he would seem forced to the view that if events exist atemporally (as he believes) then events occur atemporally. But if events occurred and existed atemporally, what would be the difference between past and future events? There would be none, which is absurd. Therefore, Silverstein should distinguish existing from occurring events or find some other way of distinguishing past from future events. It would be most plausible to say that for events or states of affairs to exist is one thing, to occur is another. One might hold that all events *exist* atemporally but that among the existing events, some have already occurred (past events) and some have not yet occurred (future events). With this distinction, moreover, it is easy to defend (C) against Silverstein's attack. (C) could be interpreted in terms of an event occurring instead of an event existing. As stated, (C) should be understood to be slightly elliptical for this: P can experience a state of affairs at some time only if it begins *to occur* before P's death. In fact, this is how I have taken it. So understood, it is no good to object to (C) that posthumous events or states of affairs exist timelessly (during a person's life). This would be logically compatible with (C). One would have to show that a person can experience a state of affairs or an event that does not begin *to occur* before the person's death. I do not see how *this* can be done. Therefore, I conclude that Silverstein's metaphysical proposal is ineffective against premise (C), whatever its merits independently.

In spite of the apparent soundness of Epicurus's argument, one might object against Epicurus's argument on the ground that it misses the point. One might claim that the badness of our deaths lies in our anticipation of losing the capacity to experience, to have various opportunities and to obtain various satisfactions. It does seem quite obvious that such anticipation is bad, for it is a source of displeasure, as much as is the experience of anticipating the tortures of the dental chair. However, the anticipation of either bad experiences or of the inability to experience *simpliciter* is something that can occur only while we are alive. It cannot occur when we are dead if being dead entails nonexistence. Therefore, we do not experience the anticipation of being dead when we are dead. So, the badness of the anticipation of death does not show the badness of death itself. This point may be understood more clearly when one compares the anticipation of dental pain to the anticipation of being dead. For the former, there are two bad experiences, the anticipation and the pain of the root canal; for the latter, there is only one bad experience, the anticipation of being dead. Indeed, Epicurus may be thought to have believed that the anticipation of death is a pointless bad, since it is a bad with no genuine basis, the object of it not being bad. Epicurus hoped that understanding this could free us from one bad, one baseless source of anxiety. One could say, I suppose, that one's death is bad, meaning that anticipation of one's death is bad. However, not only would it be unduly misleading to say this, but also, it would not be a way of undermining Epicurus's view that one's death itself is not bad for one.

Now that objections to the Epicurean argument have been shown to fail, we might think of trying to account for what seems a widespread and well-entrenched fear of death or being dead. It is perhaps useful to remind ourselves that people may fear what is not really bad for them; they might fear what they only believe to be bad for them. We might thus speculate that people fear death out of ignorance. This seems somewhat too facile and insensitive, however true. Perhaps a few conjectures may help explain the fear of being dead in a way both sympathetic to human anguish and consistent with the Epicurean view.

Lucretius offered a very interesting psychological explanation of the terror of death. He hypothesized that we have a very difficult time thinking of ourselves distinct from our bodies.

> Accordingly, when you see a man resenting his fate, that after death he must either rot with his body laid in the tomb, or perish by fire or the jaws of wild beasts, you may know that he rings false, . . . although he himself deny the belief in any sensation after death. He does not, I think, admit what he professes to admit, . . . he does not wholly uproot and eject himself from life, but unknown to himself he makes something of himself to survive. For when he in life anticipates that birds and beasts will mangle his body after death, he pities himself; for he does not distinguish himself from that thing, he does not separate himself sufficiently from the body there cast out, he imagines himself to be that and, standing beside it, infects it with his own feeling. Hence he . . . does not see that in real death there will be no other self that could live to bewail his perished self, or stand by to feel pain that he lay there lacerated or burning.[23]

Lucretius may have believed that we so habitually identify ourselves with our bodies that we have a psychologically difficult time separating ourselves from them. So we think that since bad things can happen to our bodies in death, bad things can happen to us. This way of thinking is perhaps exemplified in the custom, in some societies, of placing a dead person's body inside a sturdy, well-sealed box, fitted with comfortable bedding. Why would there be this practice if there were not at least some psychological basis for associating a living person with that person's lifeless body? If Lucretius were correct in his hypothesis, then it would help to alleviate our fear of our deaths if we could sufficiently separate ourselves from our dead bodies.

Another possible explanation for the fear of death in at least our society, broadly speaking, is that people have been exposed for so long to the thesis that there is a life after death that even if they do not explicitly accept the view, they are somehow strongly affected by it. Since they have no information about what really happens to a person after the person dies, they feel that what happens then could well be awful. Wanting desperately not to experience the awful, and not knowing that they will not, they fear. If this is so, then, ironically, fear of death has its psychological roots in the belief in a life after death.

One might try to account for our fear of death based on the fact that the conclusion of the Epicurean argument leaves plenty of room for maneuver. It would allow, for example, dying or death (possibly), but not being dead, to be bad for a person. One might hypothesize that those who view being dead as a bad for them and thus fear it do so out of confusion. They take dying or death to be bad, mistakenly identify dying or death with being dead, and then think that being dead is bad. On that basis they may fear it. Their fear could be based on a truth, that dying or death is (or could be) bad for them, and at the same time a confusion, that there is no difference between dying or death and being dead. Such a confusion might well receive aid from the fact that "death," as commonly used, is ambiguous, as I noted at the outset. Nagel's argument benefits from such a confusion. Whatever the explanation or explanations, it is obviously possible to account for our fear of death while at the same time accepting the conclusion of the Epicurean argument.

I have resurrected and reconstructed an Epicurean argument that death is not bad for one. I have given reasons for believing basic premises in the argument, and I have laid to rest all the objections of which I am aware. *(Requiescant in pace.)* Finally, I have offered conjectures which may enable us to account for our fear of being dead compatibly with the conclusion of the argument. This effort should bury the myth that death is bad for us. If we do not believe, as did many of the ancients, that a Stygian passage will take us to a nether realm of being, then, though we may not relish the idea of not being able to experience, we should find in the contemplation of our journey no cause for thanatophobia, as we might if we could reasonably believe that a disorientingly different and possibly quite displeasing set of experiences awaited us.

NOTES

1. Thomas Nagel, "Death," *Noûs,* vol. 4 (1970), pp. 73–80; reprinted as chap. 1 above.

2. Since completing this paper, I have learned of a recent paper which undertakes a defense of Epicurus. O. H. Green, "Fear of Death," *Philosophy and Phenomenological Research,* vol. 43 (1982), pp. 99–105.

3. Diogenes Laertius, *Lives of Eminent Philosophers,* vol. 2 (Cambridge: Harvard University Press, 1925), p. 651.

4. *Ibid.*

5. In fact, there is reason to expect him not to have carefully distinguished these. He wrote more for popular accessibility than for careful philosophical discussion.

6. Lucretius, *De Rerum Natura* (Cambridge: Harvard University Press,

1975), p. 254. There are many comments that prove this, but see *"scire licet nobis nil esse in morte timendum,"* at 866. The use of the phrase *"in morte"* is not eccentric, for its literary use antedates Lucretius by some 150-200 years. It occurs, for example in the Plautus play *Captivi*, at 741: *"post mortem in morte nihil est quod metuam mali."*

7. Hereafter, I shall use "death" to mean being dead, unless the context makes it clear that it is used otherwise.

8. But one might wish to review J. M. Hinton's work, *Experiences*, in which there is a useful discussion of the various senses in which the term is used (Oxford: Oxford University Press, 1973), Part I.

9. Diogenes Laertius, *Lives, op. cit.,* p. 611.

10. Mary Mothersill, "Death," in *Moral Problems,* ed. by James Rachels (New York: Harper & Row, 1971), p. 378.

11. Harry Silverstein, "The Evil of Death," *The Journal of Philosophy,* vol. 77 (1980), p. 401.

12. Thomas Nagel, "Death," *Noûs,* vol. 4 (1970), p. 76; see above, p. 26.

13. The same point is made by Harry Silverstein in "The Evil of Death," *op cit.,* pp. 414ff.

14. Nagel, "Death," *op. cit.,* p. 78; see above, p. 26.

15. L. S. Summer, "A Matter of Life and Death," *Noûs,* vol. 10 (1976), p. 160.

16. Lucretius, *De Rerum Natura, op. cit.,* p. 253 and p. 265.

17. Nagel, "Death," *op. cit.,* p. 79; see above, p. 27.

18. *Ibid.;* see above, p. 27.

19. Silverstein, "The Evil of Death," *op. cit.,* p. 413.

20. *Ibid.,* p. 418.

21. *Ibid.,* p. 417.

22. *Ibid.,* p. 419.

23. Lucretius, *De Rerum Natura, op. cit.,* p. 257.

7

Some Puzzles About the Evil of Death

Fred Feldman
University of Massachusetts

I. The Puzzles

DEATH IS NOTHING to Epicureans. They do not fear or hate death. They do not view death as a misfortune for the deceased. They think death is no worse for the deceased than is not yet being born for the as yet unborn. They say that ordinary people, who look forward to their deaths with dismay, are in this irrational. Why do they hold these odd views?

In his central argument for these conclusions, Epicurus says:

> So death, the most terrifying of ills, is nothing to us, since as long as we exist, death is not with us; but when death comes, then we do not exist. It does not then concern either the living or the dead, since for the former it is not, and the latter are no more.[1]

The argument seems to turn on what has been called "The Existence Condition"—nothing bad can happen to a person at a time unless he exists at that time.[2] If we agree that the dead don't exist, we seem driven to the conclusion that nothing bad can happen to us once we are dead. It is just a small step then to the conclusion that death itself is not bad for those who die.

Although some may find reassurance in this ancient bit of reasoning, most of us cannot help but view it as sophistry. Except in cases in which continued life would be unbearable, death is taken to be a misfortune for the one who dies. We cry at funerals; we grieve for the

Reprinted by permission of the publisher and the author from *The Philosophical Review*, 100, No. 2 (April 1991), 205–27. Copyright © Cornell University.

deceased. Especially when a young person dies, we feel that she has suffered a great misfortune. And it apparently seems to most of us that our attitude is perfectly rational. So we have our first puzzle: how can being dead be a misfortune for a person, if she doesn't exist during the time when it takes place?

According to the most popular anti-Epicurean view, death is bad for a person primarily because it deprives him of certain goods—the goods he would have enjoyed if he had not died.[3] This so-called "Deprivation Approach" thus seems to require that we make a certain comparison— a comparison between (a) how well off a person would be if he were to go on living and (b) how well off he would be if he were to die. The claim is that when death is bad for a person, it is bad for him because he will be worse off dead than he would have been if he had lived. The second puzzle arises because it appears that any such comparison is incoherent. It seems to be, after all, a comparison between (a) the benefits and harms that would come to a person if he were to live and (b) those that would come to him if he were to die. However, if he doesn't exist after his death, he cannot enjoy or suffer any benefits or harms after death. So there apparently is no second term for the comparison. Thus, the Deprivation Approach seems in a covert way to violate the Existence Condition, too.[4]

Suppose we find some coherent way to formulate the view that a person's death is a misfortune for him because it deprives him of goods. Then we face another Epicurean question: *when* is it a misfortune for him? It seems wrong to say that it is a misfortune for him while he is still alive—for at such times he is not yet dead and death has not yet deprived him of anything. It seems equally wrong to say that it is a misfortune for him after he is dead—for at such times he does not exist. How can he suffer misfortunes then?

Another problem confronts the anti-Epicurean. If we can find a coherent way to say that early death is bad for us because it deprives us of certain goods, then we probably will have found a coherent way to say that late birth also deprives us of certain goods—the goods we would have enjoyed if only we had been born earlier. Yet virtually nobody laments his late birth, or thinks it a misfortune that he wasn't born years or decades earlier. Lucretius presented a forceful statement of this puzzle. He said:

Think too how the bygone antiquity of everlasting time before our birth was nothing to us. Nature therefore holds this up to us as a mirror of the time yet to come after our death. Is there aught in this that looks appalling, aught that wears an aspect of gloom? Is it not more untroubled than any sleep?[5]

So another puzzle that must be confronted is this: if early death is bad for us because it deprives us of the goods we would have enjoyed if we had died later, then why isn't late birth just as bad for us? After all, it seems to deprive us of the goods we would have enjoyed if we had been born earlier.

There are other puzzles about the evil of death. Some of these will be addressed as we go along. But these are the main questions I mean to discuss here.

II. METAPHYSICAL AND AXIOLOGICAL ASSUMPTIONS

Before I propose my answers to these questions, I should mention some of my metaphysical and axiological assumptions. First among these, perhaps, is the assumption that there are possible worlds. I am inclined to think that a possible world is a huge proposition fully describing some total way the world might have been, including all facts about the past, present and future. Nothing I say here depends on this particular view about possible worlds. So long as it countenances an appropriate number of appropriately detailed possible worlds, any other coherent view will do as well.

I write as if a given individual may exist at several different possible worlds. This may seem controversial, but I think it is really not. Suppose Myron is an actual person. Suppose he actually smokes. I may ask you to consider some possible world in which Myron does not smoke. This may seem to commit me to the view that there are other worlds relevantly like our (concrete) world, and that in addition to being here in our (concrete) world, the actual concrete Myron (or perhaps a counterpart) is also located at these other places. That, it seems to me, would be strange.

In fact, however, I hold no such view. When I ask you to consider some world in which Myron does not smoke, I am just asking you to consider a huge proposition that fully describes some total way the world might have been, and which entails the proposition that Myron exists but does not smoke. Since it is more convenient to do so, I write in a "realistic" way about other possible worlds—as if they were giant, concrete planets far from Earth, but populated by many earthlings.

I assume that it makes sense to speak of the degree of similarity between possible worlds. Indeed, it seems to me that there are many similarity relations among possible worlds. Later I will have more to say about the details of the similarity relations that are most important for present purposes. However, if we have some particular similarity relation in mind, then it will make sense to speak of some world as being "most similar" in that way to a given world. Sometimes instead of speaking of similarity I speak of "nearness." It is just another way of expressing the same idea.[6]

Now let us briefly turn to axiology. Possible worlds can be evaluated in various ways. One sort of evaluation is "objective" and "non-relational." Suppose that the very simplest form of hedonism is true. According to this view, pleasure is intrinsically good and pain is intrinsically bad. Nothing else has any (basic) intrinsic value. Let's suppose that there is a way to measure the amount of pleasure contained in an episode of pleasure; let's suppose similarly that there is a way to measure the amount of pain contained in an episode of pain. Suppose further that the pleasure-measure and the pain-measure are commensurate, so that it makes sense to subtract amounts of pain from amounts of pleasure.[7] We can then say that the intrinsic value of a possible world is determined as follows: consider how much pleasure is experienced throughout the history of that world; consider how much pain is experienced throughout the history of that world; subtract the latter value from the former; the result is the hedonic value of the world. The simplest form of hedonism says that the intrinsic value of a world is equal to the hedonic value of that world.[8]

Another way to evaluate worlds is equally "objective," but is "person-relative." That is, instead of asking how good a world is, we ask how good it is *for a certain person*. When I speak of how good a world is for a certain person, I mean to indicate the portion of that world's goods and evils that the individual in question enjoys and suffers at that world. Suppose again that the simplest form of hedonism is true. Then the value of a world, w, for a person, s, is determined in this way: consider how much pleasure s enjoys throughout his lifetime at w; consider how much pain s suffers throughout his lifetime at w; subtract the value of the latter from the value of the former. The result is the value of w for s, or V(s,w).

I assume that these values can be expressed with numbers in such a way that higher numbers indicate greater value for the person; zero indicates neutrality for the person; negative numbers indicate badness for the person. Since V(s,w) is a measure of how well s fares at w, I sometimes refer to this as s's "welfare level" at w.[9]

There is a question concerning a person's welfare level at worlds at which he does not exist. The proposed account leaves this value undetermined. Although it plays no role in my argument, I stipulate that if s fails to exist at w, then V(s,w) = 0. This thesis is suggested by the proposed account of relativized value, since if a certain person does not exist at a world then he enjoys no pleasure there and suffers no pain there.

In fact, I do not think that a person's real welfare level is determined in the simple-minded hedonistic way I have sketched. I am inclined to think that several other factors may contribute to determining how good a world is for a person. Among other things, I suspect that the amounts of knowledge and freedom that a person enjoys, as well as the extent to which he is forced to suffer injustice, are also important. However, I prefer to proceed here on the pretense that hedonism is true. I have several reasons.

First and foremost, there is the historical reason. I am engaged in a debate with Epicurus about the evil of death. Epicurus was a hedonist. Some commentators have suggested that in order to answer Epicurus, we must reject his axiology—that his view about the evil of death is inextricably tied to his hedonism. I think this is a mistake. I want to show that, even if we accept the Epicurean axiology, we can still reject the Epicurean conclusion about the evil of death.

A second reason for assuming hedonism is strategic. The central intrinsic value-bearing properties associated with hedonism are ones that a person can have at a time only if he is alive and conscious then. I want to show how death can be an evil for the deceased even if this hedonistic axiology is assumed. Thus, I take myself to be trying to show that death may be an evil for a person even according to an axiology maximally hostile to this notion. If I succeed, it will be pretty easy to see how to extend the solution in the direction of more plausible axiologies.

It should be clear, then, that certain sorts of solution are ruled out by my axiological assumptions. I will not be able to say (as Thomas Nagel and others have suggested)[10] that death is bad in something like the way in which being the subject of nasty rumors is bad. Clearly enough, one can be the subject of nasty rumors even after one has died. If we think this is bad for a person, then we will want to say that one's welfare level at a world can be adversely affected by things that happen after one ceases to exist at that world. Another sort of example involves the failure of one's life projects. One's life projects may come unraveled after one has died. If we think this is bad for a person, then we can cite another way in which one's welfare level at a world may be reduced by things that occur after one's death.

These claims about welfare levels are controversial, and strike me as being implausible. I would rather stick to a much more hard-nosed axiology—an axiology according to which one's welfare level at a world is determined entirely by things that happen during one's life there. Thus (for purposes of illustration) I have adopted a form of simple hedonism. According to this view, if a person never learns of nasty rumors, and never suffers from them, then they don't affect his welfare level. If a person never learns that his life project has come to naught, and never suffers from this frustration, then it doesn't affect his welfare level. Only pains and pleasures can affect a person's welfare level at a world—and these he must experience during his life.

A final advantage of the hedonistic axiology is its simplicity. If we assume that the fundamental bearers of intrinsic value are experiences of pleasure and experiences of pain, and we assume that these are in principle subject to unproblematic quantification, then the determination of a person's welfare level at a possible world becomes quite straightforwardly a matter of simple arithmetic. To find s's welfare level at w, just subtract the amount of pain s suffers at w from the amount of pleasure s enjoys at w. Although the axiology is admittedly quite crude, its simplicity makes it especially useful for illustrative purposes.

I assume that any statement to the effect that something is good (or bad) for a person can be paraphrased by a statement to the effect that some *state of affairs* is good (or bad) for the person. Furthermore, I assume here that a state of affairs (such as the state of affairs of *Myron smoking*) is just a proposition (in this case, the proposition *that Myron smokes*). Thus, for present purposes, it makes no difference whether we say that a certain state of affairs obtains, or whether we say that a certain proposition is true.

In any case, instead of saying that smoking (apparently an activity) would be bad for Myron, we can say instead that *that Myron smokes* (a state of affairs) is bad for Myron. Instead of saying that a bowl of hot soup (apparently a physical object) would be good for me, we can say that what would be good for me is *that I have a bowl of hot soup,* and thus again represent the thing that is good for me as a state of affairs. I prefer to write in this way, since it induces a sort of conceptual tidiness and uniformity.

I am also going to assume that when a person dies, he goes out of existence. In fact, I think this assumption is extremely implausible. No one would dream of saying that when a tree dies, it goes out of existence. Why should we treat people otherwise? My own view is that a person is just a living human body. In typical cases, when the body dies, it continues to exist as a corpse. So the thing that formerly was a person still exists, although it is no longer alive (and perhaps no longer a person). Of course, I recognize that some people go out of existence at the moment of death—for example, those located at Ground Zero at the moment of a nuclear blast. For present purposes, I will assume that everyone does. Once again, I do this in part for historical reasons—Epicurus seems to have accepted this view about death and nonexistence—and in part for strategic reasons. I want to show how death can be bad for the deceased even on the assumptions (a) that things that directly affect a person's welfare level can happen to that person only at times when he exists, and (b) that death marks the end of existence for the deceased.[11]

III. THINGS THAT ARE BAD FOR PEOPLE

The central question here is how a person's death can be bad for him. The claim that someone's death is bad for him is an instance of a more general sort of claim—the claim that some state of affairs is bad for some person. It would be surprising if it were to turn out that we need two independent accounts of what's meant by statements to the effect that something is bad for someone: one account of the meaning of such a statement when the relevant object is the person's death, and another account of the meaning of such a statement when the relevant object is something other than the person's death. Surely the statement about death ought to be nothing more than an interesting instance of the general sort of statement. So let's consider the more general question first, and then focus more narrowly on the specific case concerning death. What do we mean when we say that something would be bad for someone?

It seems to me that when we say that something would be bad for someone, we might mean either of two main things. One possibility is that we mean that the thing would be *intrinsically* bad for the person. So if someone says that a state of affairs, p, is intrinsically bad for a person, s, he presumably means that p is intrinsically bad, and s is the subject or "recipient" of p. Given our assumed hedonistic axiology, the only things that could be intrinsically bad for someone would be his own pains. Thus, *Dolores suffering pain of intensity 10 from t1 to t3* would be intrinsically bad for Dolores.

On the other hand, when we say that something would be bad for someone, we might mean that it would be "all things considered bad" for him. At least in some instances, this seems to mean that he would be all things considered worse off if it were to occur than he would be if it were not to occur. In this case, the thing itself might be intrinsically neutral. The relevant consideration would be the extent to which it would lead to or prevent or otherwise be connected with things that are intrinsically bad for the person. Consider an example. Suppose we are interested in the question whether moving to Bolivia would be bad for Dolores. Intuitively, this question seems to be equivalent to the question whether Dolores would be worse off if she were to move to Bolivia than she would be if she were to refrain from moving to Bolivia.

Letting "b" indicate the state of affairs *Dolores moves to Bolivia*, we can say this: b would be all things considered bad for Dolores if and only if she would be worse off if b obtained than she would be if b didn't obtain. Now, if we employ the standard account of the meaning of subjunctive conditionals, together with the assumptions about values of worlds for individuals, we can rewrite this as follows: b would be all things considered bad for Dolores if and only if the value for Dolores of the nearest possible b-world is less than the value for her of the nearest possible ~b-world.[12]

Correspondingly, to say that a state of affairs would be all things considered good for a person is to say that she would be better off if it were to obtain than she would be if it were to fail to obtain. More exactly, it is to say that her welfare level at the nearest possible world where it obtains is higher than her welfare level at the nearest possible world where it does not obtain.

If we make use of the abbreviations introduced above, we can restate these claims as follows:

D1: p would be good for s if and only if $(\exists w)$ $(\exists w')$ (w is the nearest p-world & w' is the nearest ~p-world & $V(s,w) > V(s,w')$)

D2: p would be bad for s if and only if $(\exists w)$ $(\exists w')$ (w is the nearest p-world & w' is the nearest ~p-world & $V(s,w) < V(s,w')$)

If we make use of our assumption that worlds have numerical values for individuals, then we can say precisely *how bad* or *how good* something would be for someone. Suppose that if Dolores were to move to Bolivia the rest of her life would be a nightmare. Considering all the pleasures and pains she would ever experience (including the ones she has already experienced), her life would be worth + 100 points. Thus, the value for Dolores of the nearest world in which she moves to Bolivia is + 100. Suppose on the other hand that the value for her of the nearest world in which she does not move to Bolivia is + 1000. Then she would be 900 units worse off if she were to move to Bolivia. That tells us precisely how bad it would be for her to move to Bolivia. The value for her of moving to Bolivia is − 900. So the general principle says that to find the value for a person of a state of affairs, subtract the value for him of the nearest world where it does not obtain from the value for him of the nearest world where it does obtain.

Precisely the same thing happens in the case of a state of affairs that would be good for a person. Suppose it would be good for Dolores to move to Boston. To find out how good it would be for her, consider the value for her of the nearest world in which she does move to

Boston. Suppose it is + 1100. Consider the value for her of the nearest world in which she does not move to Boston. Suppose it is + 1000. Subtract the value for her of the latter from the value for her of the former. The result (+ 100) is the value for Dolores of moving to Boston.

In its most general form, then, the principle may be formulated as a principle about the overall value (good, bad, or neutral) of states of affairs for persons. The overall value of a state of affairs for a person is the result of subtracting the value for him of the nearest world where it does not occur from the value for him of the nearest world where it does occur. In other words:

D3: The value for s of p = n if and only if ($\exists$w) ($\exists$w') (w is the nearest p-world & w' is the nearest ~p-world & V(s,w) minus V(s,w') = n).

IV. The Evil of Death

The application of these ideas to the case of one's own death is straightforward. Suppose we are wondering whether it would be bad for a certain person, s, to die at a certain time, t. Then we must ask about the value for s of the possible world that would exist if s were to die at t; and we must compare that value to the value for s of the possible world that would exist if s were not to die at t. If the death-world is worse for s than the non-death-world, then s's death at t would be bad for s; otherwise, not.

Let's consider a typical example to see how this works. Suppose I am thinking of taking an airplane trip to Europe. Suppose I'm worried about accidents, hijackings, sabotage, etc. I think I might die en route. I think this would be bad for me. D3 directs us to consider the nearest possible world in which I do die en route to Europe on this trip, and to consider my welfare level at that world. I see no reason to suppose that interesting parts of my past are any different at that world from what they are at the actual world. So I assume that all my past pleasures and pains would be unaffected. The main difference (from my perspective) is that in that world I suffer some terminal pain and then a premature death, and never live to enjoy my retirement. Let's suppose that that world is worth + 500 to me—+ 500 is the result of subtracting the pain I there suffer from the pleasure I there enjoy. Next D3 directs us to consider the nearest world in which I do not die en route to Europe on this trip. The relevant feature of this world is that I do not die a painful and premature death in an airplane accident.

Suppose I there do live to enjoy many happy years of retirement. Let's suppose my welfare level at that world is + 1100. D3 implies that my death on this trip would have a value of − 600 for me. It would be a terrible misfortune.

Two points deserve mention here. One is the fact that D3 is a proposal concerning how *good* or *bad* a state of affairs is for a person, and not a proposal concerning the extent to which a state of affairs *benefits* or *harms* a person. I am inclined to suspect that the concepts of benefit and harm are in certain important ways different from the concepts of being good for and being bad for a person. One such respect might be this: it might be that it is impossible for a person to be harmed or benefitted by things that happen at times when he no longer exists. It is nevertheless still possible that something bad or something good for a person might occur at a time when the person no longer exists. D3 is not intended to have any direct implications concerning harm and benefit. It is intended to be restricted to the concepts of being good for a person and being bad for a person.

The second point is that nothing I have said here implies that death is always bad for the one who dies. Suppose a person is suffering from a painful terminal disease. Suppose he is considering suicide, and is inclined to think that death might be a blessing. He might be right. If his welfare level at the nearest world where he thus commits suicide is higher than his welfare level at the nearest world where he doesn't commit suicide, then committing suicide would be good for this person.[13] My point in formulating D3 is simply to show how it is possible for a person's death to be bad for him, not that everyone's death must be so.

Perhaps we can now see where Epicurus went wrong in his argument for the conclusion that one's death cannot be bad for him. Perhaps Epicurus was thinking that the only states of affairs that are bad for a person are the ones that are *intrinsically* bad for him. Since (given our axiological assumptions, which are intended to be relevantly like his) death is not intrinsically bad for anyone, it would follow that death is never bad for the one who dies. But even the most fervent hedonist should acknowledge a distinction between things that are intrinsically bad for a person (which he will take to be pains) and things that are bad for the person in other ways. D3 is designed to calculate an important sort of *non-intrinsic* value. It tells us the degree of *overall* badness for a person of a state of affairs. Even though my death on my imagined European trip would not be intrinsically bad for me, D3 tells us that it would be overall bad for me.

Another possibility is that Epicurus was thinking that if a state of affairs would be bad for a person, then it must at least *cause* something intrinsically bad for him. Since (given our axiological and metaphysical assumptions) nothing intrinsically bad can happen to me after my death, my death cannot cause anything intrinsically bad for me. Thus, Epicurus might have concluded that my death cannot even be extrinsically bad for me. However, D3 does not calculate extrinsic value by focusing exclusively on intrinsic goods and evils that would befall the person *as a result* of the state of affairs. Rather, it calculates the value of a state of affairs for a person by considering what would happen (whether as consequence or not) if the state of affairs were to occur, as compared to what would happen (whether as consequence or not) if it were to fail to occur. Thus, according to D3, my death would be bad for me not because it would cause me to suffer pain, and not because it would itself be intrinsically bad for me. Rather, it would be bad for me because it would deprive me of 600 units of pleasure that I would have had if it had not happened when it did. More precisely, it would be bad for me because my welfare level at the nearest world where it occurs is 600 points lower than my welfare level at the nearest world where it does not occur.

V. Some Proposed Answers

At the outset, I mentioned some questions about the evil of death. These were prompted by the Epicurean challenge. I will now attempt to answer those questions.

The first question was the question how, given that he doesn't exist after he dies, being dead can be a misfortune for a person. The simple answer is this: a state of affairs can be bad for a person whether it occurs before he exists, while he exists, or after he exists. The only requirement is that his welfare level at the nearest world where it occurs is lower than his welfare level at the nearest world where it does not occur. It may be interesting to consider an example in which something bad for a person occurs *before* the person exists. Suppose my father lost his job shortly before I was conceived. Suppose that as a result of the loss of his job, my parents had to move to another town, and that I was therefore raised in a bad neighborhood and had to attend worse schools. I would have been happier if he had not lost his job when he did. In this case, the fact that my father lost his job was bad for me—even though I didn't exist when it occurred. It was bad for me because the value for me of the nearest world where he didn't lose his job is greater than the value for me of the actual world (which, on the assumption, is the nearest world where he did lose his job). The same may be true of cases involving things that will happen after I cease to exist (although, of course, such cases will illustrate *deprivation* of happiness, rather than *causation* of unhappiness).

It should be clear, then, that the plausibility of the Existence Condition derives from a confusion. Given our hedonistic axiology, it would be correct to say that nothing *intrinsically* bad can happen to a person at a time unless he exists at that time. You cannot suffer pains at a time unless you then exist. However, even on the same axiology, the *overall* value version of the thesis is not true. That is, it would not be correct to say that nothing *overall* bad for a person can happen at a time unless he exists at that time. Perhaps some Epicureans have been induced to accept the Existence Condition because they fail to notice this distinction.[14]

The second puzzle concerns an allegedly illegitimate comparison. It may seem that I am maintaining that when a person's death is bad for him, it is bad for him because he's worse off being dead than he would have been if he had stayed alive. Yet this suggests that there is some degree of "bad-offness" that he endures while dead. However, since he doesn't exist while he is dead, he can have no degrees of "bad-offness" then. The question, then, is this: doesn't my answer presuppose an illegitimate comparison?

My answer presupposes no such comparison. I am not proposing that we compare a person's welfare level during life to his welfare level during death. I have assumed that one's welfare level at a world is determined entirely by pleasures and pains that one experiences during one's life at that world. Thus, the comparison is a comparison between one's welfare level (calculated by appeal to what happens to one during his life) at one possible world with his welfare level (also calculated by appeal to what happens to him during his life) at another possible world. I have provisionally agreed that nothing intrinsically good or bad can happen to a person at times when he does not exist.

In effect, then, my proposal presupposes what Silverstein calls a "life-life comparison."[15] To see how this works, consider again the example concerning my imagined death en route to Europe. My proposal requires us to compare the values for me of two lives—the life I would lead if I were to die on the plane trip and the life I would lead if I were not to die on the plane trip. Since (according to our assumptions) the shorter life is less good for me, my death on that trip would be correspondingly bad for me.

The third puzzle was a puzzle about dates. I have claimed that a person's death may be bad for her because it deprives her of the pleasures she would have enjoyed if she had lived. One may be puzzled about just *when* this misfortune occurs. The problem is that we may not want to say that her death is bad for her during her life, for she isn't yet dead. Equally, we may not want to say that it is bad for her after her death, for she doesn't exist then.

In order to understand my answer to this question, we must look more closely into the question. Suppose a certain girl died in her youth. We are not concerned here about any puzzle about the date of her death. We may suppose we know that. Thus, in one sense, we know precisely when the misfortune occurred. Nor are we concerned about the dates of any pains she suffered as a result of that death. We assume that there are none. The present question is, rather, a question about when her death is a misfortune for her. If Lindsay is the girl, and d is the state of affairs of *Lindsay dying on December 7, 1987*, then the question is this: "Precisely when is d bad for Lindsay?" I have proposed an account of the evil of death. According to that account, when we say that d is bad for Lindsay, we mean that the value for her of the nearest world where d occurs is lower than the value for her of the nearest world in which d does not occur. So our question comes to this: "Precisely *when* is it the case that the value for Lindsay of the nearest world in which d occurs is lower than the value for her of the nearest world in which d does not occur?"

It seems clear to me that the answer to this question must be "eternally." For when we say that her death is bad for her, we are really expressing a complex fact about the relative values of two possible worlds. If these worlds stand in a certain value relation, then (given that they stand in this relation at any time) they stand in that relation not only when Lindsay exists, but at times when she doesn't. If there were a God, and it had been thinking about which world to create, it would have seen prior to creation that d would be bad for Lindsay. In other words, it would have seen that the value for Lindsay of the relevant d-world is significantly lower than the value for Lindsay of the relevant ~d-world. And it would have seen this even though Lindsay did not yet exist at that precreation moment.

A final puzzle concerns the fact that we feel that early death is a greater misfortune for the prematurely deceased than is "late birth" for the late born, even though each may deprive us of as much happiness as the other.

Suppose Claudette was born in 1950 and will die somewhat prematurely in 2000 as a result of an accident. We may want to say that her premature death will be a misfortune for her. Consider the nearest possible world (call it "w3") in which she does not die prematurely. Suppose that at w3 she lives happily until 2035. Since she has 35 extra years of happiness in w3, her welfare level there is higher than her welfare level in the actual world. D3 yields the result that her premature death is bad for her. But now consider the claim that Claudette suffered an equal misfortune in not having been born in 1915. This fact seems to deprive her of 35 happy years too—the years from 1915 to 1950 when she was in fact born. Yet we feel uncomfortable with the idea that her late birth is as great a misfortune for Claudette as her premature death. Why is this?

Consider the state of affairs of *Claudette being born in 1915*. Call it "b." In the actual world b is false. Consider the nearest world where b is true.[16] (In other words, consider what would have happened if Claudette had been born 35 years earlier.) Call this world "w4." I see no reason to suppose that Claudette lives any longer in w4 than she does here in the actual world. Any such change in lifespan strikes me as being superfluous. I am inclined to suppose that Claudette's welfare level in w4 is slightly lower than her welfare level in the actual world— after all, in w4 she probably endures hard times during the Great Depression, and maybe even catches measles, whooping cough and other diseases that were rampant in those days. If she has just fifty years to live, she's better off living them in the second half of the twentieth century, rather than thirty-five years earlier. Thus, given my intuitive sense of how to calculate what would have happened if Claudette had been born earlier, it follows that early death is worse for Claudette than late birth. Her late birth deprived her of very little value; her early death would deprive her of a lot.

The proposed reply to Lucretius' challenge is thus based on an asymmetry between past and future. When I am asked to consider what would happen if Claudette were to die later, I hold her birthdate constant. It has already occurred, and I tend to think that unnecessary differences in past history are big differences between worlds. Thus, it is more natural for me to suppose that if she were to die later, it would be because she lives longer. On the other hand, when I am asked to consider what would have happened if she had been born earlier, I do not hold her deathdate constant. Instead, I hold her lifespan constant, and adjust the deathdate so as to accommodate itself to the earlier birthdate.

Someone might claim that I have made an unfair comparison. They might want to insist on holding lifespans constant. They might say that Claudette would be better off living longer if the extra time were tacked on to the end of her life. They might say that Claudette would not be any better off if the extra time were tacked on to the beginning of her life. (That is, if she were born in 1915 instead of 1950 but lived until 2000 anyway.) The question is vexing, since it is hard to discern Claudette's welfare levels in the appropriate worlds. My own inclination is to say that if she lives 85 happy years in each world, then her welfare level at the one is equal to her welfare level at the other. In this case,

I can't see why anyone would think it would be better for her to have the 35 years tacked on at the end of her life rather than at the beginning. When the comparison is fair, D3 generates what seem to me to be the correct results. And the results are that the deprivation of 35 happy years of life is a bad thing, whether these years would have occurred before the date at which Claudette was in fact born, or after the date on which she in fact died.

There are, after all, two ways in which we can rectify the apparently irrational emotional asymmetry. On the one hand, we can follow Lucretius and cease viewing early death as a bad thing for Claudette. On the other hand, we can at least try to start viewing late birth as a bad thing. My suggestion is that in the present case, the latter course would be preferable.

I think it must be granted that our emotional reactions toward pleasures lost by early death are quite different from our emotional reactions toward similar pleasures lost by late birth. If my proposal is right, this emotional asymmetry is irrational. To see this, consider a variant of the case involving Claudette. Suppose (to make the case very "clean") that Claudette never experienced any pleasures or pains, but that if she had died later, she would have enjoyed one especially great pleasure ("the Late Pleasure") in her old age. Suppose similarly that if she had been born earlier, she would instead have enjoyed an equally great pleasure ("the Early Pleasure"). In either case, her life would have contained exactly one pleasure.

Given natural assumptions, my proposal yields the result that Claudette's late birth was just as bad for her as was her early death. Yet I suppose that at times near the end of her life, Claudette and her friends would have been more upset about her impending early death than they would have been about her late birth. Perhaps this emotional asymmetry is to be explained by the fact that we tend to think that the past is fixed, whereas the future is still open. Thus, we may feel that there's no point in lamenting the fact that Claudette missed the Early Pleasure. On the other hand, we may feel that there was a "real chance" that she might have enjoyed the Late Pleasure. Her loss of that seems a greater misfortune.

Another possibility is that we have what Derek Parfit has called "a bias toward the future." Once they are past, we become indifferent toward our pleasures and pains; while they are still in the future, we care deeply about them.[17] If hedonism is true, this sort of asymmetry is wholly irrational. Nevertheless, it might be a deep-seated feature of human psychology.

I want to emphasize the fact that my central proposal here concerns a value-theoretic question, not a question in psychology. I mean to be discussing the question about the relative evil of early death and late birth. I have not attempted to answer the psychological question about the differences in the ways in which we react to early death and late birth. If my proposal is right, then (to a large extent) our emotional reactions may be irrational.

VI. An Objection and a Reply

In "Death and the Value of Life," Jeff McMahan considers and rejects an account of the evil of death very much like the one I mean to defend.[18] He cites a number of difficulties for any such view. One concerns a young cavalry officer who is shot and killed in the charge of the Light Brigade. According to the story, the officer was shot by someone named "Ivan." McMahan stipulates that if the officer had not been killed by Ivan's bullet, he would have died just a few seconds later by a bullet fired by Boris. McMahan says that ". . . our answer to the question of what would have happened had the officer not died when and how he did will be that he would have lived for a few seconds, and then he would have been killed. This leads to the unacceptable conclusion that his actual death was hardly a misfortune at all."[19]

McMahan goes on to offer various revisions of the original proposal, but these seem to me to be changes for the worse (and I explain why below). It seems to me that D3 generates appropriate results.

It is important to distinguish several different things that happen in this example. Let us call the gallant officer "Herbert," and let us suppose the time of his death was 3:30 p.m., October 25, 1854—or "t." Here are some states of affairs that we should distinguish:

P1: Herbert dies at exactly t.
P2: Herbert dies near Balaclava.
P3: Herbert dies in the charge of the Light Brigade.
P4: Herbert dies as a result of being shot by Ivan.
P5: Herbert dies in his youth.

It should be clear that we have five different states of affairs here. In fact, each is logically independent of each of the others. Furthermore, it should come as no surprise if some of these are worse for Herbert than others. Given the details of the story, it turns out that P1 and P4 are not very bad for Herbert. Neither of these deprived Herbert of much happiness, since if he hadn't been killed at t by Ivan, he would have been killed seconds later by Boris. It's hard to see why this calls for any alteration of D3. These states of affairs seem to me not to be very bad for Herbert. The real tragedy here is not that he died exactly at t, or that he died as a result of being shot by Ivan; the real tragedy is that he died so young. Thus, P5 should be the focus of our attention.

We must consider the nearest possible world in which P5 does not occur. Let's call it "w5." What sort of life does Herbert live there? Perhaps in w5 Herbert is one of the few survivors of the charge; perhaps he is wounded, but recovers and goes on to live a long and happy life. Of course, I don't know precisely what happens to Herbert in w5—but it is reasonable to suppose that in w5 Herbert's welfare level is significantly higher than it is here in the actual world. After all, in w5 Herbert does not die in his youth, but is otherwise as much as possible like he is here in the actual world. In any case, according to D3, the badness of P5 for Herbert is equal to the difference in value for Herbert between w5 and the actual world. This might be a significant difference. He might have led a long and happy life if he had not died in his youth.

I mentioned earlier that I think that McMahan's view is less plausible than D3. On McMahan's proposal, we are asked to consider what happens in a world far more distant than w5. McMahan asks us to consider the nearest world *in which the whole causal sequence leading up to Herbert's death* fails to occur. As McMahan remarks, in the example cited, this may mean considering a world in which the Crimean War does not occur.[20] This strikes me as being implausible. To see how it could go wrong, suppose that Herbert loved excitement. If there had been no Crimean War, he would have sought excitement elsewhere. He would have taken up mountain climbing, and would have been killed in 1853. Given these assumptions, McMahan's proposal yields the surprising result that being killed in the Crimean War was *good* for Herbert. It seems to me to make much more sense to consider a nearer world—a world in which the Crimean War occurs, Herbert participates, but does not die a premature death. w5 is supposed to be such a world, and Herbert is better off in w5 than he is in the real world.

VII. Conclusion

I have attempted to formulate a coherent answer to the ancient challenge set by Epicurus. I have claimed that there is nothing paradoxical about the idea that death may be bad for the one who dies. My answer is a version of the traditional view that death is bad (when it is bad) primarily because it deprives the deceased of goods—the goods he would have enjoyed if he had lived. I have attempted to provide my answer within a predominantly Epicurean framework. I have assumed that hedonism is true, and I have assumed that when a person dies, he goes out of existence. I have attempted to show that even if we grant these assumptions, we can still maintain that death can be evil for the deceased. I have furthermore attempted to show that if we formulate our account properly, we can provide satisfactory answers to some puzzling questions: "How can death be bad for the deceased if he doesn't exist when it occurs?" "When is death bad for the deceased?" "Is there an illegitimate comparison between the welfare of the nonexistent and the welfare of the existent?" "Why is death worse than prenatal nonexistence?" Along the way, I have also discussed the merits of some other proposed solutions to the puzzles.[21]

NOTES

1. Epicurus, "Letter to Menoeceus," trans. C. Bailey, *The Stoic and Epicurean Philosophers,* edited and with an introduction by Whitney J. Oates (New York, The Modern Library, 1940), pp. 30–31. Lucretius presents essentially the same argument. See *On the Nature of Things,* trans. H. A. J. Munro, and *The Stoic and Epicurean Philosophers,* p. 131.

2. Jeff McMahan, "The Evil of Death," *Ethics 99* (1988), pp. 32–61, at p. 33. He calls it "The Existence Requirement."

3. I am by no means the first to defend this sort of answer. Similar views are defended (or at least discussed with some enthusiasm) by a number of philosophers. See, for example, Jeff McMahan, "The Evil of Death"; Thomas Nagel, "Death," *Noûs* 4 (1970), pp. 73–80, revised and reprinted in *Moral Problems,* ed. James Rachels (New York: Harper & Row, 1975), pp. 401–409, and above, chap. 1; Roy Perrett, *Death and Immortality* (Dordrecht, The Netherlands: Nijhoff, 1987); L. S. Sumner, "A Matter of Life and Death," *Noûs* 10 (1976), pp. 145–171; Douglas Walton, *On Defining Death* (Montreal, Quebec: McGill-Queen's University Press, 1979); and Bernard Williams, "The Makropulos Case: Reflections on the Tedium of Immortality," in B. Williams, *Problems of the Self* (New York: Cambridge University Press, 1973), reprinted below as chap. 9.

4. For a vigorous defense of the claim that the standard view involves an illegitimate comparison, see Harry Silverstein, "The Evil of Death," *The Journal of Philosophy* 77 (1980), pp. 401–424.

5. *On the Nature of Things,* p. 134.

6. The locus classicus of many of these ideas is David Lewis, *Counterfactuals* (Cambridge, Mass.: Harvard University Press, 1973).

7. I attempted to present a clear formulation of this view about axiology in my *Doing the Best We Can: An Essay in Informal Deontic Logic* (Dordrecht, The Netherlands: D. Reidel, 1986). See especially Section 2.2.

8. I doubt that many moral philosophers would endorse anything like this simplest form of hedonism. Indeed, I wouldn't endorse it either. My point here

is primarily to indicate something about the structure of an axiological view—it should yield an ordering of worlds in terms of value. In an attempt to make this conception most obvious, I have assumed that there is a value function taking us from worlds to numbers. This structural approach is consistent with a wide variety of substantive axiological theories.

9. It should be obvious that in interesting cases no one could possibly calculate the value of a world for a person. On the other hand, we could have reason to believe that worlds of a certain specified sort would be uniformly *worse* for someone than worlds of some other specified sort.

10. Nagel discusses this idea in his now classic paper, "Death," cited above in note 3. A similar approach to the evil of death is suggested by George Pitcher in "The Misfortunes of the Dead," *American Philosophical Quarterly* 21 (1984), pp. 183–88.

11. Some commentators suppose that we stop existing when we die, but we don't stop "being." They also suppose that appealing to the existence/being distinction helps solve the problem about the evil of death. For an example of this approach, see Palle Yourgrau's "The Dead," *The Journal of Philosophy* 84 (1987), pp. 84–101. In this paper, I have made no such distinction.

12. I am suppressing consideration of certain complexities. One that should be addressed concerns cases in which there is no unique nearest world in which a certain state of affairs occurs—several worlds are tied for this distinction. What shall we say then?

Suppose that at the real world Dolores does not move to Bolivia. Then the real world is the nearest world in which she does not move to Bolivia. Suppose that among worlds in which she does move to Bolivia, there are two that are equally near and most near the real world. Then I want to say this: if each of these worlds is worse for Dolores than the real world, then moving to Bolivia would be bad for her; if each is better for her than the real world, then moving to Bolivia would be good for her; if one is better and the other is worse, then it's not the case that moving to Bolivia would be good for her, and it's not the case that moving to Bolivia would be bad for her; moving to Bolivia might be good for her and might be bad for her.

If all the nearest b-worlds have the same value for Dolores, then we can use this value when we compute the value of b for Dolores. On the other hand, if the nearest b-worlds differ in value for Dolores, then the computations become more problematic. One possibility would be to make use of the average value for Dolores of these nearest b-worlds. Another possibility would be to say that the value of b for her might be the result of subtracting the value for Dolores of the real world from the value for her of one of them, and it might be the result of subtracting the value for her of the real world from the value for her of another. In such a case, we would have to say that there is no number, n, such that the value of b for Dolores = n.

In what follows, I shall write as if there is always a unique nearest world. My main points are not affected by this simplifying assumption.

13. I think these remarks provide the basis for a reply to one sort of argument concerning the alleged irrationality of suicide. Some have said that sui-

cide is always irrational since it is impossible to calculate the value of death for the deceased. See, for example, John Donnelly's "Suicide and Rationality," in *Language, Metaphysics, and Death*, ed. John Donnelly, 1st. ed. (New York, N.Y.: Fordham University Press, 1978), pp. 88–105; and Philip Devine's *The Ethics of Homicide* (Ithaca, N.Y.: Cornell University Press, 1978), esp. p. 25. If what I have said here is right, the calculations are in principle possible, and some suicides are perfectly rational.

14. In "How To Be Dead and Not Care: A Defense of Epicurus," *American Philosophical Quarterly* 23 (1986) (reprinted above, chap. 6), Stephen Rosenbaum proposes an interpretation of the Epicurean argument. He suggests that one crucial premise is "A state of affairs is bad for a person *P* only if *P* can experience it at some time" (p. 218; above. p. 119). I would say that the premise is ambiguous. If taken to mean that a state of affairs is *intrinsically* bad for a person only if he can experience it, then (assuming hedonism or any other "experience-based" axiology) the premise may be true—but it is not relevant to the claim that death is bad for the one who dies, since it is most reasonable to take this as the claim that death is *extrinsically* bad for the one who dies. If the claim is understood in this more plausible way as the claim that a state of affairs can be *extrinsically* bad for a person only if he can experience it, then, as I have attempted to show, the premise is false.

15. Silverstein, "The Evil of Death," p. 405.

16. In "Death" (p. 67; this volume, p. 27), Thomas Nagel claims that late birth does not deprive anyone of anything, since no one could have been born much earlier than she was in fact born. This provides the basis for a quick answer to Lucretius. Derek Parfit makes a similar claim in *Reasons and Persons* (Oxford, England: Oxford University Press, 1984), p. 351. The argument might be based on the essentiality of origins. However, with the development of techniques for the cryopreservation of sperm and eggs, the view seems false. Even if we grant the controversial claim that each person has her origins essentially, we have to acknowledge that once the relevant sperm and egg have been frozen, it is in principle possible for her to be conceived at any time in the next thousand years or so. I grant, of course, that the issue of the essentiality of origins deserves independent discussion. I simply assume that it makes sense to speak of what would have happened if Claudette had been born earlier. This makes it possible to look more deeply into the puzzle suggested by Lucretius.

17. Derek Parfit, *Reasons and Persons*. An interesting proposal based on some Parfittian ideas can be found in "Why Is Death Bad?" by Anthony Brueckner and John Martin Fischer, *Philosophical Studies* 50 (1986), pp. 213–221.

18. McMahan (in "The Evil of Death," cited above in note 3) discusses what he calls "the revised possible goods account." This is relevantly like my proposal. He claims that it runs into the "problem of specifying the antecedent" (p. 43).

19. Ibid., p. 46.

20. ". . . we must presumably imagine that the Crimean War did not occur,

in which case the threat from Boris would not have occurred either" (ibid., p. 47).

21. Many friends provided much-needed criticism and support, for which I am thankful. I am especially grateful to Gary Matthews for his encouragement of this and related projects. Earl Conee, John Fischer, Ed Gettier, Ned Markosian, Neil Schaefer, Harry Silverstein, and the editors of *The Philosophical Review* made helpful suggestions. Earlier versions were subjected to useful criticism at Montclair State College and Drew University.

8

The Misfortunate Dead:
A Problem for Materialism

JOHN DONNELLY

University of San Diego

THE PROBLEM

IT SEEMS THAT MANY PHILOSOPHERS want to maintain that (a) death marks the irreversible end of human life such that there is no form of postmortem survival of a discarnate personality or resurrected psychophysical person, etc., and yet simultaneously uphold the pretheoretic intuition that (b) the deceased can be harmed or benefited. I wish to argue herein that (a) and (b) are a pair of inconsistent beliefs such that those philosophers must either abandon their materialistic conception of death or dismiss the pretheoretic intuition.

Of course, if one holds a dualistic perspective on death as an event in life such that there is some form of postmortem life, the problem largely vanishes, as the "dead" on such a scheme can be harmed or benefited. For instance, the famed Polish musician and patriot Ignace Jan Paderewski, who died in 1941, had expressed a wish to be buried in a free Poland. Since he believed in postmortem survival, Paderewski clearly may have suffered some posthumous harm for some fifty-one years until in July 1992 his remains were removed from Fort Myer Chapel in Virginia and flown to Warsaw for burial.

Despite holding that "death marks the permanent end not only of one's physical life, but also of one's conscious life," George Pitcher contends that the dead can be wronged, and can suffer misfortune and harm.[1] He also believes that the dead can be righted, and can gain fortune and benefit—but his analysis accentuates the negative.

Pitcher suggests there are two ways of describing the dead:

(1) One can describe the dead person as he or she was at some stage of his or her life, which Pitcher labels the "antemortem person after his death."

(2) One can describe the dead person as he or she is now, *qua* dust, which Pitcher labels the "postmortem person after his death."

Pitcher's view is that only in (1) can the dead be misfortunate, harmed, or wronged.[2]

I agree with Pitcher (to use one of his illustrations) that when a son sells his father's corpse to a medical center, he breaks a promise he had made to his father before his father's death involving a paternal request for appropriate bodily internment in the family grave. However, *contra* Pitcher, it hardly follows that "it is the living Mr. Brown who is betrayed by his son's action."[3] Leaving aside issues raised by the more morally serious aspects of *selling* (as opposed to outright scientific donation), the fact of the matter is that until the death-moment, the father (who is described by Pitcher as *unaware* of the son's plans) was not betrayed (and hence wronged), even if the son all along had the intention of selling in mind, because it was not acted upon—and could not be acted upon—until the father's death. The promise is violated by the selling (unless we are unduly Abelardian), not by the prior intention to sell. A more plausible scenario for Pitcher's thesis would be a situation in which the father made his funeral request, the son orally indicated his intent to disobey his father's wishes, and before the father could write a codicil to his will (to legally protect his corpse from his son's plans) he lapsed into what turned out to be an irreversible coma. Upon his father's death, the son then sold his father's corpse. Here the father was wronged, but while alive, not dead!

Pitcher proceeds to maintain that it is possible for something to happen after a person's death that *literally* (and not just metaphorically) harms the antemortem person described by (1). Pitcher relies on his own admittedly rather unfettered intuition in defining "an event or state of affairs [as] a misfortune for someone . . . when it is contrary to one or more of his more important desires or interests."[4] Apart from the need for greater refinement of the term *misfortune* (and the opaque use of "important"), Pitcher's analysis opens a Pandora's box of misplaced ills. For example, given Pitcher's definition, it is a misfortune for anyone with the appropriate interests/desires if they do not own a large ocean-view house in Malibu, or serve as a member of Congress, or win the jackpot in the state lottery, and so forth.

INTERESTS AND REPUTATIONS

Like some other philosophers who share a similar (materialistic) metaphysical perspective on death as the end of life (e.g., Joel Feinberg),

Pitcher analyzes *misfortunes* or *harms* as invasions of interests or desires, and seems to believe that these interests or desires are so ontologically independent of the person whose interests or desires they are that they can exist independently of her even when she is dead. That is, *interests* have become so reified, so metaphysically displaced from the wants-based sentient person whose interests they are (or, more exactly, were), that the subject of harm (or benefit) becomes the deceased person's interests or the bare logical skeleton of the antemortem person after death. This notion of free-floating *surviving interests* (a Platonic reification of interests, desires, wants, goals, projects, etc.), I believe, is incoherent, given Pitcher's metaphysical assumptions. That is, there seems to be an *intrinsic* connection between a person's *interests* (the thwarting of which can harm her) and her life, but only an *extrinsic* connection between that person's *reputation* and her life. As a result, the dead person's reputation can be harmed or benefited after her death, but her interests end with her death. Her interests necessarily die with her, but not necessarily her reputation. (Note that it is logically possible for a person to exist for the proverbial three score and ten and have no reputation during or after that life, but not for her to have no interests, one of which could be the thwarted one to have an historic reputation.) Accordingly, the proper paraphrase of the sentence

(3) The deceased philosopher Sophia has a bad reputation,

is not:

(3a) The antemortem Sophia after her death suffers interest invasion posthumously,

but rather:

(3b) The deceased philosopher Sophia is remembered unkindly.

In short, interests are *real* attributes of persons; reputations are merely *nominal*. (If so, then recent adverse publicity on Presidents Kennedy and Johnson and assorted deceased public figures could damage only their reputations, not their interests.)

To be sure, Pitcher's intuitions seem plausible. And that's the rub of our philosophical perplexity. Most of us can empathize with the current efforts of various State legislatures that are debating the topic of exploitation of the dead. If proposed legislation is adopted, there will be a resolution making it illegal for entrepreneurs to use names of deceased persons or current facsimiles of them in commercials, etc., without prior permission of their legal heirs—at least during the first fifty years of their death. (Apparently, by some *ad hoc* intuition, it is believed that in the fifty-first year of death, neither the deceased's interests nor reputation can be harmed!)

Assuredly, many of us find objectionable the intended humor on a "Saturday Night Live" television skit (irrespective of politics) that depicted the cremated ashes of Mao Tse-tung being interned in a Chinese food carryout container. But despite such unfettered intuitions, our moral sensibilities are metaphysically misplaced if we think that the deceased celebrities in question, or Mao in particular, are harmed by such depictions. No doubt our aretaic sensibilities should often be outraged by such displays, but the morally offended parties in question are the living, not the dead. We tend to think (not always correctly) that *de mortuis nil nisi bonum*, but any misfortune suffered in such circumstances is by the vulgar parodies that offend the living's deontic sense of virtue and rectitude. The dead were, perhaps, not respected, but they were not harmed. One can be disrespectful toward X without harming X. Disrespect directed toward a cadaver or an artifact is not a harming of either. Take a case of necrophilia or so-called "posthumous rape." I agree that it is morally wrong for the rapist to engage in such a perversion, but the raped (being deceased) is no more harmed here than an anatomically exact mannequin who had a sex act performed on it would be.

Another context that raises questions about harm to the dead involves the classic carnival sideshow. For example, a two-headed infant corpse known as "Ronnie and Donnie" had been displayed for many years at several carnivals. When the police attempted recently in Redlands, California, to halt this grotesque sideshow, a court overthrew their efforts on the legal technicality that the infant(s) in question was born before such exhibits were outlawed. Persuasive efforts were made to have the owner of "Ronnie and Donnie" refrain from showing the display on aesthetic grounds, as well as through appeals to a moral sense of public decency. However, the owner resisted, claiming that the show was "educational."

But do such displays, undeniably in bad taste, truly harm "Ronnie and Donnie"? I think not—at least from a materialistic, metaphysical perspective. They clearly offend the moral sensibilities of a good number of living persons, however, and therein lies the harm. (I should add that there is not always equal protection before the law in such cases. For instance, a police official at the Sonoma County Fair in 1985 did succeed in confiscating a 200-year-old male, adult mummy on the grounds of illegal desecration of human remains. But, whatever the legal verdict, the harm is done to the living, not the "mummies" in question.)

Given Pitcher's analysis of harm as an interest invasion, it seems difficult (if not impossible) for any sensitive, clear-thinking, factually aware, morally concerned, and socially involved person not to suffer numerous misfortunes in his or her life. As Camus writes, "beginning to think is beginning to be undermined." Life may be a vale of tears at times, but it is not always that burdensome in its assigned misfortunes. Given the person-relative emphasis in Pitcher's definition of *misfortune*, the end result is a non-Occamish multiplication of ills beyond compassion.

MISFORTUNE AND AWARENESS

Ironically, Pitcher seems aware of the doublethinkish gambit behind his thesis when he writes: "The view that an antemortem person can be harmed after his death is one that we all find, or can anyway be made to find, entirely plausible, if we don't stop to examine it too closely."[5]

Pitcher also claims a victim of misfortune need not be aware of it. To be sure, I do not have to personally experience an *actual* event for it to be a real misfortune for me. I can suffer or be harmed just by *imagining* what it would be like. (Of course, a purely imaginary harm is self-imposed, not other-imposed. It is self-delusion.) But Pitcher thinks I can also be a victim of misfortune even in the absence of such firsthand experience or imaginative enactment. I find it hard to see how one can suffer a misfortune when there is no phenomenal content to it, either as a privately experiential or as an imagined reality. *Contra* Pitcher, ignorance is a quasi-bliss. What you don't know or imagine can't harm you!

Of course, Pitcher et al. could argue that if there are harms or misfortunes that a person can suffer *unaware* (while alive), then surely it is not problematic to claim the same of the dead. Clearly, to grant the protasis here is to make for a smooth transition to acceptance of the apodosis. Since I want to deny, given the materialistic perspective on death, that a person can suffer a harm or misfortune totally unaware, I must try to reinforce the falsity of the protasis.

I would agree with Joan C. Callahan that an absence of harm is to be analyzed in terms of a lack of negative effect on a subject. Posthumous harms lack an effect on the decedent since there is no subject to be so affected. "Thus, lack of a subject to be affected is sufficient, but not necessary, for lack of harm, while lack of negative effect on a subject is both necessary and sufficient for lack of harm."[6] As Callahan wisely and cautiously notes, "none of this entails that certain actions which we are inclined to think are wrong because they harm the dead are not wrong. All that follows is that such actions are not wrong *because* they harm the dead."[7]

Philosophers who uphold the pretheoretic intuition that either the living or the dead can be harmed unaware rely exclusively, it seems to me, on the alleged self-evidentness or basicality of that intuition. Since I wish to question such an intuition, I confess I am able to do no other than appeal to its *counter*intuitiveness. Like my opponents, I too can appeal to illustrations to reinforce my point. But whether that deadlock or clash of intuitions can be conclusively settled is, perhaps, more a matter of psychology than of logic.

The tenacity with which people of a materialistic, metaphysical bent cling to that intuition does seem to have some *non*moot *counter*instances. For example, most wedding ceremonies, even in our age of divorce, still use the refrain "till death do us part." And hardly anyone would seriously believe that a widow who remarries causes harm to her deceased spouse by her sexual intimacies with her new husband — the Jackie Kennedy–Aristotle Onassis affair notwithstanding. Nor do we speak of the dead, say, getting older. If Smith dies in 1981 at age 78, we don't claim that he is older (i.e., 89) in 1992.

Kierkegaard writes in *Works of Love*: "You will not be able to say to one dead that he was the one who grew older and that this explains your altered relationship to him—for one who is dead does not get older. You shall not be able to say to one who is dead that he was the one who in the course of time grew cold . . . or that he was the one who became less attractive, for which reason you could love him no more. . . ."[8]

A few years back I had a female student in my class whose name was graffitied on most men's lavatory walls on campus. Janitorial erasure would just bring back the next day her name, telephone number, and accompanying obscene remarks. Suppose she had never seen this display, never heard of it directly or indirectly, never imagined it, never been treated as an object of ridicule as a result; then, despite the paradoxicality of it all, I would say she was not harmed by any of this otherwise malicious graffiti.

I am not certain how to *prove* that ignorance is blissful here, other than to appeal that dwelling on cases such as this seems to show the *counter*intuitiveness of Pitcher's pretheoretic intuition, coupled with his materialism.

However, at times, the prephilosophic intuition that a person can suffer a misfortune and not be aware of it is not so difficult to dispel. Consider the case of Corporal James Thornwell who died at age 46 and who, in 1961, was the unwitting victim of his own Army's experiments on him with LSD. The U.S. Army believed that Corporal

Thornwell stole classified documents (a charge never proven), and for over two months arranged for his kidnapping (under the guise of foreign agents) and incarceration, depriving him of proper food, light, and sanitary conditions. Because Thornwell was under the influence of LSD, he was not cognizant of the conditions of his incarceration. He did not become fully knowledgeable about such (involuntary) medical/military conscription until 1977. (Congress later awarded him monetary compensation.) Until his death, Thornwell continued to suffer from epilepsy, depression, and memory loss, and his personal life was in shambles.

Granted Thornwell was a victim of misfortune over that sixteen-year period, but was he really unaware of it? I think not! Thornwell did suffer physical and psychological anguish, but he was "unaware" of it only to the extent that he did not know its exact biochemical causal nature; he was quite aware of his misfortune.[9]

ANTICIPATORY HARMS

Pace Pitcher, there seems to be a need to place some rational constraints on what constitutes a misfortune for a person. Moreover, Pitcher does not really make a convincing case for retroactive harms that befall the dead. His various scenarios hold that the person is harmed *prior* to his death, especially when the *living* person involved is aware that the harmful event is going to occur *after* his death.

However, eristically, I think Pitcher is on to something when he writes: "So the shadow of harm that an event casts can reach back across the chasm even of a person's death and darken his antemortem life."[10]

The truth behind this dark remark, I believe, has to do with *anticipatory* harms to a person which begin to occur before his or her death, but are fully actualized after the person's death. (I will avoid any caviling on Pitcher's oxymorons of "an antemortem person after his death" or "harming a living person after his death." But even here some check needs to be placed on the misfortunes suffered from such fully unactualized possibilities, prior to posthumous nonexistence.

I would agree with Pitcher that one need not invoke the metaphysically puzzling notion of backward causation, or adopt an ontological framework like Harry Silverstein's which holds that posthumous events exist timelessly such that a person can experience states of affairs that begin after his or her death because they already exist atemporally.[11]

Instead, what is needed is something like the following:

(4) P can partially experience a fortunate or misfortunate state of affairs at some time only if it begins to partially occur before P's death.

Statement (4) allows us to recognize how the loss of reputation, the breaking of promises, vile rumors, and falsehoods could be correctly sensed as developing by the dying person, and their full instantiation occur when he or she dies. Tolstoy offers a powerful literary portrayal of this scenario in *The Death of Ivan Ilych*. In that sense of (4), the antemortem person has partially experienced the evil of death. He or she has partially experienced posthumous evil states of affairs, as objects of his or her psychological attitudes. For example, the recent civil litigation over the estate of Groucho Marx (or Liberace, Rock Hudson, etc.) could have been partially experienced by the octogenarian Marx before his death in 1977. His fears that his sexual and urinary tract problems would become public knowledge are now, after his death, a matter of court record. And if other people can truly say of a (postmortem) person's death that it was an objective misfortune (which Pitcher grants), then surely the antemortem person can say it *in* anticipation.

If we wish to speak somewhat loosely of posthumous harms, we might consider the case of an incorrect obituary notice that appears in a college alumni quarterly magazine. Suppose the mistakenly listed Mary Fourghton has appended to her obituary notice a proposed memorial scholarship fund in her name and a call for contributions to that fund. By the time Mary gets around to reading the magazine and notices this very premature announcement and informs the college to correct her listing in the next issue of the magazine, she also learns from college officials that no contributions were received for her memorial fund in the three-month interval. Here Mary is presumably harmed *in life* not only by the rather careless and mysterious way her obituary notice appeared, but also by the lack of appreciation of her life shown by the failure of any alumni to donate money in her name. In addition, she also suffers the *anticipatory harm* of recognizing what her eventual death will likely bring in the form of alumni recognition. (At least when her correct obituary listing appears, she will be beyond such misfortune.)

I think we would be speaking even less loosely of posthumous harms that occur to antemortem persons in the case of the Siamese twins Ruthie and Verena Cody. On July 19, 1991, seven-year-old Ruthie died, followed by Verena some 15 minutes later. In those 15 minutes, Verena is reported to have made some funeral requests. The girls were connected from the sternum to the navel, sharing a three-chambered heart, a liver, and parts of the intestines. In closely observing her sister's tragic death, there is a sense in which Verena also viewed her own.

A woman's giving birth to a child strikes me as an intentional action. Yet, there are medically documented cases of "brain dead" women who have given birth to children. Such women may arguably not be persons but *incubators,* albeit such a description seems jesuitical. Their death robbed them of their motherhood and could correctly be spoken of as misfortune for them. This example both seems to satisfy the requirements of (4) assuming the women lapsed into a coma in the seventh month of the gestation period, with prior awareness of her pregnancy—but also gives us a subject to attribute the evil inherent in death to, as cadavers (or dust) do not give birth! This seems to be a very close paradigm to a posthumous misfortune.

Also, in Milwaukee, the city had a law that city employees who retire must live 60 days after their retirement day to collect full pension benefits. John Pederson, 43, a veteran of 20 years on the police force, died of leukemia some two weeks before the 60-day required deadline. While fighting his terminal illness, Pederson was consumed by his interest and desire to have his *full* pension benefits bestowed on his wife. Since he failed to make the deadline, his wife received a lump sum payment of $100,000 instead of the $200,000 she would have received had he died after the deadline. Was John Pederson harmed by that settlement? If seems to me the answer is no, although he was clearly harmed in anticipation. Obviously, his wife was harmed.

Of course, for the truly gilded, the law often works wonders. For instance, actress Lynne Frederick, the widow of the late Peter Sellers, was awarded $1,000,000 in damages because the movie "Trail of the Pink Panther" insulted the memory of her deceased husband. That film used discarded clips from five previous Pink Panther films in which Sellers played Inspector Clousseau, and the film company released the new composite film two years after Sellers had died.

The high court of London ruled that Peter Sellers' contractual rights were interfered with for commercial gain, and that the producers of the film breached the Performer's Protection Act. But, again, Sellers was not harmed, except in anticipation, or benefited by the court decision. His widow may have been harmed as the beneficiary of his estate as she assumed Sellers' right to control use of his performance after his death.

HARMS AND KILLINGS

The pretheoretic intuition that there are posthumous misfortunes that can befall a deceased person is a difficult one to fully dispel. Barbara

Baum Levenbook claims that to reject such an intuition is to lose the ability to explain the harm of murder, or any killing per se.[12] (Since we are dwelling primarily on the negative, I will not discuss the contemporary belief of some philosophers who think that active euthanasia or suicide or senicide is often a *benefit* to the person so killed.) Of course, we need to keep in mind that for Pitcher, at least, if the person in question had no interest or desire for continued existence, then his death cannot be said to be a misfortune *for him*.

Levenbook raises a serious point. If one rejects the pretheoretic intuition about posthumous misfortune as compatible with materialism, then how does one explain the matter, say, of "instantaneous killings"? On the assumption that there are such events (situations where a person dies of a massive cardiac infarction, or a fatal bullet-wound to the head, etc.), does it follow that no harm was committed to the killed person because at that precise death-moment the person no longer exists? Levenbook herself analyzes harm or misfortune, *contra* Pitcher, as a loss or deprivation, and not as an interest invasion (this may well turn out to be a distinction without a difference, for one wonders how to account for any loss or deprivation except in terms of some interests, desires, plans, and so forth that have been thwarted): ". . . once the assumption that a person can lose something at the moment of his death is accepted, it is indefensible to reject the assumption that person can lose something after his death. Such a position affords no satisfactory way of explaining why the moment of his death can be a time of his loss but no time after that can be a time of his loss."[13]

The seeming paradox endemic to the matter of instantaneous killings lies in the fact that at *t,* A is both annihilated while (presumably) simultaneously having the normal interest to continue living. That is, in an instantaneous killing, the *death-moment* is virtually cotemporaneous with the misfortunate *death-producing events*. But the paradox is more apparent than real. A repenting suicide, Jones, who jumps from the Golden Gate Bridge, seems to satisfy just such a description. Suicidists, of course, are often notoriously ambivalent about their attitudes toward death. A similar situation would hold if the case in question was that of a reasonably happy, nonsuicidal window cleaner working on the 87th floor of the World Trade Center, whose support system apparatus fails, and he suddenly plummets to the street below.

Both the repenting suicide and the accident victims are harmed. But the explanation of any harm in an instantaneous killing is not unproblematic. A more precise description would need to explain that there is probably a nanosecond or millisecond gap in the otherwise cotemporality of the death-producing events with the death-moment (e.g., the bullet to the head, the massive cardiac infarction, etc.), so that the person effected is harmed in life (by the death-producing events), but once dead is beyond harm.

Levenbook writes:

> If one insists that posthumous events cannot have value for the person concerned, however, one must deny that the event that consists of the change of Jones's reputation from a good one to a bad one can have value for Jones. This is untenable. The event that consists of going from a state of affairs that is good for him to a state of affairs that is bad for him surely must have a value for him and, in particular, be bad for him. Hence, an event occurring entirely when one does not exist can be bad for him.[14]

Despite the apparent paradox, I have been claiming that posthumous occurrences cannot have value for the dead, that is, for decedents who are materialists. And I have also denied that the events that bring about a change in a deceased person's reputation have value for that person. Events occurring entirely when one does not exist cannot be bad for the deceased, although they could be misfortunate for other premortem individuals.

Levenbook maintains that her harms-as-loss account can overstep traditional epicurean objections to posthumous misfortune, and in the offing rescue the pretheoretic intuition, in a way that a Pitcherian analysis of harms-as-invasions-of-interest account cannot pull off. But, while it may be true that a living person's history and possibilities count as much as (if not arguably more than) that living person's momentary categorical state, it is not clear that a *deceased* person's past history and lost possibilities have any more value (for the deceased) than that dead person's permanent categorical state. In the latter case, given the materialistic framework, there is no value per se in the absence of a living subject or bearer.

Sophisticated attempts to devise axiological comparisons of welfare levels between possible and actual worlds so as to retain the (materialistic) view that death is evil may appear to succeed in granting legitimacy to the claim that death is evil. But such schemes principally succeed in showing how death is bad from a third-person perspective, since it is said that an individual's death is bad because it deprives that person of goods that he or she would have experienced had he or she lived in another possible world. In short, *objectively* a particular individual's death was bad, but the decedent in question did not *subjectively* suffer any misfortune after that death. Death's badness is not and cannot be experienced as bad by the decedent. To speak of states of affairs as bad (or good) for a person even when that person does not exist (either prenatally or posthumously) leads to not only a postulation of possible worlds but a multiplication of deprivations. Philosophers who would ridicule the Thomistic use of *privation* in regard to the problem of evil (i.e., evil is a lack or absence of goodness) here fail to notice or appreciate the ironic ontological similarity. After my death there really is not a continuing subject, but instead some bearerless, unexperienced void, lack, or deprivation. Such an ontology of deprivation seems to merit no pity. Again, as with the earlier Pitcherian analysis of what constitutes a misfortune, we are left with a multiplication of ills beyond compassion.

It seems to me that a consistent materialist must hold that persons cannot have experiences that extend beyond their death so that there cannot be harms, losses, or setbacks to their interests which have no consequences within their experience. A person's interests are logically linked to that person's being alive. Consider my strong interest in my children's general welfare, i.e., that overall they flourish in their private and public lives as adolescents and adults. Surely, this is a rational desire. And suppose they fail to flourish after my death. Am I posthumously harmed by such a turnabout? No! I am not harmed now (while living) because they are flourishing; and when deceased— given the materialistic presupposition—there would be no subject (i.e., me) to be so harmed. A person cannot be harmed posthumously because there is no self whose interests are then setback, no bearer for the alleged losses.

Suppose an antemortem person has a consuming interest that everyone in the world eat a daily diet of only potato chips and soda pop. Presumably no other living person shares that interest, understandably enough. And suppose, as time passes, even that single individual abandons that particular interest. Surely, that (bizarre) interest no longer exists, for it is no longer the interest of any antemortem person. Likewise, when a person dies, his or her interests, if likewise *sui generis,* die with him or her. Of course, the former *non sui generis* interests of the deceased could continue, but they would be the shared interests then of other living persons.

I agree with Don Marquis that "Levenbook's position does nothing . . . to provide us with an understanding of how it is possible for a nonexistent person to suffer a loss. The argument that it must be so, otherwise, murder would not be a harm does not resolve the issue. It merely adds to the perplexity."[15]

And I suspect that perplexity lingers because one philosopher's justification or knockdown argument is another philosopher's *reductio ad absurdum*. Philosopher X's intuition to support a particular thesis is often viewed by philosopher Y as an excellent counterexample.

For Levenbook, the following argument is cogent:

(5) If a person cannot be harmed or suffer a misfortune when dead, then, for instance, that person's murder is not a harm to said person.

(6) Said person's murder is a harm to that person.

(7) Therefore, a person can be harmed or suffer a misfortune when dead.

I, of course, contend the materialist must reluctantly accept (5). But, if so, there is reason for a materialist, however begrudgingly, to deny (6) and (7).

Pace Levenbook, I would give the above argument a *modus ponens* reading. That is,

(5) If a person cannot be harmed or suffer a misfortune when dead, then, for instance, that person's murder is not a harm to said person.

(6a) A person cannot be harmed or suffer a misfortune when dead.

(7a) Therefore, said person's murder is not a harm to that person.

Given the postulated materialistic framework, I am perplexed as to how Levenbook can speak of harm befalling "the living-person-who-was." Bizarre cases of people who die while campaigning for public office, and whose names remain on the election ballot, are not harmed (or benefited) by the election results.[16] Having no present desires or aims, they have no surviving interests that are harmed or benefited. They are neither losers nor winners, in the absence of any experienced, conscious states. There simply are no selfless, unexperienced deprivations of loss or of interests. The materialist needs to face up to this brute fact. Anything less is cryptodualism. One cannot have his or her cake and eat it too!

I believe proposed analogies between harms or benefits attributed to the dead and the environmental harms or benefits done to our various natural resources (e.g., forests, streams, mountains, oceans, etc.) which ecologists speak of are not suggestive.

Levenbook hints at this comparison in pointing out how the ordinary language oddity of speaking about a "dead person's interests" is removed or mollified by legitimate talk of the "present interests of future generations." I take it that the point of such comparisons would be that if we grant the legitimacy or linguistic appropriateness of talk of environmental harms to natural resources, we should likewise grant the acceptability of talk of the dead's being harmed. And if future generations have interests that can be thwarted, or losses that can befall them, then so too can the dead. However, the ecologists are really talking of present or future misfortunes that befall or are to be suffered by living human beings, deprived of the beauty, earthly bounty, etc., of those natural resources. The same cannot be said of the dead *qua* deceased.

But are not the dead to be accorded proper respect and moral deference? For a nonplatonic dualist, like myself, the answer is *yes*. Surely the materialists also want to answer in the affirmative, but can they do so consistently?

It seems to me that the respect owed the dead *qua former persons* is largely a matter (for a materialist) of law and custom—not any sustained rational deliberation. (Again, I underscore, this holds for a materialistic perspective, and not for many dualistic accounts with their belief in postmortem survival.) Given that law and popular culture have already eroded respect formerly paid to fetuses *qua* potential persons, it should not be surprising that the pendulum now swings toward the deceased *qua* former persons. Since most people (unfortunately) do not accord any respect to fetuses, say, regarding fitting burial rites, one wonders by parity of reasoning, why the reluctance (on the part of the materialist) to disrespect deceased, former persons?

Aristotle would dissent, apparently in the belief that the dead could be harmed by the adverse fortunes of their living descendants. He writes: "it would be odd if the fortunes of their living descendants did not for some time have some effect on the happiness of their ancestors."[17] But, unless one adopts a rather strained sociobiological criterion, the hard metaphysical reality remains, *pace* Aristotle, that the *deceased* do not have satisfied or unsatisfied interests in the "survival and well-being of descendants," or the "appropriate remembrance of family and friends," or the "success of ongoing projects." The result is that any moral deference, allegedly owed the deceased by the materialist, is based largely on the legality that sanctions last wills and testaments.

I agree that it can be a useful fiction for the materialist to continue to speak of posthumous harms or benefits. Hard metaphysical facts aside, the fostering of the belief in posthumous harms or benefits has the practical upshot of encouraging others to continue our projects after our deaths. The failure to do so can cause in some living survivors some non-idle shame (or honor).

Some Concluding Kierkegaardian Thoughts

I will close with some thoughts on the matter of moral deference to the dead, posed by Soren Kierkegaard in his *Works of Love*. Kierkegaard advises: "If you are perplexed when you consider the multiplicity of life's ways, then go out to the dead. . . . That all men are blood-relatives . . . , this kinship of life, is very often denied in life; but that they are of one mould, this kinship of death, this cannot be denied."[18]

Kierkegaard goes on to recommend visiting cemeteries both to better grasp, in general, the meaning of life, and to better understand, in particular, the significance of your love by how you relate to specific dead persons. "Therefore go out and practise it; remember one dead and learn in just this way to love the living disinterestedly, freely, faithfully."[19] Kierkegaard reminds us that if it is our duty to love those we cannot see (i.e., the dead), all the more so is it our obligation to love those we do see (i.e., the living).

Although Kierkegaard is not a materialist, he does seem to share my claim about the incoherency of the Pitcherian analysis, saying: "But when one relates himself to one who is dead, in this relationship there is only one, for one dead is nothing actual."[20] The relationship in question is entirely unilateral as the deceased *qua* object of the living person's propositional attitudes forces the living to come to grips with their own self-understanding.

Kierkegaard writes: "One who is dead is not an actual object; he is only the occasion which continually reveals what resides in the one living who relates himself to him or which helps to make clear how it is with one living who does not relate himself to him."[21]

He recommends that part of the work of love be viewed as the task of remembering the dead. Such work of love is a paradigm of *unselfish love*, for no possibility of repayment exists, as in ordinary parental love. Secondly, it is an instance of the *freest love*, as the dead cannot coerce one's love. (We often talk of love as totally free, overlooking the presence of all sorts of subtle constraints in love relationships.) And, lastly, it is a work of the most *faithful love*, as the dead do not change, so that any alteration in the nonreciprocal relationship comes from the living.

Taking a thanatological turn, and paraphrasing Kierkegaard, *mutatis mutandis*, I want to reiterate that it is not the deceased who hold the living bound, or who suffer, are harmed, or are wronged, but rather the love of the living which holds the dead fast.

It is, perhaps, a truism (at least for a materialist) to say that death has no survival value; but the phenomenon of death and our attitudes toward the deceased do confer value to survival.

NOTES

1. "The Misfortunes of the Dead," *American Philosophical Quarterly*, 21 (1984), 183. For views not unlike Pitcher's, see Joel Feinberg's *Rights, Justice*

and the Bounds of Liberty (Princeton: Princeton University Press, 1980), and his *Harm to Others* (New York: Oxford University Press, 1984). See also Roy W. Perrett, *Death and Immortality* (Dordrecht: Nijhoff, 1987).

2. While Pitcher treats the terms *harm* and *misfortune* as intensional equivalents, he thinks they are different from *wrongs* and also from *attacks.* I do not find Pitcher's distinctions to be clear. For instance, he speaks of the dead being *wronged* when, say, a trust is betrayed or the deceased are maligned. Yet, in distinguishing such *wrongs* from *attacks,* he cites as an example of an *attack* the case of a husband's revealing his deceased wife's various hitherto concealed vices, which seems equally an example of a wrong.

3. "Misfortunes of the Dead," 184.

4. Ibid.

5. Ibid., 184–85. Cf. the not uncommon judicial language of sentencing a convicted murder to life in prison, plus ten years!

6. "On Harming the Dead," *Ethics,* 97 (1987), 349.

7. Ibid.

8. *Works of Love,* trans. Howard Hong and Edna Hong (New York: Harper & Row, 1962), p. 327. "Naturally one who is dead has no rights in life" (p. 323).

9. In 1981, a cryonic storage society was found guilty of negligence and ordered to pay damages. Their stored corpses were not suitably frozen in their respective capsules. But such a legal decision does nothing to show that the dead were harmed. The misfortunes were suffered by the living relatives or friends of these neomorts, whose forlorn hopes for postponing death were thwarted.

10. Pitcher, "Misfortunes of the Dead," 187.

11. "The Evil of Death," *Journal of Philosophy,* 77 (1980), 401–24.

12. "Harming Someone After His Death," *Ethics,* 94 (1984), 407–19.

13. Ibid., 417.

14. Ibid., 418.

15. "Harming the Dead," *Ethics,* 96 (1985), 160. Incidentally, there is a move afoot to let living people *record* their views on criminal punishment should they ever be murdered. For a fee, the living can buy, say, a three-year subscription to have affidavits kept on record indicating their views on the death penalty, etc. Those affidavits which are renewable and changeable would be introduced into a trial if the person recorded should be a victim of homicide.

Apart from the legal difficulties involved in getting such affidavits introduced in a criminal proceeding (for the victim *cannot* be cross-examined by the defense), this bizarre idea may just catch some sense of postmortem harm. Again, though, the victims were harmed in life, not in death.

16. In a recent sheriff's election in San Mateo County, California, the incumbent died six weeks before the election. Yet he won the election by an 80% plurality! Ironically, the loser is declaring a victory, but the deceased incumbent can claim neither. In a 1990 November election for a judgeship in Oklahoma, the incumbent, Frank Ogden, who died on August 11, received 91% of the vote cast. Here, the losing candidate was not declared a winner by the Oklahoma Supreme Court, which declared that the judgeship can be filled

by appointment of the governor. While the penultimate case will mandate a special election, there are legal cases where, say, state officials initiate court action to attempt to fire the dead. But is this inflicting harm on the dead person? I say *no,* but the proceedings doubtlessly damage the deceased's reputation. For example, a few years back, a state worker secretly recorded a meeting with his supervisor—which is a state felony. That worker died shortly thereafter, and his widow was paid a state death benefit. The state's comptroller's office is now attempting to overturn that decision, presumably to uphold the integrity of the state tax system. But it seems to me that the deceased state employee is not harmed. No doubt his widow would be by an adverse court decision, or his relatives/friends by seeing his name tarnished in the court proceedings.

17. *Nichomachean Ethics* 1.10. Commenting on this passage, Anthony Preus claims that "fostering the practice of carrying through the projects of the dead, we encourage the possibility that our own projects will be carried out when we have passed away." *The Journal of Medicine and Philosophy,* 9 (1984), 411. But Preus' remark does not really address the underlying metaphysical issue as to whether the dead can truly be harmed. Instead he urges a kind of Pascalian, pragmatic posture of insurance, where we act as if the deceased can be harmed so as to foster the likely success of our own current interests and projects, after we are no longer alive.

18. Trans. Hong and Hong, p. 317.

19. Ibid., p. 328.

20. Ibid., p. 319. Also, "one dead is silent and says not a word . . . and perhaps he does not suffer evil either!" (p. 323).

21. Ibid. Unfortunately, Kierkegaard falls prey, at times, to a similar confusion as Pitcher et al., writing, for instance, that "one must not disturb the dead with his complaints and cries" (p. 319).

9

The Makropulos Case: Reflections on the Tedium of Immortality

BERNARD WILLIAMS

Oxford University and University of California, Berkeley

THIS ESSAY STARTED LIFE as a lecture in a series "on the immortality of the soul or kindred spiritual subject."[1] My kindred spiritual subject is, one might say, the mortality of the soul. Those among previous lecturers who were philosophers tended, I think, to discuss the question whether we are immortal; that is not my subject, but rather what a good thing it is that we are not. Immortality, or a state without death, would be meaningless, I shall suggest; so, in a sense, death gives the meaning to life. That does not mean that we should not fear death (whatever force that injunction might be taken to have, anyway). Indeed, there are several very different ways in which it could be true at once that death gave the meaning to life and that death was, other things being equal, something to be feared. Some existentialists, for instance, seem to have said that death was what gave meaning to life, if anything did, just because it was the fear of death that gave meaning to life; I shall not follow them. I shall rather pursue the idea that from facts about human desire and happiness and what a human life is, it follows both that immortality would be, where conceivable at all, intolerable, and that (other things being equal) death is reasonably regarded as an evil. Considering whether death can reasonably be regarded as an evil is in fact as near as I shall get to considering whether it should be feared: they are not quite the same question.

My title is that, as it is usually translated into English, of a play by Karel Čapek which was made into an opera by Janáček and which tells of a woman called Elina Makropulos, *alias* Emilia Marty, *alias* Ellian

Reprinted by permission from Professor Williams' *Problems of the Self* (Cambridge: Cambridge University Press, 1973), pp. 82–100.

Macgregor, *alias* a number of other women with the initials EM, on whom her father, the court physician to a sixteenth-century emperor, tried out an elixir of life. At the time of the action she is aged 342. Her unending life has come to a state of boredom, indifference, and coldness. Everything is joyless: "in the end it is the same," she says, "singing and silence." She refuses to take the elixir again; she dies, and the formula is deliberately destroyed by a young woman among the protests of some older men.

EM's state suggests at least this, that death is not necessarily an evil, and not just in the sense in which almost everybody would agree to that, where death provides an end to great suffering, but in the more intimate sense that it can be a good thing not to live too long. It suggests more than that, for it suggests that it was not a peculiarity of EM's that an endless life was meaningless. That is something I shall follow out later. First, though, we should put together the suggestion of EM's case, that death is not necessarily an evil, with the claim of some philosophies and religions that death is necessarily not an evil. Notoriously, there have been found two contrary bases on which that claim can be mounted: death is said by some not to be an evil because it is not the end, and by others, because it is. There is perhaps some profound temperamental difference between those who find consolation for the fact of death in the hope that it is only the start of another life, and those who equally find comfort in the conviction that it is the end of the only life there is. That both such temperaments exist means that those who find a diagnosis of the belief in immortality, and indeed a reproach to it, in the idea that it constitutes a consolation, have at best only a statistical fact to support them. While that may be just about enough for the diagnosis, it is not enough for the reproach.

Most famous, perhaps, among those who have found comfort in the second option, the prospect of annihilation, was Lucretius, who, in the steps of Epicurus, and probably from a personal fear of death which in some of his pages seems almost tangible, addresses himself to proving that death is never an evil. Lucretius has two basic arguments for this conclusion, and it is an important feature of them both that the conclusion they offer has the very strong consequence—and seems clearly intended to have the consequence—that, for oneself at least, it is all the same whenever one dies, that a long life is no better than a short one. That is to say, death is never an evil in the sense not merely that there is no-one for whom dying is an evil, but that there is no time at which dying is an evil—sooner or later, it is all the same.

The first argument (*De rerum natura*, 3.870ff., 898ff.) seeks to interpret the fear of death as a confusion, based on the idea that we shall be there after death to repine our loss of the *praemia vitae*, the rewards and delights of life, and to be upset at the spectacle of our bodies burned, and so forth. The fear of death, it is suggested, must necessarily be the fear of some experiences had when one is dead. But if death is annihilation, then there are no such experiences: in the Epicurean phrase, when death is there, we are not, and when we are there, death is not. So, death being annihilation, there is nothing to fear. The second argument (1091) addresses itself directly to the question of whether one dies earlier or later, and says that one will be the same time dead however early or late one dies, and therefore one might as well die earlier as later. And from both arguments we can conclude *nil igitur mors est ad nos, neque pertinet hilum*—death is nothing to us, and does not matter at all (830).

The second of these arguments seems even on the face of things to contradict the first. For it must imply that if there *were* a finite period of death, such that if you died later you would be dead for less time, then there *would* be some point in wanting to die later rather than earlier. But that implication makes sense, surely, only on the supposition that what is wrong with dying consists in something undesirable about the condition of being dead. And that is what is denied by the first argument.

More important than this, the oddness of the second argument can help to focus a difficulty already implicit in the first. The first argument, in locating the objection to dying in a confused objection to being dead, and exposing that in terms of a confusion with being alive, takes it as genuinely true of life that the satisfaction of desire, and possession of the *praemia vitae,* are good things. It is not irrational to be upset by the loss of home, children, possessions—what is irrational is to think of death as, in the relevant sense, *losing* anything. But now if we consider two lives, one very short and cut off before the *praemia* have been acquired, the other fully provided with the *praemia* and containing their enjoyment to a ripe age, it is very difficult to see why the second life, by these standards alone, is not to be thought better than the first. But if it is, then there must be something wrong with the argument which tries to show that there is nothing worse about a short life than a long one. The argument locates the mistake about dying in a mistake about consciousness, it being assumed that what commonsense thinks about the worth of the *praemia vitae* and the sadness of their (conscious) loss is sound enough. But if the *praemia vitae* are valuable—even if we include as necessary to that value consciousness that one possesses them—then surely getting to the point of possessing them is better than not getting to that point, longer enjoyment of them is better than shorter, and more of them, other things being equal, is better than less of them. But if so, then it just will not be true that to die earlier is all the same as to die later, nor that death is never an evil—and the thought that to die later is better than to die earlier will not be dependent on some muddle about thinking that the dead person will be alive to lament his loss. It will depend only on the idea, apparently sound, that if the *praemia vitae* and consciousness of them are good things, then longer consciousness of more *praemia* is better than shorter consciousness of fewer *praemia*.

Is the idea sound? A decent argument, surely, can be marshalled to support it. If I desire something, then, other things being equal, I prefer a state of affairs in which I get it to one in which I do not get it, and (again, other things being equal) plan for a future in which I get it rather than not. But one future, for sure, in which I would not get it would be one in which I was dead. To want something, we may also say, is to that extent to have reason for resisting what excludes having that thing: and death certainly does that, for a very large range of things that one wants.[2] If that is right, then for any of those things, wanting something itself gives one a reason for avoiding death. Even though, if I do not succeed, I will not know that, nor what I am missing, from the perspective of the wanting agent it is rational to aim for states of affairs in which his want is satisfied, and hence to regard death as something to be avoided; that is, to regard it as an evil.

It is admittedly true that many of the things I want, I want only on the assumption that I am going to be alive; and some people, for instance some of the old, desperately want certain things when nevertheless they would much rather that they and their wants were dead. It might be suggested that not just these special cases, but really all wants, were conditional on being alive; a situation in which one has ceased to exist is not to be compared with others with respect to desire-satisfaction—rather, if one dies, all bets are off. But surely the claim that all desires are in this sense conditional must be wrong. For consider the idea of a rational forward-looking calculation of suicide; there can be such a thing, even if many suicides are not rational, and even though with some that are, it may be unclear to what extent they are forward-looking (the obscurity of this with regard to suicides of honour is an obscurity in the notion of shame). In such a calculation, a man might consider what lay before him, and decide whether he did or did not want to undergo it. If he does decide to undergo it, then some desire propels him on into the future, and *that* desire at least is not one that operates conditionally on his being alive, since it itself resolves the question of whether he is going to be alive. He has an unconditional or (as I shall say) a *categorical* desire.

The man who seriously calculates about suicide and rejects it only just has such a desire, perhaps. But if one is in a state in which the question of suicide does not occur, or occurs only as total fantasy—if, to take just one example, one is happy—one has many such desires, which do not hang from the assumption of one's existence. If they did hang from that assumption, then they would be quite powerless to rule out that assumption's being questioned, or to answer the question if it is raised; but clearly they are not powerless in those directions—on the contrary they are some of the few things, perhaps the only things, that have power in that direction. Some ascetics have supposed that happiness required reducing one's desires to those necessary for one's existence, that is, to those that one has to have, granted that one exists at all; rather, it requires that some of one's desires should be fully categorical, and one's existence itself wanted as something necessary to them.

To suppose that one can in this way categorically want things implies a number of things about the nature of desire. It implies, for one thing, that the reason I have for bringing it about that I get what I want is not merely that of avoiding the unpleasantness of not getting what I want. But that must in any case be right—otherwise we should have to represent every desire as the desire to avoid its own frustration, which is absurd.

About what those categorical desires must be, there is not much of great generality to be said, if one is looking at the happy state of things: except, once more against the ascetic, that there should be not just enough, but more than enough. But the question might be raised, at the impoverished end of things, as to what the minimum categorical desire might be. Could it be *just* the desire to remain alive? The answer is perhaps "no." In saying that, I do not want to deny the existence, the value, or the basic necessity of a sheer reactive drive to self-preservation: humanity would certainly wither if the drive to keep alive were not stronger than any perceived reasons for keeping alive. But if the question is asked, and it is going to be answered calculatively, then the bare categorical desire to stay alive will not sustain the calculation—that desire itself, when things have got that far, has to be sustained or filled out by some desire for something else, even if it is only, at the margin, the desire that future desires of mine will be born and satisfied. But the best insight into the effect of categorical desire is not gained at the impoverished end of things, and hence in situations where the question has actually come up. The question of life being desirable is certainly transcendental in the most modest sense, in that it gets by far its best answer in never being asked at all.

None of this—including the thoughts of the calculative suicide—requires my reflection on a world in which I never occur at all. In the terms of "possible worlds" (which can admittedly be misleading), a man could, on the present account, have a reason from his own point of view to prefer a possible world in which he went on longer to one in which he went on for less long, or—like the suicide—the opposite; but he would have no reason of this kind to prefer a world in which he did not occur at all. Thoughts about his total absence from the world would have to be of a different kind, impersonal reflections on the value *for the world* of his presence or absence: of the same kind, essentially, as he could conduct (or, more probably, not manage to conduct) with regard to anyone else. While he can think egoistically of what it would be for him to live longer or less long, he cannot think egoistically of what it would be for him never to have existed at all. Hence the sombre words of Sophocles "Never to have been born counts highest of all . . ." (*Oedipus at Colonus* 1224ff.) are well met by the old Jewish reply—"how many are so lucky? Not one in ten thousand."

Lucretius' first argument has been interestingly criticised by Thomas Nagel (see Chapter 1), on lines different from those that I have been following. Nagel claims that what is wrong with Lucretius' argument is that it rests on the assumption—Nagel cites a number of plausible counter-instances—that nothing can be a misfortune for a man unless he knows about it, and that misfortunes must consist in something nasty *for* him. Against this assumption that nothing can be a misfortune for a man unless he knows about it, which would normally be thought to constitute a misfortune, though those to whom they happen are and remain ignorant of them (as, for instance, certain situations of betrayal). The difference between Nagel's approach and mine does not, of course, lie in the mere point of whether one admits misfortunes which do not consist of or involve nasty experiences: anyone who rejects Lucretius' argument must admit them. The difference is that the reasons which a man would have for avoiding death are, on the present accounts, grounded in desires—categorical desires—which he has; he, on the basis of these, has reason to regard possible death as a misfortune to be avoided, and we, looking at things from his point of view, would have reason to regard his actual death as his misfortune. Nagel, however, if I understand him, does not see the misfortune that befalls a man who dies as necessarily grounded in the issue of what desires or sorts of desires he had; just as in the betrayal case, it could be a misfortune for a man to be betrayed, even though he did not have any desire not to be betrayed. If this is a correct account, Nagel's reasoning is one step further away from Utilitarianism on this matter than mine,[3] and rests on an independent kind of value which a sufficiently Utilitarian person might just reject; while my argument cannot merely be rejected by a Utilitarian person, it seems to me, since he must if he is to be consistent, and other things being equal, attach disutility to any situation which he has good reason to prevent, and he certainly has good reason to prevent a situation which involves the non-satisfaction of his desires. Thus, granted categorical desires, death has a disutility for an agent, although that disutility does not, of course, consist in unsatisfactory experiences involved in its occurrence.

The question would remain, of course, with regard to any given agent, whether he had categorical desires. For the present argument, it will do to leave it as a contingent fact that most people do: for they will have a reason, and a perfectly coherent reason, to regard death as a misfortune, while it was Lucretius' claim that no-one could have a coherent reason for so regarding it. There may well be other reasons as well; thus Nagel's reasoning, though different from the more Utilitarian type of reason I have used against Lucretius, seems compatible with it and there are strong reasons to adopt his kind of consideration as well. In fact, further and deeper thought about this question seems likely to fill up the apparent gap between the two sorts of arguments; it is hard to believe, for one thing, that the supposed contingent fact that people have categorical desires can really be as contingent as all that. One last point about the two arguments is that they coincide in not offering—as I mentioned earlier—any considerations about worlds in which one does not occur at all; but there is perhaps an additional reason why this should be so in the Utilitarian-type argument, over and above the one it shares with Nagel's. The reason it shares with Nagel's is that the type of misfortune we are concerned with in thinking about X's death is X's misfortune (as opposed to the misfortunes of the state or whatever); and whatever sort of misfortune it may be in a given possible world that X does not occur in it, it is not X's misfortune. They share the feature, then that for anything to be X's misfortune in a given world, X must occur in that world. But the Utilitarian-type argument further grounds the misfortune, if there is one, in certain features of X, namely his desires; and if there is no X in a given world, then *a fortiori* there are no such grounds.

But now, if death, other things being equal, is a misfortune; and a longer life is better than a shorter life; and we reject the Lucretian argument that it does not matter when one dies: then it looks as though—other things always being equal—death is at any time an evil, and it is always better to live than to die. Nagel indeed, from his point of view, does seem to permit that conclusion, even though he admits some remarks about the natural term of life and the greater misfortune of dying in one's prime. But wider consequences follow. For if all that is true, then it looks as though it would be not only always better to live, but better to live always: that is, never to die. If Lucretius is wrong, we seem committed to wanting to be immortal. That would be, as has been repeatedly said, with other things equal. No-one need deny that since, for instance, we grow old and our powers decline, much may happen to increase the reasons for thinking death a good thing. But these are contingencies. We might not age; perhaps, one day, it will be possible for some of us not to age. If that were so, would it not follow then that, more life being *per se* better than less life, we should have reason so far as that went (but not necessarily in terms of other inhabitants) to live for ever? EM indeed bears strong, if fictional, witness against the desirability of that; but perhaps she still laboured under some contingent limitations, social or psychological, which might once more be eliminated to bring it about that really other things were equal. Against this, I am going to suggest that the supposed contingencies are not really contingencies; that an endless life would be a meaningless one; and that we could have no reason for living eternally a human life. There is no desirable or significant property which life would have more of, or have more unqualifiedly, if we lasted for ever. In some part, we can apply to life Aristotle's marvellous remark about Plato's Form of the Good: "nor will it be any the more good for being eternal: that which lasts long is no whiter than that which perishes in a day" (*Ethica Nicomachea* 1096B4). But only in part; for, rejecting Lucretius, we have already admitted that more days may give us more than one day can.

If one pictures living for ever as living as an embodied person in the world rather as it is, it will be a question, and not so trivial as may seem, of what age one eternally is. EM was 342; because for 300 years she had been 42. This choice (if it was a choice) I am personally, and at present, well disposed to salute—if one had to spend eternity at any age, that seems an admirable age to spend it at. Nor would it necessarily be a less good age for a woman: that at least was not EM's problem, that she was too old at the age she continued to be at. Her problem lay in having been at it for too long. Her trouble was, it seems, boredom: a boredom connected with the fact that everything that could happen and make sense to one particular human being of 42 had already happened to her. Or, rather, all the sorts of things that could make sense to one woman of a certain character; for EM has a certain character, and indeed, except for her accumulating memories of earlier times, and no doubt some changes of style to suit the passing centuries, she seems always to have been much the same sort of person.

There are difficult questions, if one presses the issue, about this constancy of character. How is this accumulation of memories related to this character which she eternally has, and to the character of her existence? Are they much the same kind of events repeated? Then it is itself strange that she allows them to be repeated, accepting the same repetitions, the same limitations—indeed, *accepting* is what it later becomes, when earlier it would not, or even could not, have been that. The repeated patterns of personal relations, for instance, must take on a character of being inescapable. Or is the pattern of her experiences not repetitious in this way, but varied? Then the problem shifts, to the relation between these varied experiences, and the fixed character: how can it remain fixed, through an endless series of very various experiences? The experiences must surely happen to her without really affecting her; she must be, as EM is, detached and withdrawn.

EM, of course, is in a world of people who do not share her condition, and that determines certain features of the life she has to lead, as that any personal relationship requires peculiar kinds of concealment. That, at least, is a form of isolation which would disappear if her condition were generalised. But to suppose more generally that boredom and inner death would be eliminated if everyone were similarly becalmed, is an empty hope: it would be a world of Bourbons, learning nothing and forgetting nothing, and it is unclear how much could even happen.

The more one reflects to any realistic degree on the conditions of EM's unending life, the less it seems a mere contingency that it froze up as it did. That it is not a contingency is suggested also by the fact that the reflections can sustain themselves independently of any question of the particular character that EM had; it is enough, almost, that she has a human character at all. Perhaps not quite. One sort of character for which the difficulties of unending life would have less significance than they proved to have for EM might be one who at the beginning was more like what she is at the end: cold, withdrawn, already frozen. For him, the prospect of unending cold is presumably less bleak in that he is used to it. But with him, the question can shift to a different place, as to why he wants the unending life at all; for, the more he is at the beginning like EM is at the end, the less place there is for categorical desire to keep him going, and to resist the desire for death. In EM's case, her boredom and distance from life both kill desire and consist in the death of it; one who is already enough like that to sustain life in those conditions may well be one who had nothing to make him want to do so. But even if he has, and we conceive of a person who is stonily resolved to sustain for ever an already stony existence, his possibility will be of no comfort to those, one hopes a larger party, who want to live longer because they want to live more.

To meet the basic anti-Lucretian hope for continuing life which is grounded in categorical desire, EM's unending life in this world is inadequate, and necessarily so relative to just those desires and conceptions of character which go into the hope. That is very important, since it is the most direct response, that which should have been adequate if the hope is both coherent and what it initially seemed to be. It also satisfied one of two important conditions which must be satisfied by anything which is to be adequate as a fulfillment of any anti-Lucretian hope, namely that it should clearly be *me* who lives for ever. The second important condition is that the state in which I survive should be one which, to me looking forward, will be adequately related, in the life it presents, to those aims which I now have in wanting to survive at all. That is a vague formula, and necessarily so, for what exactly that relation will be must depend to some extent on what kind of aims and (as one might say) prospects for myself I now have. What we can say is that since I am propelled forward into longer life by categorical desires, what is promised must hold out some hopes for those desires. The limiting case of this might be that the promised life held out some hope just to that desire mentioned before, that future desires of mine will be born and satisfied; but if that were the only categorical desire that carried me forward into it, at least this seems demanded, that any image I have of those future desires should make it comprehensible to me how in terms of my character they could be my desires.

This second condition the EM kind of survival failed, on reflection, to satisfy; but at least it is clear why, before reflection, it looked as though it might satisfy the condition—it consists, after all, in just going on in ways in which we are quite used to going on. If we turn away now from EM to more remote kinds of survival, the problems of those two conditions press more heavily right from the beginning. Since the major problems of the EM situation lay in the indefinite extension of one life, a tempting alternative is survival by means of an indefinite series of lives. Most, perhaps all, versions of this belief which have actually existed have immediately failed the first condition: they get nowhere near providing any consideration to make the difference between rebirth and new birth. But let us suppose the problem, in some way or another, removed; some conditions of bodily continuity, minimally sufficient for personal identity, may be supposed satisfied. (Anyone who thinks that no such conditions could be sufficient, and requires, for instance, conditions of memory, may well find it correspondingly difficult to find an alternative for survival in this direction which both satisfies the first requirement, of identity, and also adequately avoids the difficulties of the EM alternative.) The problem remains of whether this series of psychologically disjoint lives could be an object of hope to one who did not want to die. That is, in my view, a different question from the question of whether it will be he—which is why I distinguished originally two different requirements to be satisfied. But it is a question; and even if the first requirement be supposed satisfied, it is exceedingly unclear that the second can be. This will be so, even if one were to accept the idea, itself problematical, that one could have reason to fear the future pain of someone who was merely bodily continuous with one as one now is.[4]

There are in the first place certain difficulties about how much a man could consistently be allowed to know about the series of his lives, if we are to preserve the psychological disjointness which is the feature of this model. It might be that each would in fact have to seem to him as though it were his only life, and that he could not have grounds for being sure what, or even that, later lives were to come. If so, then no comfort or hope will be forthcoming in this model to those who want to go on living. More interesting questions, however, concern the man's relation to a future life of which he did get some advance idea. If we could allow the idea that he could fear pain which was going to occur in that life, then we have at least provided him with one kind of reason which might move him to opt out of that life, and destroy himself (being recurrent, under conditions of bodily continuity, would not make one indestructible). But physical pain and its nastiness are to the maximum degree independent of what one's desires and character are, and the degree of identification needed with the later life to reject that aspect of it is absolutely minimal. Beyond that point, however, it is unclear how he is to bring this later character and its desires into a relation to his present ones, so as to be satisfied or the reverse with this marginal promise of continued existence. If he can regard this future life as an object of hope, then equally it must be possible for him to regard it with alarm, or depression, and—as in the simple pain case—opt out of it. If we cannot make sense of his entertaining that choice, then we have not made sense of this future life's being adequately related to his present life, so that it could, alternatively, be something he might want in wanting not to die. But can we clearly make sense of that choice? For if we—or he—merely wipe out his present character and desires, there is nothing left by which he can judge it at all, at least as something *for him;* while if we leave them in, we—and he—apply something irrelevant to that future life, since (to adapt the Epicurean phrase), when they are there, it is not, and when it is there, they are not. We might imagine him considering the future prospects, and agreeing to go on if he found them congenial. But that is a muddled picture. For whether they are congenial to him as he is now must be beside the point, and the idea that it is not beside the point depends on carrying over into the case features that do not belong to it, as (perhaps) that he will remember later what he wanted in the earlier life. And when we admit that it is beside the point whether the prospects are congenial, then the force of the idea that the future life could be something that he *now* wanted to go on to, fades.

There are important and still obscure issues here,[5] but perhaps enough has been said to cast doubt on this option as coherently satisfying the desire to stay alive. While few will be disposed to think that much can be made of it, I must confess that out of the alternatives it is the only one which for me would, if it made sense, have any attraction—no doubt because it is the only one which has the feature that what one is living at any given point is actually *a life*. It is singular that those systems of belief that get closest to actually accepting recurrence of this sort seem, almost without exception, to look forward to the point when one will be released from it. Such systems seem less interested in continuing one's life than in earning one the right to a superior sort of death.

The serial and disjoint lives are at least more attractive than the attempt, which some have made, to combine the best of continuous and of serial existence in a fantasy of very varied lives which are nevertheless cumulatively effective in memory. This might be called the *Teiresias* model. As that case singularly demonstrates, it has the quality of a fantasy, of emotional pressure trying to combine the uncombinable. One thing that the fantasy has to ignore is the connexion, both as cause and as consequence, between having one range of experiences rather than another, wishing to engage in one sort of thing rather than another, and having a character. Teiresias cannot have a character, either continuously through these proceedings, or cumulatively at the end (if there were to be an end) of them: he is not, eventually, a person but a phenomenon.

In discussing the last models, we have moved a little away from the very direct response which EM's case seemed to provide to the hope that one would never die. But perhaps we have moved not nearly far enough. Nothing of this, and nothing much like this, was in the minds of many who have hoped for immortality; for it was not in this world that they hoped to live for ever. As one might say, their hope was not so much that they would never die as that they would live after their death, and while that in its turn can be represented as the hope that one would not really die, or, again, that it was not really oneself that would die, the change of formulation could point to an after-life sufficiently unlike this life, perhaps, to earth the current of doubt that flows from EM's frozen boredom.

But in fact this hope has been and could only be modeled on some image of a more familiar untiring or unresting or unflagging activity or satisfaction; and what is essentially EM's problem, one way or another, remains. In general we can ask what it is about the imagined activities of an eternal life which would stave off the principal hazard to which EM succumbed, boredom. The Don Juan in Hell joke, that heaven's prospects are tedious and the devil has the best tunes, though a tired fancy in itself, at least serves to show up a real and (I suspect) a profound difficulty, of providing any model of an unending, supposedly satisfying, state or activity which would not rightly prove boring to anyone who remained conscious of himself and who had acquired a character, interests, tastes, and impatiences in the course of living, already, a finite life. The point is not that for such a man boredom would be a tiresome consequence of the supposed states or activities, and that they would be objectionable just on the utilitarian or hedonistic ground that they had this disagreeable feature. If that were all there was to it, we could imagine the feature away, along no doubt with other disagreeable features of human life in its present imperfection. The point is rather that boredom, as sometimes in more ordinary circumstances, would be not just a tiresome effect, but a reaction almost perceptual in character to the poverty of one's relation to the environment. Nothing less will do for eternity than something that makes boredom *unthinkable*. What could that be? Something that could be guaranteed to be at every moment utterly absorbing? But if a man has and retains a character, there is no reason to suppose that there is anything which could be that. If, lacking a conception of the guaranteedly absorbing activity, one tries merely to think away the reaction of boredom, one is no longer supposing an improvement in the circumstances, but merely an impoverishment in his consciousness of them. Just as being bored can be a sign of not noticing, understanding, or appreciating enough, so equally not being bored can be a sign of not noticing, or not reflecting, enough. One might make the immortal man content at every moment, by just stripping off from him consciousness which would have brought discontent by reminding him of other times, other interests, other possibilities. Perhaps, indeed, that is what we have already done, in a more tempting way, by picturing him just now as at every moment totally absorbed—but that is something we shall come back to.

Of course there is in actual life such a thing as justified but necessary boredom. Thus—to take a not entirely typical example—someone who was, or who thought himself, devoted to the radical cause might eventually admit to himself that he found a lot of its rhetoric excruciatingly boring. He might think that he ought not to feel that, that the reaction was wrong, and merely represented an unworthiness of his, an unregenerate remnant of intellectual superiority. However, he might rather feel that it would not necessarily be a better world in which no-one was bored by such rhetoric and that boredom was, indeed, a perfectly worthy reaction to this rhetoric after all this time; but for all that, the rhetoric might be necessary. A man at arms can get cramp from standing too long at his post, but sentry-duty can after all be necessary. But the threat of monotony in eternal activities could not be dealt with in that way, by regarding immortal boredom as an unavoidable ache derived from standing ceaselessly at one's post. (This is one reason why I said that boredom in eternity would have to be *unthinkable*.) For the question would be unavoidable, in what campaign one was supposed to be serving, what one's ceaseless sentry-watch was for.

Some philosophers have pictured an eternal existence as occupied in something like intense intellectual enquiry. Why that might seem to solve the problem, at least for them, is obvious. The activity is engrossing, self-justifying, affords, as it may appear, endless new perspectives, and by being engrossing enables one to lose oneself. It is that last feature that supposedly makes boredom unthinkable, by providing something that is, in that earlier phrase, at every moment totally absorbing. But if one is totally and perpetually absorbed in such an activity, and loses oneself in it, then as those words suggest, we come back to the problem of satisfying the conditions that it should be me who lives for ever, and that the eternal life should be in prospect of some interest. Let us leave aside the question of people whose characteristic and most personal interests are remote from such pursuits, and for whom, correspondingly, an immortality promised in terms of intellectual activity is going to make heavy demands on some theory of a "real self" which will have to emerge at death. More interesting is the content and value of the promise for a person who *is*, in this life, disposed to those activities. For looking at such a person as he now is, it seems quite unreasonable to suppose that those activities would have the fulfilling or liberating character that they do have for him, if they were in fact all he could do or conceive of doing. If they are genuinely fulfilling, and do not operate (as they can) merely as a compulsive diversion, then the ground and shape of the satisfactions that the intellectual enquiry offers him, will relate to *him*, and not just to the enquiry. The *Platonic introjection*, seeing the satisfactions of studying what is timeless and impersonal as being themselves timeless and impersonal, may be a deep illusion, but it is certainly an illusion.

We can see better into that illusion by considering Spinoza's thought, that intellectual activity was the most active and free state that a man could be in, and that a man who had risen to such activity was in some sense most fully individual, most fully himself. This conclusion has been sympathetically expounded by Stuart Hampshire, who finds on this point a similar doctrine in Spinoza and in Freud: in particular, he writes, "[one's] only means of achieving this distinctness as an individual, this freedom in relation to the common order of nature, is the power of the mind freely to follow in its thought an intellectual order."[6] The contrast to this free intellectual activity is "the common condition of men that their conduct and their judgments of value, their desires and aversions, are in each individual determined by unconscious memories"—a process which the same writer has elsewhere associated with our having any character at all as individuals.[7]

Hampshire claims that in pure intellectual activity the mind is most free because it is then least determined by causes outside its immediate states. I take him to mean that rational activity is that in which the occurrence of an earlier thought maximally explains the occurrence of a later thought, because it is the rational relation between their contents which, granted the occurrence of the first, explains the occurrence of the second. But even the maximal explanatory power, in these terms, of the earlier thought does not extend to total explanation: for it will still require explanation why this thinker on this occasion continued on this rational path of thought at all. Thus I am not sure that the Spinozist consideration which Hampshire advances even gives a very satisfactory sense to the *activity* of the mind. It leaves out, as the last point shows, the driving power which is needed to sustain one even in the most narrowly rational thought. It is still further remote from any notion of creativity, since that, even within a theoretical context, and certainly in an artistic one, precisely implies the origination of ideas which are not fully predictable in terms of the content of existing ideas. But even if it could yield one sense for "activity," it would still offer very little, despite Spinoza's heroic defence of the notion, for *freedom*. Or—to put it another way—even if it offered something for freedom of the intellect, it offers nothing for freedom of the individual. For when freedom is initially understood as the absence of "outside" determination, and in particular understood in those terms as an unquestionable *value*, my freedom is reasonably not taken to include freedom from my past, my character, and my desires. To suppose that those are, in the relevant sense, "outside" determinations, is merely to beg the vital question about the boundaries of the self, and not to prove from premises acceptable to any clear-headed man who desires freedom that the boundaries of the self should be drawn round the intellect. On the contrary, the desire for freedom can, and should, be seen as the desire to be free in the exercise and development of character, not as the desire to be free of it. And if Hampshire and others are right in claiming that an individual character springs from and gets its energies from unconscious memories and unclear desires, then the individual must see them too as within the boundaries of the self, and themselves involved in the drive to persist in life and activity.

With this loss, under the Spinozist conception, of the individual's character, there is, contrary to Hampshire's claim, a loss of individuality itself, and certainly that could make an eternity of intellectual activity, so construed, a reasonable object of interest to one concerned with individual immortality. As those who totally wish to lose themselves in the movement can consistently only hope that the movement will go on, so the consistent Spinozist—at least on this account of Spinozism—can only hope that the intellectual activity goes on, something which could be as well realised in the existence of Aristotle's prime mover, perhaps, as in anything to do with Spinoza or any other particular man.

Stepping back now from the extremes of Spinozist abstraction, I shall end by returning to a point from which we set out, the sheer desire to go on living, and shall mention a writer on this subject, Unamuno, whose work *The Tragic Sense of Life*[8] gives perhaps more extreme expression than anyone else has done to that most basic form of the desire to be immortal, the desire not to die.

> I do not want to die—no, I neither want to die nor do I want to want to die; I want to live for ever and ever and ever. I want this "I" to live— this poor "I" that I am and that I feel myself to be here and now, and therefore the problem of the duration of my soul, of my own soul, tortures me [p. 60].

Although Unamuno frequently refers to Spinoza, the spirit of this is certainly far removed from that of the "sorrowful Jew of Amsterdam." Furthermore, in his clear insistence that what he desperately wants is this life, the life of this self, not to end, Unamuno reveals himself at equal removes from Manicheanism and from Utilitarianism; and that is correct, for the one is only the one-legged descendant of the other. That tradition—Manichean, Orphic, Platonic, Augustinian—which contrasts the spirit and the body in such a sense that the spiritual aims at eternity, truth and salvation, while the body is adjusted to pleasure, the temporary, and eventual dissolution, is still represented, as to fifty per cent, by secular Utilitarianism: it is just one of the original pair of boots left by itself and better regarded now that the other has fallen into disrepair. Bodies are all that we have or are: hence for Utilitarianism it *follows* that the only focus of our arrangements can be the efficient organisation of happiness. Immortality, certainly, is out, and so life here should last as long as we determine—or eventually, one may suspect, others will determine—that it is pleasant for us to be around.

Unamuno's outlook is at the opposite pole to this and, whatever else may be wrong with it, it salutes the true idea that the meaning of life does not consist either in the management of satisfactions in a body or in an abstract immortality without one. On the one hand he had no time for Manicheanism, and admired the rather brutal Catholic faith which could express its hopes for a future life in the words which he knew on a tombstone in Bilbao:

> Aunque estamos in polvo convertidos
> en Ti, Señor, nuestra esperanza fía,
> que tornaremos a vivir vestidos
> con la carne y la piel que nos cubria [p. 79].

At the same time, his desire to remain alive extends an almost incomprehensible distance beyond any desire to continue agreeable experiences: "For myself I can say that as a youth and even as a child I remained unmoved when shown the most moving pictures of hell, for even then nothing appeared quite so horrible to me as nothingness itself" (p. 28). The most that I have claimed earlier against Lucretius is not enough to make that preference intelligible to me. The fear of sheer nothingness is certainly part of what Lucretius rightly, if too lightly, hoped to exorcise; and the *mere* desire to stay alive, which is here stretched to its limit, is not enough (I suggested before) to answer the question, once the question has come up and requires an answer in rational terms. Yet Unamuno's affirmation of existence even through limitless suffering[9] brings out something which is implicit in the claim against Lucretius. It is not necessarily the prospect of pleasant times that creates the motive against dying, but the existence of categorical desire, and categorical desire can drive through both the existence and the prospect of unpleasant times.

Suppose, then, that categorical desire does sustain the desire to live. So long as it remains so, I shall want not to die. Yet I also know, if what has gone before is right, that an eternal life would be unliveable. In part, as EM's case originally suggested, that is because categorical desire will go away from it: in those versions, such as hers, in which I am recognisably myself, I would eventually have had altogether too much of myself. There are good reasons, surely, for dying before that happens. But equally, at times earlier than that moment, there is reason for not dying. Necessarily, it tends to be either too early or too late. EM reminds us that it can be too late, and many, as against Lucretius, need no reminding that it can be too early. If that is any sort of dilemma, it can, as things still are and if one is exceptionally lucky, be resolved, not by doing anything, but just by dying shortly before the horrors of not doing so become evident. Technical progress may, in more than one direction, make that piece of luck rarer. But as things are, it is possible to be, in contrast to EM, *felix opportunitate mortis*—as it can be appropriately mistranslated, lucky in having the chance to die.

NOTES

1. At the University of California, Berkeley, under a benefaction in the names of Agnes and Constantine Foerster. I am grateful to the committee for inviting me to give the 1972 lecture in this series.

2. Obviously the principle is not exceptionless. For one thing, one can want to be dead: the content of that desire may be obscure, but whatever it is, a man presumably cannot be *prevented* from getting it by dying. More generally, the principle does not apply to what I elsewhere call *non-I desire:* for an account, see my "Egoism and Altruism," *Problems of the Self,* pp. 260ff. They do not affect the present discussion, which is within the limits of egoistic rationality.

3. Though my argument does not in any sense imply Utilitarianism; for some further considerations on this, see the final paragraphs of this paper.

4. One possible conclusion from the dilemma discussed in my "The Self and the Future." For the point, mentioned below, of the independence of physical pain from psychological change, see *Problems of the Self,* p. 54.

5. For a detailed discussion of closely related questions, though in a different framework, see Derek Parfitt, "Personal Identity," *Philosophical Review,* 80 (1971), 3–27.

6. "Spinoza and the Idea of Freedom," reprinted in *Freedom of Mind* (Oxford: Clarendon, 1972), pp. 183ff.; the two quotations are from pp. 206–7.

7. "Disposition and Memory," *ibid.,* pp. 160ff.; see esp. pp. 176–77.

8. *Del sentimiento trágico de la vida,* trans. J. E. Crawford Flitch (London, 1921). Page references in the text are to the 1962 Fontana Library edition.

9. An affirmation which takes on a special dignity retrospectively in the light of his own death shortly after his courageous speech against Millán Astray and the obscene slogan "¡Viva la Muerte!" (see Hugh Thomas, *The Spanish Civil War* [Harmondsworth: Pelican, 1961], pp. 442–44).

10

De Anima

RICHARD TAYLOR

University of Rochester

SOME PHILOSOPHERS SAY that each of us has, or indeed *is*, a personal self, ego, or soul, related some way or other to his body and to the rest of the world. Just what those relationships are is much debated; but it is considered beyond doubt that there is at the very center of things this self or ego. Such, at least, is the teaching of a long and respectable philosophical tradition. It is said that this personal self came into being at a certain moment in time, and that, alas, it is going to perish at some approaching moment of time, never to exist again in the whole of eternity. Theologians say it arose as a result of God's creating it and that, if certain of God's expectations are lived up to, it can hope to go right on existing forever in some place specially reserved for it.

Other philosophers say that there is no such thing at all, that a man is nothing more than his body and that his ultimate fate, therefore, is simply the fate of his body, which is known to be dust and ashes. This teaching has the advantage of simplicity and seems generally more scientific, but since it is rather depressing, it is not so widely held.

Both schools of thought seem agreed in this, however: that a man is a finite being, distinct from everything that is not himself; that he came into being at a certain more or less identifiable moment; and that, apart from the hope nourished by religion, he is going to perish at some future moment not yet known.

Both points of view are basically mistaken on that point, though it is not easy to demonstrate this through philosophical arguments. That should be no cause for embarrassment, for philosophers have never proved anything about this, one way or another, anyway. Each imag-

Reprinted by permission from Professor Taylor's *With Heart and Mind* (New York: St. Martin's Press, 1973), pp. 122–33.

ines that he has, and dismisses those of a contrary opinion as too dense
to follow his demonstrations, but in fact all any philosopher has ever
done here is to arrange his presuppositions and prejudices in an orderly
way, then step back and say, "Behold what I have proved."

Nor is it easy to show in any other way what is wrong here. Proofs
seem to accomplish nothing, except to stimulate controversy. Nothing
can be counted on, but we might have some luck with

WALTER'S AMOEBIARY:
A PHILOSOPHICAL FABLE

Walter had an engrossing interest in microscopy, but this eventually
evolved into an interest in micro-organisms and, more particularly,
amoebae, not merely as subjects of microscopic study, but for their
own sakes. That is, he grew fond of them, studied sympathetically
their individual traits and personalities, and in time got to the point of
spending hours upon hours in their company. Of course he gave them
names: Alice, Henry, and so on. The choice of the name was in no
way guided by the sex of its possessor, for amoebae are not distinguish-
able by sex, but this did not matter. Walter found it natural and easy
to think of Alice as female, for instance, Henry as male, and so on,
considering that an amoeba's name was a perfectly reliable guide in
determining whether to refer to a given animal as *he* or *she*.

From the many hours he spent with them, Walter eventually came
to know his animals with astonishing understanding. He could pick out
Alice at once, for example, knew the circumstances of her birth and
something of her achievements, frustrations, and failures. When any
amoeba seemed sluggish or ill, he felt genuine concern, and when one
perished, it was for Walter not just the loss of something easily replaced. The amoebae, to be sure, showed little reciprocation for this
devotion and in fact exhibited no more fidelity to their owner than does
a cat, but this made no difference to Walter.

It was a harmless little hobby until Walter decided to breed the tiny
animals, with a view to improving the strain, and this led him almost
to the madhouse. Amoebae multiply rather quickly, but Walter's problems did not arise from this. They were instead metaphysical. There
were perfectly straightforward questions, the answers to which he
needed for his records, and while those answers lay right under his
nose, he somehow could not find them. He became more obsessed
with metaphysics than with his amoebae. He was beginning to think
himself deficient in intellect, but this was unjustified, for, as he eventu-

ally discovered, the questions that plagued him were questions that could not arise.

His frustrations arose in the following way. The breeder of any stock needs to know its ancestry. This would at first seem to be utterly simple for the amoeba breeder, for an amoeba has only one parent. Instead, then, of the usual family histories, with their numberless branches and ramifications, which in a few generations baffle all comprehension, the amoeba breeder would need only a simple linear record of successive parents and offspring. The breed would be improved by encouraging those with the desired traits to multiply, and by inhibiting the rest. It all seemed utterly simple. There would be no need at all to pair off prospective parents and then hope for the best, meanwhile becoming mired in the complexities of bisexual genetics.

But then arose the first problem. The amoeba reproduces simply by splitting in two. So if Henry thus divides himself, the question arises, which of the two resulting amoebae is really Henry and which is his offspring? Walter at first answered that in what seemed a perfectly straightforward, unarbitrary way. The parent, he thought, would be the larger of the two; and the offspring, the smaller. In fact it was usually quite obvious when he was on hand to witness the birth, for the offspring first appeared as a tiny bud on the parent, gradually grew larger, and then split off. There was then no problem.

But then Walter got to wondering: Why do I record the small bud as breaking off from the larger one to become its offspring, instead of thinking of the large bud as breaking away from the smaller one to become *its* offspring? Is identity a mere function of size? How do I know, to begin with, that a small bud appears on the parent amoeba? Perhaps the parent amoeba withdraws into a small bud and leaves behind the larger remains, its offspring; the parent then eventually recovers its original size and resembles its offspring. How would I ever know, in case that actually happened? How do I know it does not happen every time? So perhaps my records are all backwards, exhibiting a total confusion between parents and offspring?

Walter lost many hours and quite a bit of sleep too, pondering this question, until he hit upon a technique whereby he could, he thought, unfailingly identify any one of his animals, once and for all. He would tag them, he decided. So he developed a technique for imprinting minute but indelible colored spots on them, which could be combined in various configurations. With each animal so marked, he could then know for certain just which amoeba was before him, by checking its markings. Being thus able to distinguish any amoeba from any other, he could thereby distinguish it from any offspring, including its own. He found this particularly useful in those cases of an amoeba's reproducing by dividing itself through the middle, resulting in two animals of the same size. Had it not been for the markings, it would have been utterly impossible to tell which was the offspring, which the original. With the marking system, Walter had only to check to see which animal bore the identifying mark. That would be the parent; and the other, the offspring. He particularly rejoiced at having this system when several times he found that the offspring was in fact the larger of the two divisions, for it was in these cases the bud which bore the identifying marks. This of course confirmed his earlier fear that the larger part might sometimes be the bud that breaks off from the smaller original, so that in truth the larger of the two is the offspring and the smaller one is the parent.

This was all fine, and Walter felt entirely secure in the accuracy of his records and pedigrees, until one day a strange thing happened. One of his amoebae gave birth, but retained only half of the identifying marking, passing the other half to its offspring. Walter found himself totally unable to tell which was which. Without knowing which was the parent, his record of lineage, with respect to that particular family of amoebae, had to come to a dead end, to his dismay.

At first he thought he had minimized the chance of this ever happening again, by making the markings so tiny that it would be very unlikely that they would be divided in any fission of their bearers. But then there arose the following question, which suggested to Walter that the entire system of markings might be unreliable. What if, he thought, a parent amoeba, in shedding some and perhaps even most of its substance to give rise to a totally new individual, should at the same time shed its identifying mark, so that the very mark which was supposed to identify the parent should now be sported by its offspring? Would that not throw the records into a confusion which would be metaphysically impossible to clarify?

For quite a while Walter tried to banish this doubt by insisting that, since marks had been introduced as the very criteria of identity, no question could arise of one amoeba's transmitting its marks to another. The amoeba bearing the marks criterially distinctive of Henry, for example, would have to *be* Henry. It is by those very marks, after all, that we pick Henry out in the first place. To speak of another amoeba as having Henry's marks is to speak unintelligibly.

But like so much that passes for incisive philosophic thinking, this was soon seen to be an arbitrary fiction, from the most elementary consideration. For clearly, if one could regard a given animal as that one upon which a certain mark was bestowed, making its identity entirely a function of this, then one could by the same logic regard a given animal as one upon which a certain name is bestowed. Thus,

Henry would be whichever animal one called "Henry," and that would be the end of the matter. But surely such a solution to the problem would be worthy only of children and the most dull-witted philosophers. Our common sense tells us that there would be nothing under the sun to prevent one from flushing Henry down a drain and henceforth calling another amoeba by that name. No animal's continuing identity is ensured by a resolution to continue applying its name. But as an animal can shed its name, so also it can shed its markings—and with that obvious reflection Walter found himself back where he had begun, and on the brink of madness.

After such frustrations, Walter finally destroyed all his records, convinced they must be filled with errors. He tried other systems, but with no better luck. He had long since noted, for example, that his different amoebae displayed different personality traits, different preferences and habits, though all these were of course rather simple. When observing his amoebiary he could quite reliably distinguish one from another by these traits of character, and had in fact been partly guided by these observations in bestowing individual names in the first place. So for a time he used distinctive character traits as his guide, deciding which amoeba was Henry, which Alice, and so on, simply by how they behaved. It was not difficult, once he got to know them sufficiently well. But then one of the amoebae split, and each of the two resulting animals exhibited the character traits of the original to about the same degree. So it was again impossible to tell which was the pre-existing parent and which the offspring just come into being. It was equally impossible to regard both as having been there from the start, and just as impossible to say that each had arisen with the coming into being of the other. In fact it was impossible to say anything that had any sense to it.

If amoebae only had fingers, Walter thought, so that one could make fingerprints. But were not the distinctive marks the equivalent of fingerprints? And they did not do much good. Or if only one could communicate with amoebae at even the most rudimentary level. That would settle any doubts. If there are two similar dogs, for example, and one wants to know which is Rover, one needs only to say "Rover" and see which dog picks up his ears. But then, what if an amoeba named Henry divided into two, and each half responded to the name of Henry?

Walter finally gave up the whole enterprise of records, pedigrees, and family histories, deciding that any resolution of the problems they presented would be achieved only by metaphysicians. He went back to enjoying his pets for their own sakes, inspired by thoughts of the grandeur of even the lowliest of God's creatures, and he tried to banish metaphysical puzzles from his mind. Some of the old problems did from time to time unsettle his peace and trouble his sleep, but he resisted fairly well any temptation to try solving them.

In time the truth of things did finally dawn on Walter, however; not in the sense that any of his problems were solved, but rather, that he realized there had never been any problems there to begin with. They were all just problems that could never arise in the first place.

This enlightenment began when Walter started receiving instruction in metaphysical thinking. One of the first things he learned was that all men have souls. This is what makes them persons. If they did not have souls, they would be nothing but bodies, in principle no different from amoebae. More complicated, to be sure, but otherwise of the same order of being. Philosophers refer to this inner soul as the *self.* Since it is what thinks, it is also called the *mind.* Amoebae do not think, because they do not have any minds to think with. It is also this soul which gives men their dignity. That is why amoebae have no dignity. They lack the necessary souls. All this was of course very clear, and Walter began seeing everything in a new and much better light.

What was particularly significant for Walter, of course, was that it is on the basis of the inner self that it makes sense to distinguish one person from another in the first place. This distinction has to begin with the distinction between the self and what is not the self, which of course brings us right back again to the soul. When someone refers to *himself,* he is really referring (though he may not realize it) to his self. He as much as says so. That is, he is not referring to his body, which is only a gross physical thing, continuously changing into other things, continuously arising and perishing. He is referring to his *self.* Therefore this must be something that is not physical. It is related somehow or other to the body, no doubt. It possesses and commands the body, for example. Thus when the self commands the arm to rise, the arm does rise, and in a similar way (readily understood in one's own case) it commands the tongue to speak, instructs it in what it should say, and so on. It (the self) retains its unalterable identity throughout all the changes occurring around it in the world at large and particularly in that part of the outside world which the self refers to as its body.

The birth of the body is therefore not the origination of the person, for everyone knows that the body does not spring into being at birth. It existed before then, as part of another body. Indeed, it has always existed, mingled with other things, unlike the self itself. The person begins when there comes into being a brand new self, or what theologians appropriately call the soul, and philosophers, the mind, the ego, or simply the self. Without such minds or souls, there would only be the corporeal realm, where everything is constantly changing, where nothing is ever created or utterly perishes and where all distinctions between things are relative, as they are in the case of amoebae. In the world considered solely as corporeal, there could be no absolute distinctions between one self and another, for in such a world there would be no selves to distinguish. Hence, in such a world there could be no ultimate distinction between me and thee, mine and thine, for there would be not even the most fundamental and precious of all distinctions, that between oneself and everything else.

Walter saw, of course, that such distinctions as these, so obvious to one who has mastered the fundamentals of metaphysics, do not apply at the level of amoebae. Amoebae are not possessed of egos, selves, or souls. *That*, Walter perceived, must be why the distinction between parent and offspring was so elusive. It must be a distinction which at that level does not exist. There one finds only life assuming successive forms, wherein nothing is really born and nothing really dies—unlike that which is discovered, through metaphysics, at the higher personal level.

All this enabled Walter to see pretty clearly what had gone wrong with his attempts to keep records of amoeban ancestry. If his amoebae had possessed souls, as we do, there would have been no difficulty whatsoever. He would only have needed to keep track of souls and to record the relations of the different souls to each other.

Punch line: "Then," thought Walter, "everything would have been straightforward, perfectly simple, and above all, of course, clear."

11

On the Observability
of the Self

Roderick M. Chisholm

Brown University

I

> A traveller of good judgment may mistake his way, and be
> unawares led into a wrong track; and while the road is fair
> before him, he may go on without suspicion and be followed
> by others; but when it ends in a coal-pit, it requires no great
> judgment to know that he hath gone wrong, nor perhaps to
> find out what misled him.
>
> Thomas Reid, Inquiry into the Human Mind,
Ch. I sec. VIII

THE TWO GREAT TRADITIONS of contemporary Western philosophy—"phenomenology" and "logical analysis"—seem to meet, unfortunately, at the extremes. The point of contact is the thesis according
to which one is never aware of a *subject* of experience. The thesis in
question does not pertain to the perception of one's body. If we are
identical with our bodies and if, as all but skeptics hold, we do perceive
our bodies, then, whether we realize it or not, we also perceive ourselves. The thesis has to do, rather, with what we find when we consult
the data of our immediate experience, or when, as Hume puts it, we
enter most intimately into what we call ourselves. Thus Sartre seems
to say that, although we may apprehend things that are *pour-soi*, things
that are manifested or presented to the self, we cannot apprehend the
self to which, or to whom, they are manifested—we cannot apprehend

Reprinted by permission from *Philosophy and Phenomenological Research,*
30 (1969), 7–21.

the self as it is in itself, as it is *en-soi*.[1] And Russell has frequently said that the self or subject is not "empirically discoverable"; Carnap expressed what I take to be the same view by saying that "the given is subjectless."[2] I say it is unfortunate that the members of the two great philosophical traditions happen to meet at this particular point, of all places. For at this particular point, if I am not mistaken, both groups have lost their way.

Both traditions trace their origins, in part, to Hume.[3] I suggest that, if we are to find out what went wrong, we should turn back to the doctrines of Hume, where we will find a number of obvious, but disastrous, mistakes.

II

The first mistake was a very simple one. Consider the following remark which may be found in Hume's "Abstract of a Treatise of Human Nature": "As our idea of any body, a peach, for instance, is only that of a particular taste, color, figure, size, consistency, etc., so our idea of any mind is only that of particular perceptions without the notion of anything we call substance, either simple or compound."[4] This seems to me to be very obviously false, but many philosophers, I am afraid, tend all too easily and unthinkingly to assume that it is true.

Is it true that our idea of a peach is an idea only of a particular taste, color, figure, size, consistency, and the like, and analogously that our ideas of such things as ships, trees, dogs, and houses are ideas only of the particular qualities or attributes that these things are commonly said to have? One is tempted to say instead that our idea of a peach is an idea of *something that has* a particular taste, color, figure, size, and consistency; and analogously for the other familiar physical things. But even this is not quite right. Our idea of a peach is not an idea of something that *has* the particular qualities, say, of sweetness, roundness, and fuzziness. It is an idea of something that *is* sweet and round and fuzzy.

More pedantically, our idea of a peach is an idea of an individual x such that x is sweet and x is round and x is fuzzy. By thus using variables and adjectives, we express the fact that the object of our idea is not the set of qualities sweetness, roundness, and fuzziness, but the concrete thing that *is* sweet and round and fuzzy. We also make clear, what is essential to our idea of a peach, that the thing that is round is the *same* thing as the thing that is sweet and also the *same* thing as the thing that is fuzzy.

Leibniz saw the point very clearly when he criticized Locke's *Essay*

Concerning Human Understanding. When we consider any person or thing, he said, what comes before the mind is always a *concretum* and not a set of abstract things or qualities; we may consider something as knowing, or something as warm, or something as shining, but we do not thereby consider knowledge, or warmth, or light. The abstract things, he noted, are far more difficult to grasp than are the corresponding *concreta.*[5]

I cannot help but think that the point is a simple-minded one. "Our idea of a peach is not an idea of sweetness, roundness, and fuzziness . . .; it is an idea of something that is sweet and also round and also fuzzy. . . ." One would not have even thought of mentioning it, had not philosophers denied it and constructed fantastic systems on the basis of its negation. A small mistake at the outset, as the Philosopher said, turns out to be a great one in the end.

If the first part of Hume's observation is wrong, then so is the second. Our idea of "a mind" (if by "a mind" we mean, as Hume usually does, a person, or a self) is not an idea only of "particular perceptions." It is not the idea of the perception of love or hate and the perception of cold or warmth, much less an idea of love or hate and of heat or cold. It is an idea of that which loves or hates, and of that which feels cold or warm (and, of course, of much more besides). That is to say, it is an idea of an x such that x loves or x hates, and such that x feels cold and x feels warm, and so forth.

III

I would say that a second error we find in Hume's writings, and in the writings of those who follow him with respect to the observability of the self, has to do with the interpretation of certain data or evidence. Hume argued, it will be recalled, that he and most of the rest of mankind are "nothing but a bundle or collection of different perceptions." And in support of this "bundle theory," he cites a kind of *negative* evidence. He tells us, with respect to a certain proposition, that he *has* certain evidence for saying that he has *no* evidence for that proposition. But when he cites the evidence he *has* for saying that he has *no* evidence for the proposition, he seems to presuppose, after all, that he *does* have evidence for the proposition.

What Hume said was this: "For my part, when I enter most intimately into what I call *myself,* I always stumble on some particular perception or other, of heat or cold, light or shade, love or hatred, pain or pleasure. I never can catch *myself* at any time without a perception, and never can observe anything but the perception."[6] As Professor

Price once observed, it looks very much as though the self that Hume professed to be unable to find is the one that he finds to be stumbling— to be stumbling onto different perceptions.[7] How can he say that he does not find himself—if he is correct in saying that he finds himself to be stumbling and, more fully, that he finds himself to be stumbling on certain things and not to be stumbling on certain other things?

We must take care not to misinterpret the difficulty. The difficulty is *not* that, in formulating his evidence for the "bundle theory" of the self, Hume presupposes that there *is* a self. For this presupposition, that there is a self, is not contrary to what Hume wishes to say. The "bundle theory," after all, is not intended to *deny* that there is a self. It is intended merely to say *what* the self is and what it is not. There is a self, or there are selves, according to Hume, and what selves are are " bundles of perceptions."

The difficulty is that Hume appeals to a certain evidence to show that there are only perceptions, and that when he tells us what this evidence is, he implies not only (i) that there is, as he puts it in his example, heat or cold, light or shade, love or hatred, but also (ii) that there is *someone* who finds heat or cold, light or shade, love or hatred, and moreover (iii) that the one who finds heat or cold is *the same as* the one who finds love or hatred and *the same as* the one who finds light or shade, and finally (iv) that this one does not in fact stumble upon anything but perceptions. It is not unreasonable to ask, therefore, whether Hume's report of his fourth finding is consistent with his report of the second and the third. If Hume finds what he says he finds, that is to say, if he finds not only perceptions, but also that *he* finds them and hence that there is *someone* who finds them, how can his premisses be used to establish the conclusion that he never observes anything but perceptions?

One may protest: "But this is not fair to Hume. It is true that, in reporting his data, he used such sentences as 'I stumble on heat or cold' and 'I never observe anything but perceptions.' He did not need to express himself in this way. Instead of saying 'I stumble on heat or cold' or 'I find heat or cold,' he could have said, more simply, 'Heat or cold is found.' And instead of saying 'I never observe anything but perceptions,' he could have said, more simply, 'Nothing but perceptions are found.' He could have reported his data in this way; and had he done so, he would not have presupposed that there exists an x such that x succeeds in finding certain things and such that x fails to find certain others."

But *could* Hume have reported his data in this selfless way? Let us recall that his findings are both positive and negative and let us consider just the negative ones. It is one thing to say, modestly and empirically, "I find nothing but impressions or perceptions." It is quite another thing to say, rashly and nonempirically, "Nothing but perceptions or impressions are found." The point will be clearer, perhaps, if we consider another type of example. I may look around the room and, from where I stand, fail to see any cats or dogs in the room. If I express this negative finding modestly and empirically, I will simply say "I do not see any cats or dogs." But if I say, solely on the basis of my negative observation, "No cats or dogs are seen," then I will be speaking rashly and nonempirically and going far beyond what my data warrant. How do I know what other people or God may find? And how can I be sure that there are no unseen dogs or cats? Clearly Hume would not have been justified in saying "Nothing but impressions are to be found." And in fact he made no such subjectless report. He said, referring to himself, that *he* found nothing but impressions.

The difficulty may be put briefly. It is essential to Hume's argument that he report not only what it is that he finds but also what it is that he fails to find. But the two types of report are quite different. The fact that a man finds a certain proposition p to be true does warrant a subjectless report to the effect that p is true. For finding that p is true entails that p is true. But the fact that he fails to find a certain proposition q to be true does not similarly warrant any subjectless report about q. For one's failure to find that q is true entails nothing about the truth of q. The fact that a man fails to find that q is true entitles him to say only that *he*, at least, does not find that q is true. And this would not be a subjectless report.

What Hume found, then, was not merely the particular perceptions, but also the fact that *he* found those perceptions as well as the fact that *he* failed to find certain other things. And these are findings with respect to himself.

Referring to the view that the self is a substance persisting through time, Hume said that we have no "idea of self, after the manner it is here explain'd. For from what impression cou'd this idea be derived?" Given our first two general points, could the proper reply be this—that one may derive the idea of such a self from any impression whatever?[8]

IV

Why, then, is it so tempting to agree with Hume in his report of his negative findings?

I think we tend to reason as follows. We suppose—mistakenly, it seems to me—that if we do perceive or apprehend ourselves in our immediate experience, then such perception or apprehension must resemble in essential respects the way in which we perceive or apprehend the familiar external things around us. And then we find, in fact, that we do *not* perceive or apprehend ourselves in our immediate experience in the way in which we apprehend or perceive the familiar external things around us.

Thus whenever we perceive—say, whenever we *see*—a spatial object, then the object that we perceive has certain proper parts that we perceive and certain proper parts that we do not perceive. Suppose, for example, that I see a cat. Then we may say of that side of the cat that faces me that I see certain parts of *it*. But I do not see *all* the parts of the side that faces me (I do not see those parts I would see if I took a closer look or used a microscope) and I do not see *any* of the parts of the insides or any of the parts of the sides that face away. One of the results in changes of spatial perspective is that certain parts become seen that had not been seen before and certain parts cease to be seen that had been seen before. And so, if the distance between our body and the perceived object is not too great, we may now look over this part and now look over that. We may look more closely and scrutinize—and this means that we may now see smaller parts that we had not seen before. And analogously for the nonvisual senses. But whatever our perspective upon the perceived object may be, there will always be certain parts of the perceived object that we do perceive and certain other parts of the perceived object that we do not perceive. Moreover, and this is the important point about external perception, if we know that we are perceiving a certain physical thing, then we are also capable of knowing that we are perceiving something that is just a proper part of that thing. But the situation is different when we perceive ourselves to be thinking.

I may perceive myself to be thinking and know that I am doing so and yet be unable to know whether I am perceiving any proper part of anything that I am perceiving. It may be, for all anyone knows, that whenever I perceive myself to be thinking, I *do* perceive some part of myself. This would be the case, for example, if I could not perceive myself to be thinking without perceiving some part of my body, and if, moreover, I were identical with my body or with that part of my body. But it is not true that, whenever I perceive myself to be thinking I thereby perceive what I can *know* to be a part of myself. (Whether or not I am identical with my body or with some part of my body, I do not *know* that I am.) In short, to know that I perceive the cat to be standing, I must know that I perceive a proper part of the cat, or of the cat's body; but to know that I perceive myself to be thinking I need *not* know that I perceive what is a proper part of myself. Sartre said that the ego is "opaque"; I would think it better to say that the ego is "transparent."[9]

Ordinarily if a man can be said to perceive *that* the cat is standing, then he may also be said more simply, to perceive *the cat.* But the locution "S perceives that *a* is F" does not entail the simpler locution "S perceives *a.*"[10] Compare "Jones perceives that Smith is no longer in the room" and "Jones perceives that the lights are on next door." Could it be, then, that a man might be aware of himself as experiencing *without* thereby being aware of himself? Let us approach this question somewhat obliquely, by recalling still another familiar source of philosophical perplexity.

During the first third of this century, British and American philosophers were perplexed about the status of what they called "sense-data" or "appearances." They thought, for example, that if a man were to walk around a table, while focusing upon the white tablecloth on the top, he could experience a great variety of sense-data or appearances. Some of these entities would be rectangular like the table-top itself; they would be the ones he would sense if he were able to get his head directly above the table and then look down. Most of them, however, would be rhomboids of various sorts. If the lighting conditions were good and the man's eyes in proper order, most of the appearances would be white, like the table-cloth. But if the man were wearing rose-colored glasses, he might sense appearances that were pink, or if he were a victim of jaundice, he might sense appearances that were yellow. The other senses, as well as imagination, were thought to bring us into relation with still other types of appearances or sense-datum.

The nature and location of these strange entities, as we all know, caused considerable puzzlement, and imposing metaphysical systems were constructed to bring them together with the rest of the world. I am sure that it is not necessary now to unravel all the confusions that were involved in this kind of talk, for the sense-datum theory has been ridiculed about as thoroughly as any philosophical theory can be ridiculed. But we should remind ourselves of one of these confusions— another very simple mistake. It was the mistake that H. A. Pritchard had in mind, I think, when he used the expression, "the sense-datum fallacy."[11]

It was assumed that, if a physical thing appears white or rhomboidal or bitter to a man, then the man may be said to sense or to be aware of an appearance that *is* white, or an appearance that *is* rhomboidal, or an appearance that *is* bitter. It was assumed that if a dog presents a canine appearance, then the dog presents an appearance that *is* canine. (Thus Professor Lovejoy wrote: "No man doubts that when he brings to mind the look of a dog he owned when a boy, there is something of a canine sort immediately present to and therefore compresent with his consciousness, but that it is quite certainly not that dog in the flesh."[12]) And then it was assumed, more generally, that whenever we have a true statement of the form "Such-and-such a physical thing appears, or looks, or seems - - - to Mr. Jones," we can derive a true statement of the form "Mr. Jones is aware of an appearance which is in fact - - -." But this assumption is quite obviously false.[13] Consider the following reasoning, which would be quite sound if the assumption were true: "I know that Mr. Simione is an Italian and that he is also old and sick. I saw him this morning and I can assure you that he also appeared Italian, and he appeared old and sick as well. Therefore Mr. Simione presents an appearance which, like himself, really is Italian, and he also presents an appearance which, like himself once again, is old and sick." It is absurd to suppose that an appearance, like a man, may be Italian or old or sick; it is absurd to suppose that an appearance may be a dog; and, I think, it is equally absurd to suppose that an appearance, like a tablecloth, may be rectangular, or pink, or white.

When the philosophers thus talked about sense-data or appearances, they were, however, inadequately, reporting *something* that is very familiar to us all, and we should not let their philosophical theories blind us to the fact that there is such a going-on as sensation and that the experiences we have when we observe the familiar things around us may be varied merely by varying the conditions of observation. Suppose now we were considering this fact on its own, and without any thoughts about Hume's theory or about Hume on the observability of the self. How would we describe it if we are to avoid the absurdities of the sense-datum fallacy?

I think we would do well to compare the "grammar" of our talk about appearances with that of our talk about feelings. Consider the sentence "I feel depressed." It does not imply that there is a relation between me and some other entity; it simply tells one *how* I feel. The adjective "depressed," in other words, does not describe the *object* of my feeling; rather, if I may put the matter so, it describes the *way* in which I feel. It could be misleading, therefore, to use the longer sentence "I have a depressed feeling" in place of the shorter "I feel depressed." For the longer sentence, "I have a depressed feeling," has a syntactical structure very much like that of "I have a red book." Hence one might be led to suppose, mistakenly, that it implies the existence of *two* entities, one of them *had* by the other. And taking "a depressed feeling" as one would ordinarily take "a red book," one might also be led to suppose, again mistakenly, that the feeling which the person is said to have resembles the person in being *itself* depressed. I say one *might* be misled in these ways by the sentence "I have a depressed feeling," though I do not know of anyone who ever *has* been misled by it.

It is quite obvious, I think, that in such sentences as "I feel depressed" the verb is used to refer to a certain type of *undergoing*. This undergoing is what traditionally has been called being in a conscious state, or being in a sentient state. And the adjective, in such sentences as "I feel depressed," is used to qualify the verb and thus to specify further the type of undergoing to which the verb refers. The adjective could be said to function, therefore, as an adverb. Thus the sentences "I feel depressed" and "I feel exuberant" are related in the way in which "He runs slowly" and "He runs swiftly" are related, and not in the way in which "He has a red book" and "He has a brown book" are related. In short, *being depressed* is not a predicate of the feeling; rather, *feeling depressed* is a predicate of the man.

I suggest that the sentences "I am aware of a red appearance" and "I am experiencing a red sensation" are to be interpreted in the way in which we interpreted "I have a depressed feeling" and "I feel a wave of exuberance." Despite their grammatical or syntactical structure, neither sentence tells us that there are *two* entities which are related in a certain way. They, too, ascribe a certain type of undergoing to the person. The adjective "red," in "I am aware of a red appearance" and "I am experiencing a red sensation," is used adverbially to qualify this undergoing.[14] It would be useful, at least for the purposes of philosophy, if there were a verb—say, the verb "to sense"—which we could use to refer to this type of undergoing. Then we could say that such a sentence as "I am aware of a red appearance" tells us *how* the subject is sensing. Or, better perhaps, it tells us in which *way* he is sensing. For to be aware of "a red appearance," presumably, is to sense in one of the ways that people do when, under favorable conditions, they look at objects that are red.[15] (If we may say that a man "senses redly," may we also say that he "senses rhomboidally," or "senses rectangularly"? There is no reason why we may not—especially if we can identify one's sensing rhomboidally, or one's sensing rectangularly, with one of the ways in which a person might be expected to sense if, under favorable conditions, he were to observe objects that are rhomboidal, or rectangular.)

We may summarize this way of looking at the matter by saying that so-called appearances or sense-data are "affections" or "modifications" of the person who is said to experience them.[16] And this is simply to say that those sentences in which we seem to predicate properties of appearances can be paraphrased into other sentences in which we predicate properties only of the self or person who is said to sense those appearances. If this is correct, then appearances would be paradigm cases of what the Scholastics called *"entia entis"* or *"entia per accidens."* These things are not entities in their own right; they are "accidents" of other things. And what they are accidents *of* are persons or selves.

It is interesting to note, in passing, that Hume himself criticizes the view that appearances are modifications of persons or selves—and that, in doing so, he provides us with an excellent example of the sense-datum fallacy. First he notes the absurdity of Spinoza's view, according to which such things as the sun, moon, and stars, and the earth, seas, plants, animals, men, ships, and houses are in fact only "modifications" of a single divine substance. And then he argues that, if this Spinozistic view is absurd, then so, too, is the view that "impressions" or "ideas" are only modifications of the self. But the reason he cites for this seems clearly to be based upon the sense-datum fallacy. For, he says, when I consider "the universe of thought, or my impressions and ideas," I then "observe *another* sun, moon, and stars and earth, and seas, covered and inhabited by plants and animals; towns, houses, mountains, rivers . . ."[17] In other words, if a real dog cannot be a modification of God, then an appearance of a dog cannot be a modification of me!

Why this way of interpreting appearances? For one thing, it seems to me, we multiply entities beyond necessity if we suppose that, in addition to the person who is in a state of undergoing or sensing, there is a certain *further* entity, a sense-datum or an appearance, which is the object of that undergoing or sensing. And for another thing, when we do thus multiply entities beyond necessity, we entangle ourselves in philosophical puzzles we might otherwise have avoided. ("Does the red sense-datum or appearance have a back side as well as a front side? Where is it located? Does it have any weight? What is it made of?")

And now we may return to the question that brought us to this consideration of appearances: "Could it be that a man might be aware of himself as experiencing without thereby being aware of himself?" If what I have suggested is true, then the answer should be negative. For in being aware of ourselves as experiencing, we are, *ipso facto,* aware of the self or person—of the self or person as being affected in a certain way.

This is not to say, of course, that we do not *also* perceive or observe external physical things. It is in virtue of the ways in which we are "appeared to" by the familiar things around us, of the ways in which we are affected or modified by them, that we perceive them to be what they are. If, under the right conditions, the fields should appear green to me, then I would *see* the fields to be green.[18] And at the same time

I could become directly aware of—immediately acquainted with—the fact that I myself am modified or affected in a certain way.

If what I have been saying is true, then there are two rather different senses in which we may be said to apprehend ourselves.

The first type of apprehension was what Hume himself reported— that *he* found heat or cold, that *he* found light or shade, and that *he* did not find himself, at least in the sense in which he found heat or cold and light or shade. He found, to repeat, that there was *someone* who found heat or cold, that this same someone found light or shade, and that this same someone did not in the same sense find himself. That we apprehend ourselves in this first sense would seem to be clear whatever view we may take about the nature of appearances, or of being appeared to.

And if the particular view of appearances that I have proposed is true, then we apprehend ourselves in still another sense. For if appearances, as I have said, are "accidents" or "modifications" of the one who is appeared to, then *what* one apprehends when one apprehends heat or cold, light or shade, love or hatred, is simply oneself. Whether one knows it or not, one apprehends *oneself* as being affected or modified.

The two points may be summarized by returning to the figure of the bundle theory. One may ask, with respect to any bundle of things, what is the nature of the bundle and what is the nature of the bundled. What is it that holds the particular items together, and what are the particular items that are thus held together? Now, according to the second of the two points that I have just made, the items within the bundle are nothing but states of the person. And according to the first point, as we may now put it, what ties these items together is the fact that that same self or person apprehends them all. Hence, if these two points are both correct, the existence of particular bundles of perceptions presupposes in two rather different ways the existence of selves or persons that are not mere bundles of perceptions.

V

And there is one more simple mistake that we may note briefly.

One may grant everything that I have said ("Yes, there are those senses in which one may be said to observe the self") and yet insist, at the same time, that we really know nothing about the self which we do thus observe ("Knowing what states the self is in does not entitle you to say that you know anything about the self"). What kind of reasoning is this?

Let us recall what Kant says about the subject of experiences— about the I which, as he puts it, we "attach to our thoughts." Whenever we find ourselves thinking or judging, he said, we attach this I to the thinking or judging, and then we say to ourselves, or think to ourselves, "I think" and "I judge." Yet, although we manage somehow to "attach" the I to the thinking or judging, we do so "without knowing anything of it, either by direct acquaintance or otherwise." The I is known, he says, "only through the thoughts which are its predicates, and of it, apart from them, we cannot have any concept whatever."[19]

Kant seems to be telling us this: even if there is a subject that thinks, we have no acquaintance with it at all and we can never know what it is. And his *reason* for saying we have no acquaintance with it at all and can never hope to know what it is, would seem to be this: the most we can ever hope to know about the subject is to know what predicates it has—to know what properties it exemplifies; and apart from this—apart from knowing what predicates it has or what properties it exemplifies—we can never know anything of it at all.

During the latter part of the nineteenth century and the early part of the twentieth century, there were philosophers in the idealistic tradition who reasoned in a similar way. They seemed to say that we can never hope to have any genuine knowledge of reality. The most we can hope to know about any particular thing is to know what some of its properties or attributes are. But, they said, we can never know what the thing is that has those properties or attributes.[20] In the present century, Jean-Paul Sartre has despaired because we seem to have no access to the *en-soi*—to the self as it is in itself. Whatever we find is at best only *pour-soi*—the self as it manifests itself to itself.[21]

Despite the impressive tradition, should we not say that this is simply a muddle? The reasoning seems to be as follows.

It is noted (i) that a person can be acquainted with the subject of experience to the extent that the subject manifests itself as having certain properties. (And this we can readily accept—provided we take care not to commit at this point the first of the errors on our list above. What we should say is not merely that the subject manifests certain qualities; it is rather that the subject manifests itself *as having* certain qualities.)

Then one adds an "only" to what has just been said. One now says (ii) that a person can be acquainted with the subject of experience *only* to the extent that the subject manifests itself as having certain qualities. The "only" is thought to express a limitation. (But consider the limitation expressed by the "only" in "One can see what is only an object of sight" and "Trees are capable of growing only below the timberline.")

From these two premisses one then deduces (iii) that no one has acquaintance with the self as it is in itself.

But it is not difficult to see, it seems to me, that (ii) does not add anything to (i), and that (iii), moreover, does not follow from (i) and (ii). Indeed I would say, not only that (iii) does *not* follow from (i) and (ii), but also that the *negation* of (iii) *does* follow from (i) and (ii). From the fact that we are acquainted with the self as it manifests itself as having certain qualities, it follows that we are acquainted with the self as it is in itself. Manifestation, after all, is the converse of acquaintance: x manifests itself to y, if, and only if, y is acquainted with x. How can a man be acquainted with *anything* unless the thing manifests or presents itself to him? And how can the thing manifest or present itself unless it manifests or presents itself as having certain qualities or attributes?[22]

The muddle was neatly put by Wittgenstein. We are all naked, he said, underneath our clothes.

NOTES

1. Jean-Paul Sartre, *L'être et le néant* (Paris: Gallimard, 1948), pp. 134, 145, 652–53.

2. Bertrand Russell, *Logic and Knowledge* (London: Allen & Unwin, 1956), p. 305; Rudolf Carnap, *Der logische Aufbau der Welt* (Berlin: Weltkreis, 1928), pp. 87–90.

3. Husserl wrote of Hume: "Dessen genialer *Treatise* hat bereits die Gestalt einer auf strenge Konsequenz bedachten struckturellen Durchforschung der reinen Erlebnissphäre, [ist] in gewisser Weise also der erste Anhieb einer 'Phänomenologie'." E. Husserl, *Phänomenologische Psychologie* (The Hague: Nijhoff, 1962), p. 264. The members of the Vienna Circle traced the "scientific world-outlook" to the same source; see *Wissenschaftliche Weltauffassung* (Vienna: Wolf, 1929), p. 12.

4. Hume, *An Enquiry Concerning Human Understanding,* ed. Charles W. Hendel (New York: Liberal Arts Press, 1955), p. 194.

5. *New Essays Concerning Human Understanding,* Book II, Ch. 23, sec. 1. ". . . c'est plutôt le *concretum* comme savant, chaud, luisant, qui nous vient dans l'esprit, que les *abstractions* ou qualités (car se sont elles, qui sont dans l'object substantiel et non pas les Idées) comme savoir, chaleur, lumière, etc. qui sont bien plus difficiles à comprendre" (Leibniz, *Opera philosophica,* ed. Erdmann, p. 272).

6. *A Treatise of Human Nature,* Book I, Part iv, sec. vi ("Of Personal Identity").

7. H. H. Price, *Hume's Theory of the External World* (Oxford: Clarendon, 1940), pp. 5–6; compare P. F. Strawson, *Individuals* (London: Methuen, 1959), pp. 96–97.

8. Compare Brentano's remark about the concept of substance: "Those who say that this concept is not included in any perception are very much mistaken. Rather it is given in every perception, as Aristotle had said . . ." (Franz Brentano, *Versuch über die Erkenntnis* [Leipzig: Meiner, 1925], p 30). Referring to the thesis according to which we know only "phenomena" and not "things in themselves," he wrote: "But what does it mean to say that one apprehends something as a *phenomenon?* Simply that one apprehends it as a phenomenon to the one for whom it is a phenomenon. This means, in other words, that one apprehends that one is presented with or intuits the phenomenon in question and hence that one apprehends the one to whom it is presented, the one who intuits. But this is a thing that one apprehends in itself" (*Die vier Phasen der Philosophie* [Leipzig: Meiner, 1926], p. 92; my italics). But Brentano also held, unfortunately, that so-called external perception is "blind."

9. Jean-Paul Sartre, *The Transcendence of the Ego,* trans. Forrest Williams and Robert Kirkpatrick (New York: Farrar, Straus & Cudahy, 1957), p. 51.

10. I am indebted to Keith Lehrer for this point. I am also indebted to him and to Charles Caton for criticisms enabling me to correct an earlier version of this paper.

11. See H. A. Prichard, *Knowledge and Perception* (Oxford: Clarendon, 1950), p. 213. Compare his much earlier *Kant's Theory of Knowledge* (Oxford: Clarendon, 1909) and his "Appearances and Reality," first published in *Mind* in 1906 and republished in *Realism and the Background of Phenomenology,* ed. R. M. Chisholm (Glencoe: Free Press, 1960), pp. 143–50.

12. A. O. Lovejoy, *The Revolt Against Dualism* (New York: Norton, 1930), p. 305.

13. "The general rule which one may derive from these examples is that the propositions we ordinarily express by saying that a person A is perceiving a material thing M, which appears to him to have the quality x, may be expressed in the sense-datum terminology by saying that A is sensing a sense-datum s, which really has the quality x, and which belongs to M." A. J. Ayer, *The Foundations of Empirical Knowledge* (New York: Macmillan, 1940), p. 58.

14. Compare Thomas Reid: "When I am pained, I cannot say that the pain I feel is one thing, and that my feeling of it is another thing. They are one and the same thing and cannot be disjoined even in the imagination" (*Essays on the Intellectual Powers,* Essay I, Chapter 1).

15. But there are still two alternative interpretations of such expressions as "sensing red" or "sensing redly." (i) We might define "sensing redly" in such a way that our definiens makes explicit reference to things that are red. Using the expression in this way, we may say that no one can *know* that he is sensing redly unless he *also* knows something about red things and the ways in which they appear. Or, more empirically, (ii) we might take "sensing redly" as undefined, in which case we may say that a man who knows nothing about red things may yet know that he is sensing redly. For in this second case, the proposition connecting his sensing redly with one of the ways in which people are appeared to by things that are red would be a proposition that is synthetic.

16. And so are "thoughts." Consider a man who is thinking about a unicorn. We may say, if we choose, that he has a thought and that his thought is about a unicorn. Whether or not we say, as Meinong did, that the situation involves a relation between an existent man and a nonexistent unicorn, we should not say that the situation involves a relation between a man and a certain independent entity which is his thought. There is not *one* relation between a man and a thought, and then a *second* relation between the thought and a nonexistent unicorn. Though we say, quite naturally, that the unicorn is the object of the man's thought, it would be less misleading to say that the unicorn is the object of the man to the extent that he is thinking. For thinking, like feeling and like what we may call "sensing," is an affection, modification, or state of the man. Compare Leibniz's assertion that ideas are "affections or modifications of the mind," in his "Thoughts on Knowledge, Truth, and Ideas" in Erdmann's edition of Leibniz's *Opera philosophica*, p. 81. Sartre, too, has said that the appearance is "the manner in which the subject is affected [la manière dont le sujet est affecté]," but he adds, unfortunately, that "consciousness has nothing of the substantial [la conscience n'a rien de substantiel]." *L'être et le néant*, pp. 13, 23.

17. *Treatise of Human Nature*, Book I, Part IV, sec. v; my italics.

18. I have tried to say what these conditions are in *Theory of Knowledge* (Englewood Cliffs: Prentice-Hall, 1966), Chapter Three, and in *Perceiving: A Philosophical Study* (Ithaca: Cornell University Press, 1957). An excellent summary of this view of perception may be found in Keith Lehrer, "Scottish Influences on Contemporary American Philosophy," *The Philosophical Journal*, 5 (1968), 34–42.

19. "Durch dieses Ich oder Er oder Es (das Ding), welches denkt, wird nun nichts weiter als ein transcendentales Subject der Gedanken vorgestellt = X, welches nur durch die Gedanken, die seine Prädicate sind, erkannt wird, und wovon wir abgesondert niemals den mindesten Begriff haben können. . . . Es ist aber offenbar, dass das Subject der Inhärenz durch das dem Gedanken angehängte Ich nur transcendental bezeichnet werde, ohne die mindeste Eigenschaft desselben zu bemerken, oder überhaupt etwas von ihm zu kennen oder zu wissen." *Kritik der reinen Vernunft*, A346, A355 (ed. N. Kemp Smith, pp. 331, 337).

20. Compare A. E. Taylor: What we call one *thing* is said, in spite of its unity, to have many *qualities*. It is, *e.g.*, at once round, white, shiny, and hard, or at once green, soft, and rough. Now, what do we understand by the *it* to which these numerous attributes are alike ascribed, and how does it possess them? To use the traditional technical names, what is the substance to which the several qualities belong or in which they inhere, and what is the manner of their *inherence?* . . . The notion *that* things have a that or substance prior to their *what* or quality . . . is thus unmeaning as well as superfluous" (*Elements of Metaphysics* [5th ed.; London: Methuen, 1920], pp. 128, 133).

21. "Ainsi le Pour-soi en tant qu'il n'est pas *soi* est une présence à soi qui manque d'une certaine présence à soi et c'est en tant que manque de cette présence qu'il est présence à soi." *L'être et le néant*, p. 145.

22. Compare Leibniz again: "En distinguant deux choses dans la substance, les attributs ou prédicats et le sujet commun de ces prédicats, ce n'est pas merveille, qu'on ne peut rien concevoir de particulier dans ce sujet. Il le faut bien, puisqu'on déjà séparé tous les attributs, où l'on pourroit concevoir quelque détail. Ainsi demander quelque chose de plus dans ce pur *sujet en général,* que ce qu'il faut pour concevoir que c'est la même chose (p. e. qui entend et qui veut, qui imagine et qui raisonne) c'est demander l'impossible et contrevenir à sa propre supposition, qu'on a faite en faisant abstraction et concevant separément le sujet et ses qualités ou accidens" (*Opera philosophica,* ed. Erdmann, p. 272). *New Essays Concerning Human Understanding,* Book II, Ch. 23, sec. 2.

12

Biology and the Soul

JOHN HICK

Claremont Graduate School

THROUGHOUT THE HISTORY of the relation between science and religion the scientific theories that have proved most stimulating or most challenging to religious thought have arisen at different times within different aspects of the study of nature. In the sixteenth century, for example, the main source was astronomy; in the nineteenth century, paleontology and zoology. Fifty years ago, when Sir Arthur Eddington was writing on the nature of the physical world, his own subject of physics was the science with the most striking implications for philosophy and religion. New concepts of matter and energy, relativity theory, the principle of indeterminacy, the concept of complementarity were raising issues and suggesting speculations transcending the physicist's strict field of enquiry. Since then the biological sciences have taken a great leap forward and it is from that quarter that many of the most intriguing and disturbing new questions, and hints of possible theoretical reformulations, are coming today. Accordingly in this paper I want to look at certain aspects of contemporary biological theory in so far as these may be relevant to the religious understanding of man.

At first sight it might seem that the focus of religious interest in biology should be within the field of bio-medicine. For this has recently given rise to books with such dramatic titles as *The Biological Time-Bomb, The Bio-Medical Revolution,* and *Fabricated Man.* The reference here is to startling new methods, actual and prospective, of controlling the human genetic material, with such possibilities opening before us as the deliberate deletion of defective or unwanted genes, the cloning of human beings by producing any number of individuals with precisely the same genetic code, and even the engineering of a

Reprinted by permission from Professor Hick's *Biology and the Soul* (Cambridge: Cambridge University Press, 1972).

structure of chromosomes to a chosen specification, thereby determining in advance the characteristics which members of the next generation are to have. Within the sphere of bio-medicine itself this sudden explosion of both theory and technology can no doubt properly be described as a revolution. But whilst these new developments throw light on the nature of the human being they do not appear to throw *new* light. They dramatise facts that were already available to us, even though it may well be that many, at any rate in the theological world, had not sufficiently taken account of these facts and are now being prompted for the first time to give serious thought to their implications. But we already knew, or should have known, that the individual's psycho-physical nature is determined by a particular contingent knot, as it were, in the criss-crossing threads of genetic material as it passes down the generations. What is novel is the possibility of deliberate interference with some of the details of the process. But this new technological capability, immensely important though its practical consequences must be, does not call for a new and different picture of human nature. Men have always to some extent influenced the selection of genetic material which was to form their successors. The general fact of the transmission of characteristics has been evident from time immemorial and people have long taken account of it, in so far as they wished to, in their choice of mates. And long before there was a science of genetics mankind knew of the effects of inbreeding and had evolved prohibitions against incest and against marriage within the same tribe or extended family. Again, the thought of cloning, although revolutionary indeed as a new bio-medical technique, is not new as a fact; for we have long been familiar with the phenomenon of identical twins, and identical twins as two expansions of the same genetic code are natural clones.

Thus whilst the bio-medical revolution represents a tremendous development in technology, bringing with it immense new ethical and social problems, it does not appear to me that it revolutionises our conception of man—unless this had remained largely unaffected by the implications of the wider advances in biology during the last thirty or so years.

What then are the aspects of modern biological knowledge that bear upon the religious conception of man's nature? The particular aspect which I propose to single out for consideration is the rapidly growing understanding of the genetic process by which each of us has been uniquely formed.

What, I think, particularly strikes a layman like myself as he attends to the geneticists' descriptions of the formation of an individual, with his particular set of characteristics, is the enormous number of possible genetic codes out of which the one that is actualised has been apparently randomly selected. Behind each of us there lies an astronomical number of other possible arrangements of the same genetic material. If we confine attention for the moment to the father's contribution, there are some three to six hundred million sperm which he has launched on their race to reach and fertilise the ovum. These, say, four hundred million sperm are not however completely alike, as identical copies of each other. On the contrary, each one is unique. In each case of the millions of formations of sperm cells, through the complex process of meiotic division, a partial reshuffling of the parental genes takes place, producing unpredictable results. For a slightly different course is taken each time in the selection and arrangement of the twenty-three out of the father's forty-six chromosomes that are to constitute his sperm's contribution to the full genetic complement of a member of the next generation. The ordering of the chromosomes in the sperm cell is itself partly a matter of chance, depending upon which out of each pair of chromosomes happens to be on one side and which on the other when the two sets separate to form new daughter cells. But the degree of randomness thus introduced (calculated as at least eight million potentially different arrangements of the chromosomes) is multiplied by scattered breaks and re-formations in many of the chromosomes in the "crossing over" stage of meiosis. So it is that, of the four hundred or so million sperm cells, each carries, in its details, a different genetic code. But only one out of these four hundred million can win the race to the ovum. Nevertheless this vast number is needed if the ovum is to be fertilised. A single sperm, unsupported by its millions of companions, would not be able to make its way across the mucus area at the entry to the uterus, up the Fallopian tube, and through the membrane protecting the egg. For each sperm produces only a minute quantity of the enzyme which digests the material to be penetrated, and so only by the combined action of many is a way made through to the target. Thus hundreds of millions of sperm perish in enabling one of their number to continue in the life of a new organism.

Approximately half of the four hundred million or so sperm carry the Y sex chromosome which will result in a male embryo whilst the other half carry the X chromosome which will produce a female. And each of these two hundred or so million possible or notional males, and likewise each of the two hundred or so million possible females, is unique, differing from its potential brothers and sisters in a number of ways, mostly slight but some, arising from major mutations, far from slight.

But this family of some four hundred million potential children, only one of whom, normally, will actually be conceived and born, is really only a family of four hundred million half-children! For the sperm carries only half the total complement of human chromosomes. Meanwhile the mother has been producing egg cells, though not nearly as many as the father produces sperm cells, and usually only one at a time. Each of these eggs contains its own unique arrangement of chromosomes, and the vast range of possibilities which lies behind the formation of a particular sperm cell likewise lies behind the formation of a particular egg cell. Thus there is a further enormous multiplication in the possibilities out of which a particular genetic code is selected when it is actualised by the union of a particular sperm with a particular egg. And it is out of this astronomical number of different potential individuals, exhibiting the kinds of differences that can occur between children of the same parents, that a single individual comes into being.

Thus the process whereby a particular genetic code begins to be actualised includes, according to the geneticists, crucial elements of randomness. I presume, however, that this is not randomness in the sense in which the term is used in quantum physics. The units with which the geneticists is dealing are not the sub-atomic particles to which indeterminacy is ascribed in quantum physics, but complex molecular structures; and I take it that their individual behaviour is not unpredictable in principle, as is apparently the case with electrons, but only unpredictable in fact. I assume, then, that the "shuffling" of the chromosomes in the formation of sperm cells, and again the selection of one sperm out of some four hundred million different ones to fertilise the ovum, are random processes only in the sense that they fall outside the scope of human predictability. Presumably the continuity of cause and effect, and hence of predictability in principle, is not suspended; but the processes involved are so complex that their outcome is unpredictable in practice, and in that sense random from the human point of view. In the ensuing discussion, I shall accordingly be using the term "random" in this weaker sense.

What, then, are the implications for the nature and status of the human being of this area of randomness in the selection of a genetic code for actualisation?

From a religious point of view the randomness out of which we have come is an aspect of the radical contingency of our existence. We are not "self-made men" but products of forces at work outside and prior to ourselves. Our dependent status is ultimately traced by religious thought back to the dependence of the entire natural order upon the creative will of God. Thus far, then, our emergence out of the bewildering randomness of the genetic process is not in tension with the basic theological conception of man's absolute contingency as a created being. But on the other hand, when we stress the randomness of the process whereby we, rather than countless other possible human be-ings, have come into existence, we must ask how well this agrees with our traditional religious conception of the human being as an immortal soul. Let us therefore now turn to this idea of the soul and to the bearings of modern biological knowledge upon it.

Many different concepts of soul occur across the world and through the centuries; but in this paper I must confine myself very largely to the one prevalent in our Western and Christian culture. Here the soul has generally been equated with the individual self-conscious mind or ego, together (as we must add today) with such unconscious mental life as is able directly to influence it. Whether the soul as self is mental and in principle detachable from the body as the more Platonic strands of Western thought have affirmed, or whether it is a psycho-physical entity with indissoluble mental and bodily aspects as the more Biblical and Aristotelian strands of thought claim, is thus far an open question, and one which I shall not in this paper make any moves towards set-tling. This means leaving open also the issue between two different conceptions of human immortality, one attributing it to the mind, sepa-rated from the body at death, and the other attributing it to a re-created body-mind totality. Although I cannot defend this view here, I believe that both ideas are in fact conceptually viable: however, this is not the subject of the present paper. What is important at the moment is that in Christian thought the soul, whether detachable from the body or including the body, is the conscious, responsible ego which earns re-wards and deserves penalties, which becomes or fails to become con-scious of God by faith, and which is to enjoy hereafter the blissful life of heaven or (in the patristic and medieval tradition) to suffer eternal loss of heaven. For it is clear from Jesus' parables that the self which faces judgment after death is the same self that has lived on earth in the body. Dives and Lazarus remember their former lives and are aware of the moral appropriateness of the consequences which they encounter after death. In the parable of the sheep and the goats those who stand before the King for judgment are conscious of being the same persons who had served or who had rejected "the least of his brethren" in their earthly need. In short, the self that is to be judged hereafter and rewarded or punished in respect of choices made in this life is the conscious, responsible personal mind and will who has made those fateful choices.

Leaving aside, as I am doing in this discussion, the question of immortality, there is thus far nothing in the religious way of speaking about the self that need disturb the biologist; for the conscious personal self undoubtedly exists, and all that is so far in question is the proposal to call it (together with its unconscious depths) the soul. But a doctrine has been historically connected with this which the biologist may well feel obliged to question, namely that the soul is a metaphysical entity which has become linked with a developing human body either at conception or at some point between conception and birth. The religious heart of this doctrine is that souls—or selves—have been individually created by God for eternal fellowship with Himself. As one of the documents of the First Vatican Council of 1869–70 declared, in reaffirmation of an ancient doctrine, "God creates a new soul and infuses it into each man" (Schema of the Dogmatic Constitution on the Principal Mysteries of the Faith, Ch. 2). The point that I want to make about this traditional doctrine is that if it is to have any substance at all, so as to be worth either affirming or denying, it must entail that there are characteristics of the self which are derived neither from genetic inheritance nor from interaction with the environment. If the divinely infused soul is to have a function in the economy of human existence it must form the inner core of individuality, the unique personal essence of a human being, providing the ultimate ground of human individuation. For there would be no value in postulating a soul without content, as a mere qualityless psychic atom. Souls would not then differ from one another except numerically. Such a conception of the soul as featureless would deny all point to the notion that God has specifically created each individual human soul and endowed it with a body. For it would then be the body rather than the soul that acts as the principle of individuation, constituting one person as different from another. Everything that is distinctive of the individual would be a product of heredity and environment, and the soul would be a needless concept. It would refer at most to a metaphysical substratum, in Locke's disparaging phrase a "something, I know not what," underlying our mental life, but not to an essential self carrying the unique characteristics of the individual.

If then there is to be any point to the traditional claim that souls are special divine creations, they must be the bearers of some at least of the distinctive characteristics of the individual. These characteristics must however be ones which do not arise from the inherited genetic code. For the picture of God creating souls and infusing them into bodies involves a distinction between those characteristics that are carried by the soul and those that are already built genetically into the developing structure of the body. Thus to speak of the divinely inserted soul as any kind of real entity, playing a real part in the makeup of the human being, is to commit oneself to the claim that there are innate personal qualities which have not been inherited from one's parents but which have been implanted by God.

However, this idea of innate but not inherited qualities is highly problematic. It has long been clear, even without benefit of special scientific knowledge, that children are almost as often like a parent in basic personality traits as in purely physical characteristics. Thus it is evident that some aspects at least of one's innate character are inherited even if there should be still other aspects which represent a special divine creation. And the delimiting of the boundaries of the soul thus called for by common observation is now carried much further by the modern science of genetics. For many characteristics which might have been supposed to be attributes of the soul are now believed to be part of our genetic inheritance. Dr. Darlington lists as follows those characteristics of the human individual to which there is an important genetic contribution:

> Our hormone systems and hence our temperament, whether sanguine, melancholy or choleric; timid or courageous; observant, reflective, or impulsive. Hence our social habits, whether solitary or gregarious; affectionate or morose; settled or nomadic, useful, deranged, or criminal; hence also the company we keep, and our capacities and directions of love and hatred. Our perception and appreciation of taste, touch and smell, sound and colour, harmony and pattern. Our capacities and qualities for memory, whether for sound, sight, number or form. Our kinds and degrees of imagination, visualization and reason. Hence our understanding of truth and beauty. Hence also our educability in all these respects, or lack of it, and our capacity and choice in work and leisure.[1]

It is also maintained by many geneticists that various special aptitudes, such as those for mathematics and for music, are inherited. But if our temperamental type and character structure, our intelligence, our imaginative range and special aptitudes, all develop in directions and within limits that are genetically prescribed, it seems that this pre-established framework of possibility must be distinct from the divinely infused soul, as part of its earthly environment. The body to which the soul is said to be attached already contains genetic information selecting the personal characteristics that can and cannot be developed; and this information is part of the range of environmental factors amid which the soul is placed when it is inserted into the body. In other words we must bracket inheritance and environment together as jointly constituting the soul's world. Inheritance provides the more immediate and individual setting of the soul's life, whilst the external world provides its less immediate and more public environment—the two being of course in continual interaction and jointly constituting the concrete situation within which the soul carries on its own life of spiritual progress or regress.

The problem facing the traditional soul-theorist, then, is to indicate an adequate content and function for the soul after genetics has pared so much away.

It might be suggested, for instance, that the soul is the locus of our personal and moral freedom. The question of freewill, like that of immortality, is an immensely intricate and important subject which I cannot attempt to discuss adequately in passing. I must be content to say that I am here presupposing a real though limited human freedom; for it appears to me that however strong the arguments for universal determinism may be, the claim to know that one is totally determined must always be a self-refuting claim, since the concept of knowledge embedded in our language presupposes that the cognising mind is not totally determined. Assuming, then, the (limited) freedom of the will, might we not identify the soul with this freedom? The answer, I think, is that freedom as a purely formal condition would not be sufficient to constitute the soul as the principal of individuation. We must add to it at least the basic personal nature in virtue of which the individual exercises his freedom in one way rather than in another. We should then identify the soul with certain fundamental dispositional character-istics—presumably our basic moral and religious attitudes. Thus a con-temporary believer in the soul as a special divine creation seems led to the position that the attributes of the soul are the moral and spiritual dispositions which operate in worshipping, in valuing, in making ethical choices, and in adopting purposes and selecting ends. He will add that the material and social world of which we are a part sets the problems in the tackling of which the soul's earthly career consists, whilst our genetic inheritance, together with our acquired training and experi-ence, furnish the tools with which we tackle those problems. Of course this distinction between problems and tools, or between the outer and inner layers of the soul's environment, is only a relative one; for the tools can themselves create problems by giving rise both to good op-portunities (for example, to develop an artistic talent) and to evil temp-tations (for example, to be dominated by some animal drive or passion). Nevertheless on this view the soul remains as the core of the individual's being, his essential nature, consisting in a structure of personal and ethical characteristics which inhere, presumably, in some kind of persisting substratum or frame.

This notion coincides to a striking extent with the Indian idea of the *linga śarīra,* or "subtle body," as the bearer of a structure of moral and spiritual dispositions which are progressively reincarnated in a succession of psycho-physical individuals; and it may be instructive at this point to take note of this important Eastern conception.

The complex and profound philosophy of Advaita Vedanta, which represents the most influential school of Hindu thought today, speaks of innumerable eternal *jīvātmans* (or *jīvas*), which are ultimately identical with the Absolute, *Brahman,* but which now exist in a state of illusory separation from *Brahman.* And in this state of illusory separation the *jīvātman* has a number of bodies, thought of on the analogy of a series of sheaths enclosing the blade of a sword. One of these is the gross or physical body *(sthūla śarīra)* which begins to be formed at conception and begins to disintegrate at death. Another is the *liṅga śarīra,* usually translated, in a way that can easily mislead the Western reader, as the "subtle body." This is not a body at all in the customary Western sense of something occupying space (although in some Western esoteric and theosophical thought it is identified with an etheric or astral body). It is however bodily in the traditional Indian philosophical sense of lacking consciousness. It consists of a developing structure of moral and spiritual dispositions which is reincarnated by becoming successively associated with a series of physical bodies, whose growth it influences. As regards its contents the Eastern *liṅga śarīra* is thus the equivalent of the Western soul when this latter has been reduced by the pressures of genetic science. It differs however in that in the West the soul is not usually thought of as reincarnating in a series of bodies; and also in that the soul, as the phenomenal ego, has the quality of self-consciousness. The *liṅga śarīra,* on the other hand, is a constellation of basic dispositional characteristics which goes on from life to life but which is other than a person in that it lacks consciousness and memory. Thus the idea of the *liṅga śarīra* or subtle body is akin to the late C. D. Broad's concept of the psychic factor.[2] Broad developed this notion largely to provide a possible explanation of the phenomenon of trance mediumship. When an individual dies the mental aspect of his being persists, not however as a complete conscious personality but as a constellation of mental elements—dispositions, memories, desires, fears, etc.—constituting a "psychic factor," which may hold together for a considerable time or may perhaps quickly disintegrate into scattered fragments. Broad suggested that such a psychic grouping, sufficiently cohesive to be identified as consisting of the memories and dispositional characteristics of a particular deceased individual, may become connected with a medium in a state of trance, thus generating a temporary conscious personality which is a conflation of certain persisting mental elements of the deceased together with the living structure of the medium. The theory of reincarnation can be seen as taking this concept further—as indeed Broad himself noted[3]—and claiming that the psychic factor which separates itself from the body at death subsequently becomes fused, not with the developed life-structure of a medium but with the still undeveloped life-structure of a human embryo. It then influences the growth of the embryo as a factor additional to its physical inheritance and its external environment.

This Indian concept of the *linga śarīra* agrees with the Western idea of the soul in that both postulate the existence of innate dispositional characteristics which are not part of the individual's genetic inheritance; and the same biological comment will be relevant to both. To what extent then, let us ask, is such an idea compatible with the account of man given today by the biological sciences?

The answer seems to be that whilst it cannot be proved that the two factors of heredity and environment between them account for the entire range of the individual's character traits, it certainly seems that they do and that there is no need to postulate in addition the influence of a soul or of a *linga śarīra* carrying basic dispositional characteristics either supplied directly by God or developed in previous earthly lives. There is a good deal of established correlation, for example, between experiences in early childhood and later moral attitudes; and without spelling this out in detail it can be said to give rise to a reasonable and fairly strong presumption that a man's moral character is formed during this life, partly through learning and partly through his reactions to environmental events. His inherited physical makeup enters into the process, of course, as its necessary basis, but there is so much evidence of the formation of moral character through the individual's interaction with environmental circumstances that there is no need to postulate either ethical genes or innate ethical dispositions carried in a soul or in a *linga śarīra*. From this point of view such hypotheses are redundant. At the same time, so long as we assume the reality of human freedom it must be impossible decisively to rule out these ancient conceptions. For the basic moral and spiritual dispositions which are said to inhere in the *linga śarīra*, or in the soul, presumably actualise themselves in our fundamental choices as free beings. And so long as one man freely differs from another in his moral and spiritual attitudes it will be impossible to disprove the claim that this difference is due to basic dispositions which were either formed in previous lives or implanted by God at conception.

In view of the empirically unverifiable and unfalsifiable nature of the hypothesis the main debate has to take place on other grounds; and I shall pursue it, to the limited extent that time allows, in relation to the Western idea of the soul as a metaphysical reality which God individually creates and attaches to the body. Let us ask what hangs upon the traditional insistence on the special divine creation of each soul. What has been the significance of this idea within the Western religious understanding of man? This understanding, as it has developed through the centuries and as it has worked itself out in Western theology and philosophy, social theory and the arts, and as it has been expressed in the organisation of human life in the West, sees the human being as a unique individual who is valued and sustained by his Creator and who in virtue of his relationship to the Eternal may enjoy an eternal life. Religiously the high point in the development of the idea occurred in Jesus' teaching about God as our heavenly Father, who knows each of His human children so that the very hairs of our heads are numbered. He cares for each like a shepherd seeking a lost sheep, or a needy widow searching for a lost coin, and He lavishes His love upon each like a father welcoming back a long-lost son. Philosophically, the high points are Plato's *Phaedo,* affirming the immortality of the rational soul; Descartes' *cogito ergo sum,* taking the existence of individual self-consciousness as the necessary starting point for thought; and Kant's founding of ethics upon the free, autonomous person seen as an end in himself. In politics the idea of the inherent value of the individual human being has worked itself out in the demise of feudalism, the eventual abandonment of slavery, the gradual growth of democracy, and in the advance of women towards full social equality with men. The common theme here is the idea of the unique value of the human person as a child of God, made in the divine image, and destined to an eternal life in fellowship with God.

Now how does this Western religious valuation of man agree with the random character of the process of meiosis in the formation of the individual sperm cell, and again with the randomness of the process by which one out of some four hundred million sperm, carrying their variant genetic codes, is selected to fertilise an ovum?

We have seen the difficulty of basing the traditional Christian valuation of man upon a doctrine of the special divine creation of the soul, defined as a metaphysical entity which God infuses into the body. Are we then to justify the high value of the human individual by saying that the hand of God has been secretly at work guiding the details of the meiotic division of cells, or in aiding one particular divinely favoured sperm in its race to the ovum? To suppose this would be to invoke the "God of the gaps" in a way which recent Christian thought has for the most part renounced. God, we have been saying, is the Lord of the natural order, not merely of the gaps in the natural order. To be sure, such miraculous divine interventions cannot be disproved. If there were sufficient other grounds for maintaining such a doctrine one could maintain it. But are there good grounds for insisting upon the special divine determination of the initial genetic makeup of each human person? Is there not on the contrary a strong theological motive for *not* wanting to maintain this? For do we really want to claim that

God has specifically bestowed upon each individual the basic good and bad tendencies of character with which he is born? Would not this make Him the direct author of evil as well as good? Is it not therefore theologically preferable, as well as being in accordance with the picture indicated by the human sciences, to say that the genetic process includes a genuine element of unpredictable contingency?

We are not here in the realm of strict proof and disproof but of an informal process of probing in search of a more adequate conceptualisation of the data. As well as setting aside, as I think we must, the temptation to locate God's activity in the still unmapped intricacies of the genetic process we have also seen reasons to abandon the notion of the soul as a divinely created and infused entity. This does not however necessarily mean that the term "soul" can no longer have any proper use, but only that it should not be used as the name of a spiritual substance or entity. But we also commonly use the word as an indicator of value. "Save Our Souls," for example, the time-honoured distress signal at sea, is not only a call for help but at the same time a reminder of the value of those in danger, as fellow human beings and children of God. "You have no soul," said to an uncultured philistine, means that he lacks the capacity to appreciate value. When something is "soul-destroying" it is not the person but his values that are in danger of destruction. "Soul food" indicates the meaning of the food as a symbol of the values of the black community in its search for human justice and civil rights. And indeed I think it will be found that the word normally has a valuational connotation. It could well be that this feature of our ordinary use of the term points to its primary meaning within human communication and that the metaphysical theories of the soul are secondary, as speculative or mythological ways of affirming the unique value of the individual human person. If we accept this suggestion we shall not be opposed to the continued use of soul-language, or even to speaking of human beings as souls, or as having souls, in distinction perhaps from the lower animals; for such language will express that sense of the sacredness of human personality and of the inalienable rights of the human individual which we have already seen to be the moral and political content of the Western idea of the soul. Nor need the Church cease to strive to save souls; but the souls to be saved are simply people and not some mysterious religious entity attached to them. To speak of man as a soul is, then, to speak mythologically, but in a way which is bound up with important practical attitudes and practices. The myth of the soul expresses a faith in the intrinsic value of the human individual as an end in himself.

But let us now ask whether this valuation of humanity can continue to be religiously based once the metaphysical conception of the soul has been abandoned? In attempting to answer this question it will perhaps be best to speak from within the context of Christianity, as the faith which has historically particularly cherished and taught the idea of the sacredness of human personality and the value of men and women as rational and moral ends in themselves. Speaking, then, as a Christian theologian it appears to me that the time has come to complete the shift of emphasis in theological anthropology from the question of origins to the question of ends. It is not what man has come from but what he is going to that is important. We must assume that the picture being built up by the natural sciences of the origin of man, both individually and as a species, is basically correct and is progressively becoming more adequate and accurate as research continues. According to this picture, life on this planet began with natural chemical reactions occurring under the influence of radiations falling upon the earth's surface. Thus began the long, slow evolution of the forms of life, a process which has eventually produced man. And each human individual comes about through the partially random selection of a specific genetic code out of the virtually infinite range of possibilities contained even in the portion of genetic material lodged in his parents. This is, in broadest outline, the picture of man's beginning as it emerges from the physicists', chemists', and biologists' researches. And Christianity does not offer a different or rival account of our human origins. It says, in its Hebraic myth of man's genesis, that he has been created out of the dust of the earth; but the details of the creative process, from dust to the immensely complex religious and valuing human animal, are for the relevant sciences to trace.

If soul-language expresses a valuation of mankind, so that the soul is the human person seen and valued in this special way, then we must be prepared to renounce the idea that whereas the body has been produced by natural processes the soul has been produced by a special act of divine creation. We have to say that the soul is a divine creation in the same sense as the body—namely through the instrumentality of the entire evolution of the universe and within this of the development of life on our planet. Distinctively human mentality and spirituality emerges, in accordance with the divine purpose, in complex bodily organisms. But once it has emerged it is the vehicle, according to Christian faith, of a continuing creative activity only the beginnings of which have so far taken place.

The Biblical myth of Adam and Eve and their fall from grace, as it came to be interpreted in the mainstream of Christian tradition, cannot readily accommodate this conception. If we insist upon continuing to use the language of that tradition we have to qualify the meanings of our key terms until we no longer mean what other people hear us say.

We find ourselves speaking of a fall which did not take place at any point in time, from a paradisiacal condition which did not exist at any place. But on the other hand the alternative strand of Christian theology, which began as early as the second century A.D. in the work of some of the Greek Fathers, such as Irenaeus and Clement of Alexandria, can readily absorb the new empirical knowledge. Irenaeus distinguished between what he called the image of God and the likeness of God, and suggested a two-stage conception of the divine creation of man. The *imago dei* is man's nature as a rational, personal, and moral animal. Thus man in society, man the ethical being, man the creator of culture, exists in the image of God. It has taken many hundreds of millions of years of biological evolution to produce him, and yet even so he is only the raw material for the second stage of the creative process, which is the bringing of man, thus fashioned as person in the divine image, into the finite likeness of God. This latter state represents the fulfillment of the potentialities of our human nature, the completed humanisation of man in a society expressing mutual love. Whereas the first stage of creation is an exercise of divine power, the second stage is of a different kind; for the creatures who have been brought into existence in God's image are endowed with a real though limited freedom, and their further growth into the finite divine likeness has to take place through their own free responses within the world in which they find themselves. Human life as we know it is the sphere in which this second stage of creation is taking place; though it seems clear that if the process is to be completed it must continue in each individual life beyond our earthly three-score years and ten, whether by the survival of the mind after the death of the body or through the reconstitution of the total psycho-physical being. I have already declared my belief that both of these futures are conceivable—though I must in this context simply say this, without supporting arguments.

Such a religious interpretation of human existence is teleologically and indeed eschatologically oriented. The final meaning of man's life lies in the future state to which, in God's purpose, he is moving. And from this point of view man's lowly beginnings are not in contradiction with his high destiny. The origin of life out of the dust of the earth— or rather, in the scientifically preferred metaphor, out of the primeval soup; the emergence of the human species from lower forms of life to form the apex of the evolutionary process; the programming of the individual genetic code through an unpredictable rearranging of the chromosomes; and again the unpredictable selection of one out of hundreds of millions of sperm to fertilise an ovum, are the ways in which man has been brought upon the stage. They do not in themselves tell us what he is here for or what his future is to be. The religions, however, do profess to tell us this. The Christian faith, in the Irenaean version of its theology, suggests that this complex process whereby man has been created as a personal being in God's image makes possible his cognitive freedom in relation to his Maker. Finding himself as part of an autonomous natural order, whose functioning can at all points be described without reference to a creator, man is not compelled to be conscious of God. He has an innate tendency to interpret his experience religiously, but if he gives rein to this tendency his resulting awareness of the divine is the kind of partially free awareness that we call faith. Thus man's existence as part of the natural order ensures his status as a relatively free being over against the infinite Creator. The finite creature is able to come as a (relatively) free person to know and worship God because his embeddedness in nature has initially set him at an epistemic distance from the divine Being. Thus the process by which men and women are formed may be understood, theologically, as an aspect of the self-governing natural order on which man's cognitive freedom in relation to his Creator depends. God wills to exist an autonomous physical universe, structured towards the production of rational and personal life—an organisation of matter which may well be developing not only on this earth but on millions of planets of millions of stars in millions of galaxies. The virtually infinite complexity of the cosmic process makes it to us, as finite minds existing within it, a law-governed realm which however includes randomness and unpredictability in its details; and as such it constitutes an environment within which we may grow as free beings towards that fullness of personal life, in conscious relationship to God, which (according to Christianity) represents the divine purpose for us.

NOTES

1. C. D. Darlington, *Genetics and Man* (London: Allen & Unwin, 1964), p. 241.

2. *The Mind and Its Place in Nature* (London: Routledge & Kegan Paul, 1925), pp. 536ff.

3. Ibid., p. 551.

13

My Death

A. J. Ayer

Oxford University

What I Saw When I Was Dead

My FIRST ATTACK of pneumonia occurred in the United States. I was in hospital for ten days in New York, after which the doctors said that I was well enough to leave. A final X-ray, however, which I underwent on the last morning, revealed that one of my lungs was not yet free from infection. This caused the most sympathetic of my doctors to suggest that it would be good for me to spend a few more days in hospital. I respected his opinion but since I was already dressed and psychologically disposed to put my illness behind me, I decided to take the risk. I spent the next few days in my stepdaughter's apartment, and then made arrangements to fly back to England.

When I arrived I believed myself to be cured and incontinently plunged into an even more hectic social round than that to which I had become habituated before I went to America. Retribution struck me on Sunday, May 30. I had gone out to lunch, had a great deal to eat and drink and chattered incessantly. That evening I had a relapse. I could eat almost none of the food which a friend had brought to cook in my house.

On the next day, which was a bank holiday, I had a longstanding engagement to lunch at the Savoy with a friend who was very anxious for me to meet her son. I would have put them off if I could, but my friend lives in Exeter and I had no idea how to reach her in London. So I took a taxi to the Savoy and just managed to stagger into the lobby. I could eat hardly any of the delicious grilled sole that I ordered,

---

This article appeared in the August 28, 1988, issue of the *Sunday Telegraph*. It is reprinted with the permission of the Sunday Telegraph Ltd.

but forced myself to keep up my end of the conversation. I left early
and took a taxi home.

That evening I felt still worse. Once more I could eat almost none
of the dinner another friend had brought me. Indeed she was so
alarmed by my weakness that she stayed overnight. When I was no
better the next morning, she telephoned to my general practitioner and
to my elder son Julian. The doctor did little more than promise to try
to get in touch with the specialist, but Julian, who is unobtrusively
very efficient, immediately rang for an ambulance. The ambulance
came quickly with two strong attendants, and yet another friend, who
had called opportunely to pick up a key, accompanied it and me to
University College Hospital.

I remember very little of what happened from then on. I was taken
to a room in the private wing, which had been reserved for me by a
specialist, who had a consulting room on the same floor. After being
X-rayed and subjected to a number of tests which proved beyond question that I was suffering from pneumonia, I was moved into intensive
care in the main wing of the hospital.

Fortunately for me, the young doctor who was primarily responsible
for me had been an undergraduate at New College, Oxford, while I
was a Fellow. This made him extremely anxious to see that I recovered;
almost too much so, in fact he was so much in awe of me that he
forbade me to be disturbed at night, even when the experienced sister
and nurse believed it to be necessary.

Under his care and theirs I made such good progress that I expected
to be moved out of intensive care and back into the private wing within
a week. My disappointment was my own fault. I did not attempt to eat
the hospital food. My family and friends supplied all the food I needed.
I am particularly fond of smoked salmon, and one evening I carelessly
tossed a slice of it into my throat. It went down the wrong way and
almost immediately the graph recording my heart beats plummeted.
The ward sister rushed to the rescue, but she was unable to prevent
my heart from stopping. She and the doctor subsequently told me
that I died in this sense for four minutes, and I have no reason to
disbelieve them.

The doctor alarmed my son Nicholas, who had flown from New
York to be at my bedside, by saying it was not probable that I should
recover and, moreover, that if I did recover physically it was not probable that my mental powers would be restored. The nurses were more
optimistic and Nicholas sensibly chose to believe them.

I have no recollection of anything that was done to me at that time.
Friends have told me that I was festooned with tubes but I have never
learned how many of them there were or, with one exception, what

purpose they served. I do not remember having a tube inserted in my throat to bring up the quantity of phlegm which had lodged in my lungs. I was not even aware of my numerous visitors, so many of them, in fact, that the sister had to set a quota. I know that the doctors and nurses were surprised by the speed of my recovery and that when I started speaking, the specialist expressed astonishment that anyone with so little oxygen in his lungs should be so lucid.

My first recorded utterance, which convinced those who heard it that I had not lost my wits, was the exclamation: "You are all mad." I am not sure how this should be interpreted. It is possible that I took my audience to be Christians and was telling them that I had not discovered anything "on the other side." It is also possible that I took them to be sceptics and was implying that I had discovered something. I think the former is more probable as in the latter case I should properly have exclaimed "We are all mad." All the same, I cannot be sure.

The earliest remarks of which I have any cognisance, apart from my first exclamation, were made several hours after my return to life. They were addressed to a French woman with whom I had been friends for over fifteen years. I woke to find her seated by my bedside and starting talking to her in French as soon as I recognised her. My French is fluent and I spoke rapidly, approximately as follows: "Did you know that I was dead? The first time that I tried to cross the river I was frustrated, but my second attempt succeeded. It was most extraordinary, my thoughts became persons."

The content of those remarks suggests that I have not wholly put my classical education behind me. In Greek mythology the souls of the dead, now only shadowly embodied, were obliged to cross the river Styx in order to reach Hades, after paying an obol to the ferryman, Charon. I may also have been reminded of my favourite philosopher, David Hume, who during his last illness, a "disorder of the bowels," imagined that Charon, growing impatient, was calling him "a lazy loitering rogue." With his usual politeness, Hume replied that he saw without regret his death approaching and that he was making no effort to postpone it. This is one of the rare occasions on which I have failed to follow Hume. Clearly I had made an effort to prolong my life.

The only memory that I have of an experience closely encompassing my death, is very vivid. I was confronted by a red light, exceedingly bright, and also very painful even when I turned away from it. I was aware that this light was responsible for the government of the universe. Among its ministers were two creatures who had been put in charge of space. These ministers periodically inspected space and had recently carried out such an inspection. They had, however, failed to do their work properly, with the result that space, like a badly fitted jigsaw puzzle, was slightly out of joint.

A further consequence was that the laws of nature had ceased to function as they should. I felt that it was up to me to put things right. I also had the motive of finding a way to extinguish the painful light. I assumed that it was signalling that space was awry and that it would switch itself off when order was restored. Unfortunately, I had no idea where the guardians of space had gone and feared that even if I found them I should not be allowed to communicate with them. It then occurred to me that whereas, until the present century, physicists accepted the Newtonian severance of space and time, it had become customary, since the vindication of Einstein's general theory of relativity, to treat space-time as a single whole. Accordingly I thought that I could cure space by operating upon time.

I was vaguely aware that the ministers who had been given charge of time were in my neighbourhood and I proceeded to hail them. I was again frustrated. Either they did not hear me, or they chose to ignore me, or they did not understand me. I then hit upon the expedient of walking up and down, waving my watch, in the hope of drawing their attention not to my watch itself but to the time which it measured. This elicited no response. I became more and more desperate, until the experience suddenly came to an end.

This experience could well have been delusive. A slight indication that it might have been veridical has been supplied by my French friend, or rather by her mother, who also underwent a heart arrest many years ago. When her daughter asked her what it had been like, she replied that all that she remembered was that she must stay close to the red light.

On the face of it, these experiences, on the assumption that the last one was veridical, are rather strong evidence that death does not put an end to consciousness. Does it follow that there is a future life? Not necessarily. The trouble is that there are different criteria for being dead, which are indeed logically compatible, but may not always be satisfied together.

In this instance, I am given to understand that the arrest of the heart does not entail, either logically or causally, the arrest of the brain. In view of the very strong evidence in favour of the dependence of thoughts upon the brain, the most probable hypothesis is that my brain continued to function although my heart had stopped.

If I had acquired good reason to believe in a future life, it would have applied not only to myself. Admittedly, the philosophical problems of justifying one's confident belief in the existence and contents of other minds has not yet been satisfactorily solved. Even so, with the possible exception of Fichte—who complained that the world was his idea but may not have meant it literally—no philosopher has acquiesced in solipsism; no philosopher has seriously asserted that of all the objects in the universe, he alone was conscious. Moreover it is commonly taken for granted, not only by philosophers, that the minds of others bear a sufficiently close analogy to one's own. Consequently, if I had been vouchsafed a reasonable expectation of a future life, other human beings could expect one too.

Let us grant, for the sake of argument, that we could have future lives. What form could they take? The easiest answer would consist in the prolongation of our experiences, without any physical attachment. This is the theory that should appeal to radical empiricists. It is, indeed, consistent with the concept of personal identity which was adopted both by Hume and by William James, according to which one's identity consists, not in the possession of an enduring soul but in the sequence of one's experiences, guaranteed by memory. They did not apply their theory to a future life, in which Hume at any rate disbelieved.

For those who are attracted by this theory, as I am, the main problem, which Hume admitted that he was unable to solve, is to discover the relation, or relations, which have to be held between experiences for them to belong to one and the same self. William James thought that he had found the answers with his relations of the felt togetherness and continuity of our thoughts and sensations, coupled with memory, in order to unite experiences that are separated in time. But while memory is undoubtedly necessary, it can be shown that it is not wholly sufficient.

I myself carried out a thorough examination and development of the theory in my book *The Origins of Pragmatism*. I was reluctantly forced to conclude that I could not account for personal identity without falling back on the identity, through time, of one or more bodies that the person might successively occupy. Even then, I was unable to give a satisfactory account of the way in which a series of experiences is tied to a particular body at any given time.

The admission that personal identity through time requires the identity of a body is a surprising feature of Christianity. I call it surprising because it seems to me that Christians are apt to forget that the resurrection of the body is an element in their creed. The question of how bodily identity is sustained over intervals of time is not so difficult. The answer might consist in postulating a reunion of the same atoms, perhaps in there being no more than a strong physical resemblance, possibly fortified by a similarity of behaviour.

A prevalent fallacy is the assumption that a proof of an afterlife would also be a proof of the existence of a deity. This is far from being the case. If, as I hold, there is no good reason to believe that a god created or presides over this world, there is no good reason to believe that a god created or presides over the next world, on the unlikely supposition that such a thing exists. It is conceivable that one's experiences in the next world, if there are any, will supply evidence of a god's existence, but we have no right to presume on such evidence, when we have not had the relevant experiences.

It is worth remarking, in this connection, that the two most important Cambridge philosophers in this century, J. E. McTaggart and C. D. Broad, who have believed, in McTaggart's case that he would certainly survive his death, in Broad's that there was about a fifty-percent probability that he would, were both of them atheists. McTaggart derived his certainty from his metaphysics, which implied that what we confusedly perceive as material objects, in some case housing minds, are really souls, eternally viewing one another with something of the order of love.

The less fanciful Broad was impressed by the findings of psychical research. He was certainly too intelligent to think that the superior performances of a few persons in the game of guessing unseen cards, which he painstakingly proved to be statistically significant, has any bearing on the likelihood of a future life. He must therefore have been persuaded by the testimony of mediums. He was surely aware that most mediums have been shown to be frauds, but he was convinced that some have not been. Not that this made him optimistic. He took the view that this world was very nasty and that there was a fair chance that the next world, if it existed, was even nastier. Consequently, he had no compelling desire to survive. He just thought that there was an even chance of his doing so. One of his better epigrams was that if one went by the reports of mediums, life in the next world was like a perpetual bump supper at a Welsh university.

If Broad was an atheist, my friend Dr Alfred Ewing was not. Ewing, who considered Broad to be a better philosopher than Wittgenstein, was naif, unworldly even by academic standards, intellectually shrewd, unswervingly honest and a devout Christian. Once, to tease him, I said: "Tell me, Alfred, what do you most look forward to in the next world?" He replied immediately: "God will tell me whether there are *a priori* propositions." It is a wry comment on the strange character of our subject that this answer should be so funny.

My excuse for repeating this story is that such philosophical problems as the question whether the propositions of logic and pure mathematics are deductively analytic or factually synthetic, and, if they are analytic, whether they are true by convention, are not to be solved by acquiring more information. What is needed is that we succeed in obtaining a clearer view of what the problems involve. One might hope to achieve this in a future life, but really we have no good reason to believe that our intellects will be any sharper in the next world, if there is one, than they are in this. A god, if one exists, might make them so, but this is not something that even the most enthusiastic deist can count on.

The only philosophical problem that our finding ourselves landed on a future life might clarify would be that of the relation between mind and body, if our future lives consisted, not in the resurrection of our bodies, but in the prolongation of the series of our present experiences. We should then be witnessing the triumph of dualism, which Descartes thought that he had established. If our lives consisted in an extended series of experiences, we should still have no good reason to regard ourselves as spiritual substances.

So there it is. My recent experiences have slightly weakened my conviction that my genuine death, which is due fairly soon, will be the end of me, though I continue to hope that it will be. They have not weakened my conviction that there is no god. I trust that my remaining an atheist will allay the anxieties of my fellow supporters of the British Humanist Association, the Rationalist Press Association and the South Place Ethical Society.

Postscript to a Postmortem

My purpose in writing a postscript to the article about my 'death', which I contributed to the 28 August issue of the *Sunday Telegraph,* is not primarily to retract anything that I wrote or to express my regret that my Shakespearian title for the article, 'That undiscovered country', was not retained, but to correct a misunderstanding to which the article appears to have given rise.

I say 'not primarily to retract' because one of my sentences was written so carelessly that it is literally false as it stands. In the final paragraph, I wrote, 'My recent experiences have slightly weakened my conviction that my genuine death . . . will be the end of me.' They have not and never did weaken that conviction. What I should have said and would have said, had I not been anxious to appear undogmatic, is that my experiences have weakened, not my belief that there is no life after death, but my inflexible attitude towards that belief.

Reprinted by permission from *The Spectator,* October 15, 1988.

Previously my interest in the question was purely polemical. I wished to expose the defects in the positions of those who believed that they would survive. My experiences caused me to think that it was worth examining various possibilities of survival for their own sakes. I did not intend to imply that the result of my enquiry had been to increase the low probability of any one of them, even if it were granted that they had any probability at all.

My motive for writing the original article was twofold. I thought that my experiences had been sufficiently remarkable to be worth recording, and I wished to rebut the incoherent statement, which had been attributed to me, that I had discovered nothing 'on the other side'. Evidently, my having discovered something on the other side was a precondition of my having completed the journey. It follows that if I had discovered nothing, I had not been there; I had no right to imply that there was a 'there' to go to. Conversely, if there was evidence that I had had some strange experiences, nothing followed about their being 'another side'. In particular, it did not follow either that I had visited such a place, or that I had not.

I said in my article that the most probable explanation of my experiences was that my brain had not ceased to function during the four minutes of my heart arrest. I have since been told, rightly or wrongly, that it would not have functioned on its own for any longer period without being damaged. I thought it so obvious that the persistence of my brain was the most probable explanation that I did not bother to stress it. I stress it now. No other hypothesis comes anywhere near to superseding it.

Descartes has few contemporary disciples. Not many philosophers of whatever persuasion believe that we are spiritual substances. Those who so far depart from present fashion as not to take a materialistic view of our identities are most likely to equate persons with the series of their experiences. There is no reason in principle why such a series should not continue beyond the point where the experiences are associated with a particular body. Unfortunately, as I pointed out in my article, nobody has yet succeeded in specifying the relations which would have to hold between the members of such a series for them to constitute a person. There is a more serious objection. Whatever these relations were, they would be contingent; they might not have obtained. But this allows for the possibility of there being experiences which do not belong to anybody; experiences which exist on their own. It is not obvious to me that this supposition is contradictory; but it might well be regarded as an irreparable defect in the theory.

If theories of this type are excluded, one might try to fall back on the Christian doctrine of the resurrection of the body. But, notoriously, this too encounters a mass of difficulties. I shall mention only one or two of them. For instance, one may ask in what form our bodies will be returned to us. As they were when we died, or when we were in our prime? Would they still be vulnerable to pain and disease? What are the prospects for infants, cripples, schizophrenics, and amnesiacs? In what manner will they survive?

'Oh, how glorious and resplendent, fragile body, shalt thou be!' This body? Why should one give unnecessary hostages to fortune? Let it be granted that I must reappear as an embodied person, if I am to reappear at all. It does not follow that the body which is going to be mine must be the same body as the one that is mine now; it need not be even a replica of my present body. The most that is required is that it be generically the same; that is, a human body of some sort, let us say a standard male model not especially strong or beautiful, not diseased, but still subject to the ills that flesh is heir to. I am not sure whether one can allow oneself a choice with respect to age and sex. The preservation or renewal of one's personal identity will be secured, in this picture, by a continuity of one's mental states, with memory a necessary, but still not a sufficient, factor. I am assuming now that these mental states cannot exist on their own; hence, the need for a material body to sustain them.

I am far from claiming that such a scenario is plausible. Nevertheless it does have two merits. The first is that we are no longer required to make sense of the hypothesis that one's body will be reconstructed some time after it has perished. The second is that it does not force us to postulate the existence of a future world. One can live again in a future state of the world that one lives in now.

At this point it becomes clear that the idea of the resurrection of the body had better be discarded. It is to be replaced by the idea of re-incarnation. The two are not so very distinct. What gives the idea of re-incarnation the advantage is that it clearly implies both that persons undergo a change of bodies and that they return to the same world that they inhabited before.

The idea of re-incarnation is popular in the East. In the West it has been more generally ridiculed. Indeed, I myself have frequently made fun of it. Even now, I am not suggesting that it is or ever will be a reality. Not even that it could be. Our concept of a person is such that it is actually contradictory to suppose that once-dead persons return to earth after what may be a considerable lapse of time.

But our concepts are not sacrosanct. They can be modified if they cease to be well adapted to our experience. In the present instance, the change which would supply us with a motive for altering our concept of a person in such a way as to admit the possibility of reincarnation would not be very great. All that would be required is that there be good evidence that many persons are able to furnish information about previous lives of such a character and such an abundance that it would seem they could not possess the information unless they themselves had lived the lives in question.

This condition is indispensable. There is no sense in someone's claiming to have been Antony, say, or Cleopatra, if he or she knows less about Antony or Cleopatra than a good Shakespearian scholar and much less than a competent ancient historian. Forgetfulness in this context is literally death.

I should remark that even if this condition were satisfied, our motive for changing our concept of a person would not be irresistible. Harmony could also be restored by our changing our concept of memory. We could introduce the ruling that it is possible to remember experiences that one never had; not just to remember them in the way that one remembers facts of one sort or another, but to remember these experiences in the way that one remembers one's own.

Which of these decisions would lead us to the truth? This is a senseless question. In a case of this kind, there is, as Professor Quine would put it, no fact of the matter which we can seek to discover. There would indeed be a fact to which we should be trying to adjust our language; the fact that people did exhibit this surprising capacity. But what adjustment we made, whether we modified our concept of a person, or our concept of memory, or followed some other course, would be a matter for choice. The most that could be claimed for the idea of re-incarnation is that it would in these circumstances be an attractive option.

This time let me make my position fully clear. I am not saying that these ostensible feats of memory have ever yet been abundantly performed, or indeed performed at all, or that they ever will be performed. I am saying only that there would be nothing in logic to prevent their being performed in such abundance as to give us a motive for licensing re-incarnation; and a motive for admitting it as a possibility would also be a motive for admitting it as a fact.

The consequence of such an admission would be fairly radical, though not so radical as the standbys of science fiction such as brain transplants and teleportation. Less radical too than the speculations of mathematical physicists. These speculations titillate rather than alarm the reading public. Professor Hawking's book *A Brief History of Time* is a best-seller. Perhaps the reading public has not clearly understood what his speculations imply. We are told, for example, that there may be a reversal in the direction of the arrow of time. This would provide for much stranger possibilities than that of a re-birth following one's death. It would entail that in any given life a person's death preceded his birth. That would indeed be a shock to common sense.

14

The Faces of Immortality

KAI NIELSEN

University of Calgary

I

Is THERE AN AFTERLIFE or any reasonable possibility of an afterlife, or is belief in an afterlife—of a post-mortem existence—somehow incoherent, or is it instead merely a false belief? Given the new philosophical dispensation in the aftermath of the undermining of foundationalism, it is better for secularists such as myself to 'split the difference' and contend that conceptions of the afterlife are so problematical that it is unreasonable for a philosophical and scientifically sophisticated person living in the west in the twentieth century to believe in life eternal, to believe that we shall survive the rotting or the burning or the mummification of our 'present bodies'. There are questions of fact here, questions of interpretation of fact, and questions of what it makes sense to say which come as part of a package, and it may well be that in some instances it is not so easy to divide these questions so neatly. In a good Quinean manner I will let philosophy range over all these considerations.

If immortality is taken, as I shall take it, in a reasonably robust way and not simply as the sentimentalism that we shall live in the thoughts of others, belief in the afterlife—or so I shall argue—is so problematical that it should not be something to be believed. It is a belief, depending on how exactly the afterlife is construed, that is either fantastically unlikely to be true, or is instead an incoherent belief which could not possibly be true. Bodily resurrection, one of the reigning conceptions of the afterlife, may well, on some of its formulations, be a coherent belief (at least on some readings of 'coherent'), but it is a

---

From *Death and Afterlife*. Edited by Stephen T. Davis. Reprinted with permission of St. Martin's Press, Incorporated and The Macmillan Press, Ltd.

belief which is very unlikely indeed to be true. Its unlikelihood rests, as I shall show, on a number of grounds. One of them is, of course, the non-existence of God. If there were a God and He was what, say, Orthodox Christianity takes Him to be, we might take bodily resurrection to be a straight matter of faith.[1] Even so, I will argue, there will still be extraordinary difficulties, difficulties so great that not a few believers in God have turned away from any such conception. They have, that is, opted for belief in God without belief in immortality. In this context we should keep firmly in mind that if the grounds for believing in God are scant the grounds for believing in bodily resurrection are doubly scant. Belief in it is a considerable scandal to the intellect.

I shall, after some preliminaries, start with a discussion of bodily resurrection, go on to a discussion of disembodied existence, and finally turn to a last cluster of considerations of broadly moral and human rationales for having a concern for immortality and having a hope that it may, after all, be a reality. This last consideration will be linked to the claim made by some that belief in immortality is necessary to make life in an otherwise intolerable world have some sense in the face of what, some argue, would otherwise be human despair, a despair that is inescapable where human beings come to escape double-mindedness and face non-evasively the bleakness of their lives without God and the possibility of eternal life.[2]

II

In speaking of immortality we are speaking of the endless existence of a person after what we call her 'death' or at least the death of her body. What is agreed on all sides, and what is an inconvertible fact, is that after a time for all of us our bodies cease to be energised and left alone they will simply rot, and no matter how they are manipulated, when they are thoroughly in that state there is no evidence of their ever being re-energised. (In that respect we are not like batteries.) Believers in immortality believe that, all this to the contrary notwithstanding, we, as human beings, persons, selves, somehow do not really die but have instead an endless existence after such a deenergisation and disintegration of our bodies or (if you will) our 'earthly bodies'.

Jewish, Christian and Islamic defenders of immortality take two fundamentally different positions in their characterisation of the afterlife. The first position I shall characterise is probably the more religiously orthodox position and the second position, until rather recently, would more likely appeal to philosophers and perhaps even

to common sense since the time of Descartes, and in certain strata of
society extending down to our own time. Since I believe both views
are fundamentally defective, I shall not be concerned to take sides
with respect to them, but to be, after a characterisation of them, concerned to critique them both. The two views are, respectively, bodily
resurrection by God to eternal life, and Cartesian dualism with its
belief in an indestructible, immaterial individual self distinct from the
body in which this self is said to be housed. This self is also thought
to be capable of, without any body in which it must be housed, to exist
as a disembodied individual who is also a person.

Belief in bodily resurrection is clearly something deeply embedded
in the orthodox Judaeo-Christian-Islamic traditions. Unless we take
seriously the idea that there could be, and indeed there actually is, a
God and that He, being omnipotent, could do whatever is logically
possible, bodily resurrection is a very difficult thing in which to believe
on empirical grounds. On those grounds it just seems utterly fantastic
and no doubt is something whose reality is very unlikely indeed. However, it appears at least not to be an incoherent notion, at least if we
take an incoherent notion to be a notion which is logically impossible,
for example, 'a round square', or not understandable (comprehensible),
for example, 'Reagan sleeps faster than Thatcher'. People on such an
account, when resurrected, do not have to be radically different from
those men and women we meet on the street, including ourselves,
where as Antony Flew once put it, 'People are what you meet. We do
not meet only the sinewy containers in which other people are kept,
and they do not encounter only the fleshy houses that we ourselves
inhabit'.[3] Rather the people we meet are flesh and blood individuals:
energised, purposively acting bodies through and through a part of the
physical world (if that isn't a pleonasm).

What bodily resurrection teaches us is that we embodied beings will
survive the death of our present bodies and that our post-mortem
existence, though in certain respects it will be very different, will be,
ontologically speaking, in a manner essentially similar to our premortem existence. We will come to have, when resurrected, an energised
physical body essentially like that of our present body except that it
will be a better one, though better along familiar lines, and differing
from our present bodies in that it cannot ever wear out or become de-
energised. It must, and will, last forever. (It is like the suit in *The Man
in the White Suit.*) We have an energised body, and, as we go along
the history of our life trajectory, that body at some time ceases to be
energised and then, perhaps after considerable decay or even disintegration, gets, according to the bodily resurrection story, a refurbished
or a reconstituted body and, most importantly of all, it gets a re-

energised body as a dead battery gets recharged. We are rather like a lake, to switch the analogy, that dries up and then, on the same lake-bed, refills again. Peter Geach, a stalwart defender of bodily resurrection, forcefully puts the matter in this way:

> The traditional faith of Christianity, inherited from Judaism, is that at the end of this age the Messiah will come and men will rise from their graves to die no more. That faith is not going to be shaken by inquiries about bodies burned to ashes or eaten by beasts; those who might well suffer just such death in martyrdom were those who were most confident of a glorious reward in the resurrection. One who shares that hope will hardly wish to take out an occultistic or philosophical insurance policy, to guarantee some sort of survival as an annuity, in case God's promise of resurrection should fail.[4]

Leaving God out of it, the notions of inert bodies being re-energised or even particles of dust being brought together and formed again into a single body and then re-energised are logical possibilities (in the philosopher's sense of that phrase) and in that sense (a sense familiar to philosophers) these notions are coherent.

Of course, to say that something is logically possible is not to say much. It is logically possible that Geach might sprint from Leeds to London in three seconds or eat a thousand ears of corn in two seconds, though we better not ask for a story about how he will do these things. Similarly, it is logically possible that I might grow an aluminium exo-skeleton just as the metamorphosis in the Kafka story is, as the logical positivists used to say, consistently describable. However, that is a kind of low-order coherence if coherence at all. It is in reality no more than a necessary condition for coherence. What it does mean is that we know what it would be like to see a metallic substance spreading all over Nielsen's body and for his bones and the like to turn into something like iron rods. And we can follow the Kafka story. But we do not at all understand how such things are causally possible. They make no sense at all in terms of what we know about the world. (All we have are mental pictures here but still it does not appear that any syntactical rules have been violated.) And it is not even clear that we know what it would be like to see Geach run from Leeds to London in three seconds or even in three minutes. Suppose I were in an aeroplane at a very high altitude with very powerful binoculars. I could possibly spy out Geach at Leeds in his running shorts starting with the starter's gun and then track him as he ran—now in three seconds—to London, though, if we get specific, what it would be like to carry out such a tracking so rapidly is hard to say. However, I do know or think I know, what it would be like three seconds later—though I would have to move my binoculars awfully fast—to spy out Geach or a Geach-like replica at the outskirts of London. Given, as I remarked, the speed of his alleged running, the tracking (the very idea here) gets more obscure. What, for example, would it be like to see him running at such a speed? (But perhaps I could have a movie camera and replay the whole thing in very slow motion. Still he must have moved his arms and legs with incredible speed. And how did he do that? How is that possible? For God, all things are possible but not for Geach.)

Such stories depend for their intelligibility on their being under-described. The more we, remaining stubbornly literal, try to fill them in, the more problematical they become, namely, their intelligibility, and the less coherent they seem. (Philosophers talk of 'the limits of intelligibility' but we have no clear idea of what we are talking about here.)[5] Still, perhaps no contradictions are involved in their characterisations: problematicity and doubtful coherence yes, inconsistency no, or perhaps no. (Still, what is or isn't consistent is not always easy to ascertain.) Where no disembodiment assumptions sneak in by the back door to carry the self from one body to the next, bodily resurrection seems at least to be some kind of obscure logical possibility. Still that is not saying very much at all.

Many logical possibilities are not genuine possibilities. It is totally irrational for me to believe I can levitate, survive in the winter outside in my swimming trunks at the North Pole, or that this body of mine will go on functioning in good order indefinitely. Is it not just as irrational to believe in bodily resurrection? Well certainly it is *without* a belief in the God of Judaism, Christianity or Islam. But with it, it is not so clear. Recall that for those religions God has promised such a resurrection and for God everything is possible. God, that is, is conceived of as omnipotent which entails that He can do anything that it is logically possible to do. (But He cannot create a round square—a clear logical impossibility.) So if you can come to believe in the God of these three sister religions—and continue to conceive of Him in a fairly orthodox way—you can come, readily enough, to believe in immortality in the sense of bodily resurrection though it also may cut the other way too, for some may feel that if to believe in God one must believe in bodily resurrection then one can hardly believe in God. (Perhaps we need something like reflective equilibrium here.) If our faith commits us to things like that, it is not unnatural to believe, then it is hard to be a person of faith.

However, again an extreme Fideist, remembering his James Joyce, may believe that if it is logically possible, and indeed humanly speaking necessary, to believe in one absurdity, that is, God, it is easy enough to believe in another, that is, bodily resurrection. Still, I think that it is reasonable enough to say that, if there is a God, and if He is as He is portrayed in the orthodox Judaic, Christian and Islamic traditions, then it is not unreasonable (scandal to the intellect that it is) to believe in survival through bodily resurrection. Theologians may debate over exactly what is the least imperspicuous representation of this, but that it will occur is itself reasonable to expect *given such background beliefs*. (But we should not forget how arcane and implausible these background beliefs are, beliefs which include the idea of there being an infinite disembodied individual who is both an *individual* and omnipresent, and is an individual, and a person as well, that is transcendent to the world.)

It is, I believe, for reasons such as this that Godfrey Vesey, after arguing that bodily resurrection is a coherent notion, remarks that 'bodily resurrection is a matter of faith, not of philosophy'.[6] If one has the faith of a Jew, Christian or Moslem, one can reasonably believe in bodily resurrection, if not, not. However, philosophy, or at least reflective deliberation, need not stop just where Vesey thinks it must, for we can, and should, ask whether this faith is reasonable or indeed, for us (that is we intelligentsia), standing where we are now, knowing what we know, not irrational (viewed from a purely cognitive perspective). We should also ask, irrational or not, whether we should, everything considered, crucify our intellects and believe in God and bodily resurrection even if such beliefs are irrational. (There may be a case—a reasonable case—as we shall see later, for sometimes, if we can bring it off, having, in certain very constrained circumstances, irrational beliefs.)[7]

It is because of such considerations that I, in several books, have laboured hard and long over questions about the necessity of faith and over whether belief in God is reasonable, if we have a good understanding of what our situation is.[8] I have argued, as has Antony Flew in a rather parallel way, that belief in an anthropomorphic god is little better than a superstition, and that belief in God, when conceptualised in the non-anthropomorphic way, is incoherent.[9] The non-anthropomorphic conceptualisation is where God has come to be conceptualised, in developed Judaic, Christian and Islamic traditions, as an infinite immaterial individual, omnipresent, but still a person transcendent to the world (to the whole universe). It is this conceptualisation that we are maintaining is incoherent. It is a conception, incoherent as it is, that is beyond reasonable belief for a person in the twentieth century with a good philosophical and scientific training. (For those who are not in a good position to be cognisant of its incoherency it is another matter.)

I hasten to add, lest I seem both unreasonable and arrogant in making the above claim, that reasonable people can have, and perhaps are likely to have, *some* unreasonable beliefs. I am not saying, let me repeat, that educated religious believers are unreasonable, while I am plainly reasonable. That would be gross hubris and silliness to boot. But I am saying that their belief in God, and with that, their belief in bodily resurrection, is unreasonable. However, I am also saying that *if* it were reasonable to believe in the God of our orthodox traditions, it would not be unreasonable to believe in bodily resurrection. So I have, in my work, concentrated on belief in God, and not on immortality, taking the former belief to be the central thing on which to concentrate.

It is hardly in place for me to repeat my arguments here or to try to develop new ones. However, if, on the one hand, they, or some more sophisticated rational reconstruction of them, are sound, or, if, on the other hand, arguments against the existence of God like those of Wallace Matson or J. L. Mackie are sound, or by some rational reconstruction could be made so, then belief in bodily resurrection is unjustified. (For the same conceptualisation of God, they cannot, of course, both be sound.) I should add here that both Matson and Mackie profess (strangely it seems to me as it does to Flew as well) to have no difficulties with the intelligibility or coherence of God-talk.[10] (They are the atheist counterparts or *alter egos* of Swinburne and Penelhum.) We say that belief in the God of developed forms of these traditions is incoherent; they say, by contrast, that the belief is merely false or at least on careful scrutiny clearly appears to be false. The Matson-Mackie arguments, that is, are arguments claiming to establish that belief in God, though coherent, is unjustified, and that it is more reasonable to believe that God exists is false than to believe in God or to remain agnostic. But in either eventuality, it is unreasonable to believe in bodily resurrection. If either the Flew-Nielsen coherence arguments, or the Matson-Mackie arguments about justifying belief in God, or an appeal to faith are sound, then, given the radical diversity of putative revelations, belief in God for philosophically informed people is unreasonable. And if belief in God is unreasonable, it is surely not reasonable to believe in bodily resurrection. But if one or another of these skeptical arguments are not sound or cannot be made so with a little fiddling, and if we are justified in believing in God or perhaps justified in accepting such a belief as an article of faith, then belief in bodily resurrection seems to be reasonable *if* God is what the orthodox say He is. (I say 'seems' for, as it does to Reinhold Niebuhr and Paul Tillich, such talk might still seem to be such an intellectual affront that it would be more reasonable, and, morally, more desirable, to somehow construe the whole matter symbolically as do Niebuhr and Tillich.)

Before I leave the topic of bodily resurrection I should note that there is a felt difficulty concerning it that some, in a way that baffles me, find naggingly worrisome.[11] Suppose Sven dies and rots and eventually turns to dust and indeed further suppose his grave gets upturned and the dust, which is all that he is now, is spread randomly by the wind. God, being omnipotent, at the Last Judgment gathers these specks of dust together and reconstitutes them into an energised body that looks exactly like Sven and has all the memories Sven had, but, the objection goes, what appears is not Sven, "the very same person that died previously but merely a replica or simulacrum of him: for, since there is a time-gap between death and resurrection, during which the original body may very well have been destroyed altogether, the connecting link that would make it unambiguously the same person and not a replica will have disappeared."[12]

There are a number of things that should be said here. First, there is no reason, unless we gratuitously assume some very strange physics, to believe that the connecting link is broken: that there is not a bodily continuity. Those specks of dust scattered about and mixed with a lot of other dust are still the specks of dust of Sven, and God, being omnipotent, can readily gather up all the specks of dust and only those specks of dust that are Sven and reconstitute Sven and re-energise Sven's reconstituted corpse. For a while we have bits of Sven and then we have Sven all together again. That should not be difficult at all for God, given His intelligence and omnipotence. There is nothing there that should be *conceptually* puzzling. First we had Friday's *Globe and Mail* and then we had bits of paper scattered all over and then we had them all gathered up and pasted together into *The Globe and Mail*.

We no more need to speak of a gap-inclusive entity here than we need to speak of a gap-inclusive entity between my old battery which had gone dead and the same battery re-energised. There is no more a gap in identity between the human being first energised and then in turn de-energised and then re-energised again, than there is between the live battery, the dead battery and the battery charged up again. In both cases we maintain bodily continuity. The ashes of my pet canary, in a container on my desk, are still the ashes of my pet canary. The same physical entity transformed. God has a little more work cut out for Him in putting Sven back together again than the garage mechanic who charges my battery. (God, unlike the king's men, would have no trouble with Humpty-Dumpty.) But then again, God would not be God if He could not do it. There surely are no logical impossibilities here that omnipotence could not overcome unless perhaps omnipotence is itself an incoherent notion. (I shall assume here it is not.)

Secondly, certainly it could—and perhaps just as well—be a replica and perhaps there would be no verifiable difference between a situation describing the real Sven and a situation describing his replica. But this by now should not be in the least surprising. It is just the old story of theory being *undetermined* by data. Both descriptions make verifiable claims but perhaps there is no *further* verifiable claim that will enable us to decide between them, but post-Quinean philosophy of science has taught us to be neither surprised nor disturbed by that. There will often be a proliferation of theories all equally, or at least apparently equally, compatible with the same observed and perhaps even the same observable data. We must choose between theories on other grounds, and if Jews, Christians or Moslems have independent reason for accepting the God-centred narrative, then they can safely and reasonably ignore replica possibilities. They are not going to get certainty but then, as fallibilism has taught us, we never do in any interesting cases and, after all, why must they have certainty? They can instead be sturdy knights of faith confident that they have deflected philosophical arguments designed to show that talk of bodily resurrection is incoherent. Defeating such rationalism, they can live as persons of faith in their trust in God's promised resurrection: a promise that human beings will rise from their graves and die no more.

III

Let us now turn to an examination of a defence of immortality rooted in Cartesian dualism. That is, we will turn to claims to disembodied existence. There are Christians (Geach, for example) who vehemently reject such a conception of immortality as a philosophical myth which they take to be intellectually unsupportable and religiously unnecessary. There are other Christian philosophers who fervently wish that it would be true but are not even convinced that the very idea of disembodied personal survival is not nonsense.[13] Believers often see the claim to disembodied personal existence as a conception of Greek origin, refurbished and streamlined by Descartes. Many of them claim that it is in reality foreign to a genuinely biblical world view. Whatever may be the larger truth here, we should note that in contrast with the biblical world view, which is more communitarian in spirit, the Cartesian view nicely meshes with the intense individualism of the modern period.[14]

However, as has been pointed out, Jesus's own sayings about the afterlife are ambiguous as between the resurrection of a material body and a 'spiritual body' (whatever that means).[15] Later Christian thought has also waffled here. It has tended to teach the ultimate resurrection of our earthly bodies, no matter how long dead or in what state of decomposition, while permitting the average believer to expect an immediate transition of her soul at the moment of death.[16] Yet, a not inconsiderable number of believers, particularly *some* Protestant Christians, and, among them some philosophers, have opted (even in the age of Ryle, Wittgenstein and Dennett) for a disembodied self and the form of immortality that goes with it. Moreover, it should not be forgotten that even some atheists have believed in this form of immortality (for example, McTaggart). However, it is only against the background of a biblical world view that such a purely speculative conception, at least *prima facie* implausible, is of much interest. Christians, understandably, long for life eternal in the fellowship of God and it has come to seem to a not inconsiderable number of them that the best face that can be put on this is to see ourselves, if this can be justifiably done, as disembodied selves: spiritual continuants whose very spirituality (thinking, willing, feeling non-materially) is what makes us what we are. It is this that is our essence. This Cartesianism seems too much untutored common sense in many modern Christian environments (more likely so in Orange County than in Scarsdale) to be a clear enough notion, but many philosophers and theologians have found it very baffling indeed. Can we actually attach sense to the thesis that persons can exist disembodied? Can we be disembodied continuants who are also individuals who are, as well, persons? (Even if somehow we can attach some sense to the notion we have a long way to go to the making of it a belief that can plausibly be thought to be true.)

Hywel Lewis is just such a Christian philosopher. Lewis does not think 'that any case for immortality can begin to get off the ground if we fail to make a case for dualism'.[17] He is fully aware that many able philosophers think a belief in disembodied personal existence or in disembodied persons is an incoherent belief, devoid of any intelligible sense, and he is concerned to make a case for rejecting that (among philosophers) widely-held belief. He attempts, that is, to defend a belief in disembodied personal survival. In its classical Cartesian form it maintains that persons are real selves or souls, namely particular immaterial conscious things (continuants) which have feelings and thoughts, are capable of willing and acting and which are only contingently connected with the bodies ('physical bodies', if you will) in which they are sometimes housed.

It is this self—a self by which each person is what he is—which each of us, in our own direct, immediate experience, realises is distinct from the body and is capable of being what it is even if there is no body at all. We, the story goes, just experience ourselves as distinct from our bodies. Lewis thinks that this is just a *datum of experience*. Our sense of self-identity, which is prior to any conception we have of personal identity, just tells us that this is so. We are each directly aware of ourselves as we are directly aware of being in pain or of having a sudden thought.

A standard problem for any belief in an immaterial self is over how it is possible to individuate this self (distinguish it from other selves) since it does not have a body. Lewis in defending his view that a knowledge of an immaterial self is just a datum of awareness remarks:

> There must, then, I agree, be individuation. But how is this possible if the immaterial substances in question cannot, as the thought of them would seem to imply, 'be individuated by spatial relations'? This problem, I must now add, does not worry me a great deal, and it never has. It has always seemed evident to me that everyone knows himself to be the being that he is in just being so. We identify ourselves to ourselves in that way, and not in the last resort on the basis of what we know about ourselves. The reaction to this is sometimes to retort that we seem to be running out of arguments, and we must surely make our case by argument. This is a trying situation for a philosopher to have to meet; quite clearly he does not want to seem unwilling to argue. But argument is not everything, we have also to reckon with what we just find to be the case, we cannot conjure all existence into being by argument and we cannot, as I hope does not sound pretentious, argue against reality.[18]

It may be, as Terence Penelhum has remarked, 'that such a doctrine has no content, and just amounts to an empty assertion that our problem really does have an answer'.[19] It may be, as Godfrey Vesey and Sydney Shoemaker think, that in so reasoning Lewis in effect construes 'I' as a proper name when it is not, and when in reality it functions more like 'here' such that 'I' no more names a person than 'here' names a place.[20] On Lewis's account, even if I suffer amnesia, I do not lose the direct sense of self-identity—my direct awareness of self—of which he speaks. There just is this direct self-awareness. Vesey asserts that such a self-identification is an illusion, and so cannot give meaning to talk of personal immortality.[21] There are perfectly non-deviant uses of 'here' where 'here' does not name a place. As Vesey puts it:

> Suppose that, *although I am quite lost,* I say *to myself* 'I know where I am, I'm here'. This use of 'here', although completely uninformative, may nevertheless *seem* to be a significant, non-empty use. It borrows a facade of meaning from the informative uses. Similarly, an empty, soliloquizing, use of 'I', may 'borrow a facade of meaning from the informative, interpersonal, uses'.[22]

Suppose I am suffering from amnesia and I remember Lewis's doctrine that 'Everyone knows himself to be the being that he is in just being so', so, fortified by that, I know who I am: 'I am I'. I just find it to be the case in immediate experience that I am I. This is just something, the Cartesian story goes, we find to be so in a self-disclosure or in self-awareness. But if we recall that 'I', in standard contexts, is no more used to name a person than 'here' names a place, we should recognise the emptiness of Lewis's remark that 'Everyone knows himself to be the being he is in just being so'. It is like saying 'Everyone knows where he is, in that he can say, "I'm here" and not be wrong'.[23]

Perhaps, as J. L. Mackie thinks, things are not quite that simple (in philosophy they usually are not).[24] However, even if the above arguments about emptiness do not go through there is, I believe, a simpler objection to such an account. Suppose we grant that there is this dumb or brute self-awareness (perhaps 'inarticulate' is the better word) giving one some kind of inchoate self-identity. I am directly aware of myself in a manner similar to the way in which I am directly aware that I am thinking—like the having of a sudden thought—or having a pain. But this brute datum (if that is what it is) is just that: it does not itself carry the heavy *interpretive* weight that Lewis in effect puts on it, namely that the self of which I am aware is *immaterial* (disembodied). That is clearly an *interpretation* of the experience to which there are alternative interpretations and one would (*pace* Lewis) have to argue for that alternative. (Argument cannot stop where Lewis wants it to.) One could not rightly claim that it is just something found to be true in experience. Indeed to the extent that we do not understand 'immaterial thing', 'immaterial individual', 'disembodied person', we might think *that* interpretation is a non-starter in being only a putative interpretation.

Be that latter point as it may, what we have here, in claiming that we are directly aware of ourselves as not just a self, as something I know not what which has thoughts and feelings and initiates actions, but also as a disembodied agent, is in reality an *interpretation* and not just a datum of experience, just as much as when I say that the pain I feel is the stimulation of my C fibres I do not just report my experience but interpret it. Both are interpretations of experience. They are not direct data of experience. And if we say, misleadingly I believe, that all experiences are interpretations, then we must recognise that there are degrees of interpretiveness and grades of theoreticity. There cannot be the direct way to immortality that Lewis seeks, not even as an enabling doctrine. 'I am immortal' cannot be a matter of direct awareness in the way 'I am tired' is.

It is a rather common belief among many analytical philosophers (A. J. Ayer, Peter Strawson and Bernard Williams among them) that the very idea of a disembodied person is incoherent, for reference to a body is a necessary condition for establishing the identity of a person and for ascribing identity through time to a changing person. We indeed characteristically appeal to memory as well in determining whether a person at a later time was one and the same person as at some earlier time. But when memory and bodily criteria conflict bodily identity takes pride of place. Suppose, to take an example, Hans dies and it is alleged that his spirit lives on. However, because having a body is a necessary condition for making ascriptions of personhood, we can have no way, even in principle, of ascertaining whether there is really a disembodied Hans who is the same person as the ruddy-cheeked Hans we used to know. The very idea of a *'bodiless individual'* seems to be unintelligible.[25]

If we try to substitute memory as the primary criterion for personal identity we will fail, for we need to be able, for there to be memories at all, to distinguish between real and apparent memories, between Mildred's thinking she remembers cashing the cheque and her actually remembering it. Only genuine memories guarantee identity, not merely apparent ones. Actually remembering that I am a professor of philosophy at the University of Calgary guarantees my identity, only thinking I remember it does not. But for these to be real memories as distinct from apparent memories the events thought to be remembered must actually have occurred *and* they must have happened to the person remembering them. Memory cannot constitute personal identity or, more plausibly, be the fundamental criterion of personal identity for it presupposes that such identities have been established, that we can determine who it is that has the memories. So memory will not do the fundamental work. The only alternative—or at least the only other argument alternative—for in any fundamental way establishing personal identity is having the same body (bodily continuity).

However, are there not at least conceivable happenings that would loosen our attachment to bodily identity as a necessary condition for establishing personal identity and not only show that people, like Locke's Cobbler and the Prince, could 'exchange bodies' but that they could also exist without bodies at all? The following story is designed to show that bodiless existence is a *logical* possibility. Suppose I am a rather credulous fellow and I live in a house with a spouse, two children, my aged mother and two dogs. The house initially is a perfectly normal house, but then one day strange things, sometimes in front of us all, start happening. Lights inexplicably go on and off, doors open and close and chairs move in unaccountable ways. The happenings cannot be traced to any member of the family, to the dogs, to neighbours, to friends, or to agents whom we ordinarily would regard as people, or to the wind, or to anything like that. Suppose I, the credulous one, hypothesise that the house is haunted by a poltergeist to the considerable amusement of the more skeptical members of the family. But then suppose my son, age 16, begins to receive premonitions of what is going on. He can predict accurately when a door is going to open, a light go on, a chair at the table will move and the like. He says an invisible person, S, has talked to him. Pressed, he retracts 'talked'—no one else hears it and no tape recorder catches it. He now says rather that 'talked' is a groping way of saying S lets him know like thoughts popping into his head. But this, whatever it is, goes on with considerable accuracy for some time. My son (for example) says S told him that S is going out in the garden and sure enough the backdoor to the garden opens and closes.

Suppose, after a time, S comes out of the closet, so to say, and gives my son to understand that S is lonely and wants to belong to the family and to be accepted. After dinner, Sarah, as S tells my son she wants to be called, communicates to him that she is going to wash up, take care of the fireplace, and turn the thermostat down in the evening and up in the morning. We see, with no body around making it happen, dishes go from the table to the dishwasher, matches striking against the grate and regularly lighting the fire at the desired time and just before I get to it I see the thermostat go up in morning and down in the evening set to the required day-time and night-time temperature with no discernible hand moving the thermostat. Sarah, as we now have started to call S, lets my son know that she is beginning to feel like a member of the family. She lets him know she will be on the watch-out for us and guard us. Subsequently Sarah lets my son know that my daughter is in danger in the back yard, and indeed we rush out and discover she has fallen into the well, and at another time she warns us, again through my son, that my German Shepherd is in danger and again we rush to the back yard and find him confronted by a rattlesnake. The whole family becomes convinced, after such episodes, that Sarah is real, that she is an invisible person and a family friend. She might, if people want to talk that way, be said to have a 'subtle invisible body' that neither the family members nor the dogs can see or in any way detect, for example, no one ever bumps into her and she never steps on the dogs' paws. If such conceivable things did actually happen we might be led quite naturally and quite plausibly to use the name 'Sarah' and to think of Sarah as a person, indeed to take her to be a person albeit a disembodied person. If such things really happened there would, it is natural to say, be at least one disembodied person.[26]

If things really were so to transpire would we be justified in calling Sarah a person? Well, it would be at least plausible to say Sarah met all of Daniel Dennett's suggested conditions for personhood, namely, rationality, intentionality, propriety as the object of a personal stance, ability to reciprocate such a stance, verbal communication and a special kind of consciousness.[27] She knows, to take the elements fitting her most problematically, concern for the well-being of the family, for example, her protection of my daughter and concern for the well-being of my German Shepherd as instanced in the rattlesnake event. This gives rise to gratitude and affection and Sarah reciprocates concern with other acts, for example, at Thanksgiving various mixings mysteriously go on in the kitchen done by none of the regular family members and by no visible hands and a lovely Indian pudding emerges. And we have seen how Sarah communicates, though it is perhaps stretching things a bit to call it *verbal* communication. Sarah also seems plainly to be aware of herself and her surroundings. We identify Sarah in identifying these happenings.

Could Sarah be identified with a normal human being known to have lived a normal life? Suppose in checking the records I discover that a previous owner several years back had had a shy and retiring daughter, also called Sarah, who had died while living in what is now my house. Suppose it is further discovered from accounts about her that she had a personality very like that of 'our Sarah' and that when we ask 'our Sarah' about that young woman Sarah says that she is that very woman and leads us in the attic to a hidden box of letters from that Sarah to her parents. Under such circumstances it would be reasonable to believe that our disembodied Sarah was that very woman. So it appears at least we have described what would have to be the case to become acquainted with a disembodied person and indeed a disembodied person who had formerly had a perfectly normal body. We have given verifiable, empirical sense to the concept showing that it makes sense to speak of 'bodiless persons' and that such a concept, bizarre as it is, is an intelligible one. It has what used to be called empirical meaning.

The first thing that needs to be said about this is that, conceivable or not, things like this do not happen. Some might say this is irrelevant because, after all, what is at issue is that such talk is intelligible and this only requires that disembodied individuals be consistently describable, not that there actually be the slightest likelihood that there really are such beings. There is not the slightest chance that there are people whose skin is naturally orange and hair naturally purple but the conception, like that of 'golden mountain' or 'wooden jetliner', is perfectly intelligible. Yet we do have some understanding here in the way we do not have for 'Procrastination drinks melancholy', or 'Reagan sleeps slower than Trudeau', but then again we must remember that intelligibility, and even more obviously coherence, admits of degrees and perhaps of kinds. When we think concretely about what causally speaking would have to be in place for there to be a wooden jetliner that actually could fly we see that such a conception doesn't fit in with anything else we know. In terms of what we know about the word, it just doesn't make any sense at all and the same is true of Sarah and of Locke's story of the Cobbler and the Prince. In that perfectly standard way these accounts are incoherent. They are just stories we can tell, like certain children's stories or certain science fiction. Part of their charm (where they have any) is that they couldn't happen, and our reason for our confidence that they couldn't happen is not that we have made careful inductive investigations like looking to see if there are magpies in New York State or if the quail are different in the east of North America than in the west. Rather, our source of confidence is that these things actually obtaining just does not fit with what we know or at least reasonably believe about the world. Just how could a wooden jetliner take off or fly at 500 miles an hour at 40,000 feet? How would it stand the stress, and so on and so on? The wood would have to be remarkably hard, very different from anything we know to be wood. Such things just do not make sense and at least in this way Sarah doesn't make sense either. There are indeed more things in heaven and earth, Horatio, than is dreamt of in your philosophy. But in this context that is just empty talk. These things never happen and we would, to put it mildly, be extremely skeptical—and rightly so—of any claim that something like this did happen. People touched by modernity would not accept at face value the claim that my watch just disappeared into thin air as distinct from a claim that I had just lost it and could not find it. There cannot be wooden jetliners, Sarahs or Locke's phenomena, any more than there can be, as Evans-Pritchard was perfectly aware, Zande witchcraft substance.

However, the cobbler and the prince and Sarah aside, there are cases of alleged possession and mediumship and there is Sally Beauchamp, Dr Jekyll and Mr Hyde, and *The Three Faces of Eve*. Some cases of this sort have actually been said to have happened by noncredulous people of intellectual and moral integrity and the fictional cases have a certain verisimilitude. But in these cases, if we look at them soberly and non-metaphorically, we need not, and indeed should not, say that we have, as for example in the Eve thing, three persons caged in one body. There are not three Eves but the one Eve has a multiple personality. We should speak in these cases of a plurality of *personalities* not of *persons*. This, as J. L. Mackie points out, is much more guarded and plausible a claim to make than to say there are, mysterious as it may seem, three different persons.[28] We need not invoke disembodied existence or even dualism to handle such cases. They are bizarre and puzzling enough anyway, assuming they are not fraudulent, without adding *unnecessarily* ontological puzzlement. Here is a good place to apply the old maxim about not multiplying entities or conceptions of entities beyond need.

More generally, to return to the question about logical possibilities, we should take to heart David Wiggens's point that the concepts we use, and the particulars we identify and describe in using them, are not such that they can range over all at least putative logical possibilities. They are rather constrained by the nomological grounding of the sortal words we use.[29] We must not confuse what we can imagine or conceive with what is possible. We can *conceive* of an ice-cream cake at the centre of the sun, but such a state of affairs is *not possible*. For it to be possible the ice-cream cake, as the wooden jet, would have to have so changed that it could no longer coherently be called an ice-cream cake. In identifying any particular, say a candy bar melting in my pocket, this ability to identify and re-identify is closely tied up with our concept of what the thing in question is. We expect the bar to melt in my pocket, but the claim that it survived unmelted on the hot stove, let alone in the centre of the sun, is not a possibility that the concept allows for any more than our concept of what it is to be a wren allows for the possibility that it might fly at 60,000 feet and at the speed of 2000 miles an hour. Where we have a sortal concept it is constrained by the physical laws that apply to the exemplifications of those concepts. Copper cannot do just anything; rather it must obey the laws of nature which enable us to distinguish it as a substance. What in fact happens is the basis of all our concepts. It constrains the conceptual connections inherent in our use of language. Iron cannot melt in snow and the flesh and blood Sarah, who used to live in my house long before I lived there, cannot become a disembodied person. It *may* be that the idea of a 'disembodied person' is not contradictory—we *may* have (beyond mental pictures) understood my narrative of Sarah—but disembodied persons are neither physically nor, as some people like to talk, metaphysically possible.[30] We cannot rely on thought experiments—on various underdescribed fantasies—rather, as Wiggens puts it, we have to work back from the extensions to work out what is essential to something being the thing it is. 'For persons this extension is living, embodied, human beings'.[31] Person may not be a natural kind, but a human being—a human person—is. For our kind of natural kind, mind and character are dependent for their activities on a body in causal interaction with the world.[32] We have no coherent grounds for thinking ourselves to be immaterial substances or disembodied continuants incapable of destruction.

IV

This discussion has been metaphysical, somewhat arcane and, it seems to me, quaint. It is not the sort of thing that contributes either to the growth of knowledge or to salvation. It is, or so it seems to me, strange that people should be arguing about such things in our epoch. Yet argue they do. I think what fuels such talk is a deep human problem and I want now to turn to that. Such talk, to come at it at first indirectly, is at home against a religio-ethical background, as Pascal and Dostoevsky well saw, otherwise what we have are just some not very interesting metaphysical puzzles. After all, there is over personal identity and the like, as Derek Parfit and Thomas Nagel have shown, far more fascinating metaphysical conundrums, than the ones generated by such religious concerns, conundrums that we can, if we like doing that sort of thing, wile away our time with, if we are sufficiently leisured and undriven.[33] It is not the metaphysical puzzles about immortality but the human side of immortality that can be gripping and it is that, and that alone, that gives these arcane metaphysical investigations their point. Given our entangled lives, given the deep frustration of human hopes and aspirations, given the unnecessary hell that is the fate of many (40,000 people simply live on the streets of New York to say nothing of what goes on in Calcutta), it is surely understandable that we humans should ask 'Shall I live again?' and, noting the often utterly pointless suffering of the world, ask of those so suffering 'Shall they live again? Could there be "another world" in which they could live in some decency?'

We live in a world where 10,000 people, most of them quite unnecessarily, die of starvation each day, where people are horribly tortured and degraded and where the rich not infrequently live frivolous and expensive lives, living off the backs of the poor, and where in our part of the world Yuppidom reigns supreme. It is hard, given such a world, to just accept the fact of all those people dying in misery who have hardly had a chance to live. It is hard to accept the fact that they should just die and rot and that that is all there is to it. Of course, cognitively speaking it is easy to accept that, for what could be more obvious, but, morally speaking, it is very hard indeed to accept. The moral sense rebels at such a world.

It is easy enough for someone like myself, surrounded by a caring environment, living in comfort and having interesting work, which I can hope will have some significance, to accept the inevitability of death and my eventual utter destruction. It would be nice if it were not so and I could go on living as I am but that cannot be and others will continue after me. That is not such a hard cluster of facts to come to accept. Moreover, it is evident enough anyway.

The thing is to make something of the life I have. It can be a good and meaningful life and whether it is or not, in the circumstances in which I live, is not independent of what I do. And I can hope that I'll be lucky enough, without cancer or the like, to have my 'allotted time'. I would be frustrated if I do not and perhaps irrationally bitter, but, if I happen to be unlucky, it would just be something—and we have here the unforgettable example of Freud—to be, if I am capable of being reasonable under such circumstances, stoically accepted. But with luck nothing like that will happen to me or those close to me and I can live out my life in a meaningful and pleasant way and eventually die. What did Tolstoy get so exercised about?

I think Reinhold Niebuhr was right in turning with contempt from the egoism of healthy individuals, living what would be otherwise normal lives, having obsessive hang-ups about the fact that they will eventually die. For them to be so all important to themselves hardly inspires admiration. For those ageing Yuppies (perhaps former Yuppies is the right phrase), firmly situated in Yuppidom, who have such preoccupations, whether there is no suffering or Strindbergian or O'Neillish laceration or self-laceration, their worries are not something to inspire much sympathy or concern. The temptation is to tell them to get on with it and stop snivelling. (Dietrich Bonhoeffer had a good sense of this.)

However, for the suffering, ignorant and degraded millions, living in hellish conditions, and who have unremittingly, through no fault of their own, lived blighted lives, the inevitability, and at least seemingly evident finality, of death is another thing entirely. This, though plainly there before our eyes, is what is so hard to accept. We do not have something here which is just, or perhaps even at all, a philosopher's puzzle or a neurotic's worry. The matter of blighted lives is a very real one indeed. Five hundred million children and adults suffer from malnutrition and 800 million live, or try to live, in extreme poverty. This remains true while globally one trillion dollars is given to military spending, a spending which is astronomically beyond the needs of anything, for the various great powers principally involved, that could even remotely count as defence. Yet the World Food Council concluded in 1984 that four billion dollars a year committed internationally until the end of the century, would ensure access to food and productive lives for the 500 million people most in need, and set on track a stable world food order where among the poorer nations basket cases would not constantly pop up. However, the brute facts are that a trillion dollars a year goes into doomsday military spending and even a comparatively paltry four billion can't be found to save people from starvation and malnutrition. (Here we are reminded of the world of *1984*.)

Thinking of the callousness of it all, the hypocrisy of many great nations, the placid acceptance of this by the masses, even though such a situation is totally unnecessary, is very sickening indeed. It is understandable, given that, that people despair of the world and that there, out of despair with our human lot, arises a hope for and even faith in immortality, an immortality that will give those (along with everyone else) who never have had anything like a decent chance in life another life that is worthwhile. This is not a matter of a kind of grubby individual craving for life eternal but a longing for a morally worthwhile life for humankind as a whole. (Has our individualism and egoism dug so deep that we cannot really believe that people are genuinely capable of such hopes?)

There is a stance within Christianity, though no doubt there are similar stances within Judaism and Islam as well, often associated with Irenaean universalism, which maintains that human suffering would be irredeemably tragic if our present earthly life were not followed by another in which the suffering of each individual could be made worthwhile for that individual.[34] Suppose, in pursuing this, we ask the famous trio of questions of Kant: 'What can I know?', 'What ought I to do?' and 'What may I hope?'. Think particularly of the last one, 'What may I hope?' and then think of (to put it gently) the unhappy world that we know—keeping in mind the facts that I have just described, facts which are but some salient members of a set of deeply disquieting facts. Hopes are hard to maintain against the persistence and pervasiveness of such facts. Max Horkheimer, who certainly was no defender of a theistic world perspective, well put it when he remarked 'moral conscience . . . rebels against the thought that the present state of reality is final'.[35] Still, in the struggles of our everyday life, our hopes for a realisation, or even approximation, of a truly human society, a society of human brotherhood and sisterhood, a just society or even a rational society, are constantly being defeated. We do not, in fact, given our economic and scientific potential, have something that even remotely approximates a caring society or a just society. (It is pure propaganda for a cabinet minister to speak—boast might be a more accurate word—as one recently did of there being equality and social justice in Canada. But that is standard issue for politicians in our countries.)

Such states of affairs led Kant, Lessing, and even Voltaire, to postulate immortality in order to make some match between our hopes and what is achievable in 'this world'. It is easy to satirise such Kantian postulations of 'pure practical reason' and it is utter folly, as J. L. Mackie has well argued, to try to argue from such *hopes* to *any likelihood* at all that such a reality will come to be.[36] However, as we know from Pascal and Dostoevsky, it may be rational in certain circumstances to have a belief or to cause a belief to come to be formed (if we can) which, viewed from a purely intellectual or cognitive perspective, is an irrational belief. If I am lost in the Canadian North, and if a firm belief that I stand a good chance of getting out is, as a matter of fact, essential if I am going to have any chance at all of getting out, though in fact my objective chances are pretty slim, then it is reasonable for me to come to have that false belief if there is some possibility that I can somehow come to have it in that circumstance. (Recall Pascal on holy water and Schelling's answer to armed robbery.)

Is it similarly reasonable, given the human condition, for me to hope for human immortality in the form of universal salvation for humankind even though the objective likelihood of anything like that being the case is extremely low? In responding to this question I am going to assume that the cognitive situation *vis-à-vis* immortality is as I have claimed and argued it to be. If the situation is not as bad as I argue it is, then we should perhaps, depending on just what we believe the situation to be, draw different conclusions. But suppose I have managed to tell it like it is, then should we continue to hope, or at least wish, for immortality?

Let me describe a scenario that understandably might push a person in the direction of Pascalian hope. Imagine this person, as a humane and sensitive person, reflective and reasonable, with a good education, coming of age in the west just after the First World War. Suppose she becomes a Marxist or an Anarchist, or some other kind of socialist, and says and feels, given what is then going on in the world, that now there is hope in the world. Now imagine her living through all the times in between up to our time (1987) and now, as a rather old person, though still with sound faculties and a humane attitude, she becomes, given the world she has seen and continues to see before her, utterly disillusioned with secular struggle (including, of course, political struggle), with being able to bring that hope into the world or even to bring into the world (small isolated pockets apart, for example, Iceland or Denmark) a tolerable amount of decency. It isn't that she now comes to think that religious revival will bring it into the world—a kind of moral rearmament with God in the driver's seat. Nothing, she now believes, will bring such an order of kindliness into the world. There can be, she believes, Brecht to the contrary notwithstanding, no laying the foundations of kindliness. She has simply given up on the world. The caring for humankind and the detestation of human degradation that launched her into political struggle is still there but she has utterly lost the sense that there is hope in the world, that there will be any lasting or large-scale remedy for these ills. She doesn't as a result become a reactionary. She still supports progressive causes, though, unlike a Marxist or an Anarchist—an E. P. Thompson or a Noam Chomsky—she will no longer, given her disillusion, throw her whole life into such activities, but, while continuing to support progressive causes, turns more and more to religious concerns and thinks and feels through the issue of immortality again.

Suppose, in thinking immortality through on the cognitive side, she comes to a conclusion very similar to mine. But, unlike me, she, keeping in mind Irenaean universalism, comes passionately to hope for immortality in the form of a hope for universal salvation for humankind. Suppose further, facing non-evasively the odds, it becomes, not so much a *hope* (the odds are too dismal for that) but a *wish,* but still a wish that persistently remains with her and guides her life. Is this an attitude that it is desirable that we should come to share with her? It is certainly undesirable if it comes to block our struggling in the world, if it leads to a quietism in the face of evil: to being like Martin Luther rather than like Thomas Münzer. If that is the upshot, it is better to develop the set of attitudes that accepts that the human situation is irredeemably tragic and that we, in such a situation, in Camus's metaphor, should relentlessly fight the plague, knowing full well that the plague is always with us, sometimes striking virulently and at other times for a time remaining only latent, but always being something that will return, after an uneasy lull, to strike again in full fury. The thing to do is, acknowledging this, to unyieldingly and relentlessly fight the plague. What we should do is to tackle the most glaring ills or at least the ills we can get a purchase on, taking to heart and accepting the fact that there will be no extensive or permanent successes. We will have neither Christian nor Marxist eschatological hopes, but, like Camus, we will accept stoically an irredeemably tragic vision of the world. Doesn't this tragic sense of life square better with a non-evasive human integrity than the religious turn?

Not necessarily and perhaps not at all if the religious person takes, in a non-evasive way, a kind of Irenaean turn. Suppose she does not stop relentlessly fighting the plague and doesn't fight it *because* of the hopes/wishes she entertains for the afterlife, but fights the plague to fight evil *and* does so while still wishing for a salvation for humankind, wishing for a fate which is not irredeemably tragic and where human salvation is a reality. Isn't this way of reacting to life and to the world more desirable than sticking with a bleak Camus-like tragic vision, *if* so wishing does not lead to any self-deception about how astronomically slight the chances for salvation are, and if it doesn't weaken one's resolve to fight the plague or make one, in some other way, less effective in fighting the plague? With some people it might dull the native edge of resolution, but surely it need not. One can doggedly fight the plague *and* have such eschatological wishes as well. She can, that is, continue to fight and, utterly unblinkered, have the wish that salvation could be our lot as human beings. So held, this attitude seems at least to have everything the Camusian attitude has and something more as well and thus, everything considered, it is a more desirable attitude.

However, these are not the only alternatives. A Marxist, an Anarchist, or a revisionist socialist social democratic vision of things are not visions which are the tragic visions of an existentialist humanism or of a Freudian or Weberian view of life. If any of these forms of socialism can become and remain a reality—or can even firmly get on the agenda—and be the forms (different as they are among themselves) that Marx, Bakunin or Bernstein envisaged, or some rational reconstruction of them, without becoming like the later Stalinist *and* social democratic deformations of socialism (for example, on the social democratic side, the Wilson or Schmidt governments), then there could be hope in the world. There would be, in such an eventuality, the reasonable prospect of a decent world, or, more than a decent world order, a truly human world order where human flourishing would be extensive.

The person in our scenario turned away from such hopes because of the terrible historical events since the souring of the Russian Revolution, events such as forced collectivisation, the purge trials, the Second World War, the hegemony of Pax Americana, the Vietnam War, the rise of Islamic Fundamentalism (for example, Iran), the rise, both politically and religiously, of reactionary forms of Christianity and Judaism in American and Israel, persistent mass starvation, and the pervasiveness of doomsday war machines. She has seared into her consciousness the realisation that though we have modes of production capable of delivering plenty to the world, 10,000 starve each day, and even in the so-called First World many live, though often quite unnecessarily, very blighted lives indeed. The Russian Revolution did not spread to the west and we got instead, as Rosa Luxembourg anticipated, with the failure of its spread, on the one hand bureaucratic and authoritarian forms of statism which, if socialisms at all, are state socialisms of the worst sort and, on the other hand, matched with that we have forms of state capitalism bent on an imperialistic domination and a heartless exploitation of the world. We have, in *most* of the nations of the world, neither capitalism with a human face nor social-ism with a human face. We are, that is, caught between two very unsavory social systems indeed. The result is that we have, and quite unnecessarily, a pervasiveness of terror, a denial of autonomy and equality and massive exploitation and poverty. This picture, which *at most* is only slightly overdrawn, turns the person in our scenario, de-spairingly, to Irenaean universalism, to the hope, which for her, given her estimation of the probabilities, is little more than a wish, that there will, in an afterlife, be a universal salvation in which the sufferings of each individual could somehow be made worthwhile for that individual.[37]

What needs to be said here in response is that—given the turn of things historically, and given certain assumptions about human na-ture—however unlikely it may be that socialism on the necessary world-wide scale can be anything like the socialism of which Marx and Bakunin dreamt, it is still far more likely to become the case (to put it mildly) than is the religious eschatological dream. That is to say that something like this secular vision of the world could obtain is still vastly more likely than bodily resurrection or disembodied existence and the sustaining of Irenaean universalism. (Remember we might still have one or another of the first two things without having Irenaean universalism.) Neither the kingdom of heaven on earth nor the king-dom of heaven in a 'resurrection world' are very likely, but a kingdom of heaven on earth, of the two alternatives, is by far the least unlikely of two unlikely prospects. Moreover, there is, with the former, though *perhaps* even here the chances are rather slight, some prospect of some *approximation* of it. The other's prospects are close to being nil. This being so, the desirable thing is struggle to make that hope in the world a social reality in all the ramified ways that need to be done. What may be unlikely there is at least much less unlikely than the Irenaean thing. It may be apple pie by and by for everyone but it is at least not in the sky.

However, again there is a response from the religious wisher for immortality somewhat similar to her response to the Camusian. Could one not have the socialist thing through and through without any eva-sion at all and still have this wish for a universal salvation that need in no way be a replacement for a deflect from the struggle for a class-less society united in sisterhood and brotherhood where the conditions for both autonomy and equal liberty are maximised? There are reac-tionary atheists (for example, A. Rand and A. Flew) and there are religious Marxists or at least quasi-Marxists (for example, Gregory Baum and Dorothee Sölle). The latter have on their agenda the struggle for a classless society as much as those 'standard Marxists' who are atheists.

Marx and Bakunin were passionate atheists but there is nothing that is canonical to Marxism or Anarchism (libertarian socialism) that requires atheism, however plausible atheism may be on other grounds. Both atheism and socialism can be plausibly said to be part of the Enlightenment project. Still, that project is not such a seamless web that it is evident that one could not have socialism without atheism or atheism without socialism. There is a kind of conservative liberalism that goes well with atheism and some atheists are just plain reactionaries and there can be, and is, a socialism that is also religious. Perhaps the most coherent world view would have socialism and atheism running tandem, but that that is so is not overwhelmingly evident. There is a lot of *lebensraum* for bracketing such considerations and in practical class struggles they can perhaps be ignored. Why divide comrades over a speculative matter that may not at all effect the struggle for socialism? Religion, of course, has indeed been an opiate of the people and a bastion of reaction, but, again, that is not intrinsic to its nature, though its pervasiveness is understandable ideologically.

I think the answer to my above question is that one could be consistently committed to a socialist transformation of the world and have, as well, Irenaean hopes for the salvation of humankind. One could, as some liberation theologians are, be through and through committed to the class struggle *and* have these wishes for an afterlife of a very distinctive kind. Where this is open-eyed, with an awareness of the fantastic and perhaps even incoherent nature of the belief, and is taken as a wish and not allowed to stand in the way of class struggles and other progressive struggles (struggles around racism and sexism), there is nothing wrong with such a wish.

I *suspect* that as a matter of psycho-sociological fact such an attitude will, though perhaps only in some rather subtle ways, stand in the way of liberation—solid liberation in the world—but to the extent that it does not and to the extent it neither wittingly nor unwittingly cooks the books as to the evidence, there is no reason for atheists like myself to criticise it as unreasonable or as in anyway morally untoward, though it is not an attitude we will share even though we recognise that even in a classless, non-racist and non-sexist world order there will be human ills: children born horribly deformed, terrible accidents, a loss of partner or child and the like. It is reasonable to expect that even ills of this sort will be less frequent in such a society with its developed productive forces (including its more developed science) and greater security and greater wealth more evenly distributed. Still, such ills will always be our lot. We can lessen their incidence and surround them with a new environment, but we can never eliminate them. They will always be with us. This being so, in some ways a certain kind of belief in immortality could 'answer' to that as no secular *weltbild* could. Atheists should not blink at that fact or try to obscure its force. They should only point out that, given everything we know, it is an idle wish humanly understandable though it be.

So why not add such a hope or at least such a wish to our repertoire? For me, to speak for a moment personally, the astronomical unlikeliness of such a conception answering to anything real, coupled with the equal unlikelihood of there being a God who could ordain a certain kind of immortality, for (as the Greeks and Romans show us) not just any immortality will do, makes such hopes merely idle wishes and as such nothing to make a matter of the fabric of my life. We have better things to do than to dwell on such idle wishes. Hume, I believe, had a remarkably sane and humane mindset here as did Freud. And Hume and Freud, conservatives though they were, as well as Marx and Bakunin, can remain, without any tension at all, heroes of a contemporary intellectual wedded to the emancipatory potential of the Enlightenment project, while being fully cognisant of the dark underside of it that, on the one hand, Adorno and Horkheimer and, on the other, Foucault, have in their different ways so well exposed. There are plenty of things in both Hume and Marx that no intellectually sophisticated and informed person could accept anymore, along with central things which, with a little rational reconstruction, can be seen to be both sound—or at least arguably sound—and important, and which have forged our contemporary understanding of ourselves and our world such that for a person who has taken things to heart none of the faces of immortality provide live options.[38]

NOTES

1. Godfrey Vesey, 'Remarks,', in Stuart Brown (ed.), *Reason and Religion* (Ithaca, New York: Cornell University Press, 1977) p. 306.

2. Soren Kierkegaard, *The Sickness Unto Death,* trans. Walter Lowrie (New York: Doubleday Anchor Books, 1954).

3. Anthony Flew, 'Immortality', in Paul Edwards (ed.), *The Encyclopedia of Philosophy,* IV (New York: The Free Press, 1967) p. 142.

4. Peter Geach, *God and the Soul* (New York: Routledge & Kegan Paul, 1969) p. 29.

5. Thomas Nagel talks this way in his *The View From Nowhere* (New York: Oxford University Press, 1986) p. 23.

6. Vesey, op. cit., p. 306.

7. Derek Parfit, *Reasons and Persons* (Oxford: Clarendon Press 1984) pp. 12–13.

8. Kai Nielsen, *Contemporary Critiques of Religions* (New York: Herder & Herder, 1971); Kai Nielsen, *Scepticism* (New York: St. Martin's Press, 1973); Kai Nielsen, *An Introduction to the Philosophy of Religion* (London: The Macmillan Press, 1982); and Kai Nielsen, *Philosophy and Atheism* (Buffalo, New York: Prometheus Books, 1985).

9. Antony Flew, *God and Philosophy* (London: Hutchinson, 1966) and Antony Flew, *The Presumption of Atheism* (New York: Barnes and Noble, 1976).

10. Antony Flew, 'The Burden of Proof', in Leroy S. Rouner (ed.), *Knowing Religiously* (Notre Dame, Indiana: University of Notre Dame Press, 1985) pp. 110–14.

11. Terence Penelhum, *Survival and Disembodied Existence* (London: Routledge & Kegan Paul, 1976); Terence Penelhum, 'Survival and Identity', in Mostafa Faghfoury (ed.) *Analytical Philosophy of Religion in Canada* (Ottawa, Ontario: University of Ottawa Press, 1982) pp. 35–53.

12. Penelhum, 'Survival and Identity', p. 47.

13. Ibid., p. 53.

14. Martin Hollis, *Invitation to Philosophy* (Oxford: Basil Blackwell, 1985) pp. 119–120.

15. John Hick, *Death and Eternal Life* (London: Collins, 1976) p. 193. See also Terence Penelhum's critical notice, *Canadian Journal of Philosophy,* IX (March 1979) pp. 141–62.

16. Hick, op. cit., p. 198.

17. Hywel Lewis, 'Immortality and Dualism', in *Reason and Religion,* p. 282. Sydney Shoemaker argues in the same volume that there is a non-Cartesian dualism which is not conceptually incoherent as he believes Cartesian dualism to be. Cartesian dualism, if sound, could support disembodied existence, but, as Shoemaker sees it, it is conceptually incoherent. Non-Cartesian dualism, he argues, is conceptually coherent but it does not support disembodied existence. However, even this battened down dualism with its talk of immaterial substances being related to material substances by a quasi-spatial relationship seems of doubtful coherence, as Shoemaker half admits in a footnote on p. 268.

18. Lewis, op. cit., p. 289. Thomas Nagel, without embracing dualism, in effect reveals the rational kernel behind such an impulse. Thomas Nagel, op cit., pp. 13–37.

19. Terence Penelhum, 'Survival and Identity', op cit., p. 51.

20. Vesey, op cit., pp. 301–6 and Shoemaker, op. cit., pp. 307–11.

21. Vesey, op cit., p. 306.

22. Ibid., p. 305.

23. Ibid., p. 305 and Shoemaker, op cit., p. 311.

24. J. L. Mackie, *Persons and Values* (Oxford: Clarendon Press, 1985) pp. 15–27.

25. Penelhum, 'Survival and Identity', op cit., p. 41.

26. This little tale is adopted from a tale by G. R. Gillett, 'Disembodied Persons', *Philosophy*, 61 (237) (1986) pp. 377–86.

27. Daniel Dennett, *Brainstorms* (Montgomery, Vermont: Bradford Books, 1978) pp. 267–85.

28. J. L. Mackie, op. cit., p. 6.

29. David Wiggens, *Sameness and Substance* (Oxford, England: Basil Blackwell, 1986).

30. Gillett, op. cit., p. 384.

31. Ibid.

32. Ibid., p. 385. See, as well, Mackie, op. cit., pp. 1–27.

33. Parfit, op. cit., and Nagel, op cit.

34. John Hick, op. cit., pp. 152–66.

35. Max Horkheimer, *Critique of Instrumental Reason* (New York: Seabury Press, 1974) p. 2.

36. J. L. Mackie argues this convincingly in his 'Sidgwick's Pessimism', *Philosophical Quarterly* (1976) pp. 326–27. For a more detailed argument for this see his *The Miracle of Theism* (Oxford: Clarendon Press, 1984).

37. There is a point I pass by here made forcefully years ago by Alasdair MacIntyre. The point is this: no matter what comes after in an afterlife the sufferings of people here and now are not thereby made worthwhile. Suppose an infant at birth is born with some horrible physical defect that causes him to be wracked constantly with terrible pain. After two years of such hell he dies and goes to heaven. How does the bliss of his afterlife at all make those terrible sufferings worthwhile? They are hardly a necessary condition for this bliss. See Alasdair MacIntyre, *Difficulties in Christian Belief* (London: SCM Press, 1956) and Alasdair MacIntyre, 'The Logical Status of Religious Belief', in Ronald Hepburn (ed.), *Metaphysical Beliefs* (London: SCM Press, 1957) pp. 168–205.

38. Kai Nielsen, 'Death and the Meaning of Life' in *The Search for Values in a Changing World* (New York: The International Culture Foundation, 1978) pp. 483–90 and Kai Nielsen, 'God and Coherence', in *Knowing Religiously*, pp. 89–102.

15

Do We Need Immortality?

GRACE M. JANTZEN

University of London

THE DOCTRINE OF LIFE after death is often taken to be an essential ingredient in Christian theology. Baron Friedrich Von Hügel, when he said that 'Religion, in its fullest development, essentially requires, not only this our little span of earthly years, but a life beyond,'[1] was only echoing the words of St. Paul: 'If in this life only we have hope in Christ, we are of all men most miserable.'[2] And more recently, others, among them John Hick, have devoted much energy to a consideration of life after death. Hick writes that 'Any religious understanding of human existence—not merely one's own existence but the life of humanity as a whole—positively requires some kind of immortality belief and would be radically incoherent without it.'[3] In this article I propose to look behind the arguments for and against the possibility of life after death, to investigate the various motives for wanting it, ranging from the frivolously irreligious to the profound. I shall argue that the belief in immortality is not so central to Christian thought and practice as is often believed, and indeed that a rich Christian faith does not require a doctrine of life after death in order to be profound and meaningful.

I. SELF-REGARDING MOTIVES

To begin with the obvious, our desire for immortality is not a desire for just any sort of continued existence: the less musical among us might prefer extinction to an eternity of playing harps and singing hymns, and given a choice, we would all prefer extinction to hell. H. H. Price has offered a picture of a life after death which is entirely the product of our desires—but which might turn out to be a highly unde-

Reprinted by permission from *Modern Theology*, 1, No. 1 (1984), 33–44.

sirable state. In his description, the post-mortem world is a world in which our wishes would immediately fulfil themselves, a world whose laws 'would be more like the laws of Freudian psychology than the laws of physics.'[4] As Price points out, this might be much less pleasant than we might have thought; because our desires, when we include all those we have repressed, are not in mutual harmony. They incorporate, for instance, desires for punishment and suffering for the wrongs we have done. He offers the following grim comments: 'Each man's purgatory would be just the automatic consequence of his own desires; if you like, he would punish himself by having just those images which his own good feelings demand. But, if there is any consolation in it, he would have these unpleasant experiences because he *wanted* to have them; exceedingly unpleasant as they might be, there would still be something in him which was satisfied by them'.[5] Price's point is that if all our repressed desires suddenly came true, this would be horrifying, and we would have to set about the difficult process of altering our characters so that when we get what we want, we want what we get.

The popular desire for immortality is very little like this. Life after death is often pictured, rather, as the fulfilment of longings for pleasure: it will be a paradise where there will be no more suffering and pain, where we will be happily reunited with those we love in perpetual feasting and gladness. It must be admitted that some religious pictures of heaven reinforce this frankly hedonistic conception. In the Koran we find that heaven is a beautiful garden filled with fruits and flowers. 'There the Muslims drink the wine they have been denied on earth, wine that has no after-effects. It is brought to them by handsome youths, and dark-eyed houris wait on their every pleasure'.[6] Similar descriptions of a hedonistic paradise of feasting and delight can be found in Christian writings, except that the dark-eyed houris are conspicuously absent, probably because of Christianity's long-standing suspicion of the sorts of delights the presence of these creatures would signal.

One of the appeals of such a description of paradise is that in this eternal delight there is no more separation from those we love; we are all eternally reunited. This, however, might prove a mixed blessing. Apart from the fact that with some of those we love, the relationship improves if there are periods of space between our togetherness, there is also the consideration that heaven would not be a private party— everyone is invited. Now, what might it be like to find oneself at the heavenly feast seated next to a Neanderthal man? Surely conversation would lag, and it is doubtful whether the silences could be filled by enjoyment of the same food. Christianity has sometimes avoided this social embarrassment by consigning the vast majority of mankind to hell, but that is not a possibility with which many of us could acquiesce and still enjoy the feast.

The point behind these frivolous comments is that it is not quite so easy to give a picture of unending delight as might be thought; it is against scenarios of this sort that Bernard Williams' comments on the tedium of immortality have some point.[7] A paradise of sensuous delights would become boring; it would in the long run be pointless and utterly unfulfilling. We can perhaps imagine ways of making a very long feast meaningful; we do, after all, cope with lengthy terrestrial social occasions by choosing interesting conversational partners, and making the dinner occasions not merely for food and drink but also for stimulating discussion and for giving and receiving friendship the value of which extends beyond the termination of the dinner. But if the feasting literally never came to an end, if there were no progress possible from the sensuous enjoyment of paradise to anything more meaningful, then we might well wish, like Elina Macropolis, to terminate the whole business and destroy the elixir of youth. It is important to notice, however, that on this view survival is tedious simply because there is no progress, no point to the continued existence except the satisfaction of hedonistic desires. But this picture is much too simpleminded. Christians (and Muslims too, of course) have long recognized this, and have taken the hedonistic descriptions of the Scriptures as symbolic of something more meaningful than eternal self-indulgence, as we shall see.

Death is sometimes seen as evil because it means the curtailment of projects; immortality would be required to give significance to life because it would allow those projects to be meaningfully continued. Of course, most of our projects would not require all eternity to complete. But even in this life, one enterprise leads to another, and provided endless progress were possible, we might pursue an endless series of challenging and absorbing tasks, each one developing into another, without any risk of boredom. This might also give more point to some of our earthly projects: the painstaking acquisition of languages and techniques would be worthwhile beyond the few years we have to employ them here. This way of thinking about survival is probably more attractive to an intellectual whose current projects could easily be extended into the future, than, say, to a labourer who considers the prospect of endless projects as enough to make him feel tired already. Still, given the opportunity, perhaps he too would develop interests which he would genuinely like to pursue.

The notion that life after death would provide an opportunity for the fulfilment of projects is not, of course, presented as an argument for the likelihood of survival but as an argument for its desirability.

But does it succeed? There is considerable pull toward saying that it does, especially for those who have far more interests than they can possibly develop even assuming an average life-span. An after-life would be one in which we could all pursue what we are really interested in without worrying about earning daily bread or having the notion that the project itself is fulfilling—so that a fulfilled person is one who completes fulfilling projects—but then we have gone round in a circle. Personal fulfilment involves something like actualizing our potential, completing projects which 'do ourselves justice.' But this then is problematical again: what is meant by 'our potential'? If it means the whole variety of things that many of us would enjoy doing and could do well with suitable training, then this life is much too short for fulfilment, and immortality appears attractive.

But while this shows that immortality may be desirable (for some people in some forms) it is possible to give an alternative account of fulfilment which does not require survival. If death is seen as the limit of life, then 'death gains what significance it has, not by serving as a state characterizing things, but as a function which orders members of the limited series'.[8] Thus if we take seriously the fact that our existence will terminate, this will affect our choice about life: if we will not live forever, then we must do while we can those things which are really important to do. On this view, a fulfilled person would be a person who picked such projects for his life that were genuinely worthwhile and suitable for his abilities and aptitudes, and was able to bring them to completion: Einstein, who lived to an old age and had accomplished significant projects would be described as fulfilled, but a person who never had any projects at all, and lived in continuous aimless frustration, 'In the evening saying "Would it were morning" and in the morning saying "Would it were evening"' would not be so describable. Neither would be the person who had projects but died before he could accomplish them. We do distinguish fulfilled and unfulfilled people in these ways, without reference to immortality. This does not of course mean that immortality is not desirable, especially for those who through no fault of their own are not able to complete their projects in their life-times. But it does mean that we do not have to postulate an after-life to make sense of the very concept of fulfilled and meaningful human life.

Also, if death is a limit, this gives a significance and urgency to our choices which they would not otherwise have. If we could go on pursuing an endless series of projects, it might not matter very much which ones we chose first: we could always do others later. Nor would it matter how vigourously we pursued them—for there would always be more time—nor how challenging they were or how well they developed us and brought out the best in us—for there would always be other opportunities. But if fulfilment is something which must be reached in this life if it is to be reached at all, we will be far less cavalier about the choices we make affecting our own fulfilment, and also, very importantly, in our relationships with others for whose fulfilment we are partly responsible. A great many of our projects, and arguably the most significant of them, have to do not merely with ourselves but with others: our fulfilment is not simply a matter of, say, satisfying our individual intellectual curiosities, but is bound up with the fulfilment of family, friends, students. If we really have only this life, then enjoyment and fulfilment cannot be postponed to another, either for ourselves or for those we care about.

II. Moral Motives

It is sometimes argued that immortality is required on moral grounds. Such an argument can take the Kantian form: immortality is necessary as a postulate of practical reason. Since the *summum bonum* involves happiness as well as virtue, and since in this life we often find a disparity between the two, it is necessary to postulate a life after death where the imbalance will be redressed. Otherwise the universe is ultimately unjust, out of joint.

I do not wish to linger long over this, but simply make three points, none of them original. First, maybe we should just admit that the universe is out of joint; it hardly seems obvious, even (or especially) from the point of view of Christian theology, that it is not. Second, even if it is, that does not rob morality—even on a Kantian system—of its point. An act of intrinsic worth is still worthwhile even if it will never receive any happiness in reward; furthermore, morality retains its meaning even if we are all going to perish. (It is not pointless for the dying to show kindness to one another.) Those who say that if there is no life after death then nothing—including morality—in this life is meaningful, are implicitly admitting that there is nothing in this life which is worthwhile for its own sake, independent of eternal consequences; that everything, even love, is only a means to an end, and an end which this life cannot give. Kant himself could not have accepted such a view. Third, the Kantian view of reward has a peculiarity. What sort of happiness is it which is to be the reward of virtue? Suppose we think of it as some variant of the hedonistic paradise described earlier: then for reasons already given, the more moral one was—the more one valued that which was intrinsically good—the less happiness one would find in such ultimately pointless eternal self-indulgence. On the other hand, if Kant was speaking of the satisfactions of fulfilment rather than of hedonistic utopia, then for the one who truly pursues virtue, becoming virtuous will itself be the fulfilment; virtue will be its own reward.

A more interesting argument for the requirement of immortality arises, not from the idea that virtue needs to be rewarded, but from the fact that none of us is sufficiently virtuous. If part of the point of life is moral development, and none of us develops fully in this life, would it not be desirable for this process to continue beyond the grave? There is considerable connection between this argument and the previous ones; except that here there is no request for happiness as a compensation for virtue, but rather for fulfilment, of the very virtue that one has sought, albeit with only moderate success. There are at least two aspects of this, which I shall consider separately.

The first is encapsulated by Dostoyevsky in *The Brothers Karamazov*. Surely I haven't suffered simply that I, my crimes and my sufferings, may manure the soil of the future harmony for somebody else. I want to see with my own eyes the hind lie down with the lion and the victim rise up and embrace his murderer. I want to be there when everyone suddenly understands what it has all been for.[9] This is not a desire for happiness in any hedonistic sense, but a desire to see the point, the fruition of all one's efforts. It is a natural enough human desire, of course; yet I do not think that it can be used as an argument that morality requires immortality, for the assumption here surely is that all the toil and suffering does have a point, whether we are 'there' to understand it in the end or not. Even if we are not present at the final dénouement, this does not make working toward it less worthwhile, for once again, the value of doing that cannot depend on what we individually get out of it. Although Dostoyevsky here touches, as he so often does, a very deep nerve of desire, he surely cannot be interpreted to mean that if that desire remains forever unfulfilled, there was no meaning to the suffering in the first place.

The second aspect of the longing for immortality is the longing for perfection in virtue. This is part of what prompted the more positive conceptions of purgatory, where that was seen not as a place of retributive punishment until one had suffered proportionately to the sins one had committed on earth, but rather as a place of moral purification and advance.

> Where human spirits purge themselves, and train
> To leap up into joy celestial.[10]

This, clearly, is not an unworthy motive for desiring life after death (though in more cynical moments one might wonder how universally it is shared—how many people desire immortality because they truly want to become better). Yet it too has some problems.

In the first place, it is not obvious that simple extension of life would result in moral improvement: more time can be opportunity for deterioration as well as for advance; the person who says, 'I would be better, if only I had a little longer' is justifiably suspect. Still, although time does not automatically produce growth, it may be true that it is necessary for growth. But once again it is worth thinking about the concept of death as a limit. If immortality is denied, and if moral growth is valued, there is an urgency to moral improvement, both for oneself and for others, which might easily be ignored if it were thought that there was endless time available. And as we have already seen, it will not do to say that such moral improvement, with its struggle and frequent failure, would be worthless if all ends at death, for this would hold true only if moral improvement were a means to an end, rather than intrinsically valuable.

III. RELIGIOUS MOTIVES

Those who say that immortality will be the scene of moral progress do not, of course, usually have in mind nothing but temporal extension to bring this about: as Fichte once said, 'By the mere getting oneself buried, one cannot arrive at blessedness'.[11] Rather, they believe that in the life after death there will be some strong inducements to improvement. In Price's non-theistic purgatory the unpleasantness of getting what we want may lead us to revise our desires and characters, while according to some theistic conceptions of purgatory, the punishments for our sins will purge us—sometimes in Clockwork Orange fashion—of our innate sinfulness. The most interesting theory of inducement to moral perfection, and one that forms a bridge to specifically religious arguments for the need for immortality, is the idea that the lure of divine love, more obvious in the next life than in this one, will progressively wean us from our self-centeredness and purify us so that at last our response will be perfect love reciprocated. John Hick, in his discussion of universal salvation, argues that given the assumption that man has been created by God and is 'basically oriented towards him, there is no final opposition between God's saving will and our human nature acting in freedom'.[12] Thus God, extending his love ever again towards us, will not take 'no' for an answer but will ultimately woo successfully, not by overriding our freedom, but by winning us over so that eventually we freely choose him and his perfection. Hick says, 'if there is continued life after death, and if God is ceaselessly at work for the salvation of his children, it follows that he will continue to be at work until the work is done; and I have been arguing that it is logically possible for him eventually to fulfil his saving purpose without at any point overriding our human freedom.'[13]

But even granting Hick's basic assumptions of humanity's created bias toward God, God in loving pursuit of men and women, and endless time for 'the unhurried chase', there are still problems with his conclusion. It is not clear that genuine freedom could be preserved while still guaranteeing the ultimate result: surely if there is freedom there is always the possibility of refusal. Hick's response, presumably, would be to agree that refusal is possible but that, given his assumptions, it becomes less and less likely as time goes on. Yet significantly to the extent that theists, Hick among them, wish to use the fact of human freedom as a (partial) resolution of the problem of evil, one aspect of their defence is that, though persons were created with a bias toward God, their freedom made it possible for them to choose rebellion, thus bringing moral evil in its train: evil is the price of freedom gone wrong. I do not see how one can have it both ways: if evil choices were made in the past even when there seemed no particular reason for them, how can Hick be confident that they will not be repeated endlessly in the future, especially since in the latter case they are made by characters already considerably warped by previous evil choices? The only way that I can see out of this for Hick is by increasing the emphasis on the divine pressure, but that runs the risk of undermining the very freedom which must here be preserved.

It is important to see the implications of human freedom for a Christian doctrine of redemption. One aspect of choice not sufficiently considered is its finality. Of course decisions can sometimes be reversed: we can often change our minds. And when we do so, when there is genuine repentance and conversion, Christianity teaches that God 'makes all things new', brings creativity out of chaos, Easter out of Calvary. But the fact that we can sometimes freely change our minds is not the same as saying that in the end it makes no difference what our intermediate choices are because ultimately we will all (freely) be brought to the same goal. If it is true that whether I choose p or not-p, in the end I will get p, the idea of choice has been robbed of all significance—and that is so even if I can be persuaded that in the end it will really be p that I do want. So if I perpetually choose selfishness and distrust and dishonesty, and my character is formed by these choices, it seems perverse to say that eventually these choices will be reversed and I will attain the same moral perfection as I would have if I had all along chosen integrity and compassion. Part of what it means to be free is that our choices have consequences; it is playing much too lightly with the responsibility of freedom to suggest that these consequences, at least in their effects upon ourselves, are always reversible, even if only in the endless life to come. For that matter, if everyone is perfected, then even the consequences of our choices upon others will finally be overridden: all, in the end, will be as though no one had ever chosen evil at all. Morally revolting as is the thought of God committing people to eternal flames, one of the reasons why traditional theology has so long retained a doctrine of hell is surely to guard this aspect of freedom: there is no such thing as automatic salvation.

In spite of the strong reinforcement which the belief in immortality receives from Scripture and Christian tradition, a surprising amount can also be found which calls into question the idea that immortality is a religious requirement. In the first place, it is sometimes held that, of all the evils and suffering in this world, death is the worst. On a traditional theistic view, evil must eventually be overcome, and all the wrongs made good; and this requires that death, 'the last enemy', may not be proud. Death, too, shall die, when all who have ever lived will live again. This assumes, of course, that death is an evil; and if what I have said about death as a limit is correct, then that cannot be retained without some qualifications. Still, although death is not the worst evil, and not an unqualified evil, this does not amount to saying that it is not an evil at all; consequently in a world where evil was eradicated, death, too, would have no place.

But can this be used as an argument for a religious requirement of life after death? I am not sure that it can. If the perfect world dawns, death will perhaps not be found in it; but does this mean that death in this very imperfect world is followed by immortality? One might argue that only if it is, is God just: the sufferings of this present world can only be justified by the compensation of eternal life. But this, in the first place, is shocking theodicy: it is like saying that I may beat my dog at will provided that I later give him a dish of his favourite liver chowder. What happens after death—no matter how welcome—does not make present evil good.[14] But if life after death cannot be thought of as a compensation for otherwise unjustified present evils, surely death itself—permanent extinction—must be an evil from which a Christian may hope to escape? Well, on what grounds? We do not escape other evils and sufferings which a perfect world would not contain: why should we expect to escape this one? A Christian surely must recognize that there are many aspects of the problem of evil which he cannot explain; maybe he should just accept that death is another one. But would not death make the problem of evil not just more mysterious than it already is, but actually in principle unsolvable? Wouldn't we have to conclude that God is unjust? I don't know. If we can retain a belief in divine justice amid present evil and suffering, horrific as it is, I am not sure that relinquishing the prospect of life after death would necessarily alter the case. Of course it might tip the balance psychologically, making us 'of all men, most miserable,' but that is another matter. If the present evils can be relegated to the mysterious purposes of God, it seems presumptuous to assume that these purposes could not include our extinction.

A very persuasive argument for the requirement for immortality for Christian theology gathers up strands from several of these lines of thought, but places special emphasis on the personal love of God. If, as Christians maintain, God loves and values each of us individually, then we can trust him not to allow us to perish forever. We are worth more to him than that. Thus Helen Oppenheimer, in her discussion of problems of life after death, recognizes the great philosophical complexities regarding personal identity, resurrection, and the rest, but finally says that if we believe in God at all, we must also believe that if we keep on looking we will find the solution to these problems, because it is as unthinkable that a loving God would permit a relationship with one he loves to be severed by extinction of that loved one as it is to think that we would willingly allow our dearest friends to perish if it were in our power to provide them with a full and rich life.[15]

This approach has the merit, first, of not pretending that the puzzles of identity and/or resurrection are easily solvable, second, of treating death seriously, and third, of placing the doctrine of immortality within the context of a doctrine of personal relationship with God. Death is not seen as a mild nuisance which can be quickly left behind never to be repeated; immortality is not automatic, and could not be expected at all were it not for the intervention of an omnipotent God. It is only because Christianity stakes itself on the unfailing love of God, following the man who dared to call God 'Father' rather than 'Judge', that life after death can even be considered.

But even though this seems to me a sounder starting place, given basic assumptions of Christian theology, than the belief that human beings are endowed with naturally immortal souls, I still have problems with it. It is comforting to be told that the love of God will not allow the termination of a relationship with him; it is also much more religiously satisfying to see this relationship as of central importance, and all the descriptions of the delights of paradise as mere symbolic gropings after the enjoyment of this divine fellowship. Nevertheless, Christian theology does hold that there are other things which are precious to God and which, in spite of that, perish forever. Christian theologians increasingly recognize that it is not the case that the whole earth, every primrose, every songbird, all the galaxies of all the heavens, exist for the benefit of humanity alone. Yet if it is true that God brought about the existence of all these things and takes delight in them; then it is also true that some of the things he delights in perish forever: a popular book of natural history estimates that 99 per cent of all species of animals which have lived on earth are now extinct.[16]

We cannot have it both ways. 'Are not three sparrows sold for a farthing?' Jesus asked. 'Yet not one of them falls to the ground without your heavenly Father's knowledge.'[17] These words of Jesus have often (and rightly) been taken as his teaching of the tender concern of the Father for all his creatures; what has not been noticed so often is that Jesus never denies that sparrows do fall. If the analogy which Jesus is drawing to God's care for persons (who, he says, 'are of more value than many sparrows') is taken to its logical conclusion, the implication, surely, is not that we will not die but that our death will not go unnoticed. If a Christian admits that God allows some things which he values to perish, it will need further argument to show why this should not also be true of human beings: the primroses, presumably, are not loved less simply because they are temporary.

But perhaps they are temporary because they are loved less? Because they are not of such enduring worth to God (as human beings are) they are allowed to perish? This still leaves me uneasy. It is one thing to believe that we are individually valued by God, and valued perhaps in a way that other things are not; it is quite another to say that this value must result in our immortality. How can we be so sure? The analogy with persons we love whom we would not willingly allow to perish assumes that our relationship with God is in this respect just like our relationship with them. But even if we accept this analogy as the best we have for our relationship with God, we must still admit that there must be considerable disanalogies as well: how do we know that the case of endless preservation is not one of them? We may believe that God looks upon us with love and compassion, but that does not seem to me to be any guarantee that he wills our everlasting existence—that is a further (very large) step. We are taught, to be sure, that God wishes to bring us to eternal life; but it is a glaring confusion to equate eternal life with endless survival. As the notion of eternal life is used in the Johannine writings, for instance, it is spoken of as a present possession, a quality of life, not a limitless quantity; nor is it something that happens after death but in this present lifetime.

Furthermore, if there were no life after death, this in itself would not mean that religion would be pointless. Just as that which is morally valuable is valuable for its own sake and not for the reward it can bring, so also trust in God, if it is worthwhile at all, is worthwhile even if it cannot go on forever. A relationship with another human being does not become pointless just because at some time it will end with the death of one of the partners; why should it be thought that a relationship with God would be pointless if one day it too should end? Shneur Zalman, the Jewish founder of the Chabad, once exclaimed, 'Master of the Universe! I desire neither Paradise nor Thy bliss in the world to come. I desire Thee and Thee alone'.[18] And the hymn of Fénelon has become the common property of Christendom:

> My God I love Thee: not because I hope for heaven thereby,
>   Nor yet because who love Thee not are lost eternally . . .
> Not for the sake of winning heaven, nor of escaping hell;
> Not from the hope of gaining aught, not seeking a reward;
>   But as thyself hast loved me, O ever loving Lord . . .
> Solely because thou art my God and my most loving King.[19]

It is true, of course, that these words (and many more examples could be given) were written by men who did believe in immortality; the point, however, is that according to them, the value of the relationship with God, the vision of God, cannot be measured by measuring its temporal duration.

But perhaps it will still be objected that if God will one day allow me to perish, this shows that all the teaching about his love for me is a vast fraud—if he really loved me, he would preserve my life. I can only reply that for reasons already given, this does not seem obvious to me. I cannot forget the primroses. They perish. Must we conclude that they are not precious to God?

I am not arguing that there is no life beyond the grave or that it is irrational to hope for it or for Christians to commit their future to God in trust. But if what I have said is correct, then it would be presumptuous to be confident that life after death is a matter of course, guaranteed, whatever the problems, by the requirements of morality and religion. We should not neglect the significant change of verb in the Nicene Creed: from affirmations 'I believe in God', 'I believe in Jesus Christ', and so on, we come to the rather more tentative 'And I look for the resurrection of the dead and the life of the world to come.' Christian faith and Christian commitment bases itself not first and foremost on a hope of survival of death, but on the intrinsic value of a relationship with God, without any reservations about what the future holds—here or hereafter.

NOTES

1. Baron F. von Hügel, *Eternal Life*, 2nd edition (Edinburgh: T. & T. Clark, 1913) p. 396.

2. 1 Cor. 15:19.

3. John Hick, *Death and Eternal Life* (London: Fontana, 1976), p. 11.

4. H. H. Price, 'Survival and the Idea of "Another World" ' in J. Donnelly (ed.), *Language, Metaphysics and Death* (New York: Fordham University Press, 1978), p. 193; see below, p. 299.

5. H. H. Price, p. 192; see below, p. 298.

6. Alfred Guillaume, *Islam,* 2nd edition (Harmondsworth, Middlesex: Penguin, 1954), p. 198.

7. Bernard Williams, 'The Makropulos Case: Reflections on the Tedium of Immortality' in his *Problems of the Self* (Cambridge: Cambridge University Press, 1973), reprinted above as chap. 9.

8. James Van Evra, 'On Death as a Limit' in Donnelly, p. 25.

9. F. Dostoyevsky, *The Brothers Karamazov,* II.V.4.

10. Dante, *The Divine Comedy: Purgatory* I. 5 & 6.

11. Fichte, *Sämmtliche Werke Vol. 5* (1845–6) p. 403, quoted in Von Hügel, p. 176.

12. Hick, p. 254.

13. Hick, p. 258. 'Salvation' as Hick uses the term involves moral perfection.

14. And of course it may put a different complexion on things that were perceived as evil in our imperfect state of knowledge, so that we see that it was a necessary condition for good; but that is not at issue here.

15. Helen Oppenheimer in a University Sermon preached in St. Mary's, Oxford, in 1979.

16. Richard F. Leakey, *The Making of Mankind* (London: Book Club Associates, 1981) p. 20.

17. Matt. 10:29.

18. Quoted in Isidore Epstein, *Judaism* (Harmondsworth, Middlesex: Penguin, 1959) p. 279.

19. Quoted from *Hymns Ancient and Modern* 106.

Survival and the Idea of 'Another World'

H. H. PRICE

New College, Oxford

IN THIS PAPER I am concerned only with the conception of survival; with the *meaning* of the Survival Hypothesis, and not with its truth or falsity. When we consider the Survival Hypothesis, whether we believe it or disbelieve it, what is it that we have in mind? Can we form any idea, even a rough and provisional one, of what a disembodied human life might be like? Supposing we cannot, it will follow that what is called the Survival Hypothesis is a mere set of words and not a hypothesis at all. The evidence adduced in favour of it might still be evidence for something, and perhaps for something important, but we should no longer have the right to claim that it is evidence for survival. There cannot be evidence for something which is completely unintelligible to us.

A very great deal of work has been done on the problem of survival, and much of the best work by members of the Society for Psychical Research. Yet there are the widest differences of opinion about the results. A number of intelligent persons would maintain that we now have a very large mass of evidence in favour of survival; that some of it is of very good quality indeed, and cannot be explained away unless we suppose that the supernormal cognitive powers of some embodied human minds are vastly more extensive and more accurate than we can easily believe them to be; in short, that on the evidence available the Survival Hypothesis is more probable than not. Some people—

Originally presented as a lecture to mark the seventieth anniversary of the Society for Psychical Research, this paper was first published in the *Proceedings of the Society for Psychical Research*, 50 Part 182 (January 1953), 1–25; reprinted by permission.

and not all of them are silly or credulous—would even maintain that the Survival Hypothesis is proved, or as near to being so as any empirical hypothesis can be. On the other hand, there are also many intelligent persons who entirely reject these conclusions. Some of them, no doubt, have not taken the trouble to examine the evidence. But others of them have; they may even have given years of study to it. They would agree that the evidence is evidence of *something,* and very likely of something important. But, they would say, it cannot be evidence of survival; there *must* be some alternative explanation of it, however difficult it may be to find out. Why do they take this line? I think it is because they find the very conception of survival unintelligible. The very idea of a "discarnate human personality" seems to them a muddled or absurd one; indeed not an idea at all, but just a phrase—an emotionally exciting one, no doubt—to which no clear meaning can be given.

Moreover, we cannot just ignore the people who have not examined the evidence. Some of our most intelligent and most highly educated contemporaries are among them. These men are well aware, by this time, that the evidence does exist, even if their predecessors fifty years ago were not. If you asked them why they do not trouble to examine it in detail, they would be able to offer reasons for their attitude. And one of their reasons, and not the least weighty in their eyes, is the contention that the very idea of survival is a muddled or absurd one. To borrow an example from Whately Carington, we know pretty well what we mean by asking whether Jones has survived a shipwreck. We are asking whether he continues to live after the shipwreck has occurred. Similarly it makes sense to ask whether he survived a railway accident, or the bombing of London. But if we substitute "his own death" for "a shipwreck," and ask whether he has survived it, our question (it will be urged) becomes unintelligible. Indeed, it *looks* self-contradictory, as if we were asking whether Jones is still alive at a time when he is no longer alive—whether Jones is both alive and not alive at the same time. We may try to escape from this logical absurdity by using phrases like "discarnate existence," "alive, but disembodied." But such phrases, it will be said, have no clear meaning. No amount of facts, however well established, can have the slightest tendency to support a meaningless hypothesis, or to answer an unintelligible question. It would therefore be a waste of time to examine such facts in detail. There are other and more important things to do.

If I am right so far, questions about the meaning of the word "survival" or of the phrase "life after death" are not quite so arid and academic as they may appear. Anyone who wants to maintain that there is empirical evidence for survival ought to consider these questions, whether he thinks the evidence strong or weak. Indeed, anyone who thinks there is a *problem* of survival at all should ask himself what his conception of survival is.

Now why should it be thought that the very idea of life after death is unintelligible? Surely it is easy enough to conceive (whether or not it is true) that experiences might occur after Jones's death which are linked with experiences which he had before his death, in such a way that his personal identity is preserved? But, it will be said, the idea of after-death *experiences* is just the difficulty. What kind of experiences could they conceivably be? In a disembodied state, the supply of sensory stimuli is perforce cut off, because the supposed experient has no sense organs and no nervous system. There can therefore be no sense-perception. One has no means of being aware of material objects any longer; and if one has not, it is hard to see how one could have any emotions or wishes either. For all the emotions and wishes we have in this present life are concerned directly or indirectly with material objects, including of course our own organisms and other organisms, especially other human ones. In short, one could only be said to have experiences at all, if one is aware of some sort of a *world*. In this way, the idea of survival is bound up with the idea of "another world" or a "next world." Anyone who maintains that the idea of survival is after all intelligible must also be claiming that we can form some conception, however rough and provisional, of what "the next world" or "other world" might be like. The sceptics I have in mind would say that we can form no such conception at all; and this, I think, is one of the main reasons why they hold that the conception of survival itself is unintelligible. I wish to suggest, on the contrary, that we *can* form some conception, in outline at any rate, of what a "next world" or "another" world might be like, and consequently of the kind of experiences which disembodied minds, if indeed there are such, might be supposed to have.

The thoughts which I wish to put before you on this subject are not at all original. Something very like them is to be found in the chapter on survival in Whately Carington's book *Telepathy* (London: Methuen, 1945), and in the concluding chapter of Professor C. J. Ducasse's book *Nature, Mind and Death* (LaSalle: Open Court, 1951). Moreover, if I am not mistaken, the Hindu conception of *Kama Loka* (literally, "the world of desire") is essentially the same as the one I wish to discuss; and something very similar is to be found in Mahayana Buddhism. In these two religions, of course, there is not just one "other world" but several different "other worlds," which we are supposed to experience in succession; not merely the next world, but the next but one, and another after that. But I think it will be quite enough for us to consider just the next world, without troubling ourselves about any additional other worlds which there might be. It is a sufficiently difficult task, for us Western people, to convince ourselves that it makes sense to speak of any sort of after-death world at all. Accordingly, I shall use the expressions "next world" and "other world" interchangeably. If anyone thinks this is an oversimplification, it will be easy for him to make the necessary corrections.

The next world might be conceived as a kind of dream-world. When we are asleep, sensory stimuli are cut off, or at any rate are prevented from having their normal effects upon our brain-centres. But we still manage to have experiences. It is true that sense-perception no longer occurs, but something sufficiently like it does. In sleep, our image-producing powers, which are more or less inhibited in waking life by a continuous bombardment of sensory stimuli, are released from this inhibition. And then we are provided with a multitude of objects of awareness, about which we employ our thoughts and towards which we have desires and emotions. These objects which we are aware of behave in a way which seems very queer to us when we wake up. The laws of their behaviour are not the laws of physics. But however queer their behaviour is, it does not at all disconcert us at the time and our personal identity is not broken.

In other words, my suggestion is that the next world, if there is one, might be a world of mental images. Nor need such a world be so "thin and insubstantial" as you might think. Paradoxical as it may sound, there is nothing imaginary about a mental image. It is an actual entity, as real as anything can be. The seeming paradox arises from the ambiguity of the verb "to imagine." It does sometimes mean "to have mental images." But more usually it means "to entertain propositions without believing them"; and very often they are false propositions, and moreover we *dis*believe them in the act of entertaining them. This is what happens, for example, when we read Shakespeare's play *The Tempest,* and that is why we say that Prospero and Ariel are "imaginary characters." Mental images are not in this sense imaginary at all. We do actually experience them, and they are no more imaginary than sensations. To avoid the paradox, though at the cost of some pedantry, it would be well to distinguish between *imagining* and *imaging,* and to have two different adjectives "imaginary" and "imagy." In this terminology, it is imaging, and not imagining, that I wish to talk about; and the next world, as I am trying to conceive of it, is an *imagy* world, but not on that account an imaginary one.

Indeed, to those who experienced it an image-world would be just as "real" as this present world is; perhaps so like it, that they would have considerable difficulty in realizing that they were dead. We are, of course, sometimes told in mediumistic communication that quite a lot of people do find it difficult to realize that they are dead; and this is just what we should expect if the next world is an image-world. Lord Russell and other philosophers have maintained that a material object in this present physical world is nothing more or less than a complicated system of *appearances*. So far as I can see, there might be a set of visual images related to each other perspectivally, with front views and side views and back views all fitting neatly together in the way that ordinary visual appearances do now. Such a group of images might contain tactual images too. Similarly it might contain auditory images and smell images. Such a family of interrelated images would make a pretty good object. It would be quite a satisfactory substitute for the material objects which we perceive in this present life. And a whole world composed of such families of mental images would make a perfectly good world.

It is possible, however, and indeed likely, that some of those images would be what Francis Galton called *generic* images. An image representing a dog or a tree need not necessarily be an exact replica of some individual dog or tree one has perceived. It might rather be a representation of a *typical* dog or tree. Our memories are more specific on some subjects than on others. How specific they are depends probably on the degree of interest we had in the individual objects or events at the time when we perceived them. An event which moved us deeply is likely to be remembered specifically and in detail; and so is an individual object to which we were much attached (for example, the home of our childhood). But with other objects which interested us less and were less attended to, we retain only a "general impression" of a whole class of objects collectively. Left to our own resources, as we should be in the other world, with nothing but our memories to depend on, we should probably be able to form only generic images of such objects. In this respect, an image-world would not be an exact replica of this one, not even of those parts of this one which we have actually perceived. To some extent it would be, so to speak, a generalized picture, rather than a detailed reproduction.

Let us now put our question in another way, and ask what kind of experience a disembodied human mind might be supposed to have. We can then answer that it might be an experience in which *imaging* replaces sense-perception; "replaces" it, in the sense that imaging would perform much the same function as sense-perception performs now, by providing us with objects about which we could have thoughts, emotions, and wishes. There is no reason why we should not be "as much alive," or at any rate *feel* as much alive, in an image-world as we do now in this present material world, which we perceive by means of our sense-organs and nervous systems. And so the use of the word "survival" ("life after death") would be perfectly justifiable.

It will be objected, perhaps, that one cannot be said to be alive unless one has a body. But what is meant here by "alive"? It is surely conceivable (whether or not it is true) that *experiences* should occur which are not causally connected with a physical organism. If they did, should we or should we not say that "life" was occurring? I do not think it matters much whether we answer Yes or No. It is purely a question of definition. If you define "life" in terms of certain very complicated physico-chemical processes, as some people would, then of course life after death is by definition impossible, because there is no longer anything to be alive. In that case, the problem of survival (*life* after bodily death) is misnamed. Instead, it ought to be called the problem of after-death *experiences*. And this is in fact the problem with which all investigators of the subject have been concerned. After all, what people want to know, when they ask whether we survive death, is simply whether experiences occur after death, or what likelihood, if any, there is that they do; and whether such experiences, if they do occur, are linked with each other and with *ante mortem* ones in such a way that personal identity is preserved. It is not physico-chemical processes which interest us, when we ask such questions. But there is another sense of the words "life" and "alive" which may be called the psychological sense; and in this sense, "being alive" just *means* "having experiences of certain sorts." In this psychological sense of the word "life," it is perfectly intelligible to ask whether there is life after death, even though life in the physiological sense does *ex hypothesi* come to an end when someone dies. Of, if you like, the question is whether one could feel alive after bodily death, even though (by hypothesis) one would not *be* alive at the time. It will be just enough to satisfy most of us if the *feeling* of being alive continues after death. It will not make a halfpennyworth of difference that one will not then *be* alive in the physiological or biochemical sense of the word.

It may be said, however, that "feeling alive" (life in the psychological sense) cannot just be equated with having experiences in general. Feeling alive, surely, consists in having experiences of a special sort, namely *organic sensations*—bodily feelings of various sorts. In our present experience, these bodily feelings are not as a rule separately attended to unless they are unusually intense or unusually painful. They are a kind of undifferentiated mass in the background of consciousness. All the same, it would be said, they constitute our feeling of being alive; and if they were absent (as surely they must be when the body is dead) the feeling of being alive could not be there.

I am not at all sure that this argument is as strong as it looks. I think we should still feel alive—or alive enough—provided we experienced emotions and wishes, even if no organic sensations accompanied these experiences, as they do now. But in case I am wrong here, I would suggest that *images* of organic sensations could perfectly well provide what is needed. We can quite well image to ourselves what it feels like to be in a warm bath, even when we are not actually in one; and a person who has been crippled can image what it felt like to climb a mountain. Moreover, I would ask whether we do not feel alive when we are dreaming. It seems to me that we obviously do—or at any rate quite alive enough to go on with.

This is not all. In an image-world, a dream-like world such as I am trying to describe, there is no reason at all why there should not be *visual* images resembling the body which one had in this present world. In this present life (for all who are not blind) visual percepts of one's own body form as it were the constant centre of one's perceptual world. It is perfectly possible that visual images of one's own body might perform the same function in the next. They might form the continuing centre or nucleus of one's image world, remaining more or less constant while other images altered. If this were so, we should have an additional reason for expecting that recently dead people would find it difficult to realize that they were dead, that is, disembodied. To all appearances they *would* have bodies just as they had before, and pretty much the same ones. But, of course, they might discover in time that these image-bodies were subject to rather peculiar causal laws. For example, it might be found that in an image-world our wishes tend *ipso facto* to fulfil themselves in a way they do not now. A wish to go to Oxford might be immediately followed by the occurrence of a vivid and detailed set of Oxfordlike images; even though, at the moment before, one's images had resembled Piccadilly Circus or the palace of the Dalai Lama in Tibet. In that case, one would realize that "going somewhere"—transferring one's body from one place to another—was a rather different process from what it had been in the physical world. Reflecting on such experiences, one might come to the conclusion that one's body was not after all the same as the physical body one had before death. One might conclude perhaps that it must be a "spiritual" or "psychical" body, closely resembling the old body in appearance, but possessed of rather different causal properties. It has been said, of course, that phrases like "spiritual body" or "psychical body" are utterly unintelligible, and that no conceivable empirical meaning could be given to such expressions. But I would rather suggest that they might be a way (rather a misleading way perhaps) of referring to a set of body-like images. If our supposed dead empiricist continued his investigations, he might discover that his whole world—not only his own body, but everything else he was aware of—had different causal properties from the physical world, even though everything in it had shape, size, colour, and other qualities which material objects have now. And so eventually, by the exercise of ordinary inductive good sense, he could draw the conclusion that he was in "the next world" or "the other world" and no longer in this one. If, however, he were a very dogmatic philosopher, who distrusted inductive good sense and preferred a priori reasoning, I do not know what condition he would be in. Probably he would never discover that he was dead at all. Being persuaded, on a priori grounds, that life after death was impossible, he might insist on thinking that he must still be in this world, and refuse to pay attention to the new and strange causal laws which more empirical thinking would notice.

I think, then, that there is no difficulty in conceiving that the experience of feeling alive could occur in the absence of a physical organism; or, if you prefer to put it so, a disembodied personality could *be* alive in the psychological sense, even though by definition it would not be alive in the physiological or biochemical sense.

Moreover, I do not see why disembodiment need involve the destruction of personal identity. It is, of course, sometimes supposed that personal identity depends on the continuance of a background of organic sensation—the "mass of bodily feeling" mentioned before. (This may be called the somato-centric analysis of personal identity.) We must notice, however, that this background of organic sensation is not literally the same from one period of time to another. The very most that can happen is that the organic sensations which form the background of my experience now should be *exactly similar* to those which were the background of my experience a minute ago. And as a matter of fact, the present ones need not *all* be similar to the previous ones. I might have a twinge of toothache now which I did not have then. I may even have an overall feeling of lassitude now which I did not have a minute ago, so that the whole mass of bodily feeling, and not merely part of it, is rather different; and this would not interrupt my personal identity at all. The most that is required is only that the majority (not all) of my organic sensations should be closely (not exactly) similar to those I previously had. And even this is needed only if the two occasions are close together in my private time series; the organic sensations I have now might well be very unlike those I used to have when I was one year old. I say "in my private time series." For when I wake up after eight hours of dreamless sleep my personal identity is not broken, though in the physical or public time series there has been a long interval between the last organic sensations I experienced before falling sleep, and the first ones I experience when I wake up. But if similarity, and not literal sameness, is all that is required of this "continuing organic background," it seems to me that the continuity of it could be perfectly well preserved if there were organic *images* after death very like the organic sensations which occurred before death.

As a matter of fact, this whole "somato-centric" analysis of personal identity appears to me highly disputable. I should have thought that Locke was much nearer the truth when he said that personal identity depends on memory. But I have tried to show that even if the "somato-centric" theory of personal identity is right, there is no reason why personal identity need be broken by bodily death, provided there are images after death which sufficiently resemble the organic sensations one had before; and this is very like what happens when one falls asleep and begins dreaming.

There is, however, another argument against the conceivability of a disembodied person, to which some present-day linguistic philosophers would attach great weight. It is neatly expressed by Mr. A. G. N. Flew when he says, "people are what you meet."[1] By a "person" we are supposed to mean a human organism which behaves in certain ways, and especially one which speaks and can be spoken to. And when we say, "this is the same person whom I saw yesterday," we are supposed to mean just that it is the same human organism which I saw yesterday, and also that it behaves in a recognizably similar way.

"People are what you meet." With all respect to Mr. Flew, I would suggest that he does not in this sense "meet" *himself.* He might indeed have had one of those curious out-of-body experiences which are occasionally mentioned in our records, and he might have seen his body from outside (if he has, I heartily congratulate him); but I do not think we should call this "meeting." And surely the important question is, what constitutes my personal identity *for myself.* It certainly does not consist in the fact that other people can "meet" me. It might be that I was for myself the same person as before, even at a time when it was quite impossible for others to meet me. No one can "meet" me when I am dreaming. They can, of course, come and look at my body lying in bed; but this is not "meeting," because no sort of social relations are possible between them and me. Yet, although temporarily "unmeetable," during my dreams I am still, for myself, the same person that I was. And if I went on dreaming *in perpetuum,* and could never be "met" again, this need not prevent me from continuing to be, for myself, the same person.

As a matter of fact, however, we can quite easily conceive that "meeting" of a kind might still be possible between discarnate experients. And therefore, even if we do make it part of the definition of "a person," that he is capable of being met by others, it will still make sense to speak of "discarnate persons," provided we allow that telepathy is possible between them. It is true that a special sort of telepathy would be needed; the sort which in life produces *telepathic apparitions*. It would not be sufficient that *A*'s thoughts or emotions should be telepathically affected by *B*'s. If such telepathy were sufficiently prolonged and continuous, and especially if it were reciprocal, it would indeed have some of the characteristics of social intercourse; but I do not think we should call it "meeting," at any rate in Mr. Flew's sense of the word. It would be necessary, in addition, that *A* should be aware of something which could be called "*B*'s body," or should have an experience not too unlike the experience of *seeing* another person in this life. This additional condition would be satisfied if *A* experienced a telepathic apparition of *B*. It would be necessary, further, that the telepathic apparition by means of which *B* "announces himself" (if one may put it so) should be recognizably similar on different occasions. And if it were a case of meeting some person *again* whom one had previously known in this world, the telepathic apparition would have to be recognizably similar to the physical body which that person had when he was still alive.

There is no reason why an image-world should not contain a number of images which are telepathic apparitions; and if it did, one could quite intelligently speak of "meeting other persons" in such a world. All the experiences I have when I meet another person in this present life could still occur, with only this difference, that percepts would be replaced by images. It would also be possible for another person to "meet" me in the same manner, if I, as a telepathic agent, could cause him to experience a suitable telepathic apparition, sufficiently resembling the body I used to have when he formerly "met" me in this life.

I now turn to another problem which may have troubled some of you. If there be a next world, *where* is it? Surely it must be somewhere. But there does not seem to be any room for it. We can hardly suppose that it is up in the sky (i.e., outside the earth's atmosphere) or under the surface of the earth, as Homer and Vergil seemed to think. Such suggestions may have contented our ancestors, and the Ptolemaic astronomy may have made them acceptable, for some ages, even to the learned; but they will hardly content us. Surely the next world, if it exists, must be somewhere; and yet, it seems, there is nowhere for it to be.

The answer to this difficulty is easy if we conceive of the next world in the way I have suggested, as a dream-like world of mental images. Mental images, including dream images, are in a space of their own. They do have spatial properties. Visual images, for instance, have extension and shape, and they have spatial relations to one another. But they have no spatial relation to objects in the physical world. If I dream of a tiger, my tiger-image has extension and shape. The dark stripes have spatial relation to the yellow parts, and to each other; the nose has a spatial relation to the tail. Again, the tiger image as a whole may have spatial relations to another image in my dream, for example to an image resembling a palm tree. But suppose we have to ask how far it is from the foot of my bed, whether it is three inches long, or longer or shorter; is it not obvious that these questions are absurd ones? We cannot answer them, not because we lack the necessary information or find it impracticable to make the necessary measurements, but because the questions themselves have no meaning. In the space of the physical world these images are nowhere at all. But in relation to other images of mine, each of them is somewhere. Each of them is extended, and its parts are in spatial relations to one another. There is no a priori reason why all extended entities must be in physical space.

If we now apply these considerations to the next world, as I am conceiving of it, we see that the question "where is it?" simply does not arise. An image-world would have a space of its own. We could not find it anywhere in the space of the physical world, but this would not in the least prevent it from being a spatial world all the same. If you like, it would be its own "where."[2]

I am tempted to illustrate this point by referring to the fairy-tale of Jack and the Beanstalk. I am not of course suggesting that we should take the story seriously. But if we were asked to try to make sense of it, how should we set about it? Obviously the queer world which Jack found was not at the top of the beanstalk in the literal, spatial sense of the words "at the top of." Perhaps he found some very large pole rather like a beanstalk, and climbed up it. But (we shall say) when he got to the top he suffered an abrupt change of consciousness, and began to have a dream or waking vision of a strange country with a giant in it. To choose another and more respectable illustration: In Book VI of Vergil's *Aeneid,* we are told how Aeneas descended into the Cave of Avernus with the Sibyl and walked from there into the other world. If we wished to make the narrative of the illustrious poet intelligible, how should we set about it? We should suppose that Aeneas did go down into the cave, but that once he was there he suffered a change of consciousness, and all the strange experiences which happened afterwards—seeing the River Styx, the Elysian Fields, and the rest—were part of a dream or vision which he had. The space he passed through in his journey was an image space, and the River Styx was not three Roman miles, or any other number of miles, from the cave in which his body was.

It follows that when we speak of "passing" from this world to the next, this passage is not to be thought of as any sort of movement in space. It should rather be thought of as a change of consciousness, analogous to the change which occurs when we "pass" from waking experience to dreaming. It would be a change from the perceptual type of consciousness to another type of consciousness in which perception ceases and imaging replaces it, but unlike the change from waking consciousness to dreaming in being irreversible. I suppose that nearly everyone nowadays who talks of "passing" from this world to the other does think of the transition in this way, as some kind of irreversible change of consciousness, and not as a literal spatial transition in which one goes from one place to another place.

So much for the question "where the next world is," if there be one. I have tried to show that if the next world is conceived of as a world of mental images, the question simply does not arise. I now turn to another difficulty. It may be felt that an image-world is somehow a deception and a sham, not a real world at all. I have said that it would be a kind of dream-world. Now, when one has a dream in this life, surely the things one is aware of in the dream are not *real* things. No doubt the dreamer really does have various mental images. These images do actually occur. But this is not all that happens. As a result of having these images, the dreamer believes, or takes for granted, that various material objects exist, and various physical events occur; and these beliefs are mistaken. For example, he believes that there is a wall in front of him and that by a mere effort of will he succeeds in flying over the top of it. But the wall did not really exist, and he did not really fly over the top of it. He was in a state of delusion. Because of the images which he really did have, there *seemed* to him to be various objects and events which did not really exist at all. Similarly, you may argue, it may *seem* to discarnate minds (if indeed there are such) that there is a world in which they live, and a world not unlike this one. If they have mental images of the appropriate sort, it may even *seem* to them that they have bodies not unlike the ones they had in this life. But surely they will be mistaken. It is all very well to say, with the poet, that "dreams are real while they last"—that dream-objects are only called "unreal" when one wakes up, and normal sense-perceptions begin to occur with which the dream experiences can be contrasted. And it is all very well to conclude from this that if one did *not* wake up, if the change from sense-perception to imaging were irreversible, one would not call one's dream-objects unreal, because there would then be nothing with which to contrast them. But would they not still *be* unreal for all that? Surely discarnate minds, according to my account of them, would be in a state of permanent delusion; whereas a dreamer in this life (fortunately for him) is only in a temporary one. And the fact that a delusion goes on for a long time, even forever and ever, does not make it any less delusive. Delusions do not turn themselves into realities just by going on and on. Nor are they turned into realities by the fact that their victim is deprived of the power of detecting their delusiveness.

Now, of course, if it were true that the next life (supposing there is one) is a condition of permanent delusion, we should just have to put up with it. We might not like it; we might think that a state of permanent delusion is a bad state to be in. But our likes and dislikes are irrelevant to the question. I would suggest, however, that this argument about the "delusiveness" or "unreality" of an image-world is based on confusion.

One may doubt whether there is any clear meaning in using the words "real" and "unreal" *tout court,* in this perfectly general and unspecified way. One may properly say "this is real silver, and that is not," "this is a real pearl and that is not," or again "this is a real pool of water, and that is only a mirage." The point here is that something *X* is mistakenly believed to be something else *Y,* because it does resemble *Y* in some respects. It makes perfectly good sense, then, to say that *X* is not really *Y.* This piece of plated brass is not real silver, true enough. It only looks like silver. But for all that, it cannot be called "unreal" in the unqualified sense, in the sense of not existing at all. Even the mirage is something, though it is not the pool of water you took it to be. It is a perfectly good set of visual appearances, though it is not related to other appearances in the way you thought it was; for example, it does not have the relations to tactual appearances, or to visual appearances from other places, which you expected it to have. You may properly say that the mirage is not a real pool of water, or even that it is not a real physical object, and that anyone who thinks it is must be in a state of delusion. But there is no clear meaning in saying that it is just "unreal" *tout court,* without any further specification or explanation. In short, when the word "unreal" is applied to something, one means that it is different from something else, with which it might be mistakenly identified; what that something else is may not be explicitly stated, but it can be gathered from the context.

What, then, could people mean by saying that a next world such as I have described would be "unreal"? If they are saying anything intelligible, they must mean that it is different from something else, something else which it does resemble in some respects, and might therefore be confused with. And what is that something else? It is the present physical world in which we now live. An image-world, then, is only "unreal" in the sense that it is not really physical, though it might be mistakenly thought to be physical by some of those who experience it. But this only amounts to saying that the world I am describing would be an *other* world, other than this present physical world, and yet sufficiently like it to be possibly confused with it, because images do resemble percepts. And what would this otherness consist in? First, in the fact that it is a *space* which is other than physical space; secondly, and still more important, in the fact that the *causal laws* of an image-world would be different from the laws of physics. And this is also our ground for saying that the events we experience in dreams are "unreal," that is, not really physical, though mistakenly believed by the dreamer to be so. They do in some ways closely resemble physical events, and that is why the mistake is possible. But the causal laws of their occurrence are quite different, as we recognize when we wake up; and just occasionally we recognize it even while we are still asleep.

Now let us consider the argument that the inhabitants of the other world, as I have described it, would be in a state of delusion. I admit that some of them might be. That would be the condition of the people described in the mediumistic communications already referred to— the people who "do not realize that they are dead." Because their images are so like the normal percepts they were accustomed to in this life, they believe mistakenly that they are still living in the physical world. But, as I already tried to explain, their state of delusion need not be permanent and irremediable. By attending to the relations between one image and another, and applying the ordinary inductive methods by which we ourselves have discovered the causal laws of this present world in which *we* live, they too could discover in time what the causal laws of *their* world are. These laws, we may suppose, would be more like the laws of Freudian psychology than the laws of physics. And once the discovery was made, they would be cured of their delusion. They would find out, perhaps with surprise, that the world they were experiencing was *other* than the physical world which they experienced before, even though like it in some respects.

Let us now try to explore the conception of a world of mental images a little more fully. Would it not be a *"subjective"* world? And surely there would be many *different* next worlds, not just one; and each of them would be private. Indeed, would there not be as many next worlds as there are discarnate minds, and each of them wholly private to the mind which experiences it? In short, it may seem that each of us, when dead, would have his own dream-world, and there would be no common or public next world at all.

"Subjective," perhaps, is a rather slippery word. Certainly, an image-world would have to be subjective in the sense of being mind-dependent, dependent for its existence upon mental processes of one sort or another; images, after all, are mental entities. But I do not think that such a world need be completely private if telepathy occurs in the next life. I have already mentioned the part which telepathic apparitions might play in it in connection with Mr. Flew's contention that "people are what you meet." But there is more to be said. It is reasonable to suppose that in a disembodied state telepathy would occur more frequently than it does now. It seems likely that in this present life our telepathic powers are constantly being inhibited by our need to adjust ourselves to our physical environment. It even seems likely that many telepathic "impressions" which we receive at the unconscious level are shut out from consciousness by a kind of biologically motivated censorship. Once the pressure of biological needs is removed, we might expect that telepathy would occur continually, and manifest itself in consciousness by modifying and adding to the images which one experiences. (Even in this life, after all, some dreams are telepathic.)

If this is right, an image-world such as I am describing would not be the product of one single mind only, nor would it be purely private. It would be the joint product of a group of telepathically interacting minds and public to all of them. Nevertheless, one would not expect it to have unrestricted publicity. It is likely that there would still be *many* next worlds, a different one for each group of like-minded personalities. I admit I am not quite sure what might be meant by "like-minded" and "unlike-minded" in this connection. Perhaps we could say that two personalities are like-minded if their memories or their characters are sufficiently similar. It might be that Nero and Marcus Aurelius do not have a world in common, but Socrates and Marcus Aurelius do.

So far, we have a picture of many "semi-public" next worlds, if one may put it so; each of them composed of mental images, and yet not wholly private for all that, but public to a limited group of telepathically interacting minds. Or, if you like, after death everyone does have his own dream, but there is still some overlap between one person's dream and another's because of telepathy.

I have said that such a world would be mind-dependent, even though dependent on a group of minds rather than a single mind. In what way would it be mind-dependent? Presumably in the same way as dreams are now. It would be dependent on the *memories* and the *desires* of the persons who experienced it. Their memories and their desires would determine what sort of images they had. If I may put it so, the "stuff" or "material" of such a world would come in the end from one's memories, and the "form" of it from one's desires. To use another analogy, memory would provide the pigments, and desire would paint the picture. One might expect, I think, that desires which had been unsatisfied in one's earthly life would play a specially important part in the process. That may seem an agreeable prospect. But there is another which is less agreeable. Desires which had been *repressed* in one's earthly life, because it was too painful or too disgraceful to admit that one had them, might also play a part, and perhaps an important part, in determining what images one would have in the next. And the same might be true of repressed memories. It may be suggested that what Freud (in one stage of his thought) called "the censor"—the force or barrier or mechanism which keeps some of our desires and memories out of consciousness, or only lets them in when they disguise themselves in symbolic and distorted forms—operates only in this present life and not in the next. However we conceive of "the censor," it does seem to be a device for enabling us to adapt ourselves to our environment. And when we no longer have an environment, one would expect that the barrier would come down.

We can now see that an after-death world of mental images can also be quite reasonably described in the terminology of the Hindu thinkers as "a world of desire" *(Kama Loka)*. Indeed, this is just what we should expect if we assume that dreams, in this present life, are the best available clue to what the next life might be like. Such a world could also be described as "a world of memories"; because imaging, in the end, is a function of memory, one of the ways in which our memory-dispositions manifest themselves. But this description would be less apt, even though correct as far as it goes. To use the same rather inadequate language as before: the "materials" out of which an image-world is composed would have to come from the memories of the mind or group of minds whose world it is. But it would be their desires (including those repressed in earthly life) which determined the way in which these memories were used, the precise kind of dream which was built up out of them or on the basis of them.

It will, of course, be objected that memories cannot exist in the absence of a physical brain, nor yet desires, nor images either. But this proposition, however plausible, is after all just an empirical hypothesis, not a necessary truth. Certainly there is empirical evidence in favour of it. But there is also empirical evidence against it. Broadly speaking one might say, perhaps, that the "normal" evidence tends to support this materialistic or epiphenomenalist theory of memories, images, and desires, whereas the "supernormal" evidence on the whole tends to weaken the materialist or epiphenomenalist theory of human personality (of which this hypothesis about the brain-dependent character of memories, images, and desires is a part). Moreover, any evidence which directly supports the Survival Hypothesis (and there is quite a lot of evidence which does, provided we are prepared to admit that the Survival Hypothesis is intelligible at all) is *pro tanto* evidence against the materialistic conception of human personality.

In this paper, I am not trying to argue in favour of the Survival Hypothesis. I am only concerned with the more modest task of trying to make it intelligible. All I want to maintain, then, is that there is nothing self-contradictory or logically absurd in the hypothesis that memories, desires, and images can exist in the absence of a physical brain. The hypothesis may, of course, be false. My point is only that it is not absurd; or if you like, that it is at any rate intelligible, whether true or not. To put the question in another way, when we are trying to work out for ourselves what sort of thing a discarnate life might conceivably be (if there is one), we have to ask what kind of *equipment,* so to speak, a discarnate mind might be supposed to have. It cannot have the power of sense-perception, nor the power of acting on the physical world by means of efferent nerves, muscles, and limbs. What would it have left? What could we take out with us, as it were, when we pass from this life to the next? What we take out with us, I suggest, can only be our memories and desires, and the power of constructing out of them an image-world to suit us. Obviously, we cannot take our material possessions out with us; but I do not think this is any great loss, for if we remember them well enough and are sufficiently attached to them, we shall be able to construct image-replicas of them which will be just as good, and perhaps better.

In this connection I should like to mention a point which has been made several times before. Both Whately Carington and Professor Ducasse have referred to it, and no doubt other writers have. But I believe it is of some importance and worth repeating. Ecclesiastically minded critics sometimes speak rather scathingly of the "materialistic" character of mediumistic communications. They are not at all edified by these descriptions of agreeable houses, beautiful landscapes, gardens, and the rest. And then, of course, there is Raymond Lodge's notorious cigar.[3] These critics complain that the next world as described in these communications is no more than a reproduction of this one, slightly improved perhaps. And the argument apparently is that the "materialistic" character of the communications is evidence against their genuineness. On the contrary: as far as it goes, it is evidence *for* their genuineness. Most people in this life do like material objects and are deeply interested in them. This may be deplorable, but there it is. If so, the image-world they would create for themselves in the next life might be expected to have just the "materialistic" character of which these critics complain. If one had been fond of nice houses and pleasant gardens in this life, the image-world one would create for oneself in the next might be expected to contain image-replicas of such objects, and one would make these replicas as like "the real thing" as one's memories permitted; with the help, perhaps, of telepathic influences from other minds whose tastes were similar. This would be all the more likely to happen if one had not been able to enjoy such things in this present life as much as one could wish.

But possibly I have misunderstood the objection which these ecclesiastical critics are making. Perhaps they are saying that if the next world is like this, life after death is not worth having. Well and good. If they would prefer a different sort of next world, and find the one described in these communications insipid and unsatisfying to their aspirations, then they can expect to get a different one—in fact, just the sort of next world they want. They have overlooked a crucial point which seems almost obvious; that if there is an after-death life at all, there must surely be many next worlds, separate from and as it were impenetrable to one another, corresponding to the *different* desires which different groups of discarnate personalities have.

The belief in life after death is often dismissed as "mere wish-fulfilment." Now, it will be noticed that the next world as I have been trying to conceive of it is precisely a wish-fulfilment world, in much the same sense in which some dreams are described as wish-fulfilments. Should not this make a rational man very suspicious of the ideas I am putting before you? Surely this account of the other world is "too good to be true"? I think not. Here we must distinguish two different questions. The question whether human personality continues to exist after death is a question of fact, and wishes have nothing to do with it one way or the other. But *if* the answer to this factual question were "Yes" (and I emphasise the "if"), wishes might have a very great deal to do with the kind of world which discarnate beings would live in. Perhaps it may be helpful to consider a parallel case. It is a question of fact whether dreams occur in this present life. It has been settled by empirical investigation, and the wishes of the investigators have nothing to do with it. It is just a question of what the empirical facts are, whether one likes them or not. Nevertheless, granting that dreams do occur, a man's wishes might well have a very great deal to do with determining what the content of his dreams is to be; especially unconscious wishes on the one hand, and, on the other, conscious wishes which are not satisfied in waking life. Of course the parallel is not exact. There is one very important difference between the two cases. With dreams, the question of fact is settled. It is quite certain that many people do have dreams. But in the case of survival, the question of fact is not settled, or not at present. It is still true, however, that though wishes have nothing to do with it, they have a very great deal to do with the kind of world we should live in after death, *if* we survive death at all.

But perhaps this does not altogether dispose of the objection that my account of the other world is "too good to be true." Surely a sober-minded and cautious person would be very shy of believing that there is, or even could be, a world in which all our wishes are fulfilled? How very suspicious we are about travellers' tales of Eldorado or descriptions of idyllic South Sea islands! Certainly we are, and on good empirical grounds. For they are tales about this present material world; and we know that matter is very often recalcitrant to human wishes. But in a dream-world Desire is king. This objection would only hold good if the world I am describing were supposed to be some part of the *material* world—another planet perhaps, or the Earthly Paradise of which some poets have written. But the next world as I am trying to conceive of it (or rather next worlds, for we have seen that there would be many different ones) is not of course supposed to be part of the material world at all. It is a dream-like world of mental images. True enough, some of these images might be expected to resemble some of the material objects with which we are familiar now; but only if, and to the extent that, their percipients *wanted* this resemblance to exist. There is every reason, then, for being suspicious about descriptions of this present material world, or alleged parts of it, on the ground that they are "too good to be true"; but when it is a "country of the mind" (if one may say so) which is being described, these suspicions are groundless. A purely mind-dependent world, if such a world there be, would *have* to be a wish-fulfilment world.

Nevertheless, likes and dislikes, however irrelevant they may be, do of course have a powerful psychological influence upon us when we consider the problem of survival; not only when we consider the factual evidence for or against, but also when we are merely considering the theoretical implications of the Survival Hypothesis itself, as I am doing now. It is therefore worthwhile to point out that the next world as I am conceiving of it need not necessarily be an agreeable place at all. If arguments about what is good or what is bad did have any relevance, a case could be made out for saying that this conception of the next world is "too bad to be true," rather than too good. As we have seen, we should have to reckon with many different next worlds, not just with one. The world you experience after death would depend upon the kind of person you are. And if what I have said so far has any sense in it, we can easily conceive that some people's next worlds would be much more like purgatories than paradises—and pretty unpleasant purgatories too.

This is because there are *conflicting* desires within the same person.

Few people, if any, are completely integrated personalities, though some people come nearer to it than others. And sometimes when a man's desires appear (even to himself) to be more or less harmonious with one another, the appearance is deceptive. His conscious desires do not conflict with one another, or not much; but this harmony has been achieved only at the cost of repression. He has unconscious desires which conflict with the neatly organized pattern of his conscious life. If I was right in suggesting that repression is a biological phenomenon, if the "threshold" between conscious and unconscious no longer operates in a disembodied state, or operates much less effectively, this seeming harmony will vanish after the man is dead. To use scriptural language, the secrets of his heart will be revealed—at any rate to himself. These formerly repressed desires will manifest themselves by appropriate images, and these images might be exceedingly horrifying—as some dream-images are in this present life, and for the same reason. True enough, they will be "wish-fulfilment" images, like everything else that he experiences in the next world as I am conceiving of it. But the wishes they fulfil will conflict with other wishes which he also has. And the emotional state which results might be worse than the worst nightmare; worse, because the dreamer cannot wake up from it. For example, in his after-death dream-world he finds himself doing appallingly cruel actions. He never did them in his earthly life. Yet the desire to do them was there, even though repressed and unacknowledged. And now the lid is off, and this cruel desire fulfils itself by creating appropriate images. But unfortunately for his comfort, he has benevolent desires as well, perhaps quite strong ones; and so he is distressed and even horrified by these images, even though there is also a sense in which they are just the ones he wanted. Of course his benevolent desires too may be expected to manifest themselves by appropriate wish-fulfilment images. But because there is this conflict in his nature, they will not wholly satisfy him either. There will be something in him which rejects them as tedious and insipid. It is a question of the point of view, if one cares to put it so. Suppose a person has two conflicting desires A and B. Then from the point of view of desire A, the images which fulfil desire B will be unsatisfying, or unpleasant, or even horrifying; and vice versa from the point of view of desire B. And unfortunately, both points of view belong to the same person. He occupies them both at once.

This is not all. If psychoanalysts are right, there is such a thing as a desire to be punished. Most people, we are told, have guilt-feelings which are more or less repressed; we have desires, unacknowledged or only half-acknowledged, to suffer for the wrongs we have done. These desires too will have their way in the next world, if my picture of it is right, and will manifest themselves by images which fulfil them. It is not a very pleasant prospect, and I need not elaborate it. But it looks as if everyone would experience an image-purgatory which exactly suits him. It is true that his unpleasant experiences would not literally be punishments, any more than terrifying dreams are, in this present life. They would not be inflicted upon him by an external judge; though, of course, if we are theists, we shall hold that the laws of nature, in other worlds as in this one, are in the end dependent on the will of a Divine Creator. Each man's purgatory would be just the automatic consequence of his own desires; if you like, he would punish himself by having just those images which his own good feelings demand. But, if there is any consolation in it, he would have these unpleasant experiences because he *wanted* to have them; exceedingly unpleasant as they might be, there would still be something in him which was satisfied by them.

There is another aspect of the conflict of desires. Every adult person has what we call "a character"; a set of more or less settled and permanent desires, with the corresponding emotional dispositions, expressing themselves in a more or less predictable pattern of thoughts, feelings, and actions. But it is perfectly possible to desire that one's character should be different, perhaps very different, from what it is at present. This is what philosophers call a "second-order" desire, a desire that some of one's own desires should be altered. Such second-order desires are not necessarily ineffective, as New York resolutions are supposed to be. People can within limits alter their own characters, and sometimes do; and if they succeed in doing so, it is in the end because they *want* to. But these second-order desires—desires to alter one's own character—are seldom effective immediately; and even when they appear to be, as in some cases of religious conversion, there has probably been a long period of subconscious or unconscious preparation first. To be effective, desires of this sort must occur again and again. I must go on wishing to be more generous or less timid, and not just wish it on New Year's day; I must train myself to act habitually—and think too—in the way that I should act and think if I possessed the altered character for which I wish. From the point of view of the present moment, however, one's character is something fixed and given. The wish I have at half-past twelve today will do nothing, or almost nothing, to alter it.

These remarks may seem very remote from the topic I am supposed to be discussing. But they have a direct bearing on a question which has been mentioned before: whether, or in what sense, the next world as I am conceiving of it should be called a "subjective" world. As I have already said, a next world such as I have described *would* be subjective, in the sense of mind-dependent. The minds which experience it would also have created it. It would just be the manifestation of their own memories and desires, even though it might be the joint creation of a number of telepathically interacting minds, and therefore not wholly private. But there is a sense in which it might have a certain objectivity all the same. One thing we mean by calling something "objective" is that it is so whether we like it or not, and even if we dislike it. This is also what we mean by talking about "hard facts" or "stubborn facts."

At first sight it may seem that in an image-world such as I have described there could be no hard facts or stubborn facts, and nothing objective in this sense of the word "objective." How could there be, if the world we experience is itself a wish-fulfilment world? But a man's character *is* in this sense "objective"; objective in the sense that he has it whether he likes it or not. And facts about his character are as "hard" or "stubborn" as any. Whether I like it or not, and even though I dislike it, it is a hard fact about me that I am timid or spiteful, that I am fond of eating oysters or averse from talking French. I may wish sometimes that these habitual desires and aversions of mine were different, but at any particular moment this wish will do little or nothing to alter them. In the short run, a man's permanent and habitual desires are something "given" which he must accept and put up with as best he can, even though in the very long run they are alterable.

Now in the next life, according to my picture of it, it would be these permanent and habitual desires which would determine the nature of the world in which a person has to live. His world would be, so to speak, the outgrowth of his character; it would be his own character represented before him in the form of dream-like images. There is therefore a sense in which he gets exactly the sort of world he wants, whatever internal conflicts there may be between one of these wants and another. Yet he may very well dislike having the sort of character he does have. In the short run, as I have said, his character is something fixed and given, and objective in the sense that he has that character whether he likes it or not. Accordingly his image-world is also objective in the same sense. It is objective in the sense that it insists on presenting itself to him whether he likes it or not.

To look at the same point in another way: the next world as I am picturing it may be a very queer sort of world, but still it would be subject to causal laws. The laws would not, of course, be the laws of physics. As I have suggested already, they might be expected to be more like the laws of Freudian psychology. But they would be laws all the same, and objective in the sense that they hold good whether one liked it or not. And if we do dislike the image-world which our desires and memories create for us—if, when we get what we want, we are horrified to discover what things they were which we wanted—we shall have to set about altering our characters, which might be a very long and painful process.

Some people tell us, of course, that all desires, even the most permanent and habitual ones, will wear themselves out in time by the mere process of being satisfied. It may be so, and perhaps there is comfort in the thought. In that case the dream-like world of which I have been speaking would only be temporary, and we should have to ask whether after the next world there is a next but one. The problem of survival would then arise again in a new form. We should have to ask whether personal identity could still be preserved when we were no longer even dreaming. It could, I think, be preserved through the transition from this present, perceptible world to a dream-like image world of the kind I have been describing. But if even imaging were to cease, would there be anything left of human personality at all? Or would the state of existence—if any—which followed be one to which the notion of personality, at any rate our present notion, no longer had any application? I think that these are questions upon which it is unprofitable and perhaps impossible to speculate. (If anyone wishes to make the attempt, I can only advise him to consult the writings of the mystics, both Western and Oriental.) It is quite enough for us to consider what the *next* world might conceivably be like, and some of you may think that even this is too much.

You have noticed that the next world, according to my account of it, is not at all unlike what some metaphysicians say *this* world is. In the philosophy of Schopenhauer, this present world itself, in which we now live, is a world of "will and idea." And so it is in Berkeley's philosophy too; material objects are just collections of "ideas," though according to Berkeley the will which presents these ideas to us is the will of God, acting directly upon us in a way which is in effect telepathic. Could it be that these idealist metaphysicians have given us a substantially correct picture of the next world, though a mistaken picture of this one? The study of metaphysical theories is out of question nowadays. But perhaps students of psychical research would do well to pay some attention to them. *If* there are other worlds than this (again I emphasize the "if"), who knows whether with some stratum of our personalities we are not living in them now, as well as in this present one which conscious sense-perception discloses? Such a repressed and unconscious awareness of a world different from this one might be expected to break through into consciousness occasionally in the course of human history, very likely in a distorted form, and this might be the source of those very queer ideas which we read of with so much incredulity and astonishment in the writings of some speculative metaphysicians. Not knowing their source, they mistakenly applied these ideas to this world in which we now live, embellishing them sometimes with an elaborate façade of deductive reasoning. Viewed in cold blood and with a sceptical eye, their attempts may appear extremely unconvincing and their deductive reasoning fallacious. But perhaps, without knowing it, they may have valuable hints to give us if we are trying to form some conception, however tentative, of "another world." And this is something we must try to do if we take the problem of survival seriously.

NOTES

1. *University,* Vol. 2, No. 2, p. 38, in a symposium on "Death" with Professor D. M. Mackinnon. Mr. Flew obviously uses "people" as the plural of "person"; but if we are to be linguistic, I am inclined to think that the nuances of "people" are not quite the same as those of "person." When we use the word "person," in the singular or the plural, the notion of consciousness is more prominently before our minds than it is when we use the word "people."

2. Conceivably its geometrical structure might also be different from the geometrical structure of the physical world. In that case the space of the next world would not only be other than the space of the physical world, but would also be a different *sort* of space.

3. Sir Oliver Lodge, *Raymond Revised* (London: Methuen, 1922), p. 113.

17

Eschatological Enquiry

JOHN DONNELLY

University of San Diego

IT IS A TRADITIONAL BELIEF of orthodox Christianity that there is life after death. The more optimistic, "new-wave" Christian theologians speak of "universal salvation" (i.e., that God will grant salvation to all people in heaven), disingenuously suppressing the words of Christ that while "all are called, few are chosen." Some Platonic-minded Christians seem to think that we are naturally immortal, overlooking the sagacious counsel of Santayana that being born is a poor augury for being immortal. Of course, some secularists share these Christian sentiments, *sans* a theodicy, as witness the recent discovery, on a remarkably large scale, of "near-death experiences," and the not inconsiderable parapsychological documentation for immortality contained therein. People are not just coming out of "closets." Today it seems they are also coming out of "graves"!

Nonetheless, in general, it remains a staple of Christian theology that heaven awaits the virtuous, hell the vicious, and (although it is not often mentioned in polite theological company) purgatory awaits those who are not quite either. I suppose it is only natural, in an age of abortion and infanticide, that the always recondite and elusive notion of limbo has gone the way of a Jamaican dance!

I shall be *assuming* herein that a rational, philosophical case can be made for a Christian view of death as an *event* in life, such that talk about life after death is a distinct metaphysical possibility, and not, as Antony Flew would have it, an oxymoron. Central to a Christian's noetic structure is the belief that each person has a core of mentalistic properties (what theologians call a *soul* and parapsychologists a *discarnate personality*), which persists after bodily (i.e., cerebral) death, and can be eventually resurrected with a glorified body by an omniscient,

Reprinted by permission from *Sophia,* 24 (1985), 16–31.

omnipotent, omnibenevolent God. There seems to be considerable division in the Christian community over whether the belief is about immediate divine judgment at one's death moment, or instead concerns a final day of judgment, the *parousia*. Happily, I think one can answer affirmatively to both. That is so because God could immediately judge some persons institutionally fit for the heavenly resurrection world at the time of biological death or institutionally fit for a hellish resurrection world at that time, while other persons being neither sufficiently virtuous nor sufficiently vicious require more pre-eschatological time, and the latter would be ontologically recycled in a purgatorial mode of existence until the evidence is sufficient for an omniscient Deity to choose their eventual destination. It could be noted here that the ingenuous universal salvation theorists may have inadvertently a point, namely, that there is literally no hell. That is, God may simply annihilate the vicious, all of which is consistent with his great mercy, and as an upshot does wonders for those dolorous Malthusians who worry about over-populated resurrection worlds.

These assumptions have generated two distinct but related atheological challenges that I wish to address. I shall also (in sections V and VI) comment on some pertinent eschatological reflections of Richard Swinburne and George Wall.

I

The first challenge is presented by such authors as Homer, Mark Twain, G. B. Shaw, Bernard Williams, *et al.* They believe these Christian assumptions are mistaken, and that even Christians when shorn of these beliefs by enlightened philosophical rebirth should be glad that death marks the end of life, such that there is no life after death.

Homer in his *Odyssey* describes Ulysses as lauding Achilles' attainment of felicity, only to receive the severe reprimand from Achilles: ". . . think not death a theme of consolation; I had rather live the servile hind for hire, and eat the bread of some man scantily himself sustained, than sovereign empire hold over the shades." The irreverent Twain speaks highly of heaven's vaunted meteorology, but suggests, climate aside, hell has the only interesting company. George Bernard Shaw, equally sardonic, writes in *Man and Superman:* "Let me complete my friend Lucifer's similitude of the classical concert. . . . you will find rows of weary people who are there, not because they really like classical music, but because they think they ought to like it. Well, there is the same thing in heaven. A number of people sit there in glory, not because they are happy, but because they think they owe it to their position to be in heaven."

Bernard Williams in his *Problems of the Self* also argues that any survival hypothesis is meaningless in the sense of "without significance": ". . . from facts about human desire and happiness and what a human life is, it follows both that immortality would be, where conceivable at all, intolerable." Williams bases his view on a consideration of the (science fiction) case of Elina Makropulos. Like most of us, Elina wished to be immortal. When she was 42 and enjoying the fruits of that particularly felicitous time in her life, she strongly wished to remain 42. She had never been so happy, and could not imagine how she could ever be happier. She took an elixir, and the story catches up to her when she is 342, having been 42 for 300 years. Despite the putative panacea, she now finds her endless life a bore (her categorical desires have ceased) and suicide the only tolerable way out for her condition. Williams contends that it is not just a contingent fact about a person that her categorical desires are finite in number. But, *ex hypothesi*, suicide is not possible. Having exhausted all that 42 offered, and with no anti-elixir available, Elina suffers the misfortune of eternal forty-twoness!

Recalling the legendary case of Tithonus, who according to Greek mythology was granted immortality by Aurora, but who soon longed for death since he was not also given eternal youthfulness as well, Williams would warn every immortally youthful neo-Tithonian that boredom may be a greater evil than death, and that we may be *felix opportunitate mortis*.

Williams does not place Elina's case-history in a Christian context, but *mutatis mutandis*, his point would be especially poignant in such an eschatological situation. The first challenge then is as follows:

(1) Even allowing for the possibility of a personal post-mortem life with God, we should not look forward to it, for our fate would be much like Elina's. Boredom and general unpleasantness are intrinsic features of such an everlasting life. Our desires, wants, needs, interests, etc., are inherently exhaustible, and life in heaven would prove intolerable in the long run.

II

The *second* challenge is raised by Marxist and other scientific materialists, who argue that the Christian metaphysical framework of an afterlife fosters a general complacency with the assorted pre-mortem moral, social, political, and economic ills of daily life. Believing that this world is a vale of tears, and hoped-for deliverance awaits in the eschatological hands of God, it becomes only natural for Christians, argue the Marxists, to develop a stoical insensitivity to the mundane affairs of the proverbial threescore and ten. Undoubtedly, there is some truth herein, and the Marxists (always overlooking their own repressive regimes) are quick to point out how millions of Christians living throughout the world are regularly biting the bullet, and accepting various misfortunes that afflict them, in the Kantian hope that virtue will eventually be triumphant and vice vanquished.

The Marxist point is especially trenchant with regard to the Christian ritual of last rites. This practice, however inadvertently, reinforces the belief that any person's life can be rendered morally praiseworthy overall if they die in the right way (despite any previous pattern of non-virtuous living), and morally culpable (despite any previous pattern of virtuous living) if they do not die in the right way. Such a practice emphasizes dying *(ars moriendi)* rather than living. Christians need to be reminded here of Aristotle's caveat that one swallow does not make a spring (although I think it did, in the case of the good thief on Calvary). To be sure, dying Christians need to be reconciled to God, but that purpose is often thwarted by ersatz Pascalian-like insurance policies, issued at the midnight-hour to ensure heavenly redemption.

In short, the second objection holds:

(2) The Christian belief in an afterlife has the direct or indirect effect of diminishing the importance of pre-mortem moral, social, and political reformation, offering instead an illusory eschatological placebo, with the result that evil is tolerated in this world (the only world there is for the Marxists).

I think Christians should find both these challenges forceful and troubling, and not attempt to demythologize them away as some sort of pseudo-problem or misplaced straw argument.

III

At least one typical Christian response to the first challenge proves unsatisfactory. That is, the Christian often argues that "heaven" means "a totally blissful (peaceful, pleasant) personal, post-mortem life with God in a resurrection world." And so, when Williams *et al.*, *mutatis mutandis*, suggest that heaven will necessarily be boring or unpleasant, they are stating a contradictory claim. That is, the first challenge ultimately claims:

(3) Heaven, a totally blissful personal, post-mortem life with God in a resurrection world is not totally blissful.

Now, surely, (3) is contradictory. But can the first challenge be so easily dismissed? I think not! What is often overlooked is that if the Christian adopts such a tactic, then it follows that the positive, orthodox affirmation

(4) Heaven is not boring or unpleasant

far from stating a profound truth is instead an uninformative tautology. The so-called "good news" of Christianity promulgated by (4) is here not news at all, saying ultimately no more than

(5) Heaven is not unheavenly.

A more cautious and prudent Christian, working with a minimal definition of heaven, would leave out "totally blissful" or some equivalent expression from his or her working definition. In short, he or she would hold:

(6) Heaven refers to personal, post-mortem life with God in a resurrection world.

But, of course, the employment of (6) has the effect of re-introducing Williams' accusation with full epistemic force. For, given (6), it now makes sense to say, as the first challenge (1) does, that

(7) Heaven is boring or unpleasant.

To be sure, the Christian will deny the truth of (7), but (7) *could* be true. In any case (7) raises serious philosophical and theological questions concerning the contents of post-mortem life with God, and challenges the Christian to seriously consider "what God hath prepared for those that love him." Given the conception of heaven found in (6), conjoined with the categories of transcendence and timelessness, it might well be reasonable to believe that (7) is false. But if heaven (like hell), to quote Aquinas, is "ruled by time," then (7) is not obviously false. And since the latter view is fairly standard in Christianity, with its notion of everlasting *vs.* eternal life, (7) retains its full force. Counter-suggestions for the purpose of holding that God will not allow the virtuous to be bored or to experience misfortune in heaven overlook the importance Divine Providence constantly allots to human freedom and individual responsibility.

IV

The second challenge found in (2) is, I believe, *de jure* if not always *de facto* false. The Christian dwells simultaneously in two cities, so that while she inhabits Babylon with full legal, naturalized citizenship (like the committed Marxist), her compass is charted for Jerusalem, where by the grace of God, she hopes for conferral of non-naturalized citizenship. Christianity does not teach an aversion for this world *simpliciter*. It does not call upon one to be a mystic or a hermit. But it does issue a clarion call for good samaritanship, as the means to develop the requisite moral character essential to enjoyment of and appreciation for the affairs of heaven.

At the risk of oversimplification, it seems to me that most Christians who love God fall into two fairly distinct camps. The first, and by far the largest group, are members of what Kierkegaard termed "christendom." They are religious people who love God for the advantages found in such a relationship. God has utility for them, in light of their reflective cost/benefit analysis. Divine omnipotence generates fear in such people, which they mistakenly take to be the end (as well as the beginning) of wisdom. As a result, they worship and obey God, not out of any personal appropriation of its intrinsic worth, but due to the extrinsic rewards supposedly associated with such a lifestyle. Theirs is largely a morality of negative obligation, not positive duty. It seems to me that their love is imperfect, and their pragmatic motivation for virtue largely misplaced.

By contrast, the second group of Christians, who I believe constitute the true believers, love God because of his very nature. They understand the point of morality and religious belief, and accordingly worship and love God because of that understanding. It is not sufficient merely to *serve* God (as the first group does); one must also *know* and *love* him, as well.

Now, the first group may well find (7) true, but it is not likely the second group will so agree. Yet, I find it hard to see how God in his omnibenevolence would consign members of the first group to hell (if there be such a place), for they are, after all, rather decent types, despite their expedient ways; but it is somewhat difficult to grasp how God would grant them full citizenship in heaven. They appear to lack the proper environmental and personal fit. So, their immediate destiny seems to be that of a "second change" in purgatory; or, if heaven be their abode, (7) may well be their lot.

In theory, the two groups are mutually exclusive; but in the short run of the practical order a Christian may well move at times from one camp to another. The perimeters of each are occasionally nebulous albeit not so recondite for an omniscient God, who will judge us all. However, I find it not unreasonable to believe that God, consistent with his unswerving respect for human freedom, would constitute with a glorified body (free of physical impediment) the members of the second group who exemplified in their pre-mortem behavior a deontological love of God. There would still be the possibility of *moral* evil (sin) in heaven, and I would underscore that to forget this is to ignore the crucial lesson of Lucifer and his fallen cohorts. Because members of the second group kept the faith by virtue of their voluntary pre-mortem *imitatio Dei*, God would make them "like angels." But even angelic-type creatures are not programed by God to be good. They have their own challenges as well as their individual opportunities in the heavenly community. Indeed, a member of the second group of Christians would not want to be so programed by God as to be filled with hedonic experiences—at the expense of his or her loss of free will. And God would not in his omnibenevolence choose to fetter them. Such a programed "angel" would really be an addict, not an active agent of his or her own destiny—despite being satiated eternally by pleasurable experiences. Any such ersatz satisfactions are not personal achievements or fulfillments of a responsible person. There is nothing jesuitical about the principle that *omne ens perficitur in actu*. As St. Thomas reminds us, even the beatific vision is not a passive experience.

So, *contra* the second challenge of (2), the Christian eschatology does not entail any minimization or negation of pre-mortem striving. Devout Christians may prove stoical at times, but they are not fatalistic. Typically, as St. Augustine put it, their hearts are restless until they find their rest (peace) in God. Christian members of the second group have so prepared themselves for the next world *in this world* that the words of the Psalmist (42:1) well describe them: "as the driven hart pants after the stream of water, so longs [our] soul for you, O God." They are both *a part of* and yet *apart from* this world. They are not passive onlookers in the continuing moral, social, political, and economic process of Babylon, but instead active agents of agapism. They love God above all else, and by that love their neighbor as well. They are well prepared to avoid the Scylla and Charybdis of (1) and (2).

Acceptance of (6) seems to entail a depiction of heaven as a mode of existence in which the *possibility* of vice has not been eradicated.

Unfortunately, many Christians view the devil hypothesis as myth, but even those who do not, often fail to reflect on the moral of the Lucifer saga—a point that (1) serves to emphasize. But (1) is false, at least for members of the second group. The heavenly environment offers tasks, purposes, etc., as one strives for greater participation in the divine life. Elina became bored by the endless pursuit of *finite* pursuits, but the *visio Dei* offers *infinite* variety for imaginative, creative personal involvement.

V

Richard Swinburne seems to want to rule out any heavenly inhabitants' having unpleasant sensations.[1] If Swinburne means by this remark that God in his omnipotence has removed from his selected ones physical distress (e.g., illness) and natural disaster (e.g., hurricanes), then I would agree. But Swinburne seems to also want to include the omission of any mental distress or moral calamity, and that position, I claim, makes a mockery of the Lucifer saga. Swinburne claims "[God] will ever be able to hold our interest by showing us new facets of reality and above all his own nature."[2] But this seems to me to be on the whole true only for the second group, perhaps widening it to include devoted non-Christian theistic inquirers, as well as secular virtuous persons.

I do agree, however, with Swinburne's eschatological speculations that beatitude consists for the elect in having more than just pleasant sensations. Yet, in claiming that *full heavenly* happiness cannot make allowances for "conflicting wants," Swinburne creates a beatitude-gap for his rather heterogeneous, heavenly population. That is, while not a universal salvation theorist, Swinburne would seem to allow in members of both groups of Christians I described in section IV, as well as any honest, good-willed inquirers, be they theistic or not.[3] I suggest this creates far too great an "open admissions" policy to heaven, and plays into the hands of (1). And in suggesting that heavenly inhabitants (other than my group two) would continue to have "conflicting wants" there, albeit they are "on balance happy," Swinburne contravenes his own view that heaven is never boring or unpleasant for anyone so situated.

In short, Swinburne holds that

(8) Heavenly happiness consists in having true beliefs about intrinsically worthwhile states of affairs, and as a result, doing what one wants to be doing and having happen what one wants to have happen.

Swinburne offers a Millian-like test of the value of heavenly beatitude, and the enjoyment of non-shallow happiness, against those who raise the challenge of (1). Heaven involves a life of service, knowledge, and love of the things of God. To those like Bernard Williams who find such a prospect boring or distressful, Swinburne asks them to reflect on such likely heavenly activities and emotions, etc., and see if they cannot agree with him.[4] *Contra* Swinburne, I am afraid most people will not share his value sentiments here, yet Swinburne still seems to want them to keep their tickets.

Indeed, Swinburne avers that "heaven is not a reward for good action," but instead "for good people."[5] But surely, *pace* Swinburne, good people need more than a disposition to be virtuous; they also need to *do* good on occasion. To hold Swinburne's value system of a morality of virtue *vs.* that of a morality of obligation is to play straight into the Marxist objection of (2). *Contra* Swinburne, one builds up a character of "perfect goodness" on a foundation of good action. That is, an ethics of virtue is a necessary complement to an ethics of obligation. As William Frankena has written, "being without doing, like faith without works, is dead."[6] At times, Swinburne seems to backslide on (8).

Swinburne also finds the associated notion of hell as a resurrection world of eternal punishment for sin, to be inconsistent with divine justice. He reasons eristically "a finite number of years of evildoing does not deserve an infinite number of years of physical pain as punishment."[7] This claim strikes me as sophistical, for by the same parity of reasoning, one could argue that a finite number of years of good-doing does not deserve an infinite number of years of beatitude as a reward!

Swinburne bases a good deal of his views about heaven on the gospel of Matthew. He suggests that some persons, otherwise of good will and intention, are unable to resist the strength of certain evil mundane temptations and desires in pre-mortem life. Nonetheless, while holding that "determined pursuit of the good makes people naturally good,"[8] he also contends that such determined pursuit is not always successful. In which cases, Swinburne believes, God could reform those individuals in heaven, consistent with their free will. Since they had made those over-powering desires *extrinsic* to themselves, God could remove such obstacles in heaven, without destroying their freedom. But here Swinburne appears quite heterodoxical. Christianity teaches that one will not be tempted beyond one's strength. Indeed Matthew (11:28–30) says "Come to me all whose work is hard, whose load is heavy; and I will give you relief. . . . For my yoke is good to bear, my load is light."

I also find Swinburne's analysis of Matthew's parable of the vineyard (see 20:1–16) a paradigm case of doublethink. To be sure, this biblical passage ought to trouble philosophically minded Christians, especially its concluding non-sequitur "thus will the last be first, and the first last." This particularly dark saying seems not only inconsistent (as it stands) with divine justice, but also totally inappropriate given the context of the parable. That parable seems to ineluctably lead the reader to a conclusion that the first-and last-called faithful will be equal in God's eyes. Granted there was a seeming inequality in pay for the laborers (i.e., all received the same amount of money, but worked different amounts of time), but all are equal in enthusiastically responding to the employer's call, when elicited, to work the vineyards. Some worked much longer than others, but all served.

Swinburne, I believe, egregiously reads the parable as claiming that: "The Christian doctrine . . . is that heaven is not a reward for good action (for, as we have seen, even on the Catholic view a man can go there without having done any), rather it is a home for good people."[9] This claim cannot be exegetically based on the scriptural passage, and indeed Swinburne paradoxically seems to agree as he says (correctly): ". . . what determines whether they get their reward is their status as workers, that they are developing the vineyard (having accepted the challenge to work when it came), not how many hours work they have done."[10]

I agree! But if so, then serious doubt is cast (even by Swinburne himself) on his claim that action is less important than character, that faith is more important than works.

VI

George B. Wall, like Swinburne but with an agnostic agenda, baldly states that the Christian notion of heaven entails the absence of any moral evil therein.[11] His claim is part of a grander thesis to show that the Christian conception of heaven fails to resolve doubts about divine omnibenevolence in light of the nagging problem of evil on earth. Regarding the famous problem of evil, Wall finds the Christian often invoking what Wall terms "Panglossian Principle One," namely:

(9) it is logically impossible for God, consistent with his nature, to create a world with as much overall value as this one, but with less moral evil.

The problem with (9) is that the Christian also believes (incoherently for Wall) that it is logically possible for God to do just that, namely, create a heavenly resurrection world free of moral evil. So the acceptance of (9), coupled with the Christian notion of heaven, imperils the goodness of God, because of God's failure to create a heaven here on earth. If (9) is rejected and the Christian notion of heaven *sans* moral evil accepted, then the problem of evil seems intractable for the theist. If one does not object to the jettisoning of freedom in heaven, Wall asks, why does not the theist object to God's not jettisoning it on earth? If heaven is the best possible state for God to create, why not do so from the outset?

I have no intention of reiterating the so-called free will defense of why God allows moral evil in the world. Other philosophers have done so quite admirably, and to my mind, cogently. I do think that principle (9) is true, keeping in mind that a pre-mortem world is not the same world as a post-mortem world, and that the reference in (9) is to the former world. What strikes me as false is Wall's attribution to orthodox Christianity that acceptance of (6) entails the absence of moral evil. To think that when one attains heaven, partially due to the achievement of some degree of moral perfection, one no longer needs to be free is to misunderstand the Christian notion of heaven. The counsel, command, or ideal "to be perfect as your heavenly Father is perfect" is an endless task that the Christian is progressively engaged in, both here on earth and in heaven. Interpreted as a *command*, it tells us to *do* certain things; as an *ideal*, to aspire to *be* a certain sort of person. And freedom is a necessary condition for that aspiring eternal quest.

But Wall presses: why not a heaven without free will for its inhabitants? Surely, the Christian wants to hold

(10) God's interference with freedom in certain cases (e.g., the Exodus, the exorcising of demons, etc.) is a better state of affairs, because of the great evil otherwise involved, than his not limiting freedom.

But, *contra* Wall, acceptance of (10) is not so much evidence of "limiting freedom" as a demonstration of God's great power and glory. God, in (10), is offering a lesson to us of his divine majesty, unfortunately not always properly received, to better motivate recalcitrant persons to the proper exercise of free will and moral responsibility.

Somewhat disingenuously, Wall seems to believe that his contentions will lead more rationally minded Christians to *abandon* the conception of heaven *sans* freedom and moral evil. Wall seems to believe such a shift would be both rational and heterodoxical. I, of course, think it would be both rational and non-heterodoxical. Wall would retort that, if so, then one can somehow fall (he says "slip out") from heavenly existence. And I would agree. Wall then inquires as to where such backsliders would reside, and he introduces purgatory as the likely destination. He may well be right about purgatory, although I would not wish to rule out hell. In any case, Wall conceives of purgatory as a resurrection world in which the principal function of its inhabitants is "virtue installation," a sort of moral refueling spot, before the inevitable ascension into heaven again. I do not wish to dwell on the logic of such pareschatological states of affairs as purgatory, but would only make the claim that it is not at all obvious why purgatory must be conceived as a place of upward-mobility only.[12] It is far more appropriate, it seems to me, that purgatory, if freedom is to be prized, is a two-way street, with its eventual losers and winners. Wall, of course, thinks that if God can create a purgatorial resurrection world, then he should have done so originally: "If a purgatorial existence does a better job of virtue-installation than the present form of existence, then the purgatorial existence should have been introduced to begin with."[13]

Since I do not conceive of purgatory as Wall does, but instead view it as a "second change," I see no reason to question God's nature. I would think that a purgatorial world is quite similar to a pre-purgatorial world, much as marriage is to heterosexual co-habitation. Indeed, I would offer the dark thought (not to be pursued in this paper) that purgatory may well be co-extensive with the pre-mortem world, consisting of many persons who are being ontologically recycled (reincarnated?), having been in an earlier round neither fully formed moral agents (e.g., aborted fetuses, children who died in infancy, severely mentally handicapped individuals) nor on balance sufficiently demarcated as virtuous or vicious moral personalities. Unlike Eastern accounts of reincarnation to which purgatory has some surface similarities, the notion of purgatory does not involve any eventual annihilation of selfhood.

Wall claims that (9) rules out (10); and that (9) also excludes the Christian notion of heaven. I believe that (9) is consistent with (10) and that (9) is also consistent with the Christian notion of heaven. Wall claims also for (11) what he seeks to do with (9). That is, the Christian presumably holds:

> (11) it is logically impossible for God, consistent with his nature, to create a world with as much value as this one, but with less natural evil.

I believe that (11) is true as applied to pre-mortem life (and perhaps to purgatorial life). But (11) does not apply to heavenly life, where physical evils are absent. Wall's ultimate point is that physical evil is nonessential for soul-making, as any virtue it allegedly develops can be accomplished by the presence of moral evils alone. So Wall believes God's creating a world with natural evil in it counts against his alleged omnibenevolence. "What virtues or character traits developed through natural evil could not be equally well developed through moral evil?"[14]

I will be brief in commenting upon Wall's last point. For one, many natural evils are the product of the devil's diabolical agency, but his nefarious reach does not extend to heaven, only to the pre-mortem world (and possibly purgatory). Secondly, and inadvertently, Wall appears to concede a point to the theodicist who often points out that some putative natural evils are disguised moral evils (e.g., *famine*, as brought about by policies of multinational corporations and feudal notions of property-rights that result in the inequitable distribution of arable land, etc.; *cancer*, often brought about by industrial pollution, the intemperate use of tobacco, etc.).

Lastly, and most importantly, Wall fails to understand that if human beings are to operate as free moral agents, and build up the requisite character for heaven, then there must be physical evil in the world so that such pre-mortem persons may have the needed knowledge to bring about moral evils as well as moral good. Clearly, our principal means of getting on in this world is *via* the employment of inductive logic. But induction, to be the successful tool it is, requires in turn a certain regularity in the laws of nature. For each of us to properly mold our own destinies, we need to know the likely results of our intentional, voluntary behavior. And our control over our own destiny is predicated upon a given, inherent determinateness in nature. For example, if excessive abuse of alcohol did not produce certain adverse, physical results (ranging from nagging hangovers to cirrhosis of the liver), then none of us could be credited as responsible agents in adopting a *prudential* or *temperate* stance on the matter of alcoholic consumption.

People who have the requisite character to enter heaven have learned well the sometimes hard lessons of induction. And, while the possibility of moral evil still exists therein, God will see to it that the concomitant natural evils often associated with moral evils do not disrupt the design of his kingdom.

The possible moral evils in a heavenly resurrection world would include personal offenses, such as the *immoral sentiments of pride, jealously, envy, hatred, avarice*, etc., and possibly the ordinary range of vices that normally involve innocent victims who suffer the concomitant natural evils associated with such malevolence—but God would prevent the corresponding physical harms from being enacted. In short, a kind of ethical intentionalism would prevail, under the scrutiny of an omniscient Deity.

POSTSCRIPT

The Apostle Paul claimed that our eyes have not seen nor our ears heard what God has in store for those who love him. St. Paul also speaks, tantalizingly but vaguely, of a glorified body, a notion never metaphysically unpacked, no doubt in part due to the above remark. I share St. Paul's belief in and hope for the resurrection. I also believe that a resurrection model is the orthodox Christian eschatological view, and not any extreme dualistic views that speak of the survival of a disembodied mind—despite the curious and traditional Christian practice to pray for the *souls* of the deceased. With Aquinas, I hold that "my soul is not I." Persons, in short, are psycho-physical wholes. Prayers for resurrected persons are, of course, entirely appropriate.

Christian philosophers, in particular, need to give much more attention and reflection to what awaits a person in the eschaton. I would suggest they pay far greater metaphysical heed to the notion of divine *immediate* judgment upon biological death than to the notion of the general resurrection as the second coming. Of course, any theistic philosopher should hold that without there being an omniscient, omnipotent, omnibenevolent God any hope for personal, post-mortem survival is forlorn. Put bluntly: any hope we have for personal, post-mortem survival rests on the belief in a theistic God who can perform violation miracles.

As a preliminary sketch, I would suggest that the traditional notion (inherited from the Church Fathers) that upon biological death the individual soul persists in an interim state of temporary disembodiment (sometimes described as a kind of limbic state of incorporeality in which the soul is not even conscious of its existence!) until the general resurrection needs to be metaphysically re-examined. Clearly, the Christian philosopher needs to make a case for the irreducibility of the soul to any physicalistic explanation schemes. The soul as the form of the body is needed to provide the identity link between pre-mortem and post-mortem life. So the Christian philosopher needs to defend some sort of moderate dualism wherein persons are regarded as psycho-physical wholes. But the persisting soul's mentalistic operations (e.g., thoughts, beliefs, memories, etc.) do not guarantee personal survival of bodily death, or one is left with an immortality survival-hypothesis without the need of God and all the fantastic, often solipsistic features one can find in H. H. Price's metaphysical speculations about imagy, ideoplastic, next worlds. It is also hard to see how the interim state of temporary disembodiment (which for some deceased individuals can exist for thousands of years regardless of their pre-mortem moral merit) would not play right into the hands of the Bernard Williams-type critique. Unfortunately, such a picture is conveyed by the traditional Christian insistence on the awaited general resurrection, not to mention the fantastic metaphysical problems (however logically possible for the theistic God to perform) generated by the view that at the general resurrection God will reassemble our very pre-mortem bodily atoms, particles, quarks, etc., and reunite our souls to them. Surely, there are ways to avoid replication difficulties without resorting to such re-creation scenarios.

But what sense, however inchoate a meaning may be attached to it, can be made of the notion of a glorified body? Paul tells us (1 Cor 15:42–44): "What is sown in the earth as a perishable thing is raised imperishable. Sown in humiliation, it is raised in glory; sown in weakness, it is raised in power; sown as an animal body, it is raised as a spiritual body." I would suggest that our resurrected bodies (which God allows our persisting souls to animate upon biological death) are literally corporeal, flesh and blood simulacrum to our pre-mortem bodies, but free of any natural evils. *Contra* Paul, I believe it is false to claim that "flesh and blood can never possess the kingdom of God" (1 Cor 15:50). These resurrected bodies do not become impaired or diseased; nor do they age.

To the less than polite, non-Pauline but interesting metaphysical question as to whether a person assumes in the afterlife the age of his or her pre-mortem chronological body, I would offer this reply: the resurrection model does not require that a person have the same body or age that he or she had at biological death; but it is necessary to have a body in order to be a complete person. So if it is your happy or unhappy lot to die at the proverbial threescore and ten, it is not your perhaps infelicitous lot to live perpetually in the afterlife with the body of a septuagenarian. And, *contra* Aquinas, God does not have to reassemble all the dispersed particles that composed our human bodies in order to preserve our self-identities.

I would suggest that the heavenly resurrection world is inhabited by persons whose bodies look like those of early thirty-year-olders. I say that for at least two reasons. First of all, there is the obvious symbolic reason that that was the age of Jesus at his death. Second, I think there is considerable empirical warrant for the view that if the (pre-mortem) world cooperated (and it often does not), then people would be at the height of their mental and physical prowess at that age. Should one be reunited in heaven with one's previously deceased parents, relatives, and friends, they too would look the same age as you. Just as we occasionally say of an exceptionally erudite and wise young person that he or she is 25 going on 60, so too a person in heaven could be 33 going on a thousand-plus years. His or her intelligence and ethico-religious personality might increase, but the body would not age. A person need not then noumenally think of themselves as 33, but phenomenally they would present that physical appearance. And since so many pre-mortem persons are constantly suffering physical and psychic anguish because their physical appearances do not match their ideal bodily constructs of themselves, in heaven that would be rectified (and literally transfigured) as their ideal bodily images would correspond to reality, if God so wills.

The metaphysical contours of the heavenly resurrection world would be such that there is no physical or natural evil either in the world environment itself or in the glorified bodies of its inhabitants. But the traditional Christian resort to metaphysical libertarianism to vindicate God from the classic problem of evil needs to be consistently applied to the afterlife as well. I am speculating that we continue to have free wills even in heaven, where we are not coerced to be good or divinely programed to be virtuous. As a result, it follows that a person could be evicted from heaven. And, as I suggested earlier, I think a system of divine intentionalism reigns in heaven. An omniscient God knows our innermost thoughts, beliefs, and intentions; and should a person have *perduring* immoral sentiments—albeit no other person could be physically harmed (or victimized) by such a mind-set, that person might be evicted, being no longer fit for the community of saints.

We might rather boldly state that heaven is for lovers—lovers of God and neighbor. The likelihood of a person's being evicted from heaven, given its metaphysical parameters and the accompanying nurturing and supportive community, is indeed slim. Recall that I am postulating that we have no physical harms or impairments to contend with either in our own bodies (which are more carnal than subtle or astral) or in the resurrection world itself. So while moral intentionalism is unworkable as an ethical theory in the pre-mortem world—if it were, few if any of us could avoid damnation inasmuch as people harbor momentary, immoral sentiments quite regularly—it is tailor-made for heaven.

Suppose that a person is selected for the heavenly resurrection world, and learns that his or her predeceased parents, spouse, friends, etc., were not chosen by God. Suppose further that that person becomes resentful of God's decision, and that resentment endures for a considerable period of time. In this case, it would be entirely just for an omnibenevolent God to evict that person. But suppose that person's initial resentment proves somewhat transient as the person learns to understand and thereby accept the judgment of God. That person, it seems to me, would not be evicted.[15]

If there is a hellish resurrection world, and God does not simply annihilate the truly vicious at biological death, then I think that no modern Christian need accept the traditional, fantastic depictions of hell made famous by the likes of Dante and Milton, or the artwork of Bosch. Hell, I would suspect, could well be an inhabited planet free of physical and natural evils. Isn't hell then heaven? I think not. For in hell, a place for non-lovers, the immoral sentiments reign. There, divorced from God, is found only enmity made all the more antagonistically unbearable by the fact that a person cannot physically harm the neighbors one so dislikes or escape one's plight.

But what would a person do in heaven? I will be brief in response; but I would underscore that this strikes me as a very serious philosophical question that hardly any theologian or philosopher has dared to broach other than to rather ineffably state: experience the beatific vision. As but a rudimentary start to begin to address the question, we might reflect on a recent television commercial for a beer product that kept stressing "Live for the weekend." (Of course, the commercial was designed to get people to consume its advertised beverage during the weekend.) But there was a deep truth concealed herein. Unfortunately, many people are alienated from their work. They compartmentalize the drudgery of their weekday tasks and routine from their weekends, when ideally they can strive for some degree of self-fulfillment. And what is it we like about the weekends? In very broad strokes, it is the hope to be able to develop ourselves, to acquire knowledge, to pursue various leisurely activities in a congenial atmosphere.

I would suggest that this gives us a glimpse of what daily life is like in heaven. There the weekdays blend into the weekends. Unencumbered by any physical harms, persons are free to grow in self-knowledge, to learn more about and engage in the arts and sciences, if these activities be pleasing to God—all such activities pursued in the loving company of virtuous people, all actions *ad majorem Dei gloriam*.

NOTES

1. "A Theodicy of Heaven and Hell," in *The Existence and Nature of God,* ed. Alfred J. Freddoso (Notre Dame: University of Notre Dame Press, 1983), p. 39.

2. *Ibid.,* p. 41.

3. I should note that Swinburne demurs on Buddhists, who may well be persons of good will, but who in suppressing desire rule out the quest of heaven. He claims that God can transform those non-theists of good will who sought the good in their pre-mortem lives. But to transform the Buddhists would be impossible for God, as he would have to eradicate their moral sense of self.

4. ". . . that this is so can be seen by those of us capable of enjoying all such pleasures, comparing them for their worth." *Ibid.,* p. 40. But unfortu-

nately Williams and other highly intelligent persons holding (1) would likely demur on Swinburne's value test.

5. *Ibid.*, p. 43.

6. *Ethics* (Englewood Cliffs, N.J.: Prentice-Hall, 1973), p. 66.

7. Swinburne, "Theodicy of Heaven and Hell," p. 51.

8. *Ibid.*, p. 54.

9. *Ibid.*, p. 43.

10. *Ibid.*

11. "Heaven and a Wholly Good God," *The Personalist,* 58 (1977), 352.

12. The expression "virtue installation" unhappily fosters a picture of someone's coercing one to be moral, which I claim is inconsistent with human (or angelic) freedom. Character formation is not consistent with externally imposed behavioral modification.

13. Wall, "Heaven and a Wholly Good God," 354.

14. *Ibid.*, 355.

15. One of the implications of my speculation is that the traditional practice of praying to the saints as mediators or intercessors for us with God could be misfocused. Some of them (quite unlikely) might no longer be present in heaven.

18

Traditional Christian Belief in the Resurrection of the Body

STEPHEN T. DAVIS

Claremont McKenna College

I

ONE TRADITIONAL CHRISTIAN VIEW of survival of death runs, in outline form, something like this: On some future day all the dead will be bodily raised, both the righteous and the unrighteous alike, to be judged by God; and the guarantee and model of the general resurrection (i.e., the raising of the dead in the last days) is the already accomplished resurrection of Jesus Christ from the dead.

My aim in this paper is to explain and defend this basic view of resurrection. There are many ways it might be understood, of course, and perhaps more than one is coherent and even from a Christian point of view plausible. I shall defend one particular interpretation of the theory—an interpretation advocated by very many of the church Fathers, especially second century Fathers, as well as by Augustine and Aquinas.

It may help clarify matters if I first provide a brief map of where we will be going in this paper. After introducing the topic, I will discuss in turn what I take to be the three most important claims made by the version of the theory I wish to defend. Then I will consider one typical aspect of the traditional theory that has important philosophical as well as theological ramifications, viz., the notion that our resurrection

Reprinted by permission from *New Scholasticism* (now known as *American Catholic Philosophical Quarterly*), 62 (1988) 72–97.

bodies will consist of the same matter as do our present earthly bodies. Finally, since the version I wish to defend envisions a period of existence in a disembodied state, I will defend the theory against some of the arguments of those contemporary philosophers who find the very notion of disembodied existence incoherent.

II

There are several ways in which the basic concept of resurrection sketched in the opening paragraph can be fleshed out. One option is to understand the nature of the human person, and hence the nature of resurrection, in a basically materialist or physicalist way. Perhaps human beings are essentially material objects; perhaps some version of identity theory or functionalism is true. I am attracted to this option, and hold it to be a usable notion for Christians; but having defended elsewhere a physicalist conception of survival of death through resurrection, I will discuss it no further here.[1]

Another option is to collapse talk of resurrection into talk of the immortality of the soul. A closely related move (and a popular one in recent theology) is to interpret resurrection in a spiritual rather than bodily sense (if this in the end differs significantly from immortality). Such a view will doubtless be based on some version of mind-body (or soul-body) dualism. Let us define dualism as the doctrine which says that (1) human beings consist of both material bodies and immaterial souls; and (2) the soul is the essence of the person (the real you is your soul, not your body). It then can be added that the body corrupts at death and eventually ceases to exist but the soul is essentially immortal.

It is surprising (to me at least) that so many twentieth century Christian thinkers are tempted toward some such notion as this. For it is quite clear, both in Scripture and tradition, that classical dualism is not the Christian position. For example, the biblical view is not that the soul is the essence of the person and is only temporarily housed or even imprisoned in a body; human beings seem rather to be understood in Scripture as psycho-physical entities, i.e., as unities of body and soul. And the notion that the body is essentially evil and must be escaped from (an idea often associated with versions of classical dualism) was condemned by virtually every orthodox Christian thinker who discussed death and resurrection in the first two hundred years after the apostolic age; the Christian idea is rather that the body was created by God and is good; the whole person, body and soul alike, is what is to be saved. Finally, the biblical notion is not that we survive death because immortality is simply a natural property of souls; if we survive death it is because God miraculously saves us; apart from God's intervention death would mean annihilation for us. Thus Irenaeus says: "Our survival forever comes from His greatness, not from our nature."[2]

It would be interesting to discuss this option further, and especially to ask why so many recent and contemporary Christian theologians are drawn toward it, how they might distinguish "spiritual resurrection" from immortality of the soul, and how they might defend the theory against criticisms such as those just noted. However, I will not do so in this paper. As noted above, my aim here is rather to explore and defend a third way of understanding the traditional Christian notion of resurrection, a theory virtually all (but not quite all) of the church Fathers who discussed resurrection held in one form or another.[3] I will call this theory "temporary disembodiment."

This theory of resurrection is based on a view of human nature which says that human beings are essentially material bodies *and* immaterial souls; the soul is separable from the body, but neither body or soul alone (i.e., without the other) constitutes a complete human being. Thus Pseudo-Justin Martyr says: "Is the soul by itself man? No; but the soul of man. Would the body be called man? No, but it is called the body of man. If, then, neither of these is by itself man, but that which is made up of the two together is called man, and God has called *man* to life and resurrection, He has called not a part, but the whole, which is the soul and the body."[4] What this theory says, then, is that human beings are typically and normally psycho-physical beings, that the soul can exist for a time apart from the body and retain personal identity, but that this disembodied existence is only temporary and constitutes a radically attenuated and incomplete form of human existence.

I call the theory temporary disembodiment because it envisions the following scenario: We human beings are born, live for a time as psycho-physical beings, and then die; after death we exist in an incomplete state as immaterial souls; and some time later in the eschaton God miraculously raises our bodies from the ground, transforms them into "glorified bodies," and reunites them with our souls, thus making us complete and whole again.

Now temporary disembodiment has several theological and philosophical assets. For one thing, many Christian thinkers have seen a comfortable fit between it and the view of human nature expressed in the Bible and in the Pauline writings particularly. The Apostle seems to hold that human beings consist both of material bodies and immaterial souls, that the body is not merely an adornment or drape for the soul, and is indeed good, since it can be the temple of the Holy Spirit (I Cor. 3, 16–17; 6, 19–20), and that the soul is in some sense separable from the body (II Cor. 5, 6–8; 12, 2–3). What the body does is provide the soul with a vehicle for action in the world and expression of intentions and desires; and the soul provides the body with animation and direction.[5]

For another thing, the theory seems a neat way of reconciling the traditional view that the general resurrection does not occur until the eschaton with Jesus' statement to the good thief on the cross, *"Today you will be with me in paradise"* (Lk. 23, 43). The explanation (which naturally goes far beyond Jesus' simple statement) is as follows: The thief would be with Jesus in paradise that very day in the form of a disembodied soul, only to be bodily raised much later. The theory may also help resolve a similar tension that is sometimes said to exist in Pauline thought, with texts like I Corinthians 15 and I Thessalonians 4 pointing toward the idea of a future, eschatological, resurrection (with those who die beforehand existing till then in a kind of bodiless sleep) and texts like 2 Corinthians 5, 10 and Phillipians, 1, 23 suggesting the idea that death for the Christian is an immediate gain since one is immediately at home with the Lord. (How one can simultaneously be both "at home with the Lord" and "in an incomplete state" is a tension that perhaps remains in the theory.)

Finally, the problem of personal identity after death seems in one regard more manageable on this theory than on at least some others, for there is in this theory no temporal gap in the existence of persons (although there is a gap in their existence as complete, unified persons). There is no moment subsequent to our births in which you and I simply do not exist—we exist either as soul-bodies or as mere souls at every moment till eternity.

III

There are three main aspects of temporary disembodiment that require discussion both from a philosophical and a theological perspective. Let me now consider them in turn. The first is the notion that after death the soul exists for a time, i.e., until the resurrection, in an intermediate state without the body. The second is the notion that at the time of the parousia the body will be raised from the ground and reunited with the soul. And the third is the notion that the body will then be transformed into what is called a "glorified body."

The first main claim of temporary disembodiment, then, is that after death the soul temporarily exists without the body. This differs from physicalist concepts of resurrection in which the person does not exist at all in the period between death and resurrection. Temporary disembodiment need not be based on classical dualism as defined earlier, but is based on one tenet of classical dualism, viz., the claim that human beings consist (or in this case at least normally consist) of both material bodies and immaterial souls. (The soul is not said to be the essence of the person, however, and is said to survive death not because immortality is one of its natural properties but because God causes it to survive death.)[6]

Now almost all Christians believe that there is some kind of interim state of the person between death and resurrection. But beyond this point there are very many theological differences. Some, for example, think of the interim state as purgatorial in nature, and others do not. Some hold that spiritual change, e.g., repentance, is possible during the interim period, and others do not. Some think the soul rests or sleeps, i.e., is not active or conscious, during the interim period, and others do not. It is not part of my purpose in this paper to express an opinion on either of the first two items of disagreement. However, I will argue in regard to the third that the soul is conscious in the interim state. The biblical metaphor of sleep (cf. Luke 8, 2; I Cor. 15, 20) is not to be taken as a literal description. This is because it is difficult to make sense of the notion of a disembodied thing being in the presence of God ("Today you will be with me in paradise") if that thing is unconscious and thus unaware of the presence of God.[7] Furthermore, since sleeping is essentially a bodily activity it seems incoherent to suggest that a soul *could* sleep.

The state of being without a body is an abnormal state of the human person. This is one of the clear differences between temporary disembodiment and immortality of the soul, for the second doctrine (at least in versions of it influenced by Plato) entails that disembodiment is the true or proper or best state of the human person. On the theory we are considering, however, the claim is that a disembodied soul lacks many of the properties and abilities that are normal for and proper to human persons. Disembodied existence is a kind of minimal existence.

Which properties typical of embodied human persons will disembodied souls have and which will they lack? Clearly they will lack those properties that essentially involve corporeality. They will possess no spatial location, for example, at least not in the space-time manifold with which we are familiar. They will not be able to perceive their surroundings (using the spatial word "surroundings" in a stretched sense)—not at least in the ways in which we perceive our surroundings (i.e., through the eyes, ears, etc.). They will not be able to experience bodily pains and pleasures. They will not be able to engage in bodily activities. Taking a walk, getting dressed, playing catch—these sorts of activities will be impossible.

But if by the word "soul" we mean in part the constellation of those human activities that would typically be classified as "mental," then the claim that our souls survive death entails the claim that our mental abilities and properties survive death. This means that human persons in the interim state can be spoken of as having experiences, beliefs, wishes, knowledge, memory, inner (rather than bodily) feelings, thoughts, language (assuming memory of earthly existence)—in short, just about everything that makes up what we call personality. H. H. Price, in his classic article "Survival and the Idea of 'Another World'," argues convincingly that disembodied souls can also be aware of each other's existence, can communicate with each other telepathically, and can have dreamlike (rather than bodily) perceptions of their world.[8]

But Aquinas argues that the disembodied existence of the person in the interim state is so deficient that ultimate happiness is impossible. No one in whom some perfection is lacking is ultimately happy, for in such a state there will always be unfulfilled desires. It is contrary to the nature of the soul to be without the body, Aquinas says, and he takes this to mean both that the disembodied state must only be temporary, and that the true bliss of the human person is only attained after reembodiment, i.e., in the general resurrection. He says: "Man cannot achieve his ultimate happiness unless the soul be once again united to the body."[9]

IV

The second main claim of the theory that I am calling temporary disembodiment is that at the general resurrection, the body will be raised from the ground and reunited with the soul. As the second century writer Athenagoras says: ". . . There must certainly be a resurrection of bodies whether dead or even quite corrupted, and the same men as before must come to be again. The law of nature appoints an end . . . for those very same men who lived in a previous existence, and it is impossible for the same men to come together again if the same bodies are not given back to the same souls. Now the same soul cannot recover the same body in any other way than by resurrection."[10]

As Athenagoras stresses, the idea is that each person's selfsame body will be raised; it will not be a different and brand new body but the old body. Aquinas (echoing the argument of very many of the Fathers) notes the reason for this: "If the body of the man who rises is not to be composed of the flesh and bones which now compose it, the man who rises will not be numerically the same man."[11] Further-more, in the resurrection there will be only one soul per body and only one body per soul. As Augustine says: "Each single soul shall possess its own body."[12] Otherwise (e.g., if souls split and animate more than one body or if multiple identical copies of one body are animated by different souls) the problem of personal identity is unsolvable, and the Christian hope that we will live after death is incoherent.

The Fathers and scholastics insisted, then, that both body and soul must be present or else the person does not exist. "A man cannot be said to exist as such when the body is dissolved or completely scat-tered, even though the soul remain by itself"—so says Athenagoras.[13] And Aquinas agrees: "My soul is not I, and if only souls are saved, *I* am not saved, nor is any man."[14] Thus the Christian hope of survival is not the hope that our souls will survive death (though on temporary disembodiment that is one important aspect of it), but rather the hope that one day God will miraculously raise our bodies and reunite them with our souls.

What is it, then, that guarantees personal identity in the resurrec-tion? What is it that ensures that it will really be *us* in the kingdom of God and not, say, clever replicas of us? Aquinas argues as follows: since human beings consist of bodies and souls, and since both souls and the matter of which our bodies consist survive death, personal identity is secured when God collects the scattered matter, miracu-lously reconstitutes it a human body, and reunites it with the soul.[15] And this surely seems a powerful argument. If God one day succeeds in doing these very things, personal identity will be secure. It will be us and not our replicas who will be the denizens of the kingdom of God.

V

The third main claim of temporary disembodiment is that in the resur-rection the old body will be transformed into a "glorified body" with certain quite new properties. This claim is based primarily on Paul's discussion of the resurrection in I Corinthians 15, and secondarily on the unusual properties the risen Jesus is depicted as having in some of the accounts of the resurrection appearances (e.g., the apparent ability of the risen Jesus in John 20 to appear in a room despite the doors being locked). In the Pauline text just mentioned, the Apostle notes that some ask, "How are the dead raised? With what kind of body do they come?" His answer is an argument to the effect that the new "glorified" or "spiritual" body (*soma pneumatikon*) is a transfor-mation of the old body rather than a *de novo* creation (much as a stalk of grain is a transformation of a seed of grain, i.e., it exists because of changes that have occurred in the seed and can be considered a new state of the grain). Further, Paul argues, while the old or natural body is physical, perishable, mortal, and sown in weakness and dishonor, the glorified body is spiritual, imperishable, immortal, and sown in strength and honor. The first body is in the image of the man of dust; the second body is in the image of the man of heaven.

The term "spiritual body" might be misleading; it should not be taken as a denial of corporeality or as a last-minute capitulation to some version of the immortality of the soul as opposed to bodily resurrection. By this term, Paul means not a body whose stuff or matter is spiritual (whatever that might mean) or an immaterial existence of some sort; rather he means a body that is fully obedient to and dominated by the Holy Spirit. Paul says: "Flesh and blood cannot inherit the kingdom of God" (I Cor. 15, 50). What enters the kingdom of heaven, then, is not this present weak and mortal body of flesh and blood but the new glorified body. This new body is a physical body (Paul's use of the word *soma* implies as much),[16] and is materially related to the old body (taking seriously Paul's simile of the seed), but is a body transformed in such ways as make it fit to live in God's presence. If by the term "physical object" we mean an entity that has spatio-temporal location and is capable of being empirically measured, tested, or observed in some sense, then my argument is that the new body of which Paul speaks is a physical object.

Temporary disembodiment, then, entails that human souls can animate both normal earthly bodies and glorified resurrection bodies. Continuity between the two bodies is provided by the presence of both the same soul and the same matter in both bodies. Thus Augustine says: "Nor does the earthly material out of which men's mortal bodies are created ever perish; but though it may crumble into dust and ashes, or be dissolved into vapors and exhalations, though it may be transformed into the substance of other bodies, or dispersed into the elements, though it should become food for beasts or men, and be changed into their flesh, it returns in a moment of time to that human soul which animated it at the first and which caused it to become man, and to live and grow."[17] The matter of our present bodies may be arranged differently in the resurrection, he says, but the matter will be restored.

Many of the theologians of the early church and of the medieval period stress also the perfection of the glorified body. It will be free of every bodily defect. It will be immune to evil because fully controlled by the spirit of God. It will not suffer. It will not grow old or die. It will have "agility"—which is presumably an ability like that of the risen Jesus to come and go at will, unimpeded by things like walls and doors. It will exist in a state of fulfilled desire. It will need no material food and drink, but will be nourished by the elements of the eucharist.[18]

VI

Is the picture of resurrection just presented coherent? Is it plausible? The main objections that have been raised against it in recent philosophy revolve around the problem of personal identity. Some philosophers argue that so far as disembodied existence is concerned this problem cannot be solved. That is, they argue that if some immaterial aspect of me survives death it will not be me that survives death. Since the view of survival of death I am defending essentially involves a period of disembodied existence, I had best try to defend the view against these sorts of objections. But a prior problem must be considered first—whether the Fathers and scholastics were correct in their strong claim (I will call this claim "the Patristic theory") that if it is to be me in the kingdom of God the very matter of my original earthly body must be raised. Having discussed this point, I will then turn in Section VII to the arguments of those philosophers who oppose the notion of disembodied existence because of the problem of personal identity.

Why did Aquinas and the Fathers who influenced him insist that the same matter of my old body must be raised? Let us see if we can construct an argument on their behalf. Like many arguments in the area of personal identity, it involves a puzzle case. Suppose that I own a defective personal computer which I rashly decide to try to repair myself. Having taken it apart (there are now, say, sixty separate computer components scattered on my work bench), I find that I am unable to repair it. I call the outlet that sold me the computer, and the manager suggests I simply bring all sixty components to that office for repair. I do so, but through a horrible series of misunderstandings and errors, the sixty pieces of the computer are then sent to sixty different addresses around the country. That constitutes the heart of my story, but there are two separate endings to it. *Ending number one:* it takes three years for everything to be sorted out, for the pieces to be located and collected in one place, for the repairs to be made, and for the parts to be reassembled and restored, in full working order, to my desk. *Ending number two:* After three years of trying in vain to locate and collect the scattered pieces, the manager gives up, collects sixty similar parts, assembles them, and the resulting computer ends up on my desk.

Now I do not wish to raise the interesting question whether my computer *existed* during the three year period. I am interested in the related question whether the computer now located on my desk is *the same* computer as the one that was there three years ago. And so far as ending number one is concerned, it seems most natural to affirm that the computer I now possess is indeed the same computer as the one that I possessed before. The computer may or may not have had a gap in its existence, i.e., a period when it did not exist, but it seems clear that identity has here been preserved. And so far as ending number two is concerned, it seems most natural to deny that the computer I now possess is the same computer as the one that I possessed before. Furthermore, we would doubtless insist on this denial even if each of the sixty components the manager used to construct the computer I now possess were qualitatively identical to the sixty old components. What I now have is a qualitatively similar but numerically different computer.

Now I doubt that the Church Fathers often pondered personal identity test cases like those involving computers, and it is obvious that personal computers are different from human beings in many striking ways. But it was perhaps *the sort* of insight arrived at above that led them to take the strong stand they took on the resurrection. Only if God reassembles the very particles of which my body once consisted will it be me who is raised. Otherwise, i.e., if other particles are used, the result will be what we would call a replica of me rather than me.

But despite the above argument, does it still not seem that Aquinas and the Fathers in their strong stand have made the solution to the problem of personal identity more difficult than it need be? Even granting the point that some of the particles of the matter of which our bodies consist will endure for the requisite number of years, why insist God must re-collect it, i.e., that very matter, in the resurrection? For surely in the interim state it will be us (and not soul-like replicas of us) who will exist without any body at all; surely the Fathers and scholastics insist on this much. Thus the soul alone must guarantee personal identity; what philosophers call the memory criterion (which is typically taken to include not just memory but all one's "mental" characteristics and properties) must suffice by itself. Identity of memory, personality, and other "mental" aspects of the person are sufficient conditions of personal identity. To admit this much is not necessarily to go back on the traditional notion that the soul is not the whole person and that the whole person must be raised. It is merely to insist that the existence of my soul entails *my* existence. Otherwise talk of my existence in the interim state is meaningless.

Now I do not claim that the Patristic theory is logically inconsistent. It is possible to hold that when I die my soul will be me during the interim period but that it will no longer be me if my soul in the eschaton animates a body consisting of totally new matter, even if the new body is qualitatively identical to the old one. (Perhaps an essential property of my soul is that it can only animate *this* body—where "this body" means in part a body consisting of *these* particles. So if *per impossible* my soul were to animate a different body the result would not be me. Or perhaps every configuration of particles that can possibly constitute a human body has it as one of its essential properties that it can be animated by one and only one soul.) But while logically consistent, this view seems to me exceedingly difficult to defend; it is hard to see how the suggested theses could be argued for.

Thus so far as the problem of personal identity is concerned, it is not easy to see why a defender of temporary disembodiment cannot dispense with all talk of God one day re-collecting the atoms, quarks, or whatever of our bodies. Perhaps human beings in this regard are unlike computers. Why not say God can award us brand new bodies materially quite unrelated to (although qualitatively similar to) the old ones? If the existence of the soul is sufficient for personal identity, and if the human soul never at any moment subsequent to its creation fails to exist, it will be us who exist after the resurrection in the kingdom of God whether or not our old bodies are reconstituted.

Furthermore, it needs to be noted here that identity of particles of bodily matter does not seem necessary to perserve the identity of an ordinary human person even during the course of a lifetime. As Frank Dilley says: "We constantly replace our atoms over time and there is no reason to think that an eighty year old person has even a single atom in common with the newborn babe. If a person maintains personal identity over a process of total atom-by-atom replacement, it is difficult to see why such identity would not be preserved through a sudden replacement of all the atoms at once."[19]

Dilley's argument seems plausible, but we should notice that is does not necessarily follow. Perhaps gradual replacement of all the individual atoms of a human body is consistent with personal identity while all-at-once replacement of them is not. Perhaps some strong sort of material continuity is needed. One of the difficulties encountered by philosophers who discuss personal identity is that different persons' intuitions run in different directions. For example, in a slightly different connection, Peter Van Inwagen argues that sameness of person requires both (1) sameness of atoms and (2) regular and natural causal relationships between those atoms. So if God were now to try to raise Napoleon Bonaparte from the dead by omnisciently locating the atoms of which his body once consisted and miraculously reassembling them, the result would not be Napoleon.[20] Now I do not agree with Van

Inwagen here; I see no reason for his second stipulation. I raise his argument merely to show that his intuitions run in a different direction than do Dilley's. Since Dilley's case of sudden-replacement-of-all-the-atoms-at-once seems to constitute something *un*natural and *ir*regular, Van Inwagon would doubtless deny that in such cases personal identity would be preserved.

What if there were, so to speak, some natural way of reassembling persons out of totally new matter? Derek Parfit considers in detail a series of test cases involving an imagined Teletransporter.[21] This is a machine that is designed to send a person to distant places like Mars by (1) recording the exact state of all the body's cells (including those of the brain); (2) destroying the body and brain; (3) transmitting the information at the speed of light to Mars; where (4) a Replicator creates out of new matter a body and brain exactly like the old one. Suppose Parfit enters the machine and is "teletransported to Mars." Would the resulting Parfit-like person on Mars *be* Parfit? Here again our intuitions might differ, even in this relatively simple case (i.e., apart from complications like the original Parfit somehow surviving on earth or fifteen Parfit-like persons appearing on Mars). Those (like the Church Fathers and Aquinas) who hold to some strong requirement about bodily continuity will deny it is Parfit. Those who stress the memory criterion are free to affirm that Parfit is now on Mars. So are those (e.g., John Hick) who believe that identity is exact similarity plus uniqueness. Those who think that identity is exact similarity plus the right kind of causal origin or causal ancestry might go either way, depending on whether they think the operation of a Teletransporter constitutes an appropriate sort of causal origin for the Parfit-like person on Mars.

The moral of the story thus far, I think, is that the Fathers and Aquinas may be right in what they say about resurrection, but it is not clear that they are right. Their position may be consistent, but it does seem implausible to hold both (1) that it will be me in the interim period without any body at all (i.e., the presence of my soul is sufficient for personal identity) and (2) that it will not be me in the eschaton, despite the presence of my soul, if the body which my soul then animates consists of new matter. There may be other (perhaps theological) reasons why we should hold that it is the very matter of our old bodies that is raised, but so far as the problem of personal identity is concerned, a strong case can be made that it will not matter.

Recent and contemporary Christian theologians who discuss resurrection seem for the most part to have departed from the Patristic theory. The more common thesis is that our glorified bodies will be wholly different bodies, not necessarily consisting of any of the old matter at all. As John Hick, an articulate spokesperson for this new point of view, says: "What has become a widely accepted view in modern times holds that the resurrection body is a new and different body given by God, but expressing the personality within its new environment as the physical body expressed it in the earthly environment. The physical frame decays or is burned, disintegrating and being dispersed into the ground or the air, but God re-embodies the personality elsewhere."[22] Frequently connected with this view is an exegetical claim, viz., that by the term "the body," St. Paul meant not the physical organism but rather something akin to "the whole personality." What will be raised from the dead, then, is not the old body but rather the *person,* and in being raised the person will be given a brand new body by God.

It is not hard to see why such a view has come to be widely adopted. (1) As noted above, personal identity does not seem to require the resurrection of the old body. (2) The Patristic theory seems to many contemporary Christians to be scientifically outmoded and difficult to believe; the idea that in order to raise me God must one day cast about, locate, and collect the atoms of which my earthy body once consisted seems to many people absurd. (3) Many such theologians want to hold in any case that the kingdom of God is not spatially related to our present world. It exists in a space all its own, and so can contain no material from this spatiotemporal manifold.

I am unable to locate any philosophical or logical difficulties in the "modern" theory. It seems to me a possible Christian view of resurrection, and can fit smoothly with the other aspects of the traditional notion I am calling temporary disembodiment. Are there any theological reasons, then, for a Christian to retain the old theory, i.e., to believe that our old bodies will be raised? Two points should be made here. The first is that the most natural reading of Paul in I Corinthian 15 is along the lines of the Patristic theory. That is, Paul seems to be suggesting there that the old body *becomes* or *changes into* the new body, just as a seed becomes or changes into a plant. Thus, just as there is material continuity between the seed and the plant, so there, will be material continuity between the old body and the new; the plant is *a new form of* the seed. Note also Paul's use in verses 42 and 43 of the expression: "*It* is sown . . . *it* is raised . . .", as if the one thing (a human body) is at one time in a certain state and at a later time in another state (see also vs. 53 and 54).[23] Furthermore, as noted already, Paul's use of the term *soma* reveals that what he had in mind was a body; it is simply a lexical mistake to say that he merely meant "the whole personality," or some such thing.[24]

The second point has to do with the difficulty of God one day collecting the atoms, quarks, or whatever fundamental particles human bodies consist of. This may well be the oldest philosophical objection ever raised against the Christian notion of resurrection. Virtually every one of the Fathers who discussed resurrection tried to answer it, as did Aquinas. Such scenarios as this were suggested: What if a Christian dies at sea and his body is eaten by various fishes who then scatter to the seven seas? How can God later resurrect that body? Or what if another Christian is eaten by cannibals, so that the material of her body becomes the material of their bodies? And suppose God later wants to raise all of them from the dead, cannibals and Christians alike. Who gets what particles? How does God decide?

The move made by virtually all of the Fathers in response to this objection is to appeal to omnipotence. You and I might not be able to locate and reconstitute the relevant atoms of someone's body, not surely after many years or even centuries have passed, but God can do this very thing. And as long as (1) the basic constituents of matter (e.g., atoms) endure through time (as contemporary physical theory says they normally do); and (2) it is merely a matter of God locating and collecting the relevant constituents, I believe the Fathers were right. An omnipotent being could do that.

But with the cannibalism case and other imaginable cases where God must decide which constituent parts shared at different times by two (or even two thousand) separate persons go where, the matter is more serious. The problem does not seem insoluble, but much more needs to be said. Perhaps some constituent parts of human bodies are essential to those bodies and some are not. That is, perhaps God will only need to collect the essential parts of our bodies and use them, so to speak, as building blocks around which to reconstruct our new bodies. And perhaps omnipotence must accordingly guarantee that no essential part of one person's earthly body is ever a constituent part, or an essential part, of someone else's body. If these stipulations or ones like them are followed (e.g., Augustine's idea that atoms will be raised in that human body in which they *first* appeared[25]), it still seems that the Fathers were correct—an omnipotent being will be able to raise us from the ground.

Reacting against these and similar patristic appeals to omnipotence in order to rationalize resurrection, Paul Badham argues as follows:[26]

Given belief in a once-for-all act of creation on the pattern of Genesis 1, then the act of resurrection cannot be difficult for an all-powerful God. Given that God made the first man by direct action, the restoration of a decomposed man becomes an easy task. Given that man consists of particles, it is easy to believe that omnipotence could reassemble these particles. But today each of these premises has lost its validity, and hence the conclusions drawn from them cannot stand. That man as a species is part of a slowly evolving process of life and in every respect continuous with the processes of nature from which he has emerged does not provide a congenial background for the idea of resurrection. Further, our increasing knowledge of the incredible complexity and constant changing of our physical components makes it difficult to see the resurrection as simply involving the re-collection of our physical particles. We are not composed of building bricks but of constantly changing living matter.

It is not easy to see exactly what the arguments here are meant to be. For one thing, Badham is right that nature is incredibly complex, as are human bodies; our bodies surely do consist of constantly changing living matter. But does any of this deny—or indeed does contemporary physics deny—the idea that our bodies consist of particles? I think not. Furthermore, it is hard to see how a commitment to evolutionary theory (a commitment I make) undercuts the ability of an omnipotent being to raise us from the dead. Perhaps it does undercut a simplistic argument which we occasionally find in the Fathers, an argument which says, "Since God already did the difficult job of creating me *de novo* by assembling the particles of my body, God can also do the far easier job of reassembling them in the eschaton."[27] But surely claims about what is easy and what is hard for an omnipotent being to do are suspect anyway. The point the Fathers were making is that whatever difficulties resurrection presents are difficulties that can be overcome by an omnipotent being. That point—so I believe—still stands, and is not rendered improbable or implausible by evolution.

VII

Several philosophers have argued in recent years that the concept of disembodied existence is incoherent or at least that no disembodied thing can be identified with some previously existing human person. Antony Flew,[28] Bernard Williams,[29] D. Z. Phillips,[30] Terence Penelhum,[31] and John Perry,[32] among others, have jointly presented what might be called the standard arguments against survival of death in disembodied form. P. T. Geach[33] has similarly argued against the notion of *permanent* disembodied existence, though he supports something like the theory I am calling temporary disembodiment. Now I am inclined to hold that the standard arguments have been successfully answered by defenders of disembodied existence;[34] that is, I believe the notion of survival of death (and even permanent survival of death) in disembodied form is intelligible and logically possible. Furthermore, one result of recent discussion of the puzzle cases in the area of personal identity is that many philosophers are now prepared to defend the notion that we can imagine cases where the memory criterion will suffice by itself. But since the arguments of Flew, Williams, and Phillips, and Penelhum have been discussed thoroughly in the journals, let me instead focus on the case John Perry makes in his excellent little book, *A Dialogue on Personal Identity and Immortality.*

Perry seems, in this dialogue, to speak primarily through the character of Gretchen Weirob, a mortally injured but still lucid philosopher who does not believe in life after death. And Weirob seems to present three main arguments against the conceivability or possibility of survival of death. All are versions of arguments we find elsewhere in the literature, but the virtue of Perry's work is that they are presented with great clarity and forcefulness. Perry's first argument has to do with the soul and personal identity; the second concerns memory and personal identity; and the third is an argument about the possibility of duplication of persons.

The first argument says that immaterial and thus unobservable souls can have nothing to do with establishing personal identity. Personal identity does not consist in sameness of soul, for if it did, we would never know who we are or who others are. Since souls are not observable, no thesis having to do with souls is testable (not even the thesis, "My soul is me"). So I cannot know whether other human beings have souls, or even whether I have a soul; I have no idea whether I have one soul or several, or whether I have one soul for a time and then later a different soul. Thus there are no criteria for, and hence no way to make informed judgments about, "the same soul." It is possible simply on faith to assume criteria like, "Same body, same soul," or "Same mental traits, same soul," but since we never independently observe souls, there is no way to test these principles, and thus no reason to think they hold. But since we evidently are able to make correct personal identity judgments about persons, it follows, that personal identity has nothing to do with souls. Personal identity must instead be based upon bodily criteria. Thus, concludes Perry, no thesis about my survival of death via the survival of my soul is coherent.

Perry's second argument is that the memory criterion of personal identity, which those who believe in immortality must rely on, is never sufficient to establish personal identity. This is because of the obvious fact that memory is fallible. Without some further criterion, we will never be able to distinguish between apparent memories and genuine memories. In fact, believers in immortality are committed to a kind of circularity—they claim that genuine memory explains personal identity (that is, a purported Jones in the afterlife really is Jones just in case the purported Jones genuinely remembers from Jones's point of view

events in Jones's past), and they claim that identity marks the difference between apparent and genuine memories (the purported Jones
can have genuine memories of events in Jones's past just in case the
purported Jones *is* Jones—otherwise the memories are merely apparent memories). Thus, again, the thesis that our souls survive death,
which must rely on the memory criterion of personal identity, is
incoherent.

Finally, Perry, argues that the thesis of survival of death through
immortality is rendered incoherent by the possibility of multiple qualitatively identical persons in the afterlife. Weirob says:[35]

> So either God, by creating a Heavenly person with a brain modeled
> after mine, does not really create someone identical with me but merely
> someone similar to me, or God is somehow limited to making only one
> such being. I can see no reason why, if there were a God, He should be
> so limited. So I take the first option. He would create someone similar
> to me, but not someone who would *be* me. Either your analysis of mem-
> ory is wrong, and such a being does not, after all, remember what I am
> doing or saying, or memory is not sufficient for personal identity. Your
> theory has gone wrong somewhere, for it leads to absurdity.

When told by one of the discussants that God may well refrain from
creating multiple qualitatively identical persons in the afterlife and that
if God does so refrain the immortality thesis is coherent, Weirob replies
that a new criterion has now been added. What suffices for personal
identity (i.e., what makes it such that the purported Jones in the afterlife *is* Jones) is not just memory but rather memory plus lack of competition. An odd way for someone to be killed in the afterlife, she
remarks—all God has to do is create, so to speak, an identical twin to
Jones, and then *neither* is it Jones; Jones has not survived death. Identity is now made oddly to depend on something entirely extrinsic to
the person involved. Thus if memory does not secure personal identity
where there are two or more Jones's in the afterlife, it does not secure
personal identity at all. Weirob concludes it is best simply to abandon
any thought of survival of death—when my body dies, I die.

Perry's first argument in favor of the notion that survival of death
is incoherent is based on an element of truth, but is used by him in an
erroneous way. Throughout his book he seems illicitly to jump back
and forth between talk about criteria of personal identity and talk about
evidence for personal identity. It is surely true that the soul is not
observable, and that the presence or absence of a soul or of a certain
soul is not something for which we can successfully test. What this
shows, as I suppose, is that the soul is not *evidence for* personal identity. We cannot, for example, prove that a given person really is our
long-lost friend by proving that this person really has our long-lost

friend's soul. But it still might be true that the soul is *a criterion of personal identity*. That is, it still might be the case that the person really is our long-lost friend just in case this person and our long-lost friend have the same soul. It might even be true to say that a purported Jones in the afterlife is the same person as the Jones who once lived on earth just in case the purported Jones has Jones's soul. How we might test for or come to know this is another matter. Maybe only God knows for sure who has what soul. Maybe the rest of us will never know—not apart from divine revelation, anyway—whether the purported Jones has Jones's soul. But it can still be true that if they have the same soul, they are two different temporal episodes of the same one person.

And the claim that personal identity consists in or amounts to the presence of the soul does not rule out the possibility of our making reliable personal identity judgments on other grounds, as Weirob seems to claim it does. Those who believe in the possibility of disembodied existence need not deny that there are other criteria of personal identity (e.g., if the person before me has the same body as my long-lost friend, this person *is* my long-lost friend) and other ways of producing evidence in favor of or against personal identity claims.

Perry's second argument is also based on an element of truth—memory certainly is fallible; we do have to distinguish between apparent memories and genuine memories. So unless I have access to some infallible way of making this distinction, the mere fact that the purported Jones seems to remember events in Jones's life from Jones's point of view will not establish beyond conceivable doubt that the purported Jones is Jones (though it might count as evidence for it). As above, however, this does not rule out the possibility that memory is a criterion of personal identity—if the purported Jones does indeed remember events in Jones's life from Jones's point of view, then the purported Jones is Jones.

It is sometimes claimed that the memory criterion is parasitic on the bodily criterion and that use of the memory criterion never suffices by itself to establish identity. But such claims are surely false. We sometimes do make secure identity claims based on the memory criterion alone—e.g., when we receive a typed letter from a friend. We hold that it is our friend who wrote the letter solely on the basis of memories and personality traits apparently had by the letter's author that seem to be memories and personality traits our friend has or ought to have. Of course if doubts were to arise we would try to verify or falsify the claim that our friend wrote the letter by the use of any evidence or criterion that might seem promising. We might check the letter for finger prints; we might try to see if it was written on our friend's typewriter; we might even telephone our friend. What this shows is not that we must always rely on the bodily criterion; there are equally cases where we might try to verify an identity claim originally based on the bodily criterion by means of memories. What it shows is that in cases of doubt we will look at both criteria.

But in cases where the bodily criterion cannot be used—e.g., during the interim period postulated in temporary disembodiment—can identity claims rationally be made? Can we ever be sure that a disembodied putative Stephen Davis *is* Stephen Davis? The problem is especially acute since memory is notoriously fallible; without recourse to the bodily criterion, how can we distinguish between actual memories and purported memories? I would argue that secure identity claims can be made without use of the bodily criterion, and that this can be achieved in cases where there are very many memories from very many different people that cohere together well. The context would make all the difference. If there are, say one hundred disembodied souls all wondering whether everyone in fact is who he or she claims to be, it would be irrational to deny that their memories are genuine if they all fit together, confirm each other, and form a coherent picture. Doubt would still be conceivable, but not rational. And something like this is precisely what defenders of temporary disembodiment claim will occur during the interim period.[36]

The third or duplication argument is one that critics of disembodied existence frequently appeal to, but it is one of the advantages of Perry's *Dialogue* that he grasps the defender's proper reply to it, and then moves to deepen the objection. After the comment from Weirob quoted above, Perry has Dave Cohen, a former student of hers, say: "But wait. Why can't Sam simply say that if God makes one such creature, she is you, while if he makes more, none of them is you? It's possible that he makes only one. So it's possible that you survive." This seems to me the correct response. Of course immortality or resurrection would be difficult to believe in if there were, say, fourteen qualitatively identical Weirobs in the afterlife, each with equal apparent sincerity claiming to be Gretchen Weirob. But surely you can't refute a thesis, or the possible truth of a thesis, by imagining possible worlds where the thesis would be exceedingly hard to believe. Survival of death theses might well make good sense if in the afterlife there is never more than one person who claims to be some premortem person. And since it is possible there will be but one Gretchen Weirob in the afterlife, survival of death is possible.

In response to this point, Perry deepens the objection with Weirob's points about there now being two criteria of personal identity (memory and lack of competition) and about the oddness of God's ability to prevent someone's surviving death by creating a second qualitatively identical person. Both points seem to me correct, but do not render the survival thesis incoherent or even, as Weirob claims, absurd. What exactly is wrong with saying (in the light of God's evident ability to create multiple qualitatively identical persons) that memory plus lack of competition are criteria of personal identity? Lack of competition is a criterion that technically applies in this life as well as the next— we never bother to mention it because it rarely occurs to us that God has the ability to create multiple qualitatively identical persons here as well. And I suppose it *is* odd that God can prevent someone's survival in the way envisioned, and that personal identity is here made in part to depend on something entirely extrinsic to the person. These facts are odd, but they do not seem to me to impugn the possibility of the survival thesis.

Christians strongly deny that there will be multiple qualitatively identical persons in the eschaton. They would hold, however, that God has the ability to create such persons, so it is perfectly fair for critics to ask: How would it affect your advocacy of resurrection if God were to exercise this power? Now I prefer to hold that the existence of multiple qualitatively identical Jones's in the eschaton would place far too great a strain on our concept of a human person for us to affirm that Jones has survived death. Our concept of a person, I believe, includes a notion of uniqueness—there is and can be only one instance of each "person." Uniqueness or "lack of competition" (as Weirob puts it) is a criterion of personal identity. So I would argue at the very least that we would not know what to say if there were more than one Jones in the afterlife (perhaps our concept of a human person would have to be radically revised to include amoeba-like divisions, or something of the sort). More strongly, I would argue that Jones (the unique person we knew on earth) has not survived death.

Accordingly, I see no serious difficulty for the survival thesis here. Although the view I am defending—temporary disembodiment—does not require the coherence of any notion of permanent disembodiment (like, for example, the doctrine known as immortality of the soul), I nevertheless would hold both to be coherent. As noted above, however, Geach argues strongly that only temporary disembodiment is coherent; what alone makes the problem of personal identity manageable as regards a disembodied person is its capacity or potential eventually to be reunited with a given body. Otherwise, he says, disembodied minds cannot be differentiated.[37] If Geach is right, only temporary disembodiment is coherent—immortality of the soul is not. Or at least, those who believe in the later doctrine must add an item to their theory— perhaps something about a permanently disembodied soul permanently retaining the (forever unrealized) *capacity* to be reunited with a given body.

VIII

As can be seen from the preceding discussion, I do not consider that what I have been calling the Patristic theory is normative for Christians today. The "modern" theory seems to me an acceptable interpretation of resurrection. God's ability to raise us from the dead in the eschaton does not seem to depend on God's ability to locate and reunite the very particles of which our bodies once consisted. Nevertheless, the Patristic theory also constitutes an acceptable understanding of resurrection for Christians. The standard objections to it are answerable, and the most natural exegesis of I Corinthians 15, 35–50 supports it. Furthermore, respect for Christian tradition must (or so I would argue) grant great weight to views held by virtually all the Fathers of the church unless there is serious reason to depart from what they say. It seems to me quite possible that God will one day raise us from the dead in the very way that the Fathers and Aquinas suggest.

My overall conclusion is that the theory of resurrection I have been considering (which can be interpreted in either the Patristic or the "modern" way) is a viable notion for Christians. Temporary disembodiment seems eminently defensible, both philosophically and theologically. I do not claim it is the only viable option for Christian belief about life after death; I do claim it is an acceptable way for Christians to understand those words from the Apostles' Creed that say, "I believe in . . . the resurrection of the body."

Much contemporary philosophy in its understanding of human nature tends in a behaviorist or even materialist direction. No believer in temporary disembodiment can embrace philosophical materialism, but such believers can have great sympathy with any view which says that a disembodied person would hardly be a human person, not surely in the full sense of the word. They too embrace the notion that a disembodied person is only a minimal person, a mere shadow of a true human person—not completely unlike a person who is horribly disabled from birth or from some accident but who continues to live.

Such Christians will accordingly embrace the notion that full and true and complete human life is bodily life. That is why they look forward to "the resurrection of the body." As Pseudo-Justin says[38] "In the resurrection the flesh shall rise entire. For if on earth He healed the sickness of the flesh, and made the body whole much more will

He do this in the resurrection, so that the flesh shall rise perfect and entire."[39]

NOTES

1. See Stephen T. Davis, "Is Personal Identity Retained in the Resurrection?" *Modern Theology,* Vol. 2, No. 4 (July 1986).

2. Cyril Richardson (ed.), *Early Christian Fathers* (Philadelphia, 1953), p. 389.

3. See Harry A. Wolfson, "Immortality and Resurrection in the Philosophy of the Church Fathers," in *Immortality and Resurrection,* ed. by Krister Stendahl (New York, 1965), pp. 64–72. See also Lynn Boliek, *The Resurrection of the Flesh* (Grand Rapids, MI, 1962).

4. Alexander Roberts and James Donaldson (eds.), *The Ante-Nicene Fathers* (New York, 1899), pp. 297–298.

5. Robert H. Gundry, *Soma in Biblical Theology: With Emphasis on Pauline Anthropology* (Cambridge, Engl, 1976), p. 159.

6. Wolfson, *op. cit.,* pp. 56–60, 63–64.

7. It does not seem to make sense to speak of some disembodied thing x being "in the presence of" some other thing y, where "in the presence of" means "in the spatial vicinity of." The notion may be coherently understood, however, as something like "being acutely aware of and sensitive to." This is why I am unable to provide a sensible construal of the notion of a disembodied and unconscious person being in the presence of God.

8. H. H. "Survival and the Idea of 'Another World'," in John Donnelly (ed.), *Language, Metaphysics, and Death,* 1st ed. (New York, 1978), pp. 176–195, reprinted above as chap. 16. I do not wish to commit myself entirely to Price's theory; among others, John Hick has detected difficulties in it. See *Death and Eternal Life* (New York, 1976), pp. 265–277. But Price's main point—that disembodied survival of death is possible—seems to me correct.

9. Thomas Aquinas, *Summa contra Gentiles,* trans. by Charles J. O'Neil; Book IV (Notre Dame, IN, 1975), IV, 79.

10. Athenagoras, *Embassy for Christians and the Resurrection of the Dead,* trans. by Joseph H. Crehan, S.J. (London, 1956), pp. 115–116.

11. Aquinas, *op. cit.,* IV, 84.

12. Augustine, *The Enchiridion on Faith, Hope, and Love* (Chicago, 1961), LXXXVII.

13. Athenagoras, *op. cit.,* p. 115.

14. Cited in P. T. Geach, *God and the Soul* (London, 1969), pp. 22, 40.

15. Aquinas, *op. cit.,* IV, 81.

16. See Gundry, *op. cit.,* pp. 164ff. For this and other points made in this paragraph, see C. F. D. Moule, "St. Paul and Dualism: The Pauline Concept of Resurrection," *New Testament Studies,* Vol. 12, No. 2 (Jan., 1966), and Ronald J. Sider, "The Pauline Conception of the Resurrection Body in I Corinthians XV, 35–54," *New Testament Studies,* Vol. 21, No. 3 (April, 1975).

17. Augustine, *Enchiridion,* LXXXVIII.

18. See Irenaeus, *op. cit.,* p. 388; Augustine, *op. cit.,* XCI; Aquinas, *op. cit.,* IV, 83–87.

19. Frank Dilley, "Resurrection and the 'Replica Objection'," *Religious Studies,* Vol. 19, No. 4 (Dec., 1983), p. 462.

20. Peter Van Inwagen, "The Possibility of Resurrection," *International Journal for Philosophy of Religion,* Vol. IX, No. 2 (1978), p. 119.

21. Derek Parfit, *Reasons and Persons* (Oxford, 1986), pp. 199f. I mention here only the most simple of the test cases involving teletransportation that Parfit discusses. Nor will I consider in this paper what I take to be the central theses of Part Three of his book.

22. Hick, *op. cit.,* p. 186.

23. Commenting on Paul's argument in I Corinthians 15:53, Tertullian says: "When he says *this* corruptible and *this* mortal, he utters the words while touching the surface of his own body." Tertullian, *On the Resurrection of the Flesh,* The Ante-Nicene Fathers, Vol. III (New York, 1899), LI.

24. Gundry makes this point convincingly. See *op. cit.,* p. 186. See also Sider, *op. cit.,* pp. 429–438, and Bruce Reichenbach, "On Disembodied Resurrection Persons: A Reply," *Religious Studies,* Vol. 18, No. 2 (June, 1982), p. 227.

25. Augustine, *op. cit.,* LXXXVIII. See also *The City of God* (Grand Rapids, MI, 1956), V, XXII, 20.

26. Paul Badham, *Christian Beliefs About Life After Death* (London, 1976), p. 50. Despite my disagreement with him on this point, it must be admitted that in his book Badham does successfully rebut several unconvincing patristic arguments about bodily resurrection.

27. See, for example, Irenaeus, *Against Heresies,* The Ante-Nicene Fathers, Vol. I (Grand Rapids, MI, n.d.), V, III, 2. See also Tertullian, *op. cit.,* XI.

28. See Flew's article on "Immortality" in *The Encyclopedia of Philosophy,* ed. by Paul Edwards (New York, 1967), and the articles collected in Part III of Flew's *The Presumption of Atheism and Other Essays* (London, 1976).

29. See the articles collected in Bernard Williams, *Problems of the Self* (Cambridge, 1973).

30. D. Z. Phillips, *Death and Immortality* (New York, 1970).

31. Terence Penelhum, *Survival and Disembodied Existence* (New York, 1970).

32. John Perry, *A Dialogue on Personal Identity and Immortality* (Indianapolis, IN, 1978).

33. Geach, *op. cit.,* pp. 17–29.

34. Among others, see Richard L. Purtill, "The Intelligibility of Disembodied Survival," *Christian Scholar's Review,* Vol. V, No. 1 (1975) and Paul Helm, "A Theory of Disembodied Survival and Re-Embodied Existence," *Religious Studies,* Vol. 14, No. 1 (March, 1978). See Also Bruce Reichenbach, *Is Man the Phoenix?: A Study of Immortality* (Washington, DC, 1983).

35. Perry, *op. cit.,* p. 3.

36. I will not try to answer Perry's circularity charge noted above because

I believe Parfit has decisively done so via the notion that he calls quasi-memories. See *op. cit.*, pp. 220ff.

37. Geach, *op. cit.*, pp. 23–28.

38. Roberts and Donaldson, *op. cit.*, p. 295.

39. I would like to thank Professors John Hick, Jim Hanink, Jerry Irish, Kai Nielsen, and Linda Zagzebski for their very helpful and incisive comments on earlier drafts of this paper.

19

Survival of Bodily Death: A Question of Values

RAYMOND MARTIN

University of Maryland

Does anyone ever survive his or her bodily death? *Could* anyone? No speculative questions are older than these, or have been answered more frequently or more variously. None have been laid to rest more often, or—in our times—with more claimed decisiveness. Jay Rosenberg, for instance, no doubt speaks for many contemporary philosophers when he claims, in his recent book, to have 'demonstrated' that 'we cannot [even] make *coherent sense* of the supposed possibility that a person's history might continue beyond that person's [bodily] death'.[1]

It may seem preposterous at this late date, after thousands of years of debate, to try to add anything radically new to the philosophical discussion of survival. Surely by now it has all been said. Surprisingly, though, there is something new to add—a realization that has emerged from the recent debate over personal identity that makes it much easier to argue successfully for meaningful personal survival. This realization is that for many people the preservation of personal identity does not matter primarily in survival. What this means to the debate over survival of bodily death is that now the person who would argue for survival does not have to presuppose any particular criterion of identity and has much more latitude in terms of how the evidence for survival might be explained. The purpose of the present paper is to illustrate these claims. I shall do this by arguing for a kind of minimalist reincarnation.

Traditional arguments for reincarnation are invariably burdened with unnecessary and questionable assumptions: the vehicle for sur-

Reprinted with permission of Cambridge University Press from *Religious Studies*, 28 (1992), 165–84. Copyright © Cambridge University Press 1992.

vival is some sort of metaphysical substance or soul; there are connections of an unverifiable kind (say, karmic connections) between earlier and later people; personal survival requires identity. The argument that I shall present, by contrast, is compatible with materialism or physicalism, stands or falls on straightforward empirical grounds and dispenses with the assumption that meaningful personal survival requires identity. It is modest also in being only for the *temporary* survival of *some*—so, not for immortality or even for the temporary survival of everyone—and in resting on admittedly *incomplete and fragmentary data*—so that even if the argument is successful as far as it goes, it shows no more than that there is a *prima facie* case for actual survival that could easily be undermined later by more and better data. Even with all of these qualifications, however, the argument is still ambitious in that it is for *actual* personal survival of bodily death, something that most contemporary philosophers regard as completely beyond the pale.

I shall rely heavily on the hard work of others: on the philosophical side, on the arguments and examples of Derek Parfit and, to a lesser extent, on those of Sydney Shoemaker and Robert Nozick—none of whom, of course, has argued for *actual* personal survival of bodily death; and, on the empirical side, on the data that Ian Stevenson and his associates have collected in their investigations of children who apparently remember previous lives.[2] The argument is what I regard as the best defence of the claim that the most likely explanation of Stevenson's data implies meaningful personal survival. Although Stevenson has already used his data to argue for reincarnation, my argument will be so much more modest than Stevenson's own argument that those who find his persuasive (a group that probably does not include many professional philosophers) may well feel that I have thrown out the baby with the bath water. No matter, both arguments could be correct.

I

From 1694, when John Locke added a chapter on personal identity to his *Essay Concerning Human Understanding,* until the late 1960s British and American philosophers concerned with personal identity concentrated on a central question: What are the necessary and sufficient conditions under which *personal identity* is preserved (over time)? In 1967 the univocal focus of this nearly 300-year-old debate was shattered—probably irrevocably. What changed things was the introduction into the debate, by David Wiggins, of so-called fission examples, in which a person somehow divides (in Wiggins' account amoeba-like) into two or more qualitatively similar persons.[3] Consideration of these examples forced philosophers to face the possibility that one might survive *as* someone else whose existence one values as much as one's own and, hence, also forced them, appropriately enough, to divide two questions they had previously treated as one: the traditional question, mentioned above, and the new one: What are the conditions under which *what matters primarily in survival* is preserved (over time)? This new question was never raised earlier probably because it was simply assumed that personal identity must be what matters primarily in survival, an assumption that, if true, would guarantee that both questions have the same answer.

In the 1970s and 1980s several philosophers—including Parfit, Shoemaker, and Nozick—argued persuasively that other things matter more in survival than identity. If their arguments are correct, then there are ways of surviving (or, quasi-surviving) that do not preserve identity that are as good, or almost as good, from a person's own egoistic or self-regarding point of view, as survival that does preserve identity. This is not a new idea. In the Vedic traditions that led to Hinduism, for instance, the idea that there can be meaningful survival not as oneself but as part of a larger psychic entity is as old as recorded history. But hard-headed western thinkers have for the most part summarily dismissed such possibilities as either not responsive to western interests in personal survival or as so much mystical mumbo-jumbo. Antony Flew, for instance, who has written more extensively on survival of bodily death than perhaps any other analytic philosopher, nicely captures this dismissive attitude:

> Confronted by such an obstacle [the inevitability of bodily death] how is any such doctrine [of personal survival] to get started? Before trying to suggest an answer I wish to make a sharp, simplifying move . . . I shall . . . be taking it for granted, first, that what we are interested in is our personal post-mortem futures, if any. 'Survival' through our children and our children's children after we ourselves are irrecoverably dead, 'immortality' through the memories of others thanks to our great works, or even our immersion in some universal world-soul—whatever that might mean—may be as much as, or much more than, most of us will in fact be getting. And it may be lamentably self-centered, albeit humanly altogether understandable, that we should be concerned about more than these thin substitutes. But, for better or for worse, what we are discussing now is the possibility of our post-mortem survival as persons identifiable as those we are here and now.[4]

The sort of quick, dismissive move expressed in Flew's remarks is now obsolete. Although the seeming-possibility of meaningful personal survival without identity may be illusory, it will no longer do simply to *assume* that it is. The point must be argued.

My argument for reincarnation will stake its claim in the territory that Flew (and most other analytic philosophers) have vacated. Whether its conclusion—that some have survived *as* others to whom they are not (or may not be) identical—is a 'thin substitute' for ordinary survival (with identity) remains to be seen. It depends partly on which alternatives to ordinary survival one has in mind. (The ones I consider will be much closer to ordinary survival than those Flew mentions, particularly in that one might reasonably anticipate the future experiences of those he survives *as* in the same ways as he anticipates his own future experiences.) It depends also on how 'thick' ordinary survival is. I think, along with Parfit and some others (although for somewhat different reasons), that ordinary survival is much 'thinner' than we usually suppose, a point to which I shall return.

One of the things that makes the change of focus that comes with arguing for meaningful personal survival without identity theoretically interesting is that virtually all of the arguments that Flew and Rosenberg and others have presented against either the possibility or the actuality of survival with identity are not even relevant as objections. A plausible argument for meaningful personal survival without identity, then, can provide us with a fresh approach (at least within the context of western philosophy) to an old and relatively tired set of issues. Of course, it is controversial whether other things do in fact matter more in survival than identity. To find out one has to consider hypothetical situations, such as the fission examples, in which one is forced to choose between survival with identity and survival without it. I shall illustrate such choice situations shortly. The outcome of a full consideration of them, as I have argued at length elsewhere, is the realization that for many people some kinds of survival without identity matter as much, or almost as much, as survival with identity.[5] If this is the outcome, then to address the value *of these people* the debate over personal survival will have to shift away from its traditional focus and toward three questions that philosophers have only recently begun to discuss: What matters most importantly in survival? Under what conditions is *this* (whatever it turns out to be) preserved (over time)? Is there good evidence that *this* has ever persisted beyond someone's bodily death?

This last question is the crucial one. As indicated, I answer that, yes, for many people the persistence of their psychologies under favourable conditions (whether or not this preserves identity) may well be—if not now, at least on reflection—among the things that matter most importantly to them in survival, and there is a good enough *prima facie* case that enough of the psychologies of some people have persisted beyond their bodily deaths to make the claim of meaningful personal survival in their cases plausible.

II

The kind of fission examples that have preoccupied philosophers are, for the most part, science fiction scenarios far removed from the practical realities of day-to-day life (and death). But not completely removed. In the late 1930s some psychosurgeons began severing the corpus callosums of severe epileptics in an effort to reduce the severity and frequency of their seizures, a procedure that had the bizarre side-effect, not discovered until many years later, of creating two independent centres of consciousness within the same human skull.[6] These centres not only lacked introspective access to each other, but they could also be made to acquire information about the world, and express it behaviorally, independently of each other. Most dramatically, they sometimes differed volitionally, expressing their differences using alternate sides of the same human bodies that they jointly shared. In one frequently cited example a patient was reported to have hugged his wife with one arm while he pushed her away with the other; in another a patient tried with his right hand (controlled by his left, verbal hemisphere) to hold a newspaper in front of himself, thereby blocking his view of the TV, while he tried with his left hand to knock the paper out of the way.

The fission (and non-fission) examples that have preoccupied philosophers concerned with the possibility of survival without identity are tidier and more complete than these real life cases. They have the disadvantage of being hypothetical, but the advantage of bringing the issue of egoistic survival values into much sharper focus. Consider, for instance, an example, based on one originally presented by Shoemaker, in which you are asked to imagine that you have a health problem that will result soon in your sudden and painless death unless you receive one of two available treatments.[7] The first is to have your brain removed and placed into the empty cranium of a body that is otherwise qualitatively identical to your own. The second is to have your brain removed, divided into functionally identical halves (each of which is capable of sustaining your full psychology), and then to have each of these halves put into the empty cranium of a body of its own, again one that is brainless but otherwise qualitatively identical to your own.

In the first treatment there is a 10% chance the transplantation will take. If it does take, the survivor who wakes up in the recovery room will be physically and psychologically like you just prior to the operation except that he will know he has had the operation and he will be healthy. In the second there is a 95% chance both transplantations will take. If they do, the survivors who wake up in the recovery room will be physically and psychologically like you just prior to the operation except that each of them will know he has had the operation and each will be healthy. If the transplantation in the first treatment does not take, the would-be survivor will die painlessly on the operating table. If either transplantation in the second treatment does not take, then the other will not either, and both of the would-be survivors will die painlessly on the operating table. Suppose everything else about the treatments is the same and as attractive to you as possible; for instance, both are painless and free of charge and, if successful, result in survivors who recover quickly

Many philosophers believe that identity would be retained in the first (non-fission) treatment but lost in the second (fission) treatment. The reason for its loss in the second treatment is that identity is a transitive relationship—which implies that if one of the survivors were the same person as the brain donor, and the donor were the same person as the other survivor, then the former survivor would be the same person as the latter survivor. Yet the survivors, at least once they begin to lead independent lives, are not plausibly regarded as the same people as each other. And since it would be arbitrary to regard just one of the survivors, but not the other, as the same person as the brain donor (in the beginning they are equally qualified), it is more plausible to regard each of the survivors as a different person from the donor.

But if you would persist through the first treatment but not the second, then only by sacrificing your identity can you greatly increase the chances of someone's surviving for years who is qualitatively just like you. Would it be worth it—that is, would it be worth it for selfish (or self-regarding) reasons? Most people who consider this example feel strongly that it would be, hence (apparently) that survival without identity can matter as much, or almost as much, as survival with identity.

Some have questioned whether fission undermines identity and, hence, whether such examples can support the view that survival without identity matters as much as survival with identity. Since I have argued elsewhere that the same point can be made with non-fission examples, nothing hinges, in my view, on the debate over whether fission undermines identity, and I shall here, for expository reasons, stick to the fission case as my central example, asking the reader to focus on what is crucial about this case—not fission, but the apparently selfishly motivated trading of continued identity for other benefits.[8]

I want now to illustrate how these theoretical developments make it much easier to make a case for meaningful personal survival by considering the data that Stevenson has collected in his investigations of children who apparently remember past lives. I am using Stevenson's data because I believe it is the best evidence we have of the survival of human personality beyond the grave. The theoretical point I want to illustrate, though, is a general one that could be illustrated as well with other data, such as those gleaned from reports of mediumistic communications.

III

To begin with a specific case, consider the case of Jasbir, who was born in Rasulpur, India, in 1950, and who, when he was three and a half years old, was thought to have died of smallpox.[9] According to Stevenson's report, Jasbir's father made preparations to bury him but because of darkness postponed the burial until morning. That night he noticed stirrings in his son's body. Over a period of several weeks the boy gradually recovered enough to talk. When he did talk it was evident that he had undergone a remarkable transformation. He then stated that he was the son of Shanker of Vehedi—a person unknown to Jasbir's parents and from a relatively remote village; and he communicated many details of 'his' life and death in Vehedi, including how, during a wedding procession, he had eaten poisoned sweets given him by a man who owed him money, fell from a chariot he was riding, injured his head, and died.

Stevenson claims that Jasbir's father tried to hide Jasbir's strange claims and behaviour but news of it leaked out and about three years later came to the attention of a woman from Jasbir's village who had married a native of Vehedi. On rare occasions, at intervals of several years, she returned to Rasulpur. On one such trip in 1957, Jasbir saw her and 'recognized' her as his aunt. She then reported the incident and what she had learned of Jasbir's claims to her husband's family and also to the Tyagi family of Vehedi whose son, Sobha Ram Tyagi, had died in May, 1954, at the age of twenty-two, in a chariot accident, in the manner described by Jasbir. The Tyagis knew nothing, though, of any poisoning or debt owed Sobha Ram.

When Sobha Ram's father and other members of his family later went to Rasulpur, Jasbir reportedly recognized them and correctly identified their relationships to Sobha Ram. Jasbir was then brought to Vehedi, put down near the railway station, and asked to lead the way to the Tyagi quadrangle, which he did without difficulty. Then, over a period of several days, he demonstrated to the Tyagis and other villagers a detailed knowledge of the Tyagis and their affairs. He returned to Rasulpur reluctantly, afterward complaining that he felt isolated and lonely there and wanted to live in Vehedi, which he continued to visit from time to time, usually for several weeks in the summer.

According to Stevenson, Jasbir made twenty-two checkable statements about 'himself', almost all of which were true of Sobha Ram. For instance, Jasbir said that he was the son of Shankar of Vehedi, that he was a Brahmin (not, as Jasbir was, a Jat), that there was a peepal tree in front of his house, and that the house had a well that was half in and half outside the house (the only well of this kind in Vehedi). He said that his wife belonged to the village of Molna, that his mother was named Kela, his son Baleshwar, his aunt Ram Kali, and his mother-in-law Kirpi. And, as indicated, Jasbir explained the circumstances of Sobha Ram's death.

Stevenson claims that Jasbir recognized a total of sixteen relatives and friends of Sobha Ram and correctly identified their relationships to Sobha Ram, sometimes adding relevant details. For instance, when a man named Birbal Singh, who was teasingly called 'Gandhiji' (because he had large ears that resembled those of Mahatma Gandhi), appeared at the door, Jasbir said, 'Come in, Gandhiji'. Someone present reportedly corrected Jasbir by saying, 'This is Birbal', to which Jasbir replied, 'We call him "Gandhiji".' For their part, the Tyagis accepted Jasbir as a full member of the family and consulted him about the marriage of Sobha Ram's son and daughter. And the man Jasbir claimed killed Sobha Ram to avoid paying a debt later paid Jasbir (not Sobha Ram's family) 600 rupees.

Stevenson reports that Jasbir, after his change in personality, did not retain his original Jasbir personality. Instead, Jasbir claimed that he was Sobha Ram, behaved like Sobha Ram, and only gradually (and never fully) accepted the body and life situations of Jasbir. He continued to think of himself as a Brahmin, added Sobha Ram's Brahmin name to his Jat family name, and refused employment that was appropriate to his Jat status because he considered it beneath his dignity. Yet he continued to live most of the time with his natural parents and planned to marry in the Jat caste.

Jasbir's case differs importantly from most of the other cases Stevenson has investigated, first, in that the person whose personality Jasbir apparently took over did not die until after Jasbir was born—normally the previous personality dies first; second, in that Jasbir's personality was virtually replaced by that of Sobha Ram's—normally there is a blending of the two personalities;[10] and, third, in that Jasbir's apparent memories of Sobhra Ram's life and his identification with

Sobha Ram continued into adulthood—normally the apparent memories and identification last only a few years. Otherwise, Jasbir's case closely resembles Stevenson's other cases.

Stevenson claims, as of 1987, to have investigated about 250 'cases suggestive of reincarnation' thoroughly and to have investigated at least another thousand cases in enough detail to include them in an analysis of recurrent features. Additional cases have been investigated by Stevenson's associates. Usually Stevenson and his associates have arrived on the scene only after the families involved have attempted to verify the child's statements. Stevenson then has gathered his information after the fact, so to speak, in (apparently) carefully conducted interviews (usually involving re-interviews and cross-examination of key informants). However, in twenty-four cases (the number is continually growing) Stevenson claims that someone made a written record of what the child had said *before* anyone attempted to verify the child's statements and before the two families concerned had met.[11]

Stevenson reports that the children usually began speaking about 'their previous lives' as soon as they could speak—between two and four years old—and then stopped talking about them between the ages of five and eight. (In only a few cases—one of which is Jasbir's—did the apparent memories of the previous life continue into adulthood.) Stevenson claims that in the cases he has investigated thoroughly about 90% of the children's checkable statements about 'their previous lives' are correct.

In many cases the previous personality met a violent and early death, and events connected with or just preceding his or her death tend to be prominent among the children's apparent memories. And Stevenson reports that in 50% of the cases in which the previous personality died violently, phobias related to the previous personality's mode of death were present—for instance, if the previous personality died of drowning (or, from being shot), the subject might have a phobia of water (or, of firearms). Stevenson claims that the subjects sometimes had skills—such as sewing or the ability to repair engines—that the previous personalities also had and that the children had no normal opportunities to acquire. He also claims that birthmarks on the children corresponding closely to marks on the previous personality, often to the wounds from which the previous personality met death, are not uncommon—but, curiously, are more common in some cultures, such as the Eskimos, the Tlingits, and the Burmese, than in others.

Cultural differences are also reflected in other ways in the data—most importantly, perhaps, in that reported cases are much more common in cultures in which reincarnation is a widely shared belief than in ones in which it is not, even when the two are side by side. So, for instance, there are many more reported cases from Asia and Western Africa than from Europe and (non-tribal) North America and many more from the Druses of Lebanon than from the Christians of Lebanon. (Stevenson says he has investigated at least thirty-five (non-tribal) cases from the continental United States). The interval between the death of the previous personality and the birth of the subject is also linked to culturally determined beliefs.

With this brief indication of the rich array of descriptive data that have been (and still are being) collected by Stevenson and his associates, I want now to turn to the more theoretically interesting question of how dispensing with the assumption that meaningful personal survival requires identity affects the evaluation of competing explanations of Stevenson's data.

IV

Stevenson considers six different possible explanations of his data: fraud, cryptomnesia, paramnesia, genetic memory, extrasensory perception, and survival. Among survival explanations he distinguishes between possession and reincarnation, a distinction I shall ignore since both involve the persistence of a mind or soul which is distinct from a person's physical body and which transmigrates somehow from the deceased person to the child who apparently remembers that person's life.

Fraud. I know of no specific evidence for fraud in connection with Stevenson's data, other than what Stevenson himself mentions. Even so, it is always a possibility, either on the part of the investigators or those they investigate. And judgements about how likely it is, made ultimately against the backdrop of unstated and often unconscious assumptions about what is plausible and what not, are bound to vary from person to person. In my own admittedly subjective view, if Stevenson is as honest as he appears to be, then fraud on a scale sufficient to undermine his data is quite unlikely.

As for Stevenson himself, since 1966 he has conducted his research as a highly visible public figure, often in conjunction with research assistants, and from a relatively high profile base of operations at the University of Virginia. None of Stevenson's by now voluminous publications on these cases have the internal earmarks of investigative fraud—indeed just the opposite. Stevenson consistently comes across as someone who is willing and open to the idea of other investigators checking his cases, although few of them have actually been checked.[12] There are, of course, independent anecdotal reports of the same phenomenon, and many reports of closely related phenomena, such as adults who claim to remember previous lives.[13] (Given how common it is for adults under hypnosis to claim to remember past lives, perhaps it should not be surprising that so many children should make such claims.) Still, even if everything else about my argument for reincarnation is persuasive, one should not regard it as anything more than a *prima facie* case for survival unless and until Stevenson's data have survived the most rigorous checking by *independent* investigators.

Assuming, then, that the data as Stevenson presents them are accurate, Stevenson himself argues persuasively (at least to me) that large scale fraud on the part of his informants is unlikely. While he admits that fraud has occurred occasionally (he claims to know of three cases) he doubts it has happened often because the sort of peasant villagers that are frequently the subjects of his investigations usually lack both the time and motivation to prepare an elaborate hoax and because a successful hoax generally would require an extraordinary conspiracy involving numerous witnesses, including children, that, he thinks, his usual practice of multiple interviews would probably detect.[14] Stevenson says he has occasionally heard adults prompting the subjects— which he says he strongly discourages—but claims that it has never seemed to him to be more than an expression of adult eagerness not to have the children let the adults down by failing to say to Stevenson what the children have often said to them.

Stevenson also cites the difficulties of directing and staging some of the highly emotional scenes he claims to have witnessed.

> I cannot believe that simple villagers would have the time or inclination to rehearse such dramas as occurred in Chhatta when the family of Prakash thought—or said they thought—I favored his returning to the other family. The complexity of the behavioural features of these cases alone seems to make fraud virtually out of the question, and I prefer to pass on to other more plausible explanations of them.[15]

And we should too. My purpose is not to put the argument for reincarnation in its most convincing form but merely to put it fully and plausibly enough that it can be used to illustrate the ways in which the dynamic of the traditional debate over survival of bodily death should change.

Cryptomnesia would occur if the children acquired the information that they thought they remembered in a normal way, forgot how they acquired it, and then subsequently honestly mistook memories of this information for memories of a previous life. Stevenson claims that despite persistent trying he has generally been unable to find any significant link between the pairs of families involved in these cases and, hence, doubts that cryptomnesia could often be the explanation. He also thinks it is unlikely that young children—many of whom could barely talk when they first began relating their apparent memories—could assimilate so much information on the basis of a few overheard conversations. And he claims that many of the children investigated have revealed private information that was not known outside of the immediate families of the previous personalities. For instance, one child knew of the previous personality's attempt to borrow money from his wife, another of an occasion when the previous personality and a woman had gone to a wedding in a village (which she named) where they had had difficulty finding a latrine. Finally, Stevenson notes that it is not just information but also behavioural features of the cases that must be explained—such as the strong identifications that the subjects often make with the previous personalities.

Paramnesia. This occurs when there are certain other sorts of honest distortions and inaccuracies in the memories of those who provide information on the cases. A possible scenario, that Stevenson thinks may have obtained in a few of the cases he has investigated, involves the parents unwittingly giving their child's first few statements about the previous personality more coherence than the statements actually had:

> [The subject's parents] think of the sort of person about whom the child might be talking. Then they start searching for such a person. They find a family having a deceased member whose life seems to correspond to the child's statements. They explain to this family what their child has been saying about the previous life. The second family agrees that the child's statements might refer to the deceased member of their family. The two families exchange detailed information about the deceased person and about what the child has been saying. From enthusiasm and carelessness, they may then credit the child with having stated numerous details about the identified deceased person, when in fact he said very little, and perhaps nothing specific, before the two families met.[16]

Thus, a myth of what the child apparently remembered might develop and come to be accepted by both the families.

But this sort of scenario—and paramnesia generally—is not easily applicable in those cases in which someone had made a written record of what the child said before the accuracy of his or her statements was checked and before the two families had met. And paramnesia is unlikely also in many other cases in which Stevenson claims that he or his associates reached the scene within a few weeks or months of the initial meeting between the families and before memories of the child's previous remarks had much of a chance to fade. Add to this that the children often repeated their apparent memories many times before the families involved met and that in some cases many peoples' memories of the child's statements would have had to become distorted in the same ways, and paramnesia begins to seem less plausible as a general explanation of the data.

There is also the question of motive. Stevenson claims that many parents are reluctant to have the child's statements verified; some believe that the child could be harmed by remembering a past life, some that they could lose the child to the other family, some are reluctant to have anyone verify the children's statements about another life that was either much poorer or much more prosperous than their own, and some simply dislike encouraging behaviour that they find unattractive in the child.[17] In addition, Stevenson claims that the families of the previous personalities often have their own reasons for being reluctant to endorse the case: some, particularly wealthy families, are afraid that the subject's family means to exploit them; some dread embarrassing revelations that the subject may make about the family; still others—somewhat paradoxically—do not wish to reawaken the grief they continue to have for the deceased person.[18] Paramnesia, then, whether from ordinary forgetfulness or from motivated distortion seems an unlikely explanation of much of the data.

Genetic memory. Another possibility, at least for those cases in which the subject might be a descendant of the previous personality, is genetic (or, inherited) memory. But much of the information apparently remembered is about events—such as the deaths of previous personalities—that occurred after the previous personalities' children were conceived, and, in any case, most of the children investigated were not even genetic descendants of the previous personalities.

Extrasensory perception. Stevenson claims that ESP by itself cannot account for the behavioural features of the richer cases, including the fact that the subjects characteristically attribute their apparent memories to a previous personality with whom they identify (personation). He therefore considers ESP-with-personation as the hypothesis that most plausibly competes with survival (hereafter, I shall use the label ESP to mean ESP-with-personation). Even so, Stevenson does not think ESP would explain the selection of the person whose experiences are apparently remembered, or how—in those cases where we would have to suppose that the information apparently remembered was obtained telepathically from more than one living person who remembered it—the information came to be organized in the minds of the children who apparently remembered it in the same ways it was organized in the minds of the previous personalities, or—particularly in cultures hostile to the idea of reincarnation—why the information came to the children in the form of apparent memories, or, how, in

some cases, the children exhibited special skills or birthmarks appropriate to the previous personalities. In short, Stevenson claims that if
ESP were the explanation, it would have to be ESP 'of a very extensive
and extraordinary kind'.

Second, Stevenson claims that the cases suggestive of reincarnation
differ in various ways from what one would expect if ESP were the
explanation. Other than their apparent memories of previous lives
these children rarely exhibit any additional evidence of ESP; the phenomenology of the childrens' apparent memories is the same as that
of ordinary memory—not, say, trance-like; most of the children experience the apparent memories not as disconnected but as continuous
with their present lives; the childrens' access to information about, and
identification with, the previous lives sometimes lasts more or less
continuously for a long time—usually for years and occasionally even
for decades; and the children and also their parents often lack a plausible motive for the children to identify with the previous personalities.

In what must be one of the most knowledgeable reviews of Stevenson's data, the British psychologist Alan Gauld claims that it is 'extremely unlikely that either fraud or cryptomnesia have been more
than marginal factors in producing the correct statements and recognitions' and remarks that he is 'quite at one with Stevenson over his
doubts concerning the ESP (or super-ESP) theory'. Gauld concludes
that he does 'not find it easy to dissent' from Stevenson's claim that
his data sustain 'a rational belief in reincarnation'.[19]

V

I assume that *something* explains Stevenson's data. If his data are
accurate, then I agree with Stevenson that fraud, cryptomnesia, paramnesia and genetic memory are unlikely as explanations. That leaves
ESP and survival. There are, of course, scientific objections to ESP.
Those who weight these more heavily than I do will perhaps give the
nod to one of the explanations—such as cryptomnesia—that I would
pass over. But if they do, it is probably because they feel that one of
those explanations *must* be correct, not because there is much independent evidence that one of them actually is correct. Currently, so
far as I know, there is almost no such evidence.

Even those who weight scientific objections to ESP more heavily
than I do would probably agree that if we had more and better data
on cases suggestive of reincarnation, data of a sort that counts against
normal explanations and toward ESP or survival, that would at least
make those latter explanations *more* likely. So long as one admits that

enough good data of this sort *could* make either ESP or survival the *most* likely explanation, then disagreement over how much evidence that would take is a matter of judgement about which it is difficult and probably pointless to argue. It would be dogmatic, it seems to me, for someone to take the view that *no matter how good* the data were, they could *never* tip the balance far enough that it actually favoured either the ESP or survival explanations. As long as one agrees with that, the prudent course is simply to wait and see how good the evidence actually gets.

Whatever objections one might have to ESP as an alternative to normal explanations, these are not likely to be objections to it as an alternative to the survival explanation. So, to focus on those aspects of the argument that illustrate how the traditional debate over survival should change, I am going to set scientific qualms about ESP to one side and consider just the relative merits of ESP and survival. In my opinion, Stevenson is not in a position to dismiss ESP so easily as a possible explanation of his data. The reason is that we have virtually no basis for opinions about how ESP, if it exists, might work and, hence, no basis for claiming that it could not have produced the results Stevenson has reported. This would be so even if there were no evidence in parapsychological research that ESP might be as extraordinary and extensive as it would have to be to account for Stevenson's data. But there is *some*.

The French physician E. Osty, Director of the Institut Metapsychique of Paris from 1926 to 1938, reported incidents that would amount (according to Gauld) 'to what could justifiably be called "super-ESP" . . . without any suggestion that the information originated from spirits'.[20] And S. G. Soal, former President of the British Society for Psychical Research, reported on sittings with the famous medium Mrs. Blanche Cooper in which Soal claims she thought (as did Soal) that she was communicating with a dead Gordon Davis, but instead telepathically got information from a living Gordon Davis while simultaneously exhibiting impressive evidence of precognition. Gauld remarks that '"Super-ESP" seems an appropriate term to describe what was going on; and if it could occur in this case, why not in others, indeed in all the others that have been presented as evidence for survival?'[21] Why not indeed?

Gauld has his reasons why not—which include that Osty was careless in writing up his reports and that Gauld suspects Soal of having 'improved' the Gordon Davis case. But even if the outcome of Gauld's assessment were (which it is not) that our evidence for ESP is *always* evidence for more modest results than would be required to account for Stevenson's data—even so—since we do not know how ESP works, if we concede that it has to be taken seriously as a possible explanation (which we should *when* the competing explanation is survival), then we do not have a right to say that ESP could not be powerful enough to account for Stevenson's data. This should be clear from an analogy.

Idiot savants sometimes have extraordinary memories and equally impressive behavioural skills, such as the ability to make complicated mathematical computations quickly and accurately or to play a musical instrument proficiently with little or no training. Imagine an investigator of 150 years ago who did not have much of an idea what genes were or how they worked but who believed that he had evidence that there were genes and that a certain kind of gene—which he called a memory-gene—exercised a powerful influence on the quality and scope of every normal person's memory. Suppose he denied that memory-genes might account for the extraordinary memories and skills of idiot savants on the grounds that for a memory-gene to produce such results it would have to be not an ordinary memory-gene but a super-memory-gene—something for which, he claimed correctly, there was no evidence except in the cases of idiot savants. Imagine that he urged, instead, that the extraordinary powers of these idiot savants are more likely explained on the supposition that they draw directly on the powers of immaterial souls (many of whom were once incarnated in people who were musical or mathematical) that have somehow survived bodily death.

No one should be convinced, first, because until the investigator knows more about genes, and about memory-genes in particular, he has no business putting such limits on what genes are capable of producing and, second, because no matter how mysterious it might seem—and 150 years ago it might have seemed mysterious to the point of being almost miraculous—that genes could produce the extraordinary powers observed in some idiot savants, it could hardly be less mysterious to explain these powers by appeal to the survival of dead people.

Even Stevenson admits that ESP might have produced the results he has observed if, as he says, it were of a very extensive and extraordinary kind—for instance, if it were a kind of ESP that produced both informational and behavioural results in an organized way (so as to mimic the arrangement in a previous personality), and even produced physical effects such as the birth marks. But *how* could ESP do all this? It could if something about the previous personality directly caused the result in the subjects, who were 'selected' simply due to their unusual receptivity. The 'transmissions' could either be without intervening links (so-called action at a distance) or in the form of something like a radio-wave. We can suppose that the subjects' receptivity was such that it caused them to experience the informational aspects of these transmissions as if they were ordinary memory, which, then, in some of them did and in some did not become firmly enough implanted to resist erosion by competing influences that came later. Finally we can suppose that this receptivity in the subjects was as a special capacity distinct from the more ordinary and diffuse powers of ESP that are sometimes exhibited by others and, hence, not likely to manifest itself as a generalized capacity for ESP.

Fantastic? I agree. But if we accept Stevenson's data at face value and reject fraud, cryptomnesia, paramnesia, and genetic memory as explanations, then all of the remaining explanations are fantastic. I do not say that the explanation I have just sketched is preferable to Stevenson's survival explanation, only that, based on what we know, it is at least as likely, and hence that it would be arbitrary to reject it in favour of Stevenson's explanation. In sum, if the case for meaningful personal survival based on Stevenson's data depends on survival being the best explanation, then it fails, since for all we know his data can be explained by super-ESP.

But there is no reason that I know of to suppose that the case for meaningful personal survival based on Stevenson's data does depend on survival being the best explanation. Stevenson may feel that if ESP were the best explanation, then the identities of the people whose lives the children apparently remembered would not have been preserved. Whether he is right about that is debatable, just as it is debatable, and for much the same reasons, whether the identities would have been preserved even on Stevenson's dualistic hypothesis; Rosenberg, for instance, does not think that they would have been.

The deeper point is that it may not matter as much as survivalists, such as Stevenson, and sceptics, such as Flew and Rosenberg, seem to think whether the *identities* of the previous personalities in these cases have or have not been preserved. The new developments in personal identity theory, as illustrated in the fission example, suggest that meaningful personal survival may not require the preservation of identity. And since we have no *evidence* to support a view about *how* either a disincarnate mind or ESP (whatever these might be) could account for Stevenson's data, it is arbitrary, in our current state of ignorance, to assume that if ESP accounted for them, that would be inferior—from the point of view either of preserving identity or of sustaining meaningful personal survival—to the ways in which souls would account for his data. If this is not obvious, consider another analogy.[22]

Imagine that you are a resident of Earth at some time in the technologically distant future and that you have urgent business on Mars. You can conduct this business only by activating a Star-Trek style beamer that records exact and complete information about your body, brain, and psychology at the same time as it dematerializes you on Earth and sends the information to a receiving station on Mars. A few minutes later, the information is used on Mars to create an exact replica of you out of new, but qualitatively similar, matter. In short, the beamer is, in effect, a reincarnation machine. Suppose further that even though no one in your culture has ever known exactly how the beamer works, since it obviously preserves a person's psychology and bodily form its use is widely accepted as a way of preserving identity. You share this belief, though with some hesitation. Remembering that there are philosophers who argue that the beamer does not preserve identity—but also remembering the fission examples—you reason that whether or not the beamer preserves identity, it at least preserves what matters most to you in survival. So you drive to the transmitting station to be beamed. Once there, however, you learn that scientists have recently discovered that the beamer works in exactly the same way that super-ESP works, which, as it happens, is one of the ways I sketched above.

Would this new information make any difference to you, so far as your decision to enter the beamer is concerned? If you were satisfied that the beamer probably preserves identity, would you feel now that its claim to preserve identity had been sullied by the revelation that the information is transmitted from Earth to Mars by means of a process that also underlies super-ESP? If you were satisfied that whether or not the beaming process preserves identity it at least preserves what matters to you in survival, would you feel that it would preserve what matters to you any less if the information were transmitted by a process that also underlies super-ESP? Probably not—to both questions. But, then, super-ESP may be as good a way of ensuring meaningful personal survival as the process, whatever it is, that underlies Stevenson's survival hypothesis.

What I am suggesting is that assuming that Stevenson's data are as he presents them, then they may well provide the basis for a good argument for meaningful personal survival *whether or not* the super-ESP explanation or his survival explanation best explains them and *whether or not* the actual processes involved, on either explanation, preserve personal identity. They *will* provide such a case for anyone for whom what matters primarily in survival is simply the singular reemergence of his or her psychology—beliefs, memories, intentions, personality, and so on—after bodily death.

VI

In philosophical discussions of survival of bodily death, values often masquerade as facts, and facts are often portrayed as being more substantial than they actually are. For instance, how 'thick' or 'thin' something is as a substitute for ordinary survival, which may seem to be a factual question, depends not on how *much*—physically or psychologically—has been lost in the substitution, not even, necessarily, on whether identity has been lost, but, rather, on how much *of what matters* in survival has been lost. That is, the relevant senses of 'thick' and 'thin' have more to do, in the first instance, with our values than with either our identities or our normal circumstances, which are relevant only to the extent that we value preserving them. So, even though a great deal (quantitatively) may have been lost in some transformation, if what was lost is trivial from the vantage point of our concern for meaningful personal survival, then what emerged from the transformation is not, in the relevant sense, a thin substitute for survival, but, rather, a robust one.

The ways philosophers argue for one criterion of identity over another is often also covertly evaluative in that they rely heavily on idiosyncratic and controversial intuitive judgments about whether identity would be preserved through various sorts of bizarre transformations—the infamous puzzle cases of the personal identity literature—which are controversial in the first place because our conventions, which were formed to apply to cases that arise in normal circumstances, underdetermine what we should say about these extraordinary examples. Thus, the suspicion is unavoidable that the ways philosophers try to extend the conventions to cover the extraordinary examples generally have more to do with personal values than with objective social facts, in particular, they seem to have more to do with their feelings about whether *what matters in survival* has been preserved through the transformations depicted in the examples. If this is right, then disputes over criteria of personal identity are often simply disguised disputes over what matters in survival.

Even if it were possible, which it does not seem to be, to determine objectively how our linguistic conventions regarding personal identity should extend to cover the puzzle cases, our linguistic conventions are just that—conventions; they are not necessarily deep ontological truths. Before thinking much about how personal identity may be conventional, our identities may seem quite substantial; after thinking about it they are likely to seem more ephemeral. Nozick was right to call the puzzle cases in the personal identity literature 'a koan for philosophers'. Even the so-called facts of identity may be thinner than they first appear.

This 'lightness' of identity is surprisingly bearable. Consider, for instance, Shoemaker's example of an environmentally polluted society of the technologically distant future in which people, to keep from getting very sick, have to replace their bodies every several years with qualitatively identical ones, a procedure that in their society is regarded as routine; no more of a threat to maintaining one's identity than, say, getting one's teeth cleaned is in ours. Projecting ourselves imaginatively into such a society, it is easy for many of us to see ourselves (or our replicas) conforming without much strain to their conventions. This suggests that we could simply, and sensibly, take the view that any ways in which our social conventions might differ from those of the polluted society are not that important. By analogy, when one sees that various moral prohibitions in one's own society— for instance, against public nudity or extra-marital sex—are not shared by other societies with which one can identify without much strain, there is a natural tendency to downplay the importance of the conventions of one's own society. In the same way, when one sees that certain of our conventions regarding personal identity are not present in other (possible) societies with which one can identify without much strain, there is a natural tendency to downplay the importance of our own conventions. There is nothing inevitable about shedding such parochial values, but it is a natural and often reasonable response to exposure to attractive alternatives.

In sum, the fission examples and the other examples that have motivated the belief that identity may not be what matters primarily in survival suggest that identity, even under normal circumstances, has been overrated. In particular, they suggest that identity is not a condition of reasonably anticipating experiences in the same ways we would ordinarily anticipate our own future experiences. These suggestions may or may not be correct. To decide we will have to look freshly at—that is, re-*evaluate*—what it means to survive under ordinary as well as hypothetical circumstances. Yet among those who have tried to do this there is not now, and probably never will be, a univocal response: to some identity seems to matter a great deal, to others much less.

Whatever the outcome of this process of re-evaluation, as soon as we admit, as it seems we must, its relevance to the assessment of arguments for meaningful personal survival of bodily death, the cat is out of the bag. For then no argument for meaningful personal survival is dismissible merely on the grounds that the kind of survival it postulates would not preserve identity or that it is too 'thin' to be responsive to our egoistic interests in survival. And this means that the standard ways many philosophers have dismissed arguments for survival will no longer work. One must now consider not just whether the kind of process postulated preserves identity but also whether it preserves enough of what matters importantly in survival. In sum, when it comes to meaningful personal survival of bodily death the key question is not simply one of metaphysics, as has been assumed traditionally, but also one of values—and values that, in the end, may well vary from person to person in quite subjective ways.

Many philosophers will not welcome this conclusion. We, philosophers, love to be decisive, to settle things not just for the time being and for people with certain values rather than others, but for everyone and once and for all. We want to draw straight, definite lines. Particularly when it comes to 'nonsense', we like to dispatch it not just as unwarranted but as impossible. Yet the new developments in personal identity theory strongly suggest that for the bit of nonsense we have been discussing—meaningful personal survival of bodily death—the days of decisive dismissals are over. On this topic, many of the lines that most need to be drawn are now and henceforth probably always will be curved and blurry.[23]

NOTES

1. *Thinking Clearly About Death* (Englewood Cliffs: Prentice Hall, 1983), p. 96, emphasis added.
2. See especially Derek Parfit, 'Personal Identity', *The Philosophical Review*, LXXX (1971), 3–27, and his *Reasons and Persons* (Oxford: Clarendon Press, 1984), part III; Sydney Shoemaker, 'Persons and Their Pasts', *American Philosophical Quarterly*, VII (1970), 269–85, and his 'Personal Identity: A Materialist Account', in Sydney Shoemaker and Richard Swinburne, *Personal Identity* (Oxford: Basil Blackwell, 1984), pp. 69–152; and Robert Nozick, *Philosophical Explanations* (Cambridge: Harvard University Press, 1981), ch. 1. Stevenson's early investigations are summarized in *Twenty Cases Suggestive of Reincarnation* (Charlottesville: The University Press of Virginia, 1966; 2nd edn. 1974), but he has since (with associates) published additional data in four thick volumes—*Cases of the Reincarnation Type*: vol. 1 (1975); vol. 2 (1977); vol. 3 (1980), vol. 4 (1983)—as well as in his *Unlearned Language: New Studies in Xenoglossy* (1984) and *Children Who Remember Previous Lives* (1987), all of which were published by The University Press of Virginia. *Children Who Remember* contains a bibliography of Stevenson's many additional articles on

cases suggestive of reincarnation, including ones in *International Journal of Comparative Sociology* (1970), *Journal of Nervous and Mental Disease* (1983), and *American Journal of Psychiatry* (1979).

3. David Wiggins, *Identity and Spatio-Temporal Continuity* (Oxford: Basil Blackwell, 1967), p. 50.

4. *The Presumption of Atheism* (New York: Harper & Row, 1976), p. 104; Flew repeats this dismissive move, in almost the same words, in his Gifford Lectures, published as *The Logic of Mortality* (New York: Basil Blackwell, 1987), pp. 2–3.

5. See my 'Identity, Transformation, and What Matters in Survival', in Daniel Kolak and Raymond Martin, eds., *Self and Identity* (New York: Macmillan, 1991), pp. 289–301.

6. For a sample of the literature on commissurotomy, see Kolak and Martin, *ibid.*

7. Shoemaker, 'Personal Identity: A Materialist Account', *op. cit.*, p. 119.

8. David Lewis has questioned whether fission undermines identity by arguing for a multiple occupancy view of persons, in 'Survival and Identity', in Amélie Rorty, ed., *The Identities of Persons* (Berkeley: University of California Press, 1976), reprinted, along with 'Postscripts', in *Philosophical Papers, vol.* 1 (New York: Oxford University Press, 1983) and in Kolak and Martin, *op. cit.* John Perry has questioned the transitivity of identity in 'Can the Self Divide?' *Journal of Philosophy*, LXIX (1972), 463–88. I have argued that, so far as the importance of identity is concerned, not much depends on whether identity is lost in fission, in 'Identity, Transformation, and What Matters in Survival', *op. cit.*

9. The Jabir case is described in *Stevenson's Twenty Cases, op. cit.*, and also in *Children Who Remember, op. cit.*

10. Interestingly, philosophers sometimes argue on *a priori* grounds, apparently without considering the empirical evidence to the contrary from the psychological study of dissociation, that the blending of memories from different psychologies is impossible. See, for instance, Richard Wollheim, *The Thread of Life* (Cambridge, Mass.: Harvard University Press, 1984), pp. 112ff. (to which I have responded in 'Memory, Connecting, and What Matters in Survival', *Australasian Journal of Philosophy*, XXIV [1987], 82–97) and Marya Schechtman, 'Personhood and Personal Identity', *Journal of Philosophy*, LXXXVII (1990), 71–92.

11. In addition to the references in note 2, see Stevenson's 'Three New Cases of the Reincarnation Type in Sri Lanka With Written Records Made Before Verifications', summarized in *The Journal of Nervous and Mental Disease*, CLXXVI (1988), 741, and presented fully in *Journal of Scientific Exploration*, II (1988), 217–38.

12. Criticism of Stevenson may be found in Ian Wilson, Mind Out of Time (Victor Gollancz, 1981), pp. 58–60; William G. Roll, 'The Changing Perspectives on Life After Death', in Stanley Krippner, ed., *Advances in Parapsychological Research* (New York, 1982), vol. 3; C. T. K. Chari, 'Reincarnation Research: Method and Interpretation', in M. Ebon, ed., *Signet Handbook of*

Parapsychology (New York: New American Library, 1978); and Paul Edwards, 'The Case Against Reincarnation', a four-part article in *Free Inquiry*, vols. 6–7 (1986–7).

13. See, for instance, A. S. Pringle Patterson, *The Idea of Immortality* (Oxford: Oxford University Press, 1922), p. 107, and Alan Gauld, *Mediumship and Survival* (London: Heinemann, 1982), pp. 172–87.

14. *Children Who Remember, op. cit.,* p. 147.

15. *Twenty Cases,* 2nd edn., op. cit., p. 333. See also Stevenson's discussion of fraud in *Cases,* vol. 3, *op. cit.,* pp. 343–345.

16. *Children Who Remember, op. cit.,* pp. 150–51.

17. *Ibid.,* p. 152.

18. *Ibid.,* p. 153.

19. Gauld, *op. cit.,* p. 185.

20. *Ibid.,* p. 131.

21. *Ibid.,* p. 136.

22. This sort of example is discussed by Parfit, *Reasons and Persons, op. cit.,* pp. 199–200, and by Nozick, *op. cit.,* p. 41.

23. I am grateful to several people who offered criticisms and suggestions when I talked on the topic of reincarnation at the University of New Mexico, in March, 1991, and also to John Barresi and Ian Stevenson for written comments on an earlier version of this paper.

20

Mysticism and the
Paradox of Survival

John J. Clarke

University of Malaya

Some Current Accounts of Personal Survival

The idea of survival after death has itself survived, at least as a logical possibility, the death of many other metaphysical notions. It is not difficult to see why, for it is possible to imagine many things in connection with one's survival of death: one can picture oneself watching one's own funeral, reuniting with one's deceased friends and relatives, reflecting, dwelling on memories, and so forth. Such imaginative pictures can be painted in various thicknesses of colour. One of the most richly coloured portraits in recent years has come from John Hick.[1] His resurrection world, though sequestered from our own stretch of space and time, appears to be as richly detailed as our own. Though no longer made of physical matter, resurrected bodies are to all intents and purposes indistinguishable from our present unregenerate ones, and resurrected people therefore have no special difficulty in identifying their own or other people's bodies. The portrait is as easy as can be on our imaginations, so life-like indeed that one might sometimes wonder whether one is in this world or the next. As an example of a more sparsely drawn picture of survival one might take the notion sketched by Strawson in *Individuals*. It is possible to conceive of one's survival of bodily death, he thinks, but it would be a solitary and unenviable existence, for though one could have experiences, thoughts, and memories as at present, there would be no means

Reprinted by permission from *International Philosophical Quarterly*, 11 (1971), 165–79.

of communicating with others, embodied or otherwise, and no way of initiating changes in the world.[2]

One of the persistent problems with the notion of survival is that of understanding how an individual *person* can pass through the needle eye of death and yet still sensibly be called the same person or even a person at all. Obviously this problem becomes more acute as the detail of the picture becomes more sparse. Thus Strawson's account is not merely, as he admits, "unenticing," but borders on incoherence, for it is not intuitively obvious that the survival of my bare capacity to remember and to contemplate constitutes the survival of what could properly be called "me." The shadows he allows to pass are, one would suppose, attenuated beyond recognition. Hick's more fully drawn portrait probably has the advantage of avoiding such lines of criticism as these, but while he is more skillful in conveying persons whole and entire into the netherworld, there is one very serious deficiency in his account which has not to my knowledge been noticed and on which I propose to focus attention in this paper: his survivors remain human, all too human. It is not that we expect them for *a priori* reasons to be radically changed by this traumatic experience—though I think we would so expect—but rather that strictly speaking they do not appear to have survived death at all but merely *a* death.

Certainly from the point of view of theology such a demi-survival can be of little interest. As I understand the matter, people who have wished for and believed in the soul's survival of death have found both justification for and comfort in this belief because of some kind of change that would thereby be wrought in the soul. Whether in the context of popular theology or metaphysics, the doctrine of immortality has featured not simply as an attractive hypothesis in itself but also as providing a necessary apotheosis for a life which would otherwise be without reason or justice. If life ended with bodily death then the pains and injustices of life would render it pointless, but eternal life hereafter not only compensates for present discomforts but also supposedly gives life a rational justification which it would otherwise lack. Hick's heaven offers neither justification nor comfort. To all intents and purposes it is a replica of our present unhappy estate, without even the prospect of eternal sleep to assuage its unending course. He has in effect merely redescribed the situation from which the problem originally sprang.

There might appear to be some unfairness to Hick in this argument. It is true that his resurrection world is remarkably like our own, but he does make note of two distinctive features: firstly it is situated in a different space from our own such that it has no spatial connections with our world, and secondly its occupants are housed in bodies that

are exact replicas of their pre-resurrection abodes with the one difference that they are no longer constituted of physical matter. But it is
not very clear in what sense his world is really qualitatively different
from our own, for the claim that our bodies are identical with our
former ones, except in the one respect that they are not made of physical matter, is not an obviously meaningful one. "Being physical" is not
a property that can be added to or subtracted from entities like a coat
of paint. However, one may suppose that Hick, were he to elaborate
his picture a little more, would insist on further important differences,
and in particular he would probably want to claim that in his resurrection world pain and death no longer have dominion. This would certainly be an improvement from the point of view of the believer, and
appears to be perfectly conceivable.

However, on both points—pain and death—there are difficulties. As
far as the elimination of death is concerned, an unending existence is
not necessarily an improvement on our present one, and might even,
due to its unconscionable length, represent a considerable deterioration. Nor is it any more self-justifying, for the eternal perpetuation of
life as we know it is open to as many of the pessimist's objections as
our present finite existence. And as far as pain is concerned, "being
painful," like being physical," is not a property that can be added to
or subtracted from the world while leaving everything else as it is.
There is some sort of case here for physical pain, for while this undoubtedly serves the important biological function of a warning system, we can easily stretch our imaginations to inventing a more
congenial arrangement. But on the other hand nonphysical pain—what
we could more usefully call "suffering"—cannot be eliminated without
incurring disastrous side-effects. What I have in mind is something
like this: suffering does not have a function relative to well-being in
the way that physical pain does, for the concept of suffering is *logically*
tied to various sorts of typically human activities, unlike pain which
is contingently tied. Minimally, and roughly, we can say that being
human involves the capacity to make rational choices, and these in
turn combine the capacity to assess states of affairs and to assess one's
attitudes, desires, needs, wants, and so forth in relation to these states
of affairs. But to have choices open to one, and to be able to deliberate
about these choices in the light of what one wants and what is the
case, necessarily implies the following three possibilities: firstly that
one's beliefs about what is the case may be mistaken, secondly that
one's chosen course of action may fail to achieve its end, and thirdly
that having got what one wanted one may find that it is no longer
satisfactory or satisfying. In other words at least *some* forms of suffer-

ing are necessary for beings who make rational choices in a world more or less like our own.

Hick's model clearly cannot accommodate this difficulty. There is nothing in his account of the resurrection world which allows us to think of it as being free from suffering and hence as being in some way more acceptable than our present life. The mere elimination of pain, happy enough in itself, is inadequate, for when people have sought in an after-life an assuagement of their condition, they have sought a much deeper transformation. Cosmic engineering, tinkering about with details here and there, leaves the fundamental facts of the human condition unchanged, and hence the problem for which immortality is the supposed solution is left untouched. Furthermore, those who have found earthly life a matter of anguish and regret have often discovered the source of their dissatisfaction at an even more fundamental level, namely in the fact that we live in a world in which things are transitory and which therefore cannot give us any grounds for complete and permanent satisfaction. Such satisfaction, it has been thought, can only be gained in a world where time does not cheat us of the goals of our activities and where the very striving for the satisfaction of our needs and wants has been stilled.

Whether this represents even a coherent fantasy cannot be decided here, but at any rate it is a viewpoint which appears to underlie the Christian "heaven" and the Buddhist "nirvana," and it does at any rate point to those features of our earthly existence which have underlain many peoples' dissatisfaction with it, features which remain unredeemed in Hick's resurrection world. To sum up, then: while Hick's model does not, on the face of it, at any rate, strain our notion of personal identity, he achieves this at the expense of merely reiterating the human condition for which presumably the resurrection world is a sketch of an answer.

These deficiencies are to some extent remedied in the more economically drawn portraits of survival. Thus, in Strawson's version, suffering as a factor necessarily involved in the transactions of human persons in a spatio-temporal world has largely been removed. There are no longer any things or persons to block my choices, and indeed very few choices are still open to me to make. But on the other hand, as we have already noted, such an existence is not exactly an enviable one. Being able to dwell on one's memories presumably allows one to regret deeds one has done and also to regret that one can do nothing about the regret except simply to dwell upon it. At any rate, the possibility of suffering remains, as in the case of fully bodied existence, even if confined within narrower limits. In addition to this it is a singularly pointless existence, not one that could be considered in any way an apotheosis of earthly life, and it remains as unregenerate as the embodied life it has succeeded. One can imagine a ghostly Strawson longing for redemption from his memories and his passive experiences. But whether or not Strawson's account offers justification and comfort, there still remains the difficulty which must beset all thinly drawn portraits of survival—whether in terms of a pure ego, memory traces, stream of consciousness, intellect, will, or whatever—namely, that they demand the bending to breaking point of our usual criteria of personal identity. Whether or not it can be shown that a set of disembodied faculties represents an improvement on their previous embodied form, it is not at all clear that we can speak of a human person experiencing, remembering, deciding, choosing, desiring, and perceiving unless he is endowed with a mobile and sensitive organism.

In considering the notion of survival after death we are therefore presented with the following paradox. Either we survive with our full kit of mental and physical characteristics in more or less the same kind of world as our own, or we carry over with us a flexible list of mental characteristics only. In neither case is the problem for which survival has been offered as a solution—the problem of providing a meaningful and happy apotheosis to a supposedly miserable and senseless existence—solved. The first solution merely restates, in a large measure, the problem; the second dissolves, in varying degrees, the being for whom it is supposedly a solution. Is there any *tertium quid*? Can we offer an account of survival which takes care of both prerequisites, which allows for *persons,* not shadows or memories, to survive, and which makes such survival worthwhile? In the next section we shall explore one such possible account.

Mystical Experience as a Model

The tentative solution that I shall put forward here is in terms of a certain kind of mystical experience. First it is necessary to explain how this notion is to be employed.

It might be tempting to propound a solution to the paradox of survival on the basis of the obvious flimsiness of the concept of a person, for is it not the case that at the boundaries of the concept we are accustomed to enjoy a certain amount of freedom of manoeuvre? Where foetuses, for example, or idiots, or split personalities are concerned, we do not have a ready-made decision procedure for the application of the concept, and it might be argued that even though disembodied persons are not central cases of persons they are sufficiently close to such central cases to allow us to assimilate them to the class of persons. But clearly this will not do, for by implication it would allow us to extend quite arbitrarily any concept in any direction we wished. In general what is required for the proper extension of an empirical concept beyond its wonted domain is something like what Kant called a *schema*. According to Kant—though we do not need to borrow the notion from him in all its details—a concept remains vacuous and empty until we produce in our imagination a *schematic* representation of it, thereby providing rules for the application of the concept. To mention one analogy: if Freud's only reason for extending the concepts of "motive," "intention," "desire," and so on, was that these concepts had no fixed boundaries, then his theory of the unconscious would rightly have been rejected as arbitrary. Clearly in order to justify his extended use of these terms it was necessary for him to describe, or at any rate to provide imaginary descriptions of, examples of human activity to which these concepts, hitherto not found to be applicable, could now properly be applied, and indeed much of his work is devoted to precisely this task. What is required in our present case is something similar to this. Obviously we cannot point to actual cases of disembodied persons in the way that Freud could (in a sense) point to cases of unconscious desire, but what we can do is to point to cases of an experience, familiar at least to some earthly denizens, which, though itself not that of a disembodied person, can provide a schematic image of it. It is in this role that I have cast mystical experience.

We must next specify what we mean by "mystical experience." Certainly a wide variety of types of experience has been denoted by this term, but as far as the present paper is concerned there is no need to mention any other feature of them than their variety, for we are here interested in only one sort, namely that which is typically described in terms of *oneness and harmony with the universe*. This kind of experience, which is reduplicated in a variety of different contexts, religious and non-religious, Oriental and Western, takes its rise initially perhaps from a sense of alienation and separation of the individual from the world and from the sense of pain and anguish that arises therefrom. The type of mystical experience in question comes as a radical assuagement of this sense of alienation. The rift between the self and the world is sealed, the sense of separation along with its accompanying anguish and regret is attenuated, and the very multiplicity of the physical world itself appears to the mystic to be dissolved into oneness. In particular it is the sense of the separateness of things including oneself that disappears, to be replaced by a feeling of total unity, harmony, and tranquillity. There are of course varying degrees of oneness and serenity. At its lowest level it can be seen in experiences that can hardly be termed "mystical" at all and which are probably enjoyed sometimes by everybody and frequently by some, namely the kind of experience that involves a close unity with other persons either through love or through some form of absorbing group activity. A more specifically mystical experience—though we would not always describe it as such—can arise in the context of aesthetic contemplation, when we may become so absorbed in listening to a piece of music or in contemplating an art work that all sense of time and of involvement in real life is momentarily lost. Most typically, of course, aesthetic mysticism is associated with the contemplation of and absorption in nature. So-called "nature mystics" are not difficult to find, and one could cite the names of Wordsworth, Rimbaud, and Proust as examples of men who, without benefit of religion, have enjoyed and subsequently described states of blissful absorption in nature. In such states it is quite common that the individual ceases to experience himself as a being separate from the world and imagines that in some way he is dissolved into the object of his contemplation. Thus Tennyson describes an experience in which, as he says,

> . . . out of the intensity of the consciousness of individuality, individuality itself seemed to dissolve and fade away into boundless being, and this is not a confused state but the clearest beyond words . . . where death was an almost laughable impossibility—the loss of personality (if so it were) seemed no extinction, but the only true life.[3]

The absorption of the self into nature and the loss of a sense of the multiplicity of things is frequently accompanied by a sense of timelessness, an experience that is sometimes described as the "timeless moment." For example, much of the *Four Quartets* of T. S. Eliot appears to be devoted to the attempt to capture this feeling in words. Thomas Mann in his novel *The Magic Mountain* was similarly preoccupied, and he attempts in the following passage a "description" of the timeless moment:

> We walk, walk. How long, how far? Who knows? Nothing is changed by our pacing, there is the same as here, once on a time the same as now, or then; time is drowned in the measureless monotony of space, motion from point to point is no motion more, where uniformity rules; and where motion is no more motion, time is no longer time.[4]

And in case these examples should appear to be contrived for the sake of art rather than accurate reportage of an experience, here is a quotation in which a nineteenth-century nature mystic, Richard Jeffries, claims to describe one particular such experience: "It is eternity now. I am in the midst of it. It is about me in the sunshine; I am in it, as the butterfly floats in the light-laden air. Nothing is to come: it is now. Now is by this tumulus, on earth, now; I exist in it."[5]

There are several strands that connect together experiences of this type. They involve an experience of oneness and a corresponding loss of a sense of multiplicity in space and time, an attenuation of the sense of dualism of subject and object, the lessening or loss of one's sense of one's own separate existence, a feeling of bliss and harmony that arises from the loss of all desires and regrets, and in particular a sense of detachment which nullifies all fear of pain and death. So far I have related these experiences only to non-religious and non-metaphysical contexts, but this collection of interconnected characteristics aptly describes also the experiences of certain religious mystics and saints. Let us take Buddhism as an obvious example. The so-called Buddhist path of enlightenment, which represents an attempt to nullify craving and desire, is seen as necessarily involving the overcoming of the sense of the multiplicity of things and a loss of the sense of one's separate existence in space and time. As long as the world appears to exist externally to oneself it will inevitably constitute an object of desire and hence of suffering, and only through the obliteration of this sense of mutual externality can desire and suffering be attenuated. Such a state of desirelessness and of oneness is termed by the Buddhists *nirvana,* a condition that is to be understood, not in terms of a cosmological theory, but rather in the light of certain meditative practices along with the mental and physical discipline required to achieve the appropriate contemplative state. It is a state that can be described as one of complete and blissful detachment from a sense both of one's own self and of the external world, achieved in the first place by sustained concentration on a particular object and later by the complete removal from one's mind of all particular thoughts and ideas. The mysticism of the Upanishads moves in a similar direction. Its famous dictum *tat tvam asi* ("thou art that") sums up its denial of the reality of the self and the world and its affirmation of the ultimate oneness of things, knowledge of which is similarly the fruit of ascetic contemplation rather than of discursive thinking. Similar too is the Taoism of Lao-tze and Chuang-tze which developed independently of the Indian mystical tradition. Here too the central feature is the attainment of harmony and unity with the world through withdrawal and contemplation, "an inner experience" as one commentator has described it, "through which man and the universe interfuse as one."[6]

The West too has produced religious mystics who have given accounts of monistic experiences of a similar kind, but in the interests of economy I shall limit myself to two quotations, the first from Plotinus and the second from Meister Eckhart:

The man is changed, no longer himself nor self-belonging; he is merged with the Supreme, sunken into It; only in separation is there duality . . . no movement now, no passion, no outlooking desire; . . . reason is in abeyance and intellection and even the very self; . . . all the being calmed he turns neither to this side nor to that, nor even inwards towards himself; utterly resting he has become rest itself.

So long as the soul beholds forms . . . or herself as something formed: so long is there imperfection in her. Only when all that is formed is cast off from the soul, and she sees the Eternal One alone, then the pure essence of the soul feels the naked unformed essence of the divine unity. . . . What a noble endurance is that where the essence of the soul suffers no suggestion or shadow of difference. . . . There she entrusts herself alone to the One, free from all multiplicity and difference, in which all limitation and quality is lost and is one. This One makes us blessed.[7]

Here, then, we have our schematic model. Its advantages are two-fold. In the first place it allows us to speak of the unknown in terms of the known. It has always been a problem for metaphysicians to give sense to talk about matters which are in principle beyond direct empirical observation, and the suggestion I have put forward is that mystical experience does provide us with an imaginative schema, a *via analogica*, by which we may come to understand some of this talk. We are therefore not quite at the extreme disadvantage at which St. Paul imagined us to be when he lamented that "The eye hath not seen . . ." etc., for even though we have not seen the real stuff, we have— or some of us have—seen something like it. In this respect, of course, it is no better than the models of Hick and Strawson, for they too have tried to describe the unfamiliar in terms of the familiar, but, as I have suggested, this familiarity turns out in their cases to be a large disadvantage, for they offer us either the same course again or a similar course with the spices removed. The latter point may appear also to work to the disadvantage of our *tertium quid,* for it too, though not standardly a repetition of a previous course, lacks spice. It is certainly not what many of the faithful look forward to in the after-life, and here perhaps J. S. Mill was for once in tune with popular opinion when he admitted that the only reason for hoping for an after-life lay in the possibility of being united with one's loved ones.

But herein lies the second and perhaps most important feature of our model for if, to put it crudely, the after-life looks like a mystical experience, and if therefore it is devoid of all sense of space and of separate existences in space, and of all sense of before and after, and if therefore there can be no sense of hope or regret, no desiring or wanting, then all possibility of regretting or lamenting one's estate ceases. Not only are the conditions eliciting regret no longer present, but the very possibility of regretting anything at all has been removed. However pleasant the prospect of being reunited with Harriet, Mill has no guarantee that their love will last for all eternity, for even though their happiness might persist, the conditions for unhappiness must remain. The comfort of our new model, therefore, lies in the impossibility of discomfort, and its justification in the impossibility of ever requiring one. As Wittgenstein remarked: "The solution of the problem of life is seen in the vanishing of the problem" (*Tractatus*, 6.521).

OBJECTIONS

It is now time to consider some difficulties that the proposed model inevitably runs into. The first concerns the *language* of mystical experience. This can be approached at several levels, but undoubtedly one of the first criticisms to be voiced against the foregoing remarks is that the argument relies on a spurious similarity between a multitude of reported experiences. It is absurd, the critic might continue, to imagine that the reports of so-called mystical experiences are "pure" and objective. In fact, the language of such reports is thoroughly soaked in the doctrinal presuppositions of the reporters. There is something in this criticism that must be taken seriously, for if our *schematism* turned out to be wholly or even largely metaphysical or religious doctrine, then we would simply be begging the very question we set out to answer; it is necessary for our case that these reports should be as objective as such reports can be. But in fact they pass this test adequately enough. In the first place, as far as the Oriental examples cited are concerned, it is quite wrong to separate doctrine from experience, as if the one is learned intellectually first, as it were, and only subsequently confirmed by esoteric experience. In a sense the doctrine *is* the experience, for the experience is a necessary and a sufficient condition for understanding, the understanding itself not being "*of*" anything, but simply a state of tranquil detachment: there is nothing beyond that to know. It is true that cosmological theories have developed alongside the mystical tradition, but again it is probably a mistake to suppose that the mystical experiences came as a result of the cosmological theories. It is at least highly likely that the doctrines themselves were developed to explain the experiences and that the universal similarity of the latter helps to explain in turn the remarkable similarity between cosmological theories in diverse cultures. It should also be noted that we are relying not only on the reports of religious mystics but also on nature mystics who, though they may have no doctrinal baggage to carry along, nevertheless tell us stories which strikingly resemble those of their religious counterparts.

But still it might be urged that the argument goes wrong at a more fundamental level. Since mystical experience is not available to everyone there is no way for the detached observer to check the reports of mystics, and indeed in the last analysis the mystic appears to be going beyond the limits of what can meaningfully be said. This is a large issue and only a few brief remarks must suffice in reply. It is indeed true that the language employed by mystics to describe their experiences is pushed well to the edge of meaningfulness—as Eliot says, echoing the sentiments of many mystics themselves, "Words strain / Crack and sometimes break, under the burden."[8] But it would be incorrect to claim that their remarks were totally meaningless. No doubt we cannot appreciate fully what the mystic is trying to tell us unless we have trodden the same path ourselves, but enough of what he is saying comes through to us to enable us to be tolerably certain that we would recognize the experience if it came our way. Not everything that he says is totally foreign to us, and as has already been pointed out there is no clean break between fairly common experiences of harmony and integration with the world at the one extreme and full-blown mystical experiences at the other.

For this reason the mystic's words contain a core of meaning for us. Of course his descriptions do not function in quite the way that ordinary empirical descriptions do, but what he has to say does enable us at least to *pin-point* the experience, to place it in a certain framework and to relate it to others. This is borne out by the fact that there is a remarkable superficial resemblance between descriptions of esoteric experiences from radically diverse sources, and it would be odd if not contradictory to refuse to allow a corresponding resemblance between the experiences themselves. In other words, it is reasonable to conjecture that we are dealing here with a fairly universal feature of the human mind, namely the desire for peace, harmony, and the identification of oneself with the world, a desire which finds its highest expression in the feeling that all differences are illusory, that there is no time, no multiplicity, but that all things are really one. My claim is the minimal one that something answering to, or pin-pointed by, this sort of description has been experienced by a representative collection of people.

Objections along the foregoing lines are not, I believe, particularly strong, and though they have been dealt with briefly we can now pass on to some more powerful ones. It will no doubt have struck the reader that the mystical model is remarkably thin and sketchy by our own standards, and that therefore it ought reasonably to succumb to the same criticisms that were levelled at the Strawson model. For is it not the case that we too are allowing mere shadows—if that—to pass through death's needle eye, rather than anything that could recognizably be called a "person," let alone the "same" person who existed in a previous life? No doubt we have described a condition which represents a considerable improvement on our earthly existence. It is a state which could plausibly be called blissful (mystics have certainly thought of it as such), in which death, suffering, and indeed any vicissitude whatsoever can be of no consequence, and hence provides the comfort and justification lacking in the other models. But at the same time it looks as if we have so described this blissful condition that *persons* can no longer be sensibly described as participating in it, for one of the necessary conditions for the enjoyment of this blissful state is the attenuation of one's sense of separate existence and the feeling of absorption into some larger whole. A somewhat drastic solution to life's problems!

There are several answers that we can sketch to this objection. The first, and perhaps least telling, answer is that, typically, mystics themselves do not look upon suicide as an alternative to *nirvana,* for there would be little point in undergoing a long and difficult process in self-discipline if the same result could be achieved in a moment by means of a bare bodkin. As Schopenhauer once remarked in this connection, "The cool shades of Orcus allure him only with the false appearance of a haven of rest." More telling than this, though, is the fact that in his descriptions and reports a mystic usually ascribes his experiences to *himself,* and is grateful for the favour done to *him,* rather than to the One, or to the World Soul, or to a corpse. And further they are not only described as *his,* but as his *experiences,* and this would make no sense unless we suppose them to be the experiences of someone, and this "someone" must surely be the person describing them. When a man sets himself the task of acquiring a state of indifference and absorption, he looks forward to achieving this state for *himself,* not for someone or something else.

But there are more important considerations that can be brought in defence of our argument. It is true that the vocabulary of mystics sometimes suggests extinction both of the self and of the world, and for this reason *inter alia* mysticism has often been stigmatized as "negative" or "nihilistic." But this attitude rests on a mistake. The Zen Buddhists, for example, who have frequently had the "nihilistic" label attached to them, have considered the attainment of what they call "self-sustaining independence," not as a weary escape from a life of pain and evil, but as an attempt to experience life more abundantly. The Taoist mystics have likewise believed that in our ordinary everyday attachments to ourselves and to the objects surrounding us we become dead to the value and beauty of things, and that this value and beauty only becomes a reality for us when we have achieved tranquil unity with nature. Furthermore, only in such a state, according to the Taoists, when a man is totally emptied of himself and of his sense of the separateness of things, only then can the full powers of artistic creation in a man be released.

These do not of course reflect the views of all mystics by any means, but it is at least one representative view that mysticism is not a negation but rather some kind of affirmation of the self, the development of one's "real" or "true" self rather than its destruction. The whole vocabulary of "release," "enlightenment," and so forth, which is so typical of this form of mysticism, helps to confirm this view. To the outsider, indeed, the mystic may appear to be as good as dead, but from his own point of view the mystic has moved not from life to death but in the reverse direction. As he now sees the world, it is in ordinary experience, with its "enslavement" to the self and to particular objects, that we live a kind of twilight existence, not in the state of mystical transport where, on the contrary, he claims to have found a more fully real life. This is a view that has been maintained, as we might expect, by Christian mystics as well. Meister Eckhart, for example, who explicitly compares the mystical experience with the beatific vision, maintains that such an experience involves at one and the same time a kind of identification with God and also an affirmation of the life of the individual.[9] We can ignore the fact that this is skating over very thin logical and theological ice, for our only concern here is to show that, as far as the quality of the mystical experience itself goes, the sense of oneness of all things does not appear to exclude the sense of one's own personal identity. Rather, on the contrary, in certain forms of mysticism the two appear to be necessary concomitants of one another.

There is one final problem, which has already been mentioned in passing. It has been argued that an immortal existence, conceived in accordance with the model of a certain kind of monistic experience, not only allows us to talk sensibly of personal survival, but also offers a plausible solution to the "problem of life" with which the doctrine of personal survival has traditionally been closely tied. But one might well wonder whether the faithful, on being proffered the hope of an after-life that resembled the athletic and forbidding heights of asceticism, might no longer regard it as worth the effort. John Stuart Mill probably speaks for the average believer when he images the life to come as a continuation of all that is best in the present one. However, what the foregoing argument has tried to show is that such a conception of survival is misconceived on two counts: firstly that it must necessarily contain the suffering which it was designed to expel, and secondly that it does not represent any rational apotheosis of earthly existence. The only model which fulfills these requirements, and at the same time offers some semblance of a solution to the personal identity problem, is the one wrought from the materials of monistic experience. No doubt the believer will believe what he likes, but this model represents the only account which is fully consistent with the requirements of the problem for which it has traditionally been the solution.

Of course, it could still be argued that I am simply offering a solution to a problem of my own making, and since the believer's problem may be a different one—for example he may not be concerned about what I have called a "rational apotheosis"—he need not be concerned with my solution. In addition, the philosopher who has considered this question may also wonder whether he needs to tie down his discussion to problems concocted elsewhere: like the believer, he may surely set his own tasks. As far as the believer's objection is concerned it could be replied that if his notion of survival is to be anything more than blithely mythological then the problem as well as the solution must meet certain requirements. If the problem is posed simply as one of survival, then something like Hick's resurrection world will do; but such survival, which largely reduplicates earthly life and offers no fundamental transformation of the human condition, would represent an amusing fantasy but hardly anything of importance for philosophy or religion. And similarly for the philosopher's objection, obviously he can set his own problem and proceed to solve it, but if he deals with it as simply a question of logical possibility and nothing more—and this often *is* the manner of treatment—then his problem has no more claim on our attention than any of the other infinite number of questions of logical possibility that could be raised. If philosophical questions are in any obvious sense of the term "serious" ones, then the problem of personal survival of death must be treated as part of a more general issue that has been at the heart of religious and metaphysical thinking.

NOTES

1. "Religious Statements as Factually Significant," *The Existence of God,* ed. John Hick (New York, 1964).

2. *Individuals* (London, 1959), pp. 115–16.

3. Quoted from R. C. Zaehner, *Mysticism Sacred and Profane* (Oxford, 1957), pp. 36–37.

4. From the chapter "By the Ocean of Time" (trans. H. T. Lowe-Porter).

5. Zaehner, p. 47. F. C. Happold has collected descriptions of the experience of the "timeless moment" in his *Mysticism* (London, 1963).

6. Chang Chung-yuan, *Creativity and Taoism* (New York, 1963), Chap. 5.

7. Quoted from C. J. Ducasse, *A Philosophical Scrutiny of Religion* (New York, 1953), p. 283, and from Rudolph Otto, *Mysticism East and West* (New York, 1957), p. 59, respectively.

8. From *Burnt Norton,* said about the problem of describing an atemporal state.

9. Otto, pp. 210–11 and Ch. 4.

SELECTED BIBLIOGRAPHY

It is somewhat customary for editors of anthologies to include lengthy (often computer-generated), if not exhaustive, bibliographies. Unfortunately, such compilations are frequently too elongated to be practical (except for the most diligent scholars) and much too indiscriminate to aid the interested student. By contrast, the items in this bibliography are, I believe, both selective and tractable. All the reading suggestions listed here deal with themes inherent to the tenor of this volume and can be supplemented, if necessary, by reference to the notes in the preceding twenty essays, and the ensuing bibliographies' own suggested citations. No claim, quite obviously, is made for completeness; but a careful reading of the below-listed sources should give one an excellent feel for some basic linguistic and metaphysical problems in thanatology.

Almeder, Robert. *Death and Personal Survival: The Evidence for Life After Death*. Lanham, Md.: Littlefield Adams, 1992.

Davis, Stephen T., ed. *Death and Afterlife*. New York: St. Martin's, 1989.

Edwards, Paul, ed. *Immortality*. New York: Macmillan, 1992.

Feldman, Fred. *Confrontations with the Reaper: A Philosophical Study of the Nature and Value of Death*. New York: Oxford University Press, 1992.

Fischer, John Martin, ed. *The Metaphysics of Death*. Stanford: Stanford University Press, 1993.

Foster, John. *The Immaterial Self: A Defense of the Cartesian Dualist Conception of the Mind*. London: Routledge, 1991.

Hick, John. *Death and Eternal Life*. New York: Harper & Row, 1976.

McMullan, W. A. *Posthumous Meditations*. Indianapolis: Hackett, 1982.

The Monist (special issue on "Death and Dying"), 76 (April 1993).

Moody, Raymond. *Life After Life*. New York: Bantam, 1975.

Parfit, Derek. *Reasons and Persons*. Oxford: Clarendon, 1984.

Perrett, Roy W. *Death and Immortality*. Dordrecht: Nijhoff, 1987.

Phillips, D. Z. *Death and Immortality*. London: Macmillan, 1970.

Rosenberg, Jay F. *Thinking Clearly About Death*. Englewood Cliffs, N.J.: Prentice-Hall, 1983.

Swinburne, Richard. *The Evolution of the Soul*. Oxford: Oxford University Press, 1986.